Martha Hill

AND THE MAKING OF

AMERICAN DANCE

Martha Hill

AND THE MAKING OF
AMERICAN DANCE

Janet Mansfield Soares

WESLEYAN UNIVERSITY PRESS Middletown, Connecticut

Published by

Wesleyan University Press,

Middletown, CT 06459

www.wesleyan.edu/wespress

© 2009 by Janet Mansfield Soares

Printed in U.S.A.

5 4 3 2 1

Library of Congress

Cataloging-in-Publication Data

Soares, Janet Mansfield.

Martha Hill and the making of American dance / Janet
Mansfield Soares.

 p. cm.

Includes bibliographical references and index.

ISBN 978-0-8195-6899-1 (cloth: alk. paper)

1. Hill, Martha, 1900-1995. 2. Dance teachers—United
States—Biography. 3. Dance—Study and teaching
(Higher)—United States—History—20th century.
4. Modern dance—United States—History.
I. Title.

GV1785.H54S63   2009

792.8092—dc22

[B]   2009000994

Wesleyan University Press is a member of the
GreenPress Initiative. The paper used in this book
meets their minimum requirement for recycled paper.

For Archie,

Our children, Sabrina and Tristan,

and theirs,

Daniella, Justina, Olivia, and Will

Contents

Preface and Acknowledgments

Surprises come at odd moments when writing a biography that shares one's own history. I knew Martha for forty of her ninety-four years and became adept at second-guessing what she was going to say. As a student, I studied her every action in admiration—and she knew it. She mentored practically every aspect of my professional life in dance. Martha was the person I most wanted to emulate in my own career. As a dance composition teacher encouraging new choreographers under Martha's leadership at Juilliard, I appreciated her faith in me. As a dancer and choreographer myself, I began to view the whole field of contemporary dance as shaped by a few significant contributors.

After completing a book on Louis Horst—a labor she heartily approved of—it was as if Martha, now in her eighties, had predestined me to be her biographer. As research progressed, I was amazed that although Hill's and Horst's lives were related in time, proximity, and mission, his bore little resemblance to my new subject. Both were important twentieth-century missionaries for a new "modern" dance. If Horst was the one who gave dance aesthetic vision—or "morality," in ballet giant Lincoln Kirstein's words—I marveled at the evidence that it was Martha who provided a great deal of structure and direction to the fledgling American art form of modern dance.

But if Horst made sacrifices for "the sake of dance," they were easy by comparison. He loved women, making music, and good food, and all abundantly filled his rich life. In contrast, Martha's lean physicality matched her relentless determination to support dance at great personal cost.

Impeccably honest, Martha was forthright, yet discreet. A natural beauty with distinctive good looks, she exuded confidence. She always dressed stylishly, mixing elegance and practicality. For as long as I knew her, her silver-streaked hair was placed in a signature asymmetrical knot secured with a velvet ribbon. Only her sensible shoes belied the former dancer's need for comfort over fashion.

Martha's commanding midwestern voice pronounced each thought with authority and sureness. A good communicator, her manner was both outgoing and optimistic. She listened and responded graciously, but always to the point. From her majestic height of five-foot-seven, she made direct eye contact when she spoke to men, then tilted her head jauntily downward as she conversed with women shorter than her.

It has been said that women are impossible biographical subjects because their lives are full of secrets. I soon discovered that the subject of this book harbored many. A master of deflection, by keeping herself out of the limelight, Martha was able to wield extraordinary power.

It is paradoxical that someone so pivotal to the legitimatizing of indigenous contemporary dance would lead so unconventional a personal lifestyle. Recalling her two years of performing with Martha Graham as "a most thrilling time," Martha told me, "My being a professional dancer was frowned upon even though I was teaching dance." While describing her upbringing and her "daring" move to Greenwich Village "where things were freer," she revealed her deep emotional need for independence.[1] For Martha, dance was the most intensely consuming factor of her life: it was also the one liberating agent that made all the difference.

Poised in her position as artistic director emerita of the Juilliard Dance Division at Lincoln Center for the Performing Arts, Martha told me in 1987, "Besides dancing, talking is what dancers love to do best." But when I pressed her for an interview, she was politely reticent. "Why?" she asked. I explained that I was writing an article in honor of her thirty-three years at Juilliard. After two false starts (a Capezio Award to attend, and when she deems my son's fever a priority) I began to wonder if anything resembling a formal meeting would ever happen. Nervously, I typed out a list of queries, knowing that Martha was an expert at weighing words. She was usually the one to ask the questions.

At last, the first interview. Martha glanced at my list and suggested that she might just as well reply with notes in the margins where appropriate. Her extraordinary ability to sidestep the unnecessary had always been a strong point. As she spoke in a practiced way about her own background, I began to suspect that Martha had always possessed certain natural abilities and had learned to use them as a leader from the moment she entered the uncharted world of dance as a young adult. "I like to say, my major is people," Martha revealed at the end of her life. "That's my talent. I am good about understanding and reconciling different points of view. I'm a sort of catalyst—pushing things ahead. That's always been my role."[2]

At Juilliard, I had observed that very quality: breezing down the corridor of the school, program copy in hand, on the way to wherever the dancers were, or rummaging through stacks of clippings and correspondence piled high on her desk, Martha was happiest when she made things happen. "I am not a writer," she confessed, "I am a doer. I have never been interested in reliving the past. She surprised me by adding, "But lately, I do see the need for setting the facts straight." Feeling more confident, I pressed Martha to speak of things I had always been curious about. But having been in the business of developing the fine art of dance for more than three-quarters of a century, Martha had a wealth of facts to get straight. (So many, I would later find out, were intertwined with major events in its development that they created a very messy manuscript for years to come.) A stickler for extracting names and framing them within the context of their time, she recalled dates and details of events in her rich past. This session and the ones that followed offered a rare opportunity to flesh out the circumstances surrounding the key players in the development of America's modern dance.

When excerpts from the interview were published in the *Juilliard Journal*, Martha barely mentioned it. Instead she wrote on a celebratory program I asked her to sign, "So many experiences together! So many projects and events!! And you so young! Martha." The next day we were at a dance showcase of student works in a Juilliard studio, viewing the raw energy of budding talents with intense pleasure. I saw that she savored every movement. I wondered then, about the predicament of reliving the past in a field so devoted to the present.

I began to suspect that Martha Hill, who had accomplished so much, had stayed forward-looking with fresh ideas precisely because she did not look back. For her, there was always more to do tomorrow. When mentioning her belated marriage to her longtime lover, Martha's expression changed briefly to one of nostalgia. Moments later, she was back to the realities of the day, reminding me that when the school year finished she was off to Alaska, Israel, and then Australia as adviser to emerging dance companies. It was Martha's way of continuing to spread the gospel of dance. These were new frontiers for modern dance as she saw it, reminiscent of breakthroughs she had helped generate in the 1930s and 1940s in the United States, and she wanted to spark their growth in whatever way she could.

Another five years passed before the idea of a biography surfaced. Long practiced at concealing her private life from public view, a memoir might be engaging, she said, if it illustrated the social and cultural circumstances surrounding her life in dance. "I am a product of my experiences," she offered. "My life within its social context is an interesting story." Unexpectedly, a closer study uncovered deep hurts and silent motives—shocking revelations, not because they were unique among artists, but because Martha worked so hard to dismiss and conceal them.

Like many of her contemporaries, Martha did not view herself as a feminist, yet she was a perfect model of one. From the moment she made an irrevocable break from the values of her family, her ideas were her own. As a woman, Martha waged private battles against the "uprightness" of an ingrained midwestern morality, as she dealt with conflicted feelings of shame and wickedness. Her own affairs of the heart were seldom revealed to others.

If relinquishing a performance career was Martha's deepest regret, possibly it was also the reason for the longevity of her success in the field. In order to survive on her own, she abandoned the career she coveted most. She did this at the very point when a modernist movement was developing in all of the arts. As a member of an inner circle of talents, she seized the opportunity to bring forth a parallel vitality for America's new dance. In the process, she shaped environments in which its major artists thrived.

Selfless within a community of egocentrics, even-tempered among high volatiles, and ever-positive in the direst situations, Martha found the strength to arbitrate in the most wrenching circumstances among artists and their producers. Among them, it was Martha who had, in Bennington poet and Martha's lifelong friend, Ben Belitt's words, "the terrible gift of the gaze"—the one who saw the potential of "the body's unwearied uplift."[3]

Other writers have claimed Martha Hill as a prime mover for American dance, but none have attempted a full-length biography. I am amazed at how many hidden pieces of the puzzle there were in this writing project. Exploring the "whys and wherefores" of a life in the performing arts with zigzagging chronologies set into monthly calendars, schedules, clippings of reviews, endless student lists, correspondence, and unpublished manuscripts offered tangled clues. Selective memories, most particularly Martha's own, have served as artifacts, along with audiotaped interviews and salvaged fragments on film to be studied, questioned, and sometimes simply accepted at face value. This book is a portrait, "warts and all," of a woman and her contemporaries. Underlying the portrait is an attempt to reveal the narrow lineage of American dance history.

To a large extent, this book is the story of America's indigenous brand of contemporary concert dance, from college gymnasium to theater, and then to performing arts centers around the world. And it is revealed through the story of a person who was at the center of it all.

I am especially grateful to the following organizations and individuals for their assistance in my research: National Endowment for the Arts, Humanities Division; Barnard College, Columbia University; the staff of the New York Public Library, Lincoln Center for the Performing Arts, Jerome Robbins Dance Division; Jeni Dahmus, archivist, the Juilliard School; Noreen McBride, librarian, East Palestine Memorial Public Library; reference/archives librarians at Bennington Library and Salem Library; Catherine Phimasy and Nova M. Seals at

Connecticut College Charles E. Shain Library; the staff of Duke University Lily Library; Heather Briston at University of Oregon Library; Patty Nicholas at Fort Hays State University, Forsyth Library; Gene Gavin, Wadsworth Atheneum, Arubach Library; George Livingston of the Willard Library; Christina Bickford, Barnard College Library; Lynn Alexander and Richard Conroy of the Old Lyme Phoebe Griffin Noyes Library; fine agent Maria Carvainis, Renée D'Aoust, Beth Foster, Katie Higham-Kessler, Bill Hill, George McGeary, Dianne McPherson, Barbara Palfy, Sabrina Soares Roberts, Rhonda Rubinson, Arthur Faria Soares, and Henry Van Kuiken. My gratitude goes to Director and Editor-in-Chief of Wesleyan University Press, Suzanna Tamminen, for her guidance and expertise.

It is said that dance is the most imperfect of art forms. Also, the most formidable and demanding one: from moment to moment any part of its execution is subject to total collapse. It is this risk-taking in dance that ignites audiences and engages the dancer as an artist. Yet this most daring, most temporal, and most sensual of the performing arts thrives in an environment of stern discipline. The dichotomy between free and bound is always present in dance: it is perhaps the deep opposition to inertia as the primary mission that makes a dancer's life story so compelling.

Martha Hill's dance ancestors were Loie Fuller, Isadora Duncan, and Ruth St. Denis. Her contemporaries were Martha Graham, Hanya Holm, and Doris Humphrey. Together this band of zealots defied the pervasive European tradition and claimed legitimacy for America's indigenous art form of modern dance. They were proselytizers for dance—not with words, but with actions. These women had a different notion of art dancing, far removed from the increasingly worn discipline of ballet. They emerged promisingly at the turn of the twentieth century from what might be viewed as meager offerings in American culture and commercial theater. They were pioneers with a new conception for dance that plotted a path for others to follow.

All of them began their careers as performers: dancing, choreographing, and staging their own work. At first, they took on these multiple roles not by choice, but by necessity. (This evolution was dramatically different from the European concept of the creation of a ballet, where the female as the prima ballerina was the extraordinary but submissive subject of the male ballet master.) Throughout their lives, dance remained a marginal art form. They constantly confronted issues of body image and gender, yet these women were hell-bent on creating their own history. In a sense, they invented themselves.

New forms of aesthetic, or interpretive, dance were first created for the stage by the early solo "artistes"—Fuller, Duncan, and St. Denis—during a time when audiences craved human images of great beauty (or, at the least, a titillating glimpse of ankle or bare shoulder).

At the turn of the twentieth century Illinois-born Loie Fuller's idea of emulating dancing images of goddesses was soon deemed an appropriate pastime for women of college age. Her butterfly-inspired illuminations first delighted audiences in Paris. Fuller's own eclectic background began in 1875 as a thirteen-year-old "temperance performer," where she learned to "hold the stage" by extemporizing in solo presentations.

But it was the San Franciscan, Isadora Duncan (1878–1927), who would not dance in the form of unearthly creatures but as an expressive woman of her own time.[1] Duncan set out to fulfill that promise guided by a nonconformist mother who found ways to press her children into artistic livelihoods in order to support the family. In 1898 and 1899 Isadora began dancing as the "society pet" of the Vanderbilts' gatherings for New York City's Four Hundred.

Draped in diaphanous gowns, Duncan continued to charm European audiences at soirees with her barefoot performances to Chopin etudes. Isadora's performances in the United States with Walther Damrosch's New York Symphony in 1908 excited American artists, intellectuals, and kinetic ideologists spellbound by the depth of her expression. In 1916, returning as a more mature dancer, she startled American audiences with her war allegories. Dancing to the music of Beethoven and Wagner, she presented, in her words, the struggle against adversity that was her call to arms. Her dramatic *La Marseillaise*, through "visceral action and visceral reaction to outward movement," was novel. She searched for "emotional truth" to "discover the roots of [the] impulse toward movement as a response to every experience."[2] These were ideas that were close to those developed by the expressionist Mary Wigman in Germany between the world wars, although the results were very different. Both Duncan and Wigman would have a strong impact on America's dance history.

At this time few had viewed the European ballet companies that occasionally toured the United States. Ballet was distinctly a curiosity, with Anna Pavlova's touring company attracting select audiences hungry for a glimpse of Europe's finer cultural offerings. The average American went for bawdier entertainments, such as carnival acts and minstrel shows or the occasional Gilbert and Sullivan operetta. The country's patriotic love of celebrations and parades fostering civic pride and expressions of identity took hold in the American Pageant movement of the early twentieth century. Communities held spirited political rallies and local events that included dance, poetry, and staged dramatic action. (Pageantry had even become a subject for study at Columbia's Teachers College, as physical education leaders were often called upon to help organize groups in local public events.)

Ruth St. Denis had gained recognition as a solo artist in the 1890s as a skirt dancer, and then with touring road shows produced by David Belasco, who renamed Ruthie Dennis "St. Denis" because of her "virginal ways." With a Pre-Raphaelite aura, St. Denis combined the sensual with the exalted body, the two opposites of nineteenth-century female morality. In one historian's view, her image as a professional dancer was defined primarily by her sexuality, which, along with her portrayal of the mother figure, produced a kind of transcendence that captured audiences of the day.[3] St. Denis first saw Fuller dance at the 1900 Paris Exposition Universelle and even joined her company briefly. But she would find greater inspiration in the Eastern mysticism and "beautiful austerities" of the Japanese dancer Sada Yacco.

During this period of what might be considered aesthetic naïveté in the United States, fads ran more toward Tin Pan Alley's ragtime and the savvy "tea dance" routines of the trendsetting couple Irene and Vernon Castle. St. Denis decided she needed a partner in order to perform at the popular afternoon soirees and chose Ted Shawn. With the birth of Denishawn came the first professional American dance troupe to make a deep impression on its audiences. Showmanship was the priority: Shawn and St. Denis strove for high art in their dance works but more often settled for popular theater, as they toured the vaudeville circuit cross-country from 1914 to 1931.

In 1915, as the company flourished, Shawn organized a Denishawn school in Los Angeles—claiming it to be the first professional school for American dance—as a business venture and training ground for company dancers under "Miss Ruth's" tutelage. Featured among the cast of thousands in D. W. Griffith's film *Intolerance,* the school gained a quick reputation as a convenient source for Hollywood's latest starlets. From a nucleus of Denishawn's stars came a generation of new dancers and choreographers eager to proclaim themselves the next wave of American leaders. Among them, Martha Graham joined the Denishawn ranks in 1919, two years after Doris Humphrey.

American dance as we know it was essentially developed by these dancers as one by one they became matriarchs in the field of dance. All envisioned dance as an independent performing art; all became teachers and mentors, consumed with the belief that they must create their own personal movement vocabularies. The one thing these dancers had in common was their need to express and perfect their art using the most complex and mysterious instrument on earth: the human body. The kind of dance these women championed dug beneath "empty formalisms" to bring forth movement and gesture designed to reflect the human condition.

It was the revolutionaries Fuller, Duncan, and St. Denis, followed by the "pioneering" efforts of their offspring, Graham and Humphrey, that first appealed to Martha Hill as a member of Martha Graham's all-female dance group. A torchbearer for the others in her generation beginning in the early 1930s, Hill worked to position dance as a valued artistic practice, one that belonged in the sociocultural life of campuses and arts centers in the United

States and around the world—and one that would gradually shape a cultural identity of its own.

All of these women were pioneers of modernism, but it was Martha Hill who, with her colleagues, managed to transform a many-faceted group of eccentrics into a community of talents with a single goal: to assure the survival of contemporary dance into a new millennium. Martha Hill did not take the path her dance predecessors had so brilliantly undertaken. Her work would go beyond the narrow scope of the individual artist's domain. She would orchestrate greater causes.

What distinguishes Martha's accomplishments is that she moved the field of dance from a solitary, self-serving venture to one that opened doors for others while insisting on the best. By midcentury there was no one else so able to take her vision of dance into the conservatory setting of the Juilliard School of Music. After the school's move to Lincoln Center and with the reestablishment of the American Dance Festival, she was able to establish dance as an art form deserving of a place in the arts complexes emerging across the country.

Martha took on every aspect of educating dancers and dance audiences, "seeding" dance in colleges, conservatories, and dance centers across the country. At the same time, she made possible the creation of some of the most enduring dance repertory of the twentieth century. Certainly, Martha Hill is in the very warp and weave of America's dance fabric.

PART I

Bible Belt to Academe

Martha Hill liked to say that on her mother's side, she came from the same branch of Todds as Abraham Lincoln's wife, Mary. Of Scottish and Irish extraction, her mother, Grace Todd, was born and raised in East Palestine, Ohio. Early records, however, show that Grace's paternal ancestors were Mennonites who left Zurich, Switzerland, because of religious oppression. Samuel, the son of Alexander Todd, was one of the early settlers of Baltimore County in Maryland.

In 1794 with a friend, Jacob Lyon, Samuel built a flat-bottom boat at Old Fort Redstone on the Monongahela (a river in the United States that flows north) on which they floated, continuing down the Ohio River with their families. When a sudden rise occurred, they docked temporarily along the shore, but when the water went down the boat settled over a stump that punctured the bottom. The accident determined a settlement for the Todds on the north side of the Ohio River above Smith's Ferry.[1] Salt was found when drilling for water, and its production became a lucrative business at ten dollars a barrel and the chief means of support for the pair and their families. According to *History of Columbiana County, Ohio*, Saline Township was established in 1816. Its center, Salineville, incorporated in 1848, showed little growth until the completion of the Cleveland and Pittsburgh Railroad, and the subsequent development of the coal-mining interests that laid the foundation for the area's future prosperity.

A Todd married a Lyon in 1812, parenting eight children. Their second child, Samuel B., married Nancy Fitzsimmons in 1839 and produced nine offspring. One of the five boys, Thomas Taggart Todd, married Eugenia Catherine (Jenny) Sheets in 1876. The Taggart and the Sheets families figure prominently in the area's history: in 1803 both John Taggart and Frederick Sheets were registered owners of large parcels of rich farming land. It is recorded that in 1853, John served as an elder for what in 1842 was the Associate Reform Presbyterian congregation, later becoming the United Presbyterian Church. The families continued to be influential when East Palestine incorporated in 1875 and one B. F. Sheets was elected to the village council. The town was named "Palestine" by the wife of a doctor who felt that the quiet beauty of the little town and the "virtuous simple life of its people," recalled "holy memories." Because there was already a Palestine in Ohio, the prefix "east" was added when the government granted the town a post office.[2]

Thomas and Eugenia had three children, Fred, Grace, and Hugh, before Thomas died suddenly in 1882 at age thirty-two, when Grace, Martha's mother, was four years old. Remarried three years later to Daniel Faulk, "Eugenia" bore two more children: Olive, born in 1887, and Florence in 1894. The situation was an unfortunate one for Grace, who resented the addition of her young stepsisters to the family: "She had an unhappy childhood," Martha's youngest brother, Bill Hill believed.

On Martha's paternal side, four Hill brothers who were Huguenots also left Switzerland for religious freedom, immigrating to the United States seventeen years earlier than the Todd family. They first settled in Strasburg Township, Pennsylvania, later moving to Churchville in Butler County and purportedly supplied provisions to Washington during the Revolution. One of ten children, Martha's grandfather, Shiloh Hill, born in 1825, married twice, siring ten children each time. His second marriage was to Mary Emily Weaver (herself the eighth of twelve children, and related to one of the signers of the Declaration of Independence). The couple ran a gristmill in Baghdad, Pennsylvania, that became the social gathering place for families in the area. An "Indian fighter," a hunter, and a frontiersman, he was said to have preached "white magic" on the banks of the Kiskiminetas River. "There was a lot of black magic being practiced, and he was the one that sort of eliminated it," Bill explained.[3]

Martha's father, Grant, the fifth of Shiloh's second set of ten children, was born in 1868. Four of the sons operated the Stull, Hill, Coulter Company in Leechburg. "Dad ran the Coulter's concession [supply store] to the mines from there."[4] One of Grant's sisters, Ruth, taught Latin and French in the high school. Known for her eccentricities, she put the fear of God into her pupils as they learned conjugations, according to one of her lackluster students whose father owned the "other" hardware store in town: the Hill and McGeary families were archrivals. Later, Miss Hill was doubly stern with young George McGeary.[5]

For generations none of the Hills ventured out of Leechburg before Martha's father left home. She called him "a limitedly adventuresome young man because he was the only one of his family who left Pennsylvania to try his fortune in Ohio." Having grown up in Leechburg, Armstrong County, and an area rich with bituminous coals, "Dad went to work for Lewis Hicks, who owned a lot of property," Bill Hill remembered.

When Grace met Grant, "she was a stunning young woman from the village and he was quite a catch coming from Pennsylvania," Martha explained. Grace was seventeen and had just graduated from high school; Grant was ten years older. He escorted her to church socials, and together they participated in missionary work. Once he proposed, Grace excitedly itemized the furniture she planned to buy for his approval in preparation for their life together. Their marriage took place in 1897 at their proudly furnished apartment on North Market Street, East Palestine. After the ceremony they celebrated with a dinner reception for twenty-one guests.

The couple soon became staunch Presbyterians (although Grant was raised as a Lutheran), and solid citizens of the town. As the superintendent of the Prospect Hill Coal Company, also known as the Carbon Hill Coal Mine, which mined and shipped gas and steam coal, Grant was able to support Grace in comfort. They were well respected in this small town halfway between Pittsburgh and Cleveland that boasted 2,493 residents in its 1900 census, and after several years they rented "the Frazer house" on North Park Street. There the first of four children, Martha (named Grace Martha), was born on 1 December 1900, in her words, "in this restricted community" of "home and the church . . . under the watchful Victorian eye" of the period. Her christening took place in the imposing new United Presbyterian Church completed that year.

Grace proudly recorded births and deaths in her diary as carefully as her notations of properties they rented. A second child, Mary Katherine, was born in 1904 "at the Whittenburger house" on East Martin Street. In 1907 a third child, Grant Eugene (called Eugene or Gene), was delivered "in Lawrence house." Katherine's traumatic death at the age of five was brought about by spinal meningitis in 1909. According to Martha, it "broke her mother's heart," and intensified Martha's love of her brother. Throughout, Grace and Grant found solace in their deepening belief in the church.

Martha always exhibited proper demeanor as a child, beautifully dressed in crisp, white pinafores, with fancy ribbons in her tidy braids. She was a bright child with doleful eyes; rather than inheriting the letter-perfect features of her mother, she was more a Hill in looks. The eldest, she was expected to maintain a sense of place, purpose, and mission—qualities that stayed with her throughout her life. With charity, fortitude, honesty, and good faith key to Martha's upbringing, she counted church socials as the liveliest happenings during her childhood.

At six years old, Martha played Bach's *Two-part Inventions* during her piano lessons with teachers who were graduates of Oberlin College. She was also coached in singing at an early age. Her teacher was a friend of her father's from Pittsburgh who taught voice every weekend in the family parlor. "Father was a minstrel show buff. All of his family were amateur musicians—very good ones. They all played piano and they all sang, so that there was a great deal of music around the house." Family outings included attending music concerts and plays in Pittsburgh and Cleveland, pleasurable diversions in a childhood of churchgoing and strict rules. She remembered attending an exposition in Pittsburgh where she saw "a skirt dancer following Loie Fuller" in a production of Maurice Maeterlinck's *The Bluebird*. And on another occasion in East Palestine, Martha was spellbound by "a very beautiful dancer in green lights, performing a copy of Pavlova's 'Dragonfly.' From that point on I knew I wanted to dance."[6]

Martha described herself as a Bible Belt child. "I am a product of my experiences, beginning in an unsympathetic Ohio village with all its restrictions and taboos." With abolitionists and "Holy Rollers" in their heyday, many Presbyterian testimonials attributed their "downfall" to "modern" dancing as well as to drinking and cardplaying. When evangelist Billy Sunday came to revival meetings at the Ohio campgrounds, the Hills were there to hear him preach against dance halls as "the most damnable, low-down institution[s] on the face of God's earth [causing] more ruin than anything this side of hell."[7] Frightened by his exhortations, Martha asked her parents, "Do you mean that I can't even dance with my own brother?" "Correct!" was the response. Although Martha held her feelings in check, she admitted, "I would go to the railway station to watch the trains going east, longing for the day when I could be on my own." Sunday's praise of marriage and motherhood (and denigration of any other female endeavor) only served to increase Martha's brewing desire for independence.

As a firstborn female who received all the attention her doting parents could give, Martha gained a natural sense of herself that normally only boys during that period had the opportunity to develop. Very bright and willing to learn, "she was Dad's little girl," her brother observed. At the same time, her impassive mother presented a model to a girl with a healthy ego of what she did not want to be.

Martha's one secret idol was her stepaunt, Olive Faulk Price, her mother's half sister, an actress onboard the prosperous showboat *Water Queen* who had studied some dance. In 1910 Olive married Steven E. Price, whose father owned eight different "floating palaces" that toured up and down the Missouri River. The couple was given the *Columbia* as a wedding present, and Mrs. Price became its efficient program director.[8] Much to the mother's chagrin, Martha admired her free-spirited aunt, and yearned to be like her: "I adored her from afar! She was my inspiration about dance." Martha's brother Bill recalled, "Olive wasn't talked about because in a small Ohio town shows and dancing were wicked. My mother was quite a WCTUer [Women's Christian Temperance Union]. She never approved of her."

Determined to do well in school, Martha was an excellent student who demonstrated leadership during her high school years. She reveled in the readings of Cicero and Virgil in her Latin classes (and was the pride of her spinster aunt Ruth back in Leechburg), learned German as well as plane and solid geometry and "all the rest of it," she recalled. As a freshman at East Palestine High, Martha played "the Nurse, who lives on the campus" in the school play, *The Hero of the Grid Iron* and in her essay, "Freshman History," for the 1915 *Ephanian* she spoke for the forty-five other classmates, claiming that "we shall have climbed one rung higher on the ladder of our school life and in the three remaining years we shall endeavor to be faithful and useful helpers to our school." Grace and Grant built their own stately two-story home on Haight and Union Streets in the neighboring town of Salem, and when the family moved there in 1915, Martha began her sophomore year at Salem High School.

The *Reveille Echo* reported on 9 March 1916 that Martha was elected secretary after the formation of "high school Bible study classes" for girls to be held (at the same time as the classes for boys) on Friday nights.[9] An article in the paper on 15 April 1916 noted in the column "High School News" that the basketball girls planned to hold a party at the home of Martha Hill, where a "good time is in store for every girl who practiced." The 1916 *Ephanian* yearbook pictures Martha front and center with her sophomore class.

When the son of "EPO's" shoestore owner wanted to court her, Martha, shy around the opposite sex, would have nothing to do with him. Martha later recalled, "Every time a boy wanted to take me out my mother asked me if he was a Presbyterian."[10]

Thriving on any physical activity, Martha played team sports and was elected captain of the woman's field hockey team. The oddly indented bridge of her diminutive nose, which gave her otherwise wholesome appearance a distinction of its own, was caused by a sports accident in her junior year. Whacked by an opponent's hockey stick, she lost a front tooth and suffered a broken nose. She was hospitalized to repair a deviated septum, and the accident left her with a self-conscious habit of touching her nose that few detected throughout her life. None were privy to the knowledge that she had a false tooth except her family and her dentist.

Martha's sympathetic classmates at Salem High School elected the bright sportswoman valedictorian of their senior class, and she gallantly delivered an address "Americanization," at her graduation. To Martha's chagrin, at forty-one, Grace had unexpectedly become pregnant for a fourth time. Lewis Todd was born just as Martha was making plans to attend college. A precocious child, he was soon nicknamed by his "nanny" after "Kaiser Bill" who had terrorized Europe. However, he was legally named after Lewis Hicks, Grant's "investor who was now in the steel business." But the second son remembered that it was Gene who remained "the fair-haired boy. Dad gave him anything he wanted."

Although athletics had taken a less attractive turn, Martha continued to harbor a passion for dancing and theater, and refused an academic scholarship from the University of Ohio. "I wanted to dance. I wanted a professional school out of sheer orneriness. It was outside the pale. Dance was not the thing one did."[11] Preoccupied by the new arrival in the family, her parents finally agreed to enroll her in a program at the Battle Creek Normal School of Physical Education in Battle Creek, Michigan. "Although they did not approve of dance, they approved of learning physical education. That was okay," Bill explained. Martha Hill's life in dance began under the propriety of academics. It was her only available means for fulfilling a vague but passionate desire to express herself physically in movement.

At a period when progressive ideas were emerging among educators, the American university had begun to engage students in the process of their own education and had recast itself as a learning laboratory. Self-discipline, self-reliance, and individualism were bywords for a new generation of educators seeking a better quality of life for their students. Schools began to consider matters of the body and physical education, and later dance, as independent academic disciplines—a result of the trend to develop the "service" university.

American artists and scholars alike were highly charged by new archaeological discoveries of the savage as well as the civilized. A revival of ancient studies encouraged an appreciation for the total human being in mind, body, artistic inclinations, and expressive qualities. The American Delsarte movement taught "techniques for expression" drawn from Frenchman François Delsarte's system of developing individual abilities through gesture, posture, and movement.[12]

Increasing numbers of young women in fashionable seminaries and coeducational universities were in need of programs for every aspect of healthy living. In response, educational publications now championed the ability of dance to enlarge one's emotional life. By 1910, John Dewey (1859–1952) was the acknowledged leader of progressive change in education. Part of the antitraditional movement against formalism that was asserting itself, Dewey believed that experience shaped and directed the abilities of an individual's development. "Learn by doing," became the motto, and it was one that gave a strong advantage to dance advocates of the time.[13] Suddenly, American dance claimed its own unique history by including the practice of national folk dances as an artful expression of the beauty of the body, along with a particular passion for clogging. Dance as an art-based discipline in higher education would have to wait for Martha Hill's ideas to take shape.

The school Martha's father chose for her college education was one of three that included nursing and home economics in its curriculum. Instituted by Dr. John Harvey Kellogg, a health reformer affiliated with the Battle Creek Sanitarium, Dr. Kellogg's Temple of Health offered "an intensive course for the perfection of technical skill." Grant Hill had been called in by one of the Kelloggs to review a mining property in upstate Michigan, where he heard that the Battle Creek College's one-year school of physical education was to expand into a two-year course of study. Additionally, Grant was impressed by the Kellogg brothers' doings: Dr. Kellogg's brother Will went on to make cornflakes, the cornerstone of a multimillion-dollar breakfast food industry.

John Harvey Kellogg lectured widely and had written a sex education manual, *Plain Facts about Sexual Life*, in 1877. An eccentric who preached abstinence from alcohol and meat products, he abhorred obesity. He always dressed completely in white. "He'd lecture us in these white serge suits. I can still see him giving us a talk about how awful it was to eat meat," student Barbara Page Beiswanger recalled. "He preached sexual abstinence as well."[14] He did, however, attempt to construct a scientific foundation in his teachings, while advocating the importance of "diet, cleanliness, exercise, fresh air, and rest"—bywords of Martha's first professional training.[15]

At Battle Creek, Martha was particularly enamored of the dancing teacher, Marietta J. Lane, "a very beautiful redhead" who, according to the school catalogue, taught folk, aesthetic, and interpretative dancing as well as Swedish gymnastics, kinesiology (the physiology of movement), and a subject called "anthropometry."[16] Registering for every dance and related anatomy course offered, including physiology, physical diagnosis, medical gymnastics, and the "theory of hydrotherapy" (water treatments), Martha was particularly drawn to every sort of movement experience she could find.

Kellogg's students mixed with patients, who were called "guests." The patients were often exhausted wealthy patrons and luminaries, and all were kept busy with a regimen of sports, exercise, rest, lectures, and special treatments. These years of freeing the spirit and caring for the body, would catapult the impressionable Martha into the "dancing for health" arena. "Suddenly I found this beautiful thing in dance. . . . Instead of the body being a carnal thing, it was a beautiful instrument. Dance became a great releasing thing to me. It was related to nature, to the theater always, and not to the sports field." From then on, she would strive to make dance a recognized art form, not placed into college study under the guise of physical fitness.

Martha's first semester of college coincided with the invasion of the influenza epidemic in the fall of 1918, just as the end of World War I seemed imminent. Students were pressed into service as aides at nearby Camp Custer, a major transfer center for the army. Martha biked six miles to and from the hospital to assist the Red Cross volunteers caring for repatriated soldiers, along with many in training that had pneumonia and were dying. She recalled spending hours rolling bandages, while becoming aware of the realities of the world outside of the gymnasium. On 11 November 1918, the war was over. She felt a strange mixture of relief and mourning as parades of rejoicing passed the grim stacks of wooden boxes beside the freight trains of Battle Creek's Michigan Central tracks.

During this period, Martha enthusiastically observed the increasing numbers of "liberated" women around her who had entered the workforce as volunteers and as professionals committed to the war effort. Women's colleges, the new interest in physical culture, and the ratification of the Nineteenth Amendment in 1920 granting women the right to vote—all would press women Martha's age into a new realm of possible careers past the traditional "women's" professions of teaching or nursing. With the end of World War I, their vision was irrevocably expanded beyond provincialism. As Martha and others stepped into the world of professionals, they took advantage of expanding opportunities in an arena where women were forging their own identities.

However taken she was with dance, Martha was a very active college student at the renamed (in 1919) Kellogg School of Physical Education. She played soccer during her first year at school, and varsity basketball and hockey in the second, winning her the nickname "Trippie" in Battle Creek's 1920 yearbook *Discus*. She served as the athletic association's treasurer, associate editor of *Discus*, vice president of the "43" club (newly formed by ten dormitory mates who, after happy months together, were "forced to seek rooms in different cottages"), and was a member of the Sigma Sigma Psi Honorary Society and Delta Psi Kappa. Her senior photograph is accompanied by the following words: "Martha is one of those girls who can accomplish more in a few minutes with seemingly no effort than most people can in a week. She holds a much-to-be envied record in both theoretical and practical work—especially dancing. And the best part of it is that Martha is not the slightest bit spoiled." As a guard on the varsity basketball team, the yearbook commented on Martha's "long, lean," and "lanky" physique, adding, "She is a clean cut, steady player and always there when needed. We are betting on a successful career for Martha."

Now holding a two-year degree, Martha extended her studies for a third year, "even dissecting a cadaver" in her science laboratory work, to earn a "life teaching certificate" awarded by the state of Michigan. (Although, according to local newspapers, a local woman was teaching ballet in her private studio, there is no evidence that Martha ventured out to study with her.) While on trips to neighboring cities, however, she did encounter her first performances by professional dance companies. She recalled seeing Pavlova on her last tour, performing her *Dying Swan*; Martha was impressed by her "fiery, sensuous duets with Mikhail Mordkin" on an improvised stage in Kalamazoo, Michigan, as well as by performances by Fokine and Fokina. She later spoke of these viewings as "high points in an art that was quite dead" in the United States at that time.[17]

In the fall of 1921 Martha took over Marietta Lane's teaching position in Battle Creek College's expanded three-year curriculum as assistant in dancing and athletics. (Lane would go on to start the first exercise program at the Elizabeth Arden salon). "My very first job. I had to teach a little bit of golf or something on the side, but then I made dance so popular, I didn't have to do that."

The combination of her enthusiasm and the midwestern openness of her voice with its clear diction easily commanded attention, without the slightest hint of bossiness. One of her first students, Barbara Beiswanger, remembered the "marvelous training" that Hill gave her in ballet. "This was my first experience in dance and there I learned what it meant to find the joy of movement, led by a noted and radiant teacher."[18] Remarkably, despite her own meager studies at Kellogg in ballet, Martha was able to convey the subject with conviction and authority.

In the twenties, friendships among women were not questioned. Romances between women were considered innocent foreplay that did not preclude eventual marriage. The Great War had left campuses man-deprived. Onscreen kisses were chaste while filmmakers drew up contracts with moral clauses and played by the rules of the heartland. "It girl" Clara Bow became the flapper heroine and Parisian Coco Chanel's silk crepe chemises were copied in the Sears catalogue. Actresses such as Tallulah Bankhead, Katharine Cornell, and Greta Garbo epitomized the glamorous world of Hollywood; yet for those in the know, their lesbian experiences were just as intriguing.

Another Kellogg student (and fellow "43"er) also interested in dance was Mary Jo Shelly from Grand Rapids, Michigan, who arrived in 1919, and graduated in the spring of 1922. A witty conversationalist and a bright scholar, Mary Jo—with a tea rose complexion that revealed her English heritage and inquisitive eyes—reveled in filling notebooks with poetic references and philosophical quotes. She would become one of Martha's lifelong friends, and the single most important figure in shaping Martha's career for years to come. Intelligent and inquiring schoolmates, they sought out like minds in literature as well as the arts, and yearned to be part of New York's bohemian culture while studying body sciences in a school for women. They excitedly discussed the Woman's Peace Party of New York and its panoply of suffragists and socialists. Militant feminists of the time were characterized by the press as wearing bobbed hair and believing in relationships out of wedlock, now coined "free love." All were exhilarating ideas to Martha.

Unlike Mary Jo, once Martha left home, she had no interest in returning save for perfunctory visits to family gatherings on occasions of deaths and reunions. The few photographs of the Hill siblings together show the well-heeled Martha and Gene with their packed suitcases ready to depart, and youngster Bill playfully joining them on the front lawn. She found little need to spend time with her parents, although she kept tabs on her younger brothers, happy to offer advice or support when they asked for it.

While on Kellogg's faculty, Martha became interested in dressage and horsemanship, and at twenty-one met and fell in love with a handsome banker and polo player. Their liaison progressed happily with their shared interest in horseback riding: "I used to go to his ranch and ride." But when he suggested that their relationship might become more serious, Martha pulled back. And her brother Bill recalled: "There was another man who was an economist and a Rhodes scholar who was a next-door neighbor. She didn't want anything to do with him either." Marrying and settling down to a life of domesticity was the farthest thing from her mind, particularly at a time when a woman's marriage meant her contract would be terminated in many school systems. Martha's career would be over.

With sure skill for organization, while in Michigan, Martha also trained children in ballet classes and choreographed extravaganzas at Goguage Lake's summer festivals in Battle Creek. A willing worker, Martha tie-dyed vats of fabric, directed mothers with the sewing, and kept track of huge orders from Chicago costume houses as she organized and helped stage the panoramas and sketches, moving large ensembles with numbers of small children, dressed as dragonflies and fairies.

Martha answered an advertisement for a job at the Kansas State Teachers College of Hays, Kansas (now Fort Hays State University), and was hired as director of physical education for women for the fall of 1923. Most likely her experience with children at Goguage Lake made her an attractive candidate for the position. Her Kansas curriculum vitae states that in preparation, she took correspondence courses "at Columbia and with the Vestoff-Serova Russian School of Dancing."

During this period, physical education teachers, encouraged by their institutions, routinely attended refresher courses during summer sessions in order to stay current with rapid changes in dance pedagogy. To improve her skills as a technician, Martha traveled to the Rocky Mountain Dancing Camp (soon to be retitled Perry-Mansfield School of the Theater and Dance) in Steamboat Springs, Colorado. There she studied ballet with Edna McRae, who had been trained by Adolph Bolm. (Edna's vivid recollection of Martha that summer was of "our tennis games on the old concrete court. Why this is so, I do not know, for my skill at tennis was nil."[1] And then there was horsemanship with Charlotte Perry, and movement technique with Portia Mansfield, who combined Louis H. Chalif–inspired Russian ballet with her own "plastic Greek and interpretive work," according to a 1921 tour reviewer.[2]

Martha's new job at Kansas State was on a campus established in 1902 that consisted of several imposing granite-block buildings set on a desolate stretch of plains. Her terrain became the massive gymnasium, well fortified with Swedish gymnastics apparatus, including barbells and Indian wands. The Picken Hall auditorium contained a small but elegant proscenium stage and an apron large enough for a six-foot concert grand. The college's 1924 yearbook,

Reveille, stated, "Miss Hill took charge of the department this year, but in this short time has won the love and admiration of every girl on the campus." It is clear from the many photographs of Dutch dances, parades of wooden soldiers, and cakewalks on its "dancing" pages, that competitive sports quickly became a sideline activity after her arrival.

One of Martha's responsibilities was to create dances for the Festival Week of "music, dance and oratorio." In spring 1924 the new 3,500-seat Sheridan Coliseum, designed as "a mecca for music lovers" was completed, in time for the festival's sixth season, under the music direction of Henry Edward Malloy, whom Martha greatly admired. Billed in its program as "a marvelous array of talent singing western Kansas into tune," it opened the Easter week with Handel's *Elijah* and closed with his *Messiah,* sung by a participating chorus of 531. Martha's contribution was a three-act "aesthetic dance program," *The Kingdom of Happiness: A May Day Fantasy.*

A mammoth project with a huge cast, the nearly two-page program synopsis describes children gathering in celebration to perform sword and maypole dances. In act 2, the children's search leads them into foreign lands where they watch dances performed in wooden shoes, a traditional Mexican dance, a Saint-Saëns mazurka, and a Russian bridal dance to music by Tchaikovsky—all performed by Martha's college student group. Act 3 contains sequences called "Spirit of the Sea" (set to music by Debussy); "The Flowers" and "The Butterflies" (music by Grieg); and concludes with a sunset scene (music by Dvořák. "People came from all over the plains of Kansas in buckboards, wagons, and trucks to the events," Martha recalled, "with room and board and nursery care available for weeklong visitors."

During her three years at Kansas State, Martha maintained a heavy teaching schedule. She also conducted long hours of rehearsals where she organized group sequences and transitions around the dances by Veronine Vestoff and Sonia Serova (deciphering from their instruction manuals, which arrived by mail from Manhattan, complete with costume designs and sheet music.)[3] By today's standards one might view the Russian couple as charlatans, but such long-distance mentorships were common during that period. "We study a pupil's physique [through photographs sent with applications], and we know she can do some things and can't do others. We fit our routine to the dancer's body, and she is made a better dancer," Vestoff explained to a writer for *The Dance Magazine.*[4]

Between semesters, Martha traveled to Chicago to improve her ballet technique with Edna McRae, who had established a school there in 1923. But with little time to create her own choreographic steps and no idea about how to start the process, what artistic encouragement she received was from two new colleagues the next year: an assistant, Edith Ballwebber, who had been a former student of Martha's from Kellogg; and a lanky, bespectacled pianist, Mark Hoffman, who had just been hired by the music department. After graduating from Chicago Musical College, Mark had spent a year studying and concertizing in Berlin, and another as head of the piano department at Lethbridge Conservatory in Alberta, Canada.

The fun-to-be-with musician with a gadfly personality also served as Martha's recital pianist, and he became her "dear friend." (Ironically, their romance somewhat mirrored a more significant one then taking place between a pianist and a dancer: Louis Horst and Martha Graham.[5] Unlike Horst, however, whose zealous crusade against romanticism affected Graham, Hoffman seemed to have no particular interest in modernizing Hill's ideas about music and dance.) Later, she casually mentioned that she always "had boyfriends in relation to her work." Her first year in Kansas had been lonely, but with Hoffman she could share her enthusiasm for the arts.

Now titled "professor" and sporting a bobbed haircut, Martha faced another major production assignment. In April 1925, the Kansas State Teachers College Bulletin announced that in conjunction with that year's music festival, Martha Hill would direct "an elaborate interpretative or classic dance" with costuming, lighting effects, and the dance itself . . . worked out with a degree of finesse not often found in amateur productions." Its success no doubt influenced Martha's confidence and spawned her desire to stage performance series and festivals throughout her career.

The production was again in three sections with part 1 taking place in "somebody else's garden." Part 2 was a Greek festival at Olympia, complete with sacrificial ceremonies. During this production in the huge Sheridan Coliseum, Mark or her music director Malloy might have discussed Stravinsky's *Sacre du Printemps* (produced by Diaghilev's Ballets Russes more than a decade earlier) with Martha; if they did, however, what had set the European dance world on fire had evidently not reached Kansas. (That same year, Louis Horst was frustrated by the same lack of interest among musicians in Vienna.)

Martha relied on Serova's "famous composers of dance creations" for her routines, along with some studies by Portia Mansfield such as her *Rhythmic Games;* she also choreographed a piece to Schubert's *Unfinished* Symphony. Of the many dance sections Martha staged, only a solo, *Columbine que Flirte,* was credited to Denishawn, which by this time was another popular resource selling dance studies of its own. Part 3 ends the evening in "The Toy Shop" where "dolls and toys waken and there is a gay frolic."[6] In a 1989 interview, when

Agnes de Mille scolded her for being so incredulously innocent about the ballet scene before 1925, Martha meekly confessed that she was "putting things together for myself," barely aware of Denishawn either.

Steeped in her college commitments, that year's yearbook praised Martha for having "greatly increased the course of study of the Physical Education Department" and raising the requirements for majors and minors.[7] This time the dance photographs show women in tutus, in tunics carrying garlands, and children in rabbit costumes. With the production finished, totally exhausted, both Edith and Martha went off to Perry-Mansfield in the Rockies for the summer.

The spring semester of 1926 would be the last one in Kansas for both Martha and Mark. Martha had continued to arrange dances in Scottish kilts and baroque costumes on a seesaw. But, although she appreciated Malloy's high praise for her work in his extravaganzas, teaching in the stern atmosphere of the physical education department had disenchanted her of working in a vaudevillian format. Having strengthened his repertoire, Mark presented a solo recital as part of the 1926 music festival, playing Schubert, Brahms, Granados, and John Alden Carpenter. Although he was made "professor of piano and composition" and was obviously a great asset to the music department, like Martha he suffered from wanderlust. The two commiserated about their futures. Vowing to seek a more challenging life in the arts, Mark accepted another teaching position at the University of Mississippi and Martha ventured east on her own.

Martha may have been searching for a fresh start as a "proper" student, but she could never quite release herself from the urge to combine her love of music with her attraction to the formality of ballet. The geometry at their roots and their logical methodologies of patterning made them "safe" territories. Her appreciation of their abstract qualities, devoid of emotional expression, seemed to suit her persona. Perhaps for the same reason, she loved to square dance.

Passionate outbursts were to be controlled: sentimentality and affectation embarrassed Martha and would continue to do so throughout her life. ("I never saw her cry," one of Martha's closest friends confessed.) Her tendency to pull away from confrontation also kept her behind the scenes as a performer. It would not be appropriate for a teacher to perform with her students, she reasoned. Sadly, except for classroom demonstrations on the lawns and the gymnasiums at Kellogg, Martha had not yet ventured in front of an audience.

Martha's family had moved to Versailles a year earlier: "right in the center of Missouri, halfway between Kansas City and St. Louis, near the Begnall Dam where they were mining for lead and zinc. Our house on North High Street was not too far from town," Bill recollected. Gene went to the University of Missouri in Columbia for a year in preparation for West Point. "I remember him coming home once or twice," Bill said. He saw even less of Martha. "I think I knew them as siblings, in a sense. But they'd visit for a couple of days and then were gone." One of his few recollections of Martha was when he was five: she and Edith Ballwebber stayed for a few days on their way back from Chicago. They had purchased fabrics and leotards in the city, and spent their stay "doing a lot of dying of clothes, hanging them to dry in the backyard," Bill remembered.

Despite misgivings, in the summer of 1926 Grant Hill surprised his daughter by "staking" her to a full three months of dance study in New York City. If her father worried that dance was the work of the devil, he had nonetheless given her five hundred dollars with reluctant approval. Still, "He never let people know that I was a dancer. It was never his subject of conversation or of announcement," Martha told Teresa Bowers in 1979. Twenty-five-year-old Martha stayed at the Three Arts Club on West Eighty-fifth Street, every day checking the job notices posted in its lobby. After a brief hire by a film company for a day shoot, in which she donned a bathing suit and lounged at a pool on Long Island, she found a teaching position at Saint Bartholomew Community House to help pay room and board.[8] Martha would manage to earn enough to extend her stay in New York City to almost a year.

Martha began taking ballet lessons at Louis Chalif's studio at his Temple of Terpsichore on West Fifty-seventh Street, which he claimed was one of the first ballet schools established in the United States.[9] As a subscriber to *Dance Lovers Magazine,* she knew of his reputation as the president of the American Society of Teachers of Dancing and of his prominence as an "authority on the art of terpsichore," which occupied "undoubtedly one of the most magnificent studios of dancing in the world."[10] Having studied Chalif's five textbooks on her own and tackled more of his "600 Clearly Described Dances" (as advertised in the magazine that July), she was ready to seek out other studios.[11]

Also having completed a series of lessons-by-mail with one of Pavlova's Russian partners, Konstantin Kobeleff, Martha was invited to a two-week intensive program that was part of his Normal Course for Teachers of Dancing, which she thought was "very effective." But she was suddenly apprehensive when confronted with the competition in Manhattan. Because of her height in pointe shoes, Martha, at five-feet-seven in stocking feet, began to realize the improbability of her ever going on the ballet stage. Still, Kobeleff helped her to gain confidence. "He liked me very much."

"I also studied with Vestoff and Serova, as somebody who didn't know much about ballet might have done." Although welcomed into their 47 West Seventy-second Street studio to learn "dances of all descriptions," as a teacher who had been one of their best "home study" customers, Martha soon began to doubt the validity of their profitable enterprise. Trained under the tutelage of his father who had been a ballet master in various Moscow theaters, Vestoff had left Russia in 1910 to become a solo dancer with the Metropolitan Opera House. He started teaching in California, then Chicago, and finally New York. "He gives the best in him to the many ambitious girls who come to him for instruction," a writer for *The Dance Magazine* wrote in July 1926, quoting him as saying, "American girls are excellent dancers. They understand quickly and are strong, but they are cursed with impatience. . . . Dancing holds a wonderful promise of a career for a woman, I think . . . the girl who studies with the idea of teaching others will find a tremendous field."[12] (He could have been speaking directly to Martha Hill.) Years later, when de Mille compared notes with her on their early training, Martha defended Vestoff to de Mille's outrage: "I was his best dancer. He loved me, so I loved studying with him. He was very good to me." De Mille retorted that his teaching was "very careless!"[13]

Martha continued to scout out new teachers, at first more interested in improving her pedagogy than in mastering her own skills as a dancer. "I saw other people at the East Fifty-ninth Street building where Kobeleff and Luigi Albertieri taught," she explained, believing that much of what she learned was by observation. "I think you're born with a bent toward teaching, because teaching is a sharing with somebody else. You observe what works and what doesn't work in your own schooling."[14]

Observation rather than participation also meant that while Martha saved money by not actually taking class, she also realized how far behind she was technically. She soon made her way to the Carnegie Hall studios, where she studied "free" expression with "Isadorable" Anna Duncan, having attended her first appearance at the Guild Theatre. ("Her simple and natural form of classic dancing" made her "the loveliest and most classical of the Duncan dancers," according to *The Dance Magazine*.)[15] Bird Larsen was another "great person in the early days of modern dance who taught in that building," and Martha very much admired her work.

Part of the education in Manhattan that her father never guessed he was paying for was Martha's social awakening, contributing to her sense of herself as a young artist. By eating at the counter at Child's in the Village or the self-serve Automat on Fifty-seventh Street and walking everywhere, Martha managed to save enough to see talkies such as *The Jazz Singer* (with Al Jolson crooning "Toot, Toot, Tootsie" in blackface), along with Broadway's latest shows. "I could go to Grey's Drug Store at Times Square at one o'clock and pick up a ticket for the second balcony of any theater for under a dollar! I went to everything!"[16]

In the summer of 1926, Martha and Mary Jo teamed up again to continue their degree work at Teachers College, Columbia University, moving into a campus dormitory room "on the fire escape and opposite the elevator shaft" at Whittier Hall on New York City's Amsterdam Avenue. Mary Jo, having just completed her B.A. at the University of Oregon, where she had been an instructor since 1924, now began working on a master's degree. She planned to return to Oregon as director of the physical education department. Both understood the importance of maintaining their connection within an "old-girl" gymnasium system—one that would guarantee their security as single-woman professionals. "Instead of a hateful field filled with dull gymnastics and sports, a really alive field of brilliant, remarkable groups of women were administrators of physical education. At first, most coming out of Boston," Martha explained, referring to Sargent School of Physical Education (originally Dudley Sargent Boston Normal School of Gymnastics).

At Teachers College, Martha, Mary Jo, and their Kellogg and University of Oregon colleague Edith Ballwebber enrolled into Gertrude Colby's program in the School of Practical Arts within the physical education department. The school's catalog that year listed a variety of movement classes, with a heavy dose of physical exercise for health, physiology, and applied anatomy along with Colby's natural dancing and problems in natural dancing.[17] Classmates who would graduate in 1927 and go on to teach at the college were Mabel Ellsworth Todd and Lulu Sweigard, both becoming major influences to dance educators. Dance studies included clogging and "original" etudes demonstrating "free rhythms and techniques with scarves, spirals, and body swaying" to music by Beethoven and Schubert. Colby's classes used musical structures as compositional models, paralleling phrases, accents, and climaxes for dance content—ideas that Martha had been using in her own teaching for several years.

That November, the daughter of a friend of her father's gave Hill a ticket to see Martha Graham's second recital in Manhattan at the Klaw Theatre on West Forty-fifth Street. The seventeen short works on the program interspersed Graham's solos to music by Scriabin and Satie that gave an indication of what was to come. In this historic concert, her trio of women performed interlude pieces to Mendelssohn and in *Alt-Wien* to music arranged by Louis Horst. The aforementioned reviewer for *The Dance Magazine*, who had praised Anna Duncan, in the same article pronounced that Graham's "talent is for making pictures." He added that the work of this "blessed damozel . . . from Rochester" was "pretty but lacked force."[18] These words certainly must have provoked some antagonism from the ever soul-searching choreographer.

But what Martha saw at the Klaw Theatre changed her life. "It was instant conversion! That was it," she explained. "I realized it was possible to communicate serious ideas in movement. It was what I was looking for." Long after the performance was over, she found herself walking the streets of New York, far from the theater, so moved she scarcely knew where she was, Hill told a friend. She immediately sought out lessons with Graham at the John Murray Anderson–Robert Milton School of the Theatre on East Fifty-eighth Street. Louis Horst accompanied class at the piano. He would become a much-requested musician among dancers, soon playing for the German expressionists Yvonne Georgi and Harald Kreutzberg and American newcomers now giving solo recitals, including Agnes de Mille and Helen Tamiris as well as Graham. A charmer and guardian of young women, he befriended Martha Hill.[19] He also saw to it that she was counseled against threats of city life—and that career-killer for all dancers: marriage. Hill knew from dressing-room conversations that Graham and Horst were lovers. (Louis had suffered from a failed marriage, a "mistake" made in his Denishawn days.)[20] Graham would later reveal, "All of my life I have been a devotee of sex, in the right sense of the word. Fulfillment, as opposed to procreation, or I would have had children. . . . I couldn't control being a dancer. I knew I had to choose between a child and dance, and I chose dance."[21] (This point of view would become Martha Hill's as well.) Although Louis liked to pronounce that he and Graham "lived together," he also praised the glories of a single toothbrush in his bachelor quarters. Louis had a room at the Great Northern Hotel across from Carnegie Hall; Graham, a studio with a tiny alcove for sleeping on Fifth Avenue at Tenth Street, one of a series of Spartan abodes she would inhabit over the next few years.

"Graham was doing things straight out of Miss Ruth's Denishawn," Hill remembered. Sitting cross-legged on a little platform in a Chinese robe as her mentor Miss Ruth had done, Graham had her students practice at the barre and work on "the calls" crossing the floor as well as more lyrical phrases. But Martha Hill was most struck by the personal, emotional core of Graham's teaching.

Martha Hill's years of dry university teaching in Michigan and Kansas had only increased her desire to devote her life to dance. Now her stay in Manhattan had widened her view of the world both aesthetically and emotionally. In this freer environment, where women openly maintained liaisons with women and men with men, Martha felt more comfortable in her own relationship with Mary Jo.

Distinctions between deep friendship and overt sexual partnering had suddenly come into focus in the theater scene with Edouard Bourdet's new play, *The Captive*. In it, lesbian love "walked out on the New York stage." The conservative press now had a cause and a headliner. The *New York American*'s was "Wipe Out Those Evil Plays Now Menacing the Future of Theater."[22] The Society for the Suppression of Vice closed the show. A month later, the New York State Supreme Court ruled that the stage must not portray "grossly immoral human emotions." Soon afterward the Penal Code of 1909 was amended to bar plays dealing with sexual degeneracy or sex perversion.

Martha, Mary Jo, and their friends were alarmed when the more relaxed social mood of the Roaring Twenties that had encouraged freedom of expression was suddenly threatened. These women who had managed to separate from the Victorian mores of their childhood now felt the threat of conservative backlash. Having escaped the harsh moral climate that Martha had so detested in East Palestine, she now witnessed outright oppression of another set of ideals that had become important to her.[23]

Martha had been a servant to the passion of others: her parents, Kellogg in Michigan, and Malloy in Kansas. Now she had found Martha Graham who, fearing nothing, fiercely fought for her own beliefs as an artist. Graham was the role model she had been searching for.

In weighing her chances of a successful career as a professional dancer, Martha analyzed her own natural gifts as a mover. "I was a jumper, with a lighter, springy quality—an allegro dancer with a long back. I had trouble with adagio movements, and weighted actions. I struggled with leg extensions. My développés were not particularly high. I had good feet and I was taller than most. I think I was a competent dancer but my ballet background always seemed to get in the way." Frustrated with her limitations, but determined not to admit failure to her parents, Martha observed that others took menial jobs such as waitressing in order to continue as a dancer, something she was unwilling to do. Her self-doubt was compounded by an inability to release the passion she felt into the movement she loved—a requisite that she knew existed in the best dancers. Ever practical, she also knew that her ability as a college teacher was still her most promising asset, giving her a respectable profession that made a decent wage.

However much Martha savored the theories of the progressive educators John Dewey and Harold Rugg as she raced from classroom to studio, by the end of the 1927 spring semester her money had run out. No doubt at Mary Jo's recommendation, Martha was called to a job interview with the dean of the University of Oregon. "We talked and talked very excitedly about Oregon. I'd never been that far west. He offered me a job. My credentials were a little more impressive because I had a musical background, and I was intellectually interested in what was going on in the arts." At the same time Elizabeth Arden had offered her a job, recommended by Marietta Lane. "Elizabeth was keeping me dangling a bit, holding out the opportunity maybe of going to London, or her shops in Paris—where I'd [also] never been—but I thought 'bird in hand,' so I went to Oregon. I needed to make a living so that I could [return] to study with Martha. It was my meal ticket."[24]

As she was crossing the country anyway that summer, Martha decided to take a summer course at the University of Wisconsin with the prominent dance education figure Margaret (Marge) Newell H'Doubler, wanting to experience her teaching methods.[25] H'Doubler supporters praised their master teacher's ability to nurture creativity and to relieve the "stress" of producing "concert dancers which has cursed dance studios for years." Not a dancer herself, but a physical educator, "H'Doubler was never really a fan of dance as an art form," biographer Janis Ross writes. H'Doubler had been told in 1921 by "a very image-conscious interim president" that "he would not have the university known as 'a dancing school.' After that, the studio was never thought of as a stage, but as a space for movement."[26]

But the experience for Hill was negative: "The summer confirmed my belief in Martha Graham. At Wisconsin, they never used anything below their waists. Everything was arms. No torso. That would be too erotic. I liked [H'Doubler] when I got old enough to be more generous, but I disliked very much the way she sentimentalized what she did. That was what we were against . . . what we were breaking down."[27]

Martha traveled by rail to Oregon to begin the fall term, greeted by her colleague Mary Jo, with whom she would share living quarters. Together, they took on teaching responsibilities in "rhythmic work" and envisioned the brave new direction dance might take. In the meantime, Martha planned her own courses. Their discussions were all the more poignant when they received the news from France of Isadora Duncan's tragic death. (When her scarf caught in the wheel of a roadster, her neck snapped). In a clever move to show the way "by contrast," Martha and Mary Jo arranged a week's visit by H'Doubler to the campus: students were polite, but not impressed.

One of them was the former student of Martha's from Battle Creek, Barbara Beiswanger, who moved on to the University of Oregon at the same time and remembered her good fortune at finding Martha on the faculty there. "Martha

Hill greatly inspired me with her philosophical approach, on top of the anatomical, physiological, and psychological approaches to dance. [She] emphasized the elements of dance and the understanding of the musical structure, which she beautifully presented to her students so that we had a good musical background as well as an understanding of movement and dance."[28]

Martha's demeanor as a college teacher now exuded independence and she knew the importance of one's appearance. On a very limited budget, she chose her wardrobe and hairstyle as carefully as she chose her friends. Her long limbs, square shoulders, and uncomplicated good looks gave her the attributes of a fashion model. She created a sophisticated persona for herself, with the individuality of a young Katharine Hepburn (minus the trousers). Although she made her living teaching in gymnasiums, Martha emulated the style of the "white-gloved" faculty women with whom she taught—a necessity for commanding respect. Practiced in every detail, she slipped into smartly designed jersey dance attire for studio teaching.

Dance student Bessie Schönberg recalled that Martha was "lovely to be with and lovely to look at" and "a quite different person from her predecessor."[29] Having taken a course in

> clumsy tunics of heavy rayon jersey and bands across our foreheads . . . [and] many classes spent in how to handle yards of chiffon, I learned that a new, young teacher was expected . . . and that she was a modern dancer from New York. It was in everlasting gratitude that this turned out to be Martha Hill. . . . Fresh from her studies with Martha Graham, she had made a transition in her dance thinking and . . . was deeply caught up in this new direction . . . discovering movement in the body and the spine. She was lithe and quick . . . very well put together. She imbued her body with strength and elegance, in a very fluid and beautiful way. A very stimulating teacher, [she was] down-to-earth, straightforward and very alive. She insisted on correctives and discipline. And move we did. The great lesson that Martha Hill taught us [was] to learn to love to move, to learn to move with exuberance, with passion, with speed, with control. . . . Everything was possible.[30]

In the summer of 1928, Martha went with Mary Jo to the University of Chicago, where she taught technique and took an aesthetics course with De-Witt H. Parker. "Wherever I went I took courses. It was like money in the bank," she later explained. The pair then returned to Manhattan, both heading back for more coursework at Columbia's Teachers College, and to Graham's studio to take classes. (Mary Jo decided after a few lessons that dance was not her calling.)

Martha found that Graham's technical style had significantly changed:

When I first came to Graham, it was a little simpler, because she was closer then to her Denishawn days; but when I came back from out west, it was terribly exciting to see all these changes. [Graham] gradually built the idea of discovering, not inventing, and the idea of an economy of means. She would do less and less to say more and more. We danced on a dime, doing most of the class on about four-foot square, just the stride of our feet, using the torso, thrusting the torso, throwing the leg across, and wrenching ourselves, experimenting, cutting down. At the end of the class she would let us go running around the room like maenads—mad figures running to be released.

The concert scene, too, was growing to swift adulthood. John Martin began writing about dance for the *New York Times* in 1927. Helen Tamiris, ever committed to social justice, had produced her first *Dance Moods* solo concert in 1927. Doris Humphrey was about to break away from her Denishawn roots: she would soon premier her classic *Water Study* (a group work in silence inspired by the ebb and flow of ocean waves) in her first independent concert.

That summer, while working toward a Bachelor of Science degree, Martha pecked away at Columbia's required core academics. Sharpening her own philosophic view in an end-of-term paper for Professor John Gassner's popular course in theater history, she substantiated her view that dance must establish itself as a separate art form. In "A Study on the Nature of the Dance," she wrote, "Until it has realized more of its own potentialities, it cannot bring a worthy contribution to the other arts. It should establish itself as a pure art, accomplishing a unity and simplicity of expression through the use of its medium, the human body, in dance forms that take into consideration the principles of form, balance, contrast, evolution, and organic unity. . . . and yet there must be much more than form. A dance must be the embodiment of a desire, expressed through a sensuous medium yet transcending its necessary form and becoming communicable to others by virtue of its unity, clarity, and objectivity of expression."[31]

In appreciation of her contributions as a faculty member at the University of Oregon, Martha was appointed an assistant professor, "without a degree," when she returned for a second year of teaching. By then, she had clarified her ideas about the art she was determined to serve. Still, Martha remained firm in her desire to return to Manhattan, "all the while writing back and forth and saving money so that I could return to the city."

PART II

New Dance

Dancing with Graham, 1929–1931

Along with Mary Jo and Bessie, savings in hand, Martha did finally venture back to Manhattan the next summer, at the beginning of the major economic depression of 1929. Yet Martha was
joyful: "These were exciting times. We were avid to learn anything in any art.
We went to concerts and galleries. We taught, talked, and lived dance." Martha's
range of cultural interests had grown considerably since her last stay two years
earlier. This time, with Mary Jo, she thrived in Manhattan's cosmopolitan
world and its arts and ideas, admiring Edward Steichen's photographs, reading
F. Scott Fitzgerald and André Malraux, intrigued by Marlene Dietrich's films,
absorbing New York's panoply of choices—hearing jazz in Harlem one night
and attending Yiddish theater in lower Manhattan the next.

As Prohibition was not repealed until 1933, Martha's social life in college
circles consisted of "dry" soirees and innocent evenings with friends who, like
her, had developed a taste for tobacco. Nonetheless, gin or hard cider would
often appear, courtesy of a local bootlegger, and somebody always seemed to
know of a parlor down a back alley where hard liquor was available. Despite
soapbox preachers' warnings, the 1920s brought a fun-loving easiness to the
social scene, with dance marathons, Charleston competitions, and escapes to
boisterous roadside inns in Ford Model As complete with rumble seats.

But the mood of the country was increasingly bleak, with thousands of jobs
disappearing every day. With political corruption and organized crime critically undermining police departments, illicit drinking establishments proliferated, and legally proscribed sex between men was virtually ignored. If Martha
was a prime example of President Hoover's cry for self-reliance and individual
initiative—the very ethos of white, Protestant culture—she was one of the fortunate ones, and she knew it. When the apple-shippers' association came up
with the scheme to sell apples to the unemployed on credit at $1.75 a crate, six
thousand peddlers appeared on the street corners of New York City, hawking
apples at a nickel apiece. Into the early 1930s, with hunger strikes, lynchings,
and mob violence making headlines, the situation became dire. Still, the Depression was not so great a hardship for artists, according to Louis Horst, because they lived on practically nothing anyway.

In that summer of 1929, soon after the trio arrived in New York City, Graham invited Martha Hill into her company of women. There she reveled in the
exhilaration of rigorous rehearsals where Graham and her group explored new

movement ideas. Her work as a dancer with Graham would become the most significant influence in her life: "It was cultish in a way, I suppose, a kind of hero worship, but not holding her aloof. I could have gone to Doris, I could have stayed with ballet, I could have done other things, but the minute I went to Martha [Graham] I just said, 'Here I am. I believe in you.' This was what I'd been looking for—the look, the aesthetic, the belief behind the look. We never questioned Martha [Graham] about her approach to her art. We were much more imbued with a higher spirit. I ate and slept dance. It was a passion."

Martha's first year as a dancer working on the concert scene was very productive. "We had input in what Martha [Graham] was doing. She let us improvise. . . . It was such fun. We would take an idea, Martha would do something and we'd do something. [Graham's] early movement seemed right artistically . . . what she was saying and the way she was saying it."

Graham had earlier created political statements in her solos *Revolt* (1927) and *Immigrant: Steerage: Strike* (1928). When Martha Hill joined the group, she learned *Heretic* and *Vision of the Apocalypse,* dances that had premiered at the Booth Theatre on 14 April 1929. She understood Horst's influence on Graham, and credited his fascination for the German artists Käthe Kollwitz and George Grosz for the "violent things [Graham] was doing."

The first thing Martha learned in the studio was *Prelude to a Dance* to a Honegger score. It was not unusual for Graham to experiment and set materials on her group before distilling the final product into a solo for herself. This work led to her 1929 solo, *Dance,* a "clarion call of her new thinking," according to Bessie Schönberg, who described it as "credo" made up of action only between the shoulders and knees. "Martha Hill used to say, 'She looks as if she dared anybody to move her feet.'" Watching the dance from the wings would be a revelatory experience that both dancers never forgot.[1]

But Martha Hill's first big appearance was as one of the Oppressors with Graham in the title role of *Heretic,* set to Horst's arrangement of an old Breton song, repeated six times. "The group makes a phalanx, shoulder to shoulder, tight against Martha, she would come and beg us, we would break and wait, and make a shape, then rise into relevé and burst out into the next movement. At the end Martha [falls] down, the group again forms a phalanx, and with the thumping of our heels, it was very exciting to be part of. Louis rehearsed us. He was a very good and very tough rehearsal director. Every arm, every head had to be just so."

If Graham's *Heretic* had completed her stylistic voyage toward a limited movement palette, it was also shaped by the limitations of her dancers' bodies. Most were trained within a physical education regime and possessed strong thighs and torsos but little foot articulation or ability for leg extension. Chore-ographing for their limited movement range meant flexed feet stepping per-cussively onto the floor and simple but dramatically timed gestures performed for the group held in tight unison as a foil against Graham's outcast figure. The precursor of such later works as *Primitive Mysteries, Heretic* set the look of soloist against chorus in Greek mode (also used in the stark "breadline" cross-ings in "Steps in the Street" from *Chronicle* in 1935). It would be a composi-tional technique that Graham used for years to come to frame the central choreographic action of solos and duets.

While others in the Group had families or husbands to support them, Hill was one of the few on her own financially. To tide her over during the summer months, she taught dance several afternoons a week to immigrant children at Greenwich House in the Village, much like her earlier job at Saint Bartholo-mew's. Confident that cultural barriers could be crossed through movement, she taught Irish clog dancing, country reels, and American square dancing. Al-though few of her students understood English, Martha delighted in watching them perform these dances as enthusiastic young Americans.

In the fall of 1929, Mary Jo joined the faculty of Teachers College as an instructor teaching the theory and practice of dance. Taking an apartment at 32 Washington Square West, Martha happily joined her as her roommate. If Shelly preferred the company of women and harbored a romantic interest in Martha during those years, this proximity guaranteed, if not intimacy, then the ability to maintain their close friendship. Perceptions about women living to-gether were changing radically, with "lavender marriages" now a drawing-room topic. With the 1928 publication of Radclyffe Hall's *The Well of Loneliness,* the "veil of silence" was suddenly lifted: women's love for women was now actually labeled "lesbian." During the early 1930s, in contrast to today's redefined atti-tudes, college women did not overtly seek a particular lifestyle or want to be categorized because of their love lives even if they did display lesbian behavior.[2] Such was particularly true of Martha, who would never give the slightest indi-cation that her relationship with Mary Jo was anything more than platonic, al-though others assumed that they were a couple over the next fourteen years.

Needing to earn a living, Martha applied for a job teaching physical educa-tion to junior and senior high school students at Teachers College's experi-mental Lincoln School. Not officially hired until the 1930–31 academic year, she recalled having to "push" because she didn't have a union card in public ed-ucation.[3] "They kept me dangling. I made up my mind. I'd say, 'Either tell me yes or tell me no because I've got to get something else.' I was then dancing with Martha [Graham] and I needed a job to maintain myself in New York, and this was the best possible job one could think of in the city." She explained, "I was able to do that because school was out at three-thirty in the afternoon, and then I would go and take class at Martha [Graham's] and we'd have late rehearsals."[4]

But other conflicts arose. Martha Hill would finally learn about Stravinsky's *Le Sacre du Printemps* firsthand when Léonide Massine came to audition the company in his search for a chorus of nineteen women. Graham was to dance the role of the Chosen Maiden for performances at the Metropolitan Opera House in April 1930. "I was chosen but had to give it up or give up my job, which I would have been glad to do, but in those days it was an ethical responsibility and you couldn't drop out . . . midyear."[5]

"I began to work myself out of ballet via music," Martha Hill explained, by discovering Emile Jaques-Dalcroze's eurythmics. She began to study with Elsa Findlay and Nellie Reuschel at the Institute of Musical Art, which was later to become the Juilliard School of Music. This study of movement in relation to music involved a system of rhythmic exercises designed to increase feeling for movement inherent in music. It was a method that Martha found helpful in her teaching for years to come. "Elsa amused me because she would say, 'You there, you Graham,' because I'd absorbed enough of Graham at that point that she recognized it, and I said, 'Miss Findlay, I wish Martha Graham would think that,' because I was having a very difficult time working out of the ballet idiom into Martha [Graham's] style of movement."[6]

Martha continued to work with Graham in a whirlwind of rehearsals, experimenting with "inner feelings" through improvisations with "sounds, words, intensities of emotion, and qualities of energy," after which the choreographer, according to Dorothy Bird, abstracted for "essence" to give these experiments form.[7] Alongside Hill, the large company of women included Louise Creston, Ailes Gilmour (who was sculptor Isamu Noguchi's sister; their Irish mother worked as a seamstress for Graham), Betty Macdonald, Evelyn Sabin, and Rosina Savelli (the original three dancers who had been with Graham from 1926), as well as Bessie Schönberg (who suffered a knee injury shortly after the season, sadly ending her performing career). Soon after, Gertrude Shurr (a dancer with a degree from Sargent in physical education), would become a strong influence on Graham's developing technique and Anna Sokolow (drawn from Graham's and Horst's first classes at the Neighborhood Playhouse) joined the Group. Graham was "very clairvoyant, very humanly aware of the feelings and experiences of the people in her company," Hill recalled.

The Group diligently prepared for an ambitious week of shared concerts at the Maxine Elliott Theatre, produced by the new "coalition of forces"

(Humphrey, Tamiris, Weidman, and de Mille), under the name of Dance Repertory Theatre. The idea of a shared concert series was initiated by Tamiris, who wanted to create a producing unit for modern dance. As pianist, Horst enthusiastically joined Tamiris as cofounder in this first attempt to organize and bring various aspects of American dance to the public. He recalled, "It was a very vibrant period—very historical because we tried to get together. It kept me busy! I was playing for all of them, going from Martha Graham's studio to every other."[8] Hill shared Horst's enthusiasm for the project: "It was really a great community feeling as we worked together to make something happen."

Graham and her dancers prepared *Moment Rustica, Visions of the Apocalypse, Sketches from the People,* and *Heretic* for different programs, as well as *Project in Movement for a Divine Comedy,* based on William Blake's illustrations for Dante's *Inferno.* Graham, still fairly inexperienced as an ensemble choreographer, was beset by problems in *Project* rehearsals, a situation made worse by lack of a score to lean on. Horst later asserted the work to be Graham's only one choreographed in silence, although originally a "conductorless" orchestra was to have accompanied the piece. Schönberg remembered that when they got together, it didn't work. Too late: the only thing left was to perform it in silence. Of the Group's ensemble works, the 1929 *Heretic* received excellent press, with the *New York Telegram* reporting "cheers and bravos at the fall of the curtain."[9] But it was Graham's powerful solo—her "dance of sorrows" *Lamentation* to an Anton Kodály score—that was clearly the highlight of the season.

If personally gratified by the critical success her own work received, Graham nonetheless felt the "intense criticism of the esthetic purpose of the organization."[10] These shared concerts would mark the beginning of her choreographic rivalry with Doris Humphrey who, as a dancer, had been St. Denis's favored darling of Denishawn, much to Graham's chagrin. But Doris and the then titled "Doris Humphrey, Charles Weidman and the Concert Group" also had entered into this project wearily.[11] She wrote to her parents on 29 October 1929, "It has seemed necessary to incorporate, and of course I hate that idea because organization has come to be such a hateful thing. . . . And besides I haven't much faith in Martha Graham. She is a snake if there ever was one. In spite of all misgivings, it is the best thing to do—the thing is to be ready for double crossing."[12] Graham would remain Humphrey's nemesis throughout her career.

Hill was aware of these tensions through her conversations with Gertrude Shurr, who had recently defected from the Humphrey-Weidman company to join Graham. This deep-rooted animosity that had festered in their Denishawn days was not lost on Hill, who would take on the role of mediator between Graham and Humphrey over the next years.

Despite mixed emotions among the choreographers, it was evident to Horst that the members of the Dance Repertory Theatre were the "accepted leaders," with Humphrey and Graham "more on one line. Martha was more dramatic and Doris, more purely choreographic. They were always going in one way together, but in their own way."[13]

The companies, with Agnes de Mille invited to join the roster, continued to rehearse throughout the fall of 1930, preparing for the upcoming second Dance Repertory Theatre week of performances scheduled for the Craig Theatre. Martha Hill recalled, "Sometimes we would rehearse until two o'clock in the morning, setting up a whole section of a dance, and we would come back to the next rehearsal and Martha [would say], 'It isn't going to work. We're going to throw it away and start all over again,' and we would experiment on something new to discover the source, the basic thing in movement." Hill was inspired by Graham's descriptive ideas for *Primitive Mysteries*: "She would bring all kinds of American Indian things—books on saints of the Southwest and figures of the saints—to look at and talk about. All of us were affected by the beauty, the economy of means which [to us] was very contemporary."

Primitive Mysteries premiered on 2 February 1931, greatly overshadowing the impressive array of other works. Graham's sixteen dancers also performed on the four programs in *Bacchanale* to a Wallingford Riegger score, and repeats of *Heretic, Moment Rustica, Project in Movement for a Divine Comedy,* and *Sketches from the People*.

Hill remembered the thrill of being onstage with Graham as the central figure of the Virgin in *Mysteries*: "You felt the intensity of [Graham] in her performances, and tried not to cross the direction of [her] gaze, which was so intense, particularly on her entrances or exits. I worried sometimes that Martha was so much a part of what she was projecting that for curtain calls she would walk right into the pit, because she was totally a part of what she was doing." Dancer May O'Donnell, who joined the company in 1932, also described the "powerful concentration" of Graham's movement in *Primitive Mysteries*. "There was this walk, for hours . . . a kind of inner motivation. . . . You never showed your extensions in the modern dance. Not at all. [I]t had to start back with basics to make a point. . . . You couldn't move very much, but you could get dynamic oppositions of lines, of pull in the body and the tensions of lines that made it—like a piece of sculpture."[14]

Primitive Mysteries received twenty-three curtain calls, Martha recalled. "I think we were surprised at the tumult of it. [Graham] distrusted the importance of it and was getting all upset. But we were serious artists, serving the art. Oh, we liked a good review, but we wouldn't have given a damn if it wasn't."

Martha recollected wonderful Christmas parties with the Graham Company during this time. One, in particular, was held in the luxurious brownstone apartment on Central Park South that Edith Isaacs (the editor of *Theatre Arts Monthly*) had given over to Graham to live and rehearse in for a year. "Husbands and friends were invited and with Louis at the piano [Graham] danced and improvised old Denishawn things. Hugo Burgomasto, the flutist, brought his homemade wine, and we all got a little tipsy. Being part of this close-knit group was a great feeling," Hill reminisced about her new dance family. "This was an exciting period. Martha [Graham] encouraged all of us to discover in all directions. I am forever grateful, not only [for her] giving me so much professionally, but personally too. She was so very, very personal. Martha changed my life."

Hill took on the stage name of Martha Todd for the Graham performances that season to keep her performing life a secret from disapproving professors. Yet their attitude only redoubled her belief in the legitimacy of dance as an art form that should be honored by the academic establishment.

When the season ended, Martha accepted a part-time teaching position at New York University. With jobs more scarce as the economic slide continued, following the Wall Street crash of October 1929, she was glad for the income. "I was very fortunate," she said, but at the same time, lamented her inevitable decision. "I had to choose to either go with Graham or teach. Graham's whole development was really burgeoning at that time and so you had to be free. I had to resign, giving up a life of performance because I had to make a living. For me, it was a matter of economy rather than artistic principle. I would have preferred to be a professional dancer. One [job] paid and one didn't so there was little choice. . . . I'll never forget being in the balcony and seeing Graham's next performance. I was so happy to be able to see it from the audience's point of view, but so sad not to be backstage."[15]

Finding herself in the polar opposite worlds of academics and bohemians, Martha was determined to take on the task of merging the two. Accepted into a world of like-minded independent women educators, she saw that a bright future in dance might be charted at precisely the right time in America's cultural history.

Her teaching began that summer in New York University's graduate studies summer camp at Sloatsburg, New York, on Lake Sebago. Footage from that first summer of teaching shows close-up shots of dancers sitting on the grass drumming tom-toms. Canoes can be glimpsed passing in the background.

One dancer strikes a large gong as nine others holding hands begin a rhythmic swinging pattern, moving to the right, left, right, then right to right. Some wear short skirts; others are costumed in jersey dresses as they perform upper-body swings, accenting skyward with their fists. In a circular formation the women fall to their knees, then move forward in plodding lunges followed by triplets in circular paths. The group follows Hill, their leader, as she demonstrates a short, light traveling pattern. A close-up shows her in a one-piece, light-colored leotard, her straight, fine, shoulder-length hair secured by a dark headband. Tall and thin, she demonstrates prances, skips, and leaps, and then a solo phrase, interjecting contractions and percussive gestures. An assertive mover, her long legs and arms akimbo, she is clearly exhilarated by the sheer joy of moving.

In the fall, Martha was hired as a part-time instructor with NYU's School of Education in the Department of Health, Physical Education, and Recreation. Its location in Greenwich Village at the school's main campus meant that she and Mary Jo now had a strong reason to stay in the part of Manhattan "where anybody in dance wanted to be. Living in the Village where things were freer was thought to be very daring." From the turn of the century, the Village had grown as a bohemian enclave for freethinkers challenging the morals of American provincialism. Even if this pair of bachelor girls did not read the leftist paper *The Masses* as regularly as some of their associates, it was the literary and artistic subculture and the easy acceptance of women on their own that appealed to them.

Martha had secured a monthly wage when the economic scene was increasingly bleak. Mary Jo, too, accepted a job with a decent salary, joining the faculty of New College, Columbia University's latest educational experiment. For the next three years, the program sparked brief optimism for its expansion of progressive thinking. As its physical education director and one of ten full-time professors hired for its first (1932–33) year, Mary Jo supervised courses that emphasized the study of communities and fostered global studies. In the master's degree program, students participated in an open-ended curriculum that included fieldwork in New York City's settlement houses, in Appalachia, and abroad.[16]

Louis Horst, who would soon find quarters a few blocks away from Graham's studio, at 63 East Eleventh Street, praised Hill's good sense at sharing costs with Shelly. "Martha Graham thinks about a telephone as something with which to call her mother in California, not as a bill to be paid at the end of the month!" Hill recalled Horst declaring, knowing that it was the musician who paid Graham's outstanding bills (often drawing from fees collected from his freelance work with other dance artists).[17] It was also Martha Hill's now steady salary and bank account balance that guaranteed Graham's loan for her New York seasons. Hill explained that into the 1940s "Martha [Graham] borrowed at the start of the year. Every year we went to the City Bank there on the corner of Thirteenth and Fifth Avenue for a loan. Because I had a job at the university I used to cosign a note. It was a very different period. We were very crazy people then," she conceded. "If we could find the money to exist and to carry on the work we wanted to do, we were happy."[18] Although Graham bargained for costume fabrics on Orchard Street, Hill knew that Graham's own clothing came from New York's best department stores. If more frugal than Graham, Hill too had become somewhat fashion-conscious, choosing her tailored outfits wisely.

Students recalled Hill's teaching style at New York University: "She was beginning to experiment in all different approaches to composition and new techniques. No one had taken the professional dance's technical point of view [before] and put it into an educational situation . . . superbly." "Indefatigable," Martha taught "quite a different kind of dance" from H'Doubler's University of Wisconsin style to which Theodora (Teddy) Wiesner (who came from Wisconsin to New York University to work on a master's degree) was accustomed. H'Doubler, who now wielded strong influence, had taken an interim step of situating dance within physical education. Yet she remained limited by that approach. Students recognized that Martha had other ideas. "Martha did all of the analysis and planning of the elements of space and time and rhythm. Nobody had ever done that before." Teddy wore "a little Grecian tunic" to her first dance class. Later, Martha went home and told Mary Jo, "'I'm going to get that Teddy Wiesner out of that tunic before very long,' and she did."[19] Now pulling dance out of the gymnasium and placing it into the larger theater, music, and art world had become Martha's primary goal.

Martha's dance vocabulary drew upon what she had learned in her studies with Findlay and Graham, interspersed with the use of swings, lunges, and falls, contrasting dynamics, and choral-group shifts that were Germanic in style, more akin to Kurt Jooss's material. Except for the tendency to include percussive accents throughout each phrase, Hill's movement choices were very much like the ones Humphrey had made in *Water Study* and *Passacaglia*. She also drew upon Graham's classroom vocabulary of prances, skips, contractions, and tilts.

Throughout, Hill never lost sight of her one condition for teaching (and judging) dancers. Regardless of body type, raw physicality—that special ingredient that first drew her to emulate Martha Graham—remained supreme.

Working under Jay B. Nash, professor of education and head of the Department of Health, Physical Education, and Recreation (though himself a recent arrival on campus), Martha taught "Methods of Teaching Dancing," "Creative Dancing," "Clogging and Folk Dancing," and "Elementary Creative Dancing." All were two-hour courses that met once a week that first semester.[20] "I was full-time then although I was called part-time," Martha explained, subtly acknowledging her lack of title and rank. "What I enjoyed about NYU was the opportunity to work with more mature students who were serious about the business of dance." But if taking the position at NYU renewed her chance to stay in New York, once again she had retreated to an academic position, knowing that the continuation of her life as a dancer was remote. Graham had placed increasing demands on her dancers that Martha Hill could no longer fulfill. Her brief career onstage now ending, Hill resigned herself to a serving rather than a self-promoting role.

Ruth Lloyd, one of Martha's first accompanists at NYU, began her lifelong friendship with Martha as a senior who needed to make money to finish her degree. She was first a pianist for Louise Baylis, whose specialty was clog and tap according to the NYU catalog, although Ruth remembered the course as one in "alertness." "She was quite satisfied with my playing, because, as my husband used to say, my head was full of the world's worst music, and I could play anything she suggested. Then I played for Martha Hill. She was teaching 'Methods of Teaching Tap Dancing,' although I don't think she could tap much herself. The thing that surprised me so was that she had a great pile of scores and wanted to use what I considered great music. It was probably only moderately great, but I felt that if a charming young woman like her had all this music, there must be some validity to what she was trying to do."[21]

Ruth spoke about the great difference Martha made in her feeling about teaching. "The student was important—more important, maybe—than the teacher. She pushed them in their own way. She didn't insist, as most people among the professional dancers did, who wanted a certain type of person and wanted them to look the same way. I think she tended somehow to cut through one's resolutions. Martha let them find their own way out, with often very good results." Ruth appreciated the fact that she "didn't have to give anything up to fit Martha Hill's ideas about dance. It was a quality that made her successful."[22]

Recently married to a pianist, Norman Lloyd, who needed a job, Ruth suggested he go to NYU "and not bother with anybody but Martha Hill. After he was hired, Martha was always our friend." Ruth continued, "We saw her quite frequently in an informal way, and gradually through her we got to know Doris, Charles, and of course, Martha Graham and Louis." While others found collective living arrangements—Graham was with Horst and Humphrey's entourage managed together as a kind of commune—for Martha, it was Mary Jo Shelly whose intellectual and moral support she needed and relied upon. Ruth recalled, "One had a feeling that Mary Jo was always pulling for Martha somehow. She did everything she could to help her. Their living situation was quite refined. Stable."[23]

Martha and Mary Jo were a team, unwilling to be diverted by social distractions that might lead to romantic involvement with men, marriage, and children. In this, they were like many other achievement-oriented women of that era. As Lillian Faderman, in her book *Surpassing the Love of Men,* wrote of long-term women partners: "They divided duties not on the basis of sex-role stereotypes but on the basis of natural talents or inclination or time; and they pooled emotional, physical, and financial resources not better to enable one of them to go out into the world and strive, but to allow them both to do so . . . fostering rather than hampering . . . their pioneering activities toward worldly success while also fulfilling all their personal needs."[24] "I never believed Martha wanted children," a lifetime friend noted.[25] Queried about this, her brother responded, "No, I can't see Martha as a mother figure. And her mother wouldn't have instilled it in her."

As roommates, the women plotted enthusiastically for the success of the new dance they saw in concerts on Sunday evenings. (These dark nights in Broadway theaters were available for recitals at affordable rents.) The pair often invited friends to their apartment afterward to talk over what they had seen. Shelly later wrote about the dance scene, "Innovation suddenly began intruding upon a comfortably quiescent classical style, overthrowing tradition from content to costume, breaking all the established rules, provoking consternation along with excitement."[26]

While at Teachers College, Martha and Mary Jo had begun coauthoring a book on dance theory. "At the time John Martin was defining modern dance. We thought it was terrible that he wanted to call it the modern dance. We wanted to write our own definition." The word "modern," drawn from the organizers of the Museum of Modern Art, was understood to mean "contemporary, or art of the present," at least, according to curator Glenn Lowry.[27] In the working title for their manuscript, the authors used "new" rather than "modern" as the preferred adjective. "Sources and Characteristics of the New Dance" was "a theory book to sort out definition," Martha explained. The first chapter begins, "Dance is the Matrix Art. . . . The history of the dance is both a written and an unwritten record because dance has impermanent form and has never found means of perpetuating itself as has music. . . . It has conserved its folk quality even in its most formal periods because it is an art that has been handed down directly from dancer to dancer, without suffering translation. The history of the dance is a history of great and lesser persons who have been its instruments."[28]

After graduating from Teachers College, Hill and Shelly continued to theorize about dance: Martha would come up with ideas and jot them down. Mary Jo would clarify, edit, and type a treatise aimed toward developing support for a new direction in dance, and the importance of dance throughout history. Meant to serve as a position paper on the importance of dance as an independent art in society, it instead provided a blueprint for their future endeavors. It might have equaled John Martin's 1933 *The Modern Dance* in depth and content, yet they set it aside. "We decided [dance] was changing so fast we couldn't keep up with it." It was never published. "We had other things to do."

When Barnard College held a dance symposium in February of 1932, it was the first of its kind in the Northeast. Shelly, representing Barnard's neighboring New College, lent academic strength in her guidance of the symposium's events, and it was there that New York University's Hill with her group of students first impressed critics and administrators alike. Martha surmised, "We were somewhat revolutionary, I suppose, at that time, in the whole picture of the dance because my training had composited the ballet with Martha Graham. Also, seeing everything that was going on in the dance world, I was striking out on my own."[1]

In search of a faculty member to create a dance program for an innovative new college in Vermont of which he would be president, Robert Devore Leigh (who had briefly served on Barnard's faculty) introduced himself to Martha. "He came up to me and said, 'I want to talk to you.' He saw what I did at that symposium. He loved dance and music. . . . He was really avid about the avenues of expression for the human spirit. So he had probably seen enough in dance so he had some basis for judgment."[2]

Leigh asked Hill to accompany him to Bennington's unfinished campus on a windy March weekend in 1932. It was her first time of many hundreds more on the Rutland Railroad "Up-Flier," as Benningtonians called it. "This was my first view of New England. The barn still had hay in it, and Cricket Hill, the farmer's house on the estate, was being used as headquarters. We had lunch there, and then we walked around." Hill recalled the steel skeleton of the Commons building looking like a setting for *Mourning Becomes Electra*. "And there were all these fields and the beginning of the dormitories." (Later, Martha told de Mille that when Frank Lloyd Wright came to visit the finished campus, "he thought that the school had done a horrible thing, being geographically true, but not true to the times and the new faith in architecture.")[3]

Afterward, they were driven to the train station in Albany. "We ate dinner on the train . . . and we talked about the state of education and what his dreams were about Bennington and where dance would be in the commonwealth of the arts there. He said, 'I propose that you consider coming part-time because I know you're thinking in your mind that you do not want to leave New York.' He was quite right to sense . . . that I had reservations about cutting loose from New York City where everything was going on. So I said, 'That sounds very exciting,' and we talked about . . . what I would do. I was young and inexperienced."[4] She admitted that the campus at first look seemed far away and uninviting, but she was intrigued that Leigh was "in the business of way-breaking" in his call for "high intellectual standards freed from the dry and stuffy aspects that had been the pattern for women's colleges." And Leigh's offer gave Martha an opportunity she could not resist.

While keeping her part-time position at New York University, Martha served as Bennington's first dance department chairman as part of the Arts and Music Division for the 1932–33 academic year along with teaching duties. The school started up with eighty-seven students. More than a third chose to study dance along with their academic courses.[5]

"At Bennington I was supported in everything that I believed in," Martha said. It was "very brave" for the school to open its doors in the economic climate of October 1932, when in the following March the banks would close. How long Martha's new source of employment would last seemed rather shaky as the Depression worsened. As poet and literary man Ben Belitt later commented, "The operative word here . . . is 'risk.' Bennington was risky. Students were risky. And everything could fail dismally. [Dance as art] had never been part of a college curriculum before . . . so there was risk in the untried addition. The exciting thing was that you entered a whole thermal force of risk—that risk was a force field for creation."[6]

Reflecting on her first year at the college, she recalled, "I went to Bennington in order to have the freedom to be my own person. As Louisa May Alcott said of herself, 'I'd rather be a free spirit and paddle my own canoe.'" Hill adjusted to her split week on the faculties of two colleges and kept that routine until 1951. She arrived by train on Thursday and returned to Manhattan on Sunday (teaching Friday afternoons and Saturdays and, two years later, adding Thursdays). "In quite a few of the eighteen years I commuted, there was only an 8:00 A.M. train up and . . . a 3:30 P.M. down. The trainmen would look for me each week." During the first part of the week she dealt with the rigors of city life and then, like Alcott, paddled her "own canoe" in Vermont, all the while calculating a future for dance.

One of the big events of the season back in Manhattan was the opening program of Radio City Music Hall at Rockefeller Center. On 27 December 1932, the new theater presented an array of the country's best concert artists, Martha Graham and her group among them. Martha recalled that it would be one of the first of many conflicts between the modern dance and the commercial desires of producers and paying customers. It was after midnight when they finally performed *Choric Dance for an Antique Greek Tragedy: A Chorus of Furies* with Horst playing his "original music" at the keyboard, as conductor

Leopold Stokowski and his weary orchestra sat it out. Dancer Ailes Gilmour recalled that its producer, Samuel L. ("Roxy") Rothafel had wanted them to perform behind a "steam curtain" for visual effect, but Graham explained that the woolen costumes would shrink and immobilize the dancers. When the management took Graham off the program for subsequent performances, Hill moved into action: "We diehards made a point of calling the box office to place a ticket order for a theater party. I'd ask when the group would be performing. To the answer, 'Martha Graham isn't on the schedule' in protest I said, 'Graham isn't on? Well then, cancel!'"[7] Outraged, Hill resolved to bandstand for the cause. The event made a dramatic impression on her, both literally and figuratively. Initially saddened because she herself was not performing in the production, Martha suddenly saw the dancing she loved so much in sharp perspective. The dancers looked like fleas scrambling across the giant stage. It was a rude awakening for Martha Hill, and one that spurred her on to find more appropriate circumstances.

In the spring of 1933, at John Martin's popular New School lecture series, Hill proselytized, "Anything good in the dance is likewise good in art and education." She reflected years later, "From the beginning, I imported the best dance to the university setting." Her first opportunity to do so was during that spring at Bennington, when she helped to organize meetings, seminars, demonstrations, and concerts that included dance in a symposium on modernism in the arts—although she admitted that the highlight of the event was an evening with jazz musician Leadbelly.

In the fall of 1933, despite widening poverty and unemployment in their midst, Martha's circle of dance artists and academics were optimistic about the progressive ideas of the newly elected president Franklin Delano Roosevelt. His New Deal legislation ended the bank crisis—thirty-eight states had closed their banks—and began to restore public confidence. Encouraged with the promise of an upturn in the economy, Leigh secured permission from Bennington's trustees to seek an appropriate summer enterprise.

"Bennington, first and foremost," Martha stated, "was a liberal arts college. Therefore, dance was a field that one would study as one would study literature or any other field." She added,

it was the first time dance had equal status with the other theater arts. The great idea of that time was that dance in education was no different from dance in art. Dance would be on a sort of intellectual parity with other endeavors. That was the new thing. That wasn't true at NYU or any other place. We were the first. Sarah Lawrence [where Marion McKnighten had begun to organize residencies for both Graham and Horst] was making a great bid in developing the arts, too, but there were no departments of dance alone. Margaret H'Doubler started a dance major at Wisconsin much earlier, but that was under physical education and was strongly oriented toward education.[8]

For Martha, the idyllic campus in Bennington, Vermont, seemed very removed from the social problems clearly visible on Manhattan's streets and an ideal location to start something new.

On a Saturday stroll, passing Cricket Hill, now a faculty residence, Leigh stopped by to talk to Hill. She remembers:

> I had just washed my hair and was drying it when he approached me for ideas. I said, "Well, several other arts—music, drama, writing—had found congenial summer homes in New England. Why not dance and why not at Bennington? Why don't we have a dance school?" He responded, "You know, that's a very good idea, because in New England we have painting schools behind every bush, with a lot of theater going on and music here and there." He said he'd think about it. Next fall he said, "Remember that idea about a dance school? Let's have a meeting. Mrs. Leigh knows Mary Jo Shelly, who's a friend of yours. Let's get Mary Jo to come and have a meeting."[9]

Also present was another of Martha's "very best friends" who had been adviser to women and assistant medical director at the University of Oregon, Wilmoth Osborne. Wilmoth, who "billeted on journeys across the Atlantic in a men's section because her name was strange for a woman," was also a friend of the Leighs from their years at Reed and had been hired as the first medical officer of Bennington.[10] The group of planners for a summer session included Leigh's wife, Mildred, who was always amused by Martha's way as "a gregarious and democratic" member of the faculty. Martha admitted, "If a party started for four or five, it was likely to end up being twenty and thirty, because I liked that sort of thing."[11] In the same fashion, the first meeting organized by Martha took place in Wilmoth's apartment, where plans for the summer program were launched among familiar faces and rounds of martinis.

In a kind of credo to explain the summer school within the context of education, Shelly wrote for a Bennington publication that in the last five or six years she had noticed that many colleges had followed the trend toward adapting modern dance into their programs. "The change in the style of dance is taking place at a time when interest in the dance in this country, both inside and outside the school, is greater than ever in its history." The shift in educational thinking now placed the body and the emotions in "almost as good educational standing as the mind." Mary Jo concluded, "the tenets of the modern dance are more thoroughly compatible with the best in contemporary educational thinking than have been those of any other form of dance. . . . The period just beginning is the first in which dance is likely to find itself identified as an art." She names the promising indications for the future as the growing rapport between the dance artist and the dance teacher, the rising standards in dance teaching, and the gradual disappearance of the sharp line between dance as a part of physical education and the other arts in the school. Shelly's "disappearance of the sharp line" smooths over her worry about growing conflicts among dance people "dancing for art's sake" and those in physical education promoting proper exercise and good health.[12]

For the 1934 start of the Bennington Summer School of the Dance, Mary Jo was to become Martha's administrative director. The formality of the title belied the reality of the job. As Mary Jo put it, "Go do whatever comes next, and do it fast." Martha's university background gave her the knowledge she needed to create her own "temple" for dance at Bennington College. But throughout the establishment of Bennington's Summer School of Dance, unquestionably, it was Mary Jo who used her already powerful connections within the college circuit. "Mary Jo was so absolutely essential to translate all into the proprieties of institutional and pedagogical discourse, [because] Martha was a moving exemplar of dance rather than concoctor of treatises. For her, the 'graphics' of the 'chorus' were visual, and all that was visual was volatile," Belitt believed. Martha's success as a director would rely on Shelly's steady right hand as administrator.

Belitt termed John Dewey's educational theories "the Gospel According To John. Don't *talk* of a future or theorize about its viability—do it! Can you think of anyone more *American* in their matrix-for-a-*do*ing than Martha Hill or Mary Jo Shelly? Nothing furtive or subversive or incongruous—just a midwestern spaciness and verve." Martha would soon cultivate her belief that the true writing for dance was choreographic, and Belitt would be her fondest supporter. Her inclination was collaborative in spirit for the good of the community, with ideas that fit comfortably into the idealized notions of progressive thought of the day.

Leigh had instructed Hill to "get the best there is" for a faculty, and she did. As visiting staff, along with a bevy of talented dance musicians, they were expected to serve as both artists and teachers. Martha quickly lured whom she considered the "best," each for two-week sessions. "Within weeks she had convinced those dancers she believed would be the leaders for a future for modern dance in America to come," according to Shelly. Hill talked to Graham first, and then Humphrey and Weidman, through the couple's company manager Pauline Lawrence, and finally, to Hanya Holm. "They all knew Bennington because each of them had been there to perform. And they knew me, although I was very suspect in the first place in the modern dance because I had been a ballet dancer; and then I was suspect in the modern dance because I had been in Martha's company, and that was the time when one gave one's allegiance to a single group. I felt that I had to build confidence. Not with Martha, of course, but with Doris, Charles, and Hanya. But everybody agreed to give this a trial."

Belitt, soon to become the oracle of the group, recalled, "Hers was the improbable task of placating a faculty of competing innovators, each with her own aesthetic for exploring an option in a simultaneous search for mastery. Instead of provoking an irreconcilable confrontation of egos, she somehow managed to transform a many-faceted collaboration of eccentrics into a single-minded community of talents and assure its survival into a new millennium."

Graham, of course, was Hill's essential first choice—a position no one questioned. She was a luminary "in the great sense," Ruth Lloyd confirmed.[13] Holm, who had danced with Wigman's company in Germany for ten years before she came to Manhattan to set up a New York branch of the Wigman School in 1931, recalled in 1981, "I was fresh from Germany, a stranger . . . a little odd fitting in the rhythm because my rhythm was different. It was the first time I came in touch with the top vibrancies, and I was confronted with Americans who all took their own power and desire."[14]

Doris Humphrey's considerable choreographic talent had been evident throughout her years with Denishawn as soloist and assistant to St. Denis beginning with her *Soaring* in 1920. Breaking away and establishing a company in 1928 with Denishawn partner, Charles Weidman, the couple began to produce some of the most respected dance work on the recital scene. Charles's choreographic output had included pieces such as his 1931 *Happy Hippocrite* (after a Max Beerbohm story rewritten as a musical pantomime ballet by Herbert Elwell in 1928) and *Ringside,* which was infused with lively, physically demanding movement. And it was his rare sense of humor that complemented Doris's effort to make modern dance "a theater art of our time," as Belitt saw it. "Charles was an entertainer. He was a vaudevillian that came into good hands."[15] The combination was perfect. Doris's *Water Study* (1928), *Air for the G String* (1928), *Life of the Bee* (1929), *The Shakers* (1931), and *The Pleasures of Counterpoint* (1932) revealed her genius at formal composition, able to move waves of dancers, elegantly and with power.

Both accomplished dancers from their Denishawn days, in order to pay the rent, while leading their large ensemble group, the couple also took jobs in opera and on Broadway when the opportunity arose. Norman Lloyd understood the difficulty of mixing commercial and noncommercial work: "Doris and Charles were working with the Theatre Guild staging things. She did Gluck's *Orpheus* at the Philadelphia Opera and Shubert revues like *Americana,* and each time they would lose a couple of members of their group when they suddenly realized you could earn real money dancing in a show."[16]

  Their growing reputation as serious artists notwithstanding, they could laugh at each other on occasion, in what Doris called "Peep Shows." Charles would entertain friends with hilarious parodies of his colleagues. Using an enema tube, he performed St. Denis's *Cobras;* wearing white briefs with a bright green fig leaf, he sucked in his gut to imitate Ted Shawn. For Martha Graham he sucked in his cheeks, threw a noose over a beam and pulled. He wore a red mop on his head as a protesting Tamiris, and made fun of himself counting.[17]

  In contrast to Charles's slapstick nature, the very solemn José Limón had come on the scene to study at their studio; within months he was dancing minor roles with the company. José and Charles were soon lovers. After a romantic encounter on a cruise ship respite to Trinidad, Doris, too, found a partner, having met Englishman and second officer on the SS *Dominic.* They married a year later on 10 June 1932. Charles Francis Woodford (called Leo) was eight years Doris's junior. Although away at sea most of their married life, Leo would be a calming force, and a loving, if absentee father to their son, Charles Humphrey Woodford, born 8 July 1933. With Leo back at sea shortly after their marriage and for the next seven years, Doris returned to her communal lifestyle in a seven-room apartment at 31 West Tenth Street shared with Weidman, Lawrence, Limón, and an occasional baby nurse. Getting away from a hot summer in New York City for a residency at Bennington was a godsend to all of them.

  For the summer venture, Martha was eager to implement solidity for every aspect of dance. She wisely invited New York City's leading dance critic and modern dance advocate, John Martin, to develop a dance history and critical writing course for the curriculum. The idea of having Martin teach, she affirmed, was "elemental . . . a natural. . . . Who else would we have had? John coalesced in words for us. He was our spokesman for the new movement."[18]

  Their own theory writings were now stored away; for Martha and Shelly, the real work of the day would be to support the artists' creations. Martha recalled, "We were busy seeing that the dances were getting done, so we didn't get around to formulating our beliefs into words. We danced our beliefs." Belitt, who would soon be their colleague at Bennington, surmised, "They conceded to a higher authority. Someone who was more literate as a critic of proven eloquence and elegance; who was a distinguished dance commentator: a professional. Why shouldn't they? They said, 'to each his own!' They knew they were in good hands and were glad to defer. Martin knew that dance merited a place on a college campus, however others might dismiss it as a frivolity just to dance around!" And Belitt might have added that Martin had the advantage of the *New York Times* behind him.

Louis Horst would be the school's authoritative figure for anything pertaining to dance composition or music for dance. Hill increasingly came to rely on Graham's mentor as the majordomo of her group of hires: "Louis was the dean of that part of the curriculum in the area of music. . . . it began simply and then expanded very, very much as was necessary." The "pessimistically hopeful" Horst had just begun in February 1934 to publish *Dance Observer* as an advocate sheet for modern dance. Martha and Mary Jo willingly joined his first staff. "The new dance has grown up and thrown away its baby rattles of 'self expression,'" Ralph Taylor confidently reported in the magazine's second issue. It was the experienced Horst with his determination to make a bona fide art form of the new modern dance to which these fellow advocates deferred.

When asked whether people like Horst and Graham felt comfortable coming into such a community, Belitt responded, "Who else would invite them for a summer of dance? Who else would set them up this way? Who else would say: the main thing we expect of you is the creation of dancers and dances? (Who else would they invite to the indignities and tedium of training unskilled, unselected beginners in a routine that was collegiate in its disciplines, but not professional?)"

The group's enthusiasm for the new project notwithstanding, Hill had second thoughts about the summer-school plans. "I was very fearful because I was afraid that Bennington would lose its shirt. I did not want to be responsible for a great loss to a school that was being very generous to the art I loved. I wanted to see the school of the dance go forward, but not at the expense of Bennington." President Leigh firmly allayed her fears by saying, "If you get sixty students you'll be able to pay your bills." Leigh had calculated a 4 percent return to the college on its capital investment for the use of the campus and suggested that a minimum of forty-three students paying $190 apiece would house and feed the faculty and staff, who would be reimbursed for what it would cost them to get there and back.

The school issued an announcement to "magnetize" students generated from the college's New York office to help the situation. (The office had originally been concerned with the logical business of raising endowment funds for a college that blithely opened in the Depression without one.) "When the forty-third registration came, we relaxed. When the sixty-fifth came, we celebrated. With the arrival of the hundred and third, we closed enrollment. There were no more beds," Martha remembered. Mary Jo gave her a book on contemporary art for the occasion. "We knew we had an original and world-shaking, and timely idea."[19]

"What happened at Bennington . . . has come to seem inevitable. Actually, the launching of the Bennington School of the Dance in 1934 resembled more an act of faith than a predestined success. At that date no one even imagined the Festival, which later emerged to make dance history of the first order," Mary Jo wrote in her manuscript about Bennington in 1957.

"In retrospect, there could not have been a more felicitous falling out of cir-cumstances—the time, the place, the people—for the creation of a new center for the already burgeoning American dance," Martha wrote years later in prep-aration for her lecture "Bennington, an Historic Milepost."[20] The film voice-over for National Educational Television's *USA: Dance. Four Pioneers* (first aired in 1965) perhaps put it best: "The dance revolution was fought on many fronts, but the key battle took place at Vermont's Bennington College. Over the span of seven summers the modern dance movement grew from adolescence to maturity."[21]

If "everything fell into place in the journey to Bennington for Martha Hill and Mary Jo Shelly, as a posse of two," as Ben Belitt said, "that place was very chary." The February 1934 issue of the *Bennington College Bulletin* stated the new program's intent (penned by Hill and Shelly): "The Bennington School of the Dance will be initiated during the summer of 1934 as a center for the study of the modern dance in America . . . designed to bring together leaders and students interested in an impartial analysis of the important contemporary trend in the dance." Further, a variety of viewpoints among artists would reveal "the essentials of modernism in the dance, . . . the modern dance, in common with the other arts of the period, as a diversified rather than a single style."[1] The opportunity was "the best dance news to be had," according to Bessie Schönberg.[2] Norman Lloyd concurred, "Aside from Perry-Mansfield, there was nothing like it in the country. The timing was right."

Today hundreds of colleges offer a dance curriculum that very much resembles Bennington's first summer offerings. In 1934, at that historic beginning, the "program of work" for a full session of six weeks included Fundamental Techniques, Dance Composition, Music and the Dance, Teaching Methods and Materials, and Production as well as a survey of dance history and critical theory under John Martin's direction.

Enrolled in the first season of Bennington's summer dance program was a small but valiant army ready to serve in the name of a rapidly growing American art form. Those registered were all women: less than one-third were actually undergraduate students. Those who were undergraduates came from colleges such as New College at Columbia, Connecticut College, Purdue, Sarah Lawrence, Skidmore, Smith, Vassar, and Wellesley as well as Bennington. The rest were teachers (Ruth Alexander from Ohio University; Ruth Bloomer, University of Oregon; Marian Streng, Barnard; Marian Van Tuyl, the University of Chicago; and Marion Knighten, Sarah Lawrence; Hood, McGill, Mount Holyoke, Oberlin, Swarthmore, and the University of California also were among the colleges represented). The directors correctly figured that this impressive array of "professional" women would return to their respective colleges as serious advocates, multiplying the impact of the cause.

"If the highest percentage were teachers of dance, the true diversification was one of personalities and aptitudes," Shelly asserted, adding that out of the

103 enrolled, "no two went back where they came from with an identical sense of accomplishment but, for certain, none went back unaffected by so intense and kaleidoscopic an experience."

In that first cool New England summer in Vermont, the beauty of the location and the accommodations would far surpass each student's expectations. As the Up-Flyer pulled into the quaint North Bennington train station, transport was waiting for dancers and their trunks. Hill and Shelly gave an eight-page memo to each new arrival, covering everything from the cleaning of rooms to film-developing services. Making their stay even more appealing, a five-dollar fee covered six weeks of golfing, swimming, and tennis at the Mount Anthony Country Club. (To an amateur champion golfer like Marian Streng, this was unbelievable good luck.) Clear warnings against guests in the dormitories were stated so as not to cause havoc with housekeeping; however, meals were available for visitors at forty cents for breakfast, fifty cents for lunch, and seventy-five cents for dinner. "There are no house rules," the memo states. After the 1:00 A.M. doors-locked curfew, the night watchman provided a key. A "hairdressing" shop was open six days a week.

Students danced for one-and-a-half hours daily under the direction, in Shelly's words, of "the up-and-coming modernists for a new dance." Sessions divided students into groups with "little or no previous experience in the modern dance" or "a foundation in the modern dance." As the mimeographed handout for the first session explained, each week one of the artists and their assistants would present their own approach "to the modern dance through technique, analysis and discussion" with emphasis on the "consideration of dance as an art form."[3]

Graham, Holm, Humphrey, and Weidman were soon labeled The "Big Four" and each felt the weight of their mission. With Graham the leader of the pack, Hanya Holm was chosen as the distinguished exponent of Wigman's influential style of German modern dance. Martha Hill later explained, "Hanya brought something to the U.S. which we were very much lacking. We in America are 'doers.' We make the leg lift. We hit the stage, and we make something happen with little reference to the space in which we do it. One of Hanya's particular gifts was to bring to us a space consciousness. She had a discipline about space that was fresh to us."[4]

Hanya recalled, "Bennington was a beginning. . . . It was also a job in attitude, point of view, behaviorism, spiritual values, [about] the whole human being . . . which had to be kind of re-educated to think in a different way." Attracting students who might otherwise travel to Germany to study with the great dance expressionist, Hanya vowed to teach her Bennington students that the intent was to use the body "not only as a form, shape and pattern, but using it in its own right," with "no taboo. . . . In the modern dance, style was created by the reasons underlying what you were dancing about. And that created an entirely different set of movements. So every time it's a new battle, it's a new fight, there's a new agony. It is a new heartache. It's a new birth and always that pain connected with it."[5]

Weidman, under Humphrey's wing, had emerged as a voice of authority, as well. "We became possible because of two revolts. One was the revolt against the 'eeses,'" referring to the Japanese and Chinese dances the couple performed with Denishawn. "Why don't we have a dance which would be indigenous of this country, rough that it may be—that we could take all over and say 'this is America dancing?' We were very strong. We were revolutionists."[6] If others found his choreographic work lightweight, Mary Jo was particularly fond of Weidman's quick wit, which contributed a much-needed sense of humor into the mix of personalities, most of whom took themselves very seriously.

At first, their teaching was definitely a grassroots proposition. Martha Hill remembered the problems Norman Lloyd had explaining the rudiments of music to his class of dancers. "'The dot after a note adds half the value of the note to the note. Are there any questions?' he asked, and one hand went up. 'I don't understand at all.' So then Norman demonstrated by cutting an apple into slices to illustrate his point. The student responded, 'Yes, I understand, but I don't agree with it.' That's where we stood in 1934!"

"You can't imagine the lively primitive quality in the early populations of Bennington," Ruth Lloyd later quipped. "Sometimes you just took them by the hand and tried to get them to walk in a steady pulse. The joke was that the advanced classes were advanced in age only, but there was marvelous spirit that first year of Bennington." Even if distracted by the "primitive" nature of the students, Norman and Ruth were "absolutely bowled over" by the whole modern dance scene. "It was fresh—the thing that you'd been waiting to happen."

Martha Hill, with Shelly at her side, soon developed an uncommon ability to organize people, places, and concerts while keeping calm under trying circumstances. But for the directors, upsets were to be expected. Shelly recalled, "Fifteen-year-olds did not want to room with forty-nine-year-olds: the ages of the students spanned three generations. One student could not sleep after one night because of the quarter-hour soundings of the Commons clock."

Bessie did recall raised eyebrows from the Bennington locals at first. It was Mildred Leigh's self-appointed responsibility to keep the faculty in line "almost as though we had to live up to our New England setting and not be 'gypsies' in the midst of this whole progressive education. In the first year, being very free spirits, we had suntan leotards that would look very nude on the campus, and it was noised all about the village that we had a nudist colony. They took all this in stride, and the trustees of Bennington College were marvelous."[7]

The winsome Norman later reflected that during his summers at Bennington, there were on occasion some strained relationships with Vermont's Yankee stock. He made occasional trips to a clothing store during the first years when nobody would pay any attention to him. "It was almost as if we didn't exist. People after me got waited on and I'd still be there. But after about the sixth summer, they recognized me! We were outsiders coming in and taking over. It never became the kind of community thing where local people would come to see the dancers. Audiences were generally New Yorkers, [the school was] good for business, but not for encouraging aesthetics among the locals."

If Martha and Mary Jo were more pressed to maintain a sense of propriety within the college environment, nearly all of Martha's closest colleagues subscribed to a bohemian lifestyle with little concern for their appearance once offstage. Even Martha Graham wore bobby socks and solid walking shoes on occasion. Cotton dresses, with cardigan sweaters for the cool nights were de rigueur for concertgoing after a day in leotards and dance skirts. A historic group photograph shows the entire student body lined up on the Commons Building's front stairs, with Horst (Spud in his lap), Graham, Shelly, Hill, the Lloyds, and Schönberg in the front row.

Once given the opportunity of going to Bennington, all relished the idea. More to the point, they needed the work. For these artists, their impassioned love for dance meant serious limitations on their way of life in a world struggling to recover from the Depression: few could afford much past the month's rent, or shared expenses for Pauline's delicious suppers with "enough spaghetti for everyone." Most lived within two city blocks in Greenwich Village. "We used to say," Hill joked, "if a bomb ever went off at West Eleventh Street, that would be the end of modern dance in America."

All of the artists struggled financially, taking work where they could get it. As Limón described it, for them, money was "something one needs to pay for food, shelter, studios, costumes, dancers, musicians, and other costly things. One works hard to earn that money, but one doesn't devote one's life to making money just to put in the bank or make more money."[8] The creation of an equitable pay scale for artists at Bennington, so that everyone felt compensated and happy with their working situation, sat squarely on Martha's shoulders, and she quickly learned how to manage the financial arrangements to everyone's satisfaction. There was never a complaint registered for more salary in these early years: to work under her leadership was considered a privilege.

For Martha, the summer school was the realization of a dream to draw together rival artists in an all-out effort to propagate the idea of modern dance as an innovative new medium. "The first year, with great tact, she scheduled Graham and her rivals so that they would not meet, but thereafter this precaution was scrubbed with no resulting turbulence," Bennington President Thomas Brockway later noted in his history of the college.[9] Martha made sure that everything was "even-steven" for each group; as a result, the atmosphere at Bennington was congenial and relaxed. For her own part, Martha was determined to make Bennington as utopian an environment as possible. Later she herself expressed her surprise at how smoothly the summer ran:

[The artists] got along very well, working noon and night on their own things, and they would give [in] to each other when it was necessary. All were assured of three meals a day and a roof over their heads in beautiful country air and landscape, able to work much faster [than in New York City] because everything was concentrated. There was great energy-saving. It was just like more of the same in one sense, but somebody else was paying for it, and it wasn't as much work.

"We had a gathering place we called the store where we would go for a drink. Martha [Graham] and Louis would have tea until Louis would look at his watch and say, 'Time to go.' He was the countereffect to anything romantic or decorative; he was a schedule custodian," Hill recalled. She had built her own reputation as a taskmaster:

They used to tease me: "If Martha ever leaves this earth, we'll see yellow tablets of foolscap notes coming down from the clouds saying, 'Don't forget to do this. Tell someone to do that.'" I think Martha [Graham], Louis, and I felt that same sort of responsibility to get [things] done.

"Louis was originally hired to teach for one week, and he got so involved with the project that he decided he would stay for six, for the price of one," Norman Lloyd said. In the first year some of the people from "prestige" positions in colleges and universities who took Louis's class were "very embarrassed to have direct criticism of what they were doing in front of their colleagues," according to Martha. "So Bessie and I went into Louis's class and did the assignments right along with everybody, and Louis would come down very hard on us because he was very direct and very honest, and also terribly amusing as a critic." She recalled his bellowing from the keyboard after one student's attempt, "Many are called but few are chosen!"

Life at Bennington was rough on the musicians as well, but they recognized the school's mission to support a tight musical connection. Ruth and Norman Lloyd were hired to accompany classes, for "room and board and sixty dollars for both." But living for six weeks at Bennington was "a real bonanza," Norman reflected. "It was a wonderful discovery at that particular time of our life . . . [of] the whole ambience about dance. There were so many movements in the arts in America in the 1920s and 1930s: poetry, literary, painting. American dance was one of the most important movements of the time, and [we] were part of it."

The seldom-needed infirmary was cleared out to become a pressroom for the criticism course, with a typewriter assigned to every student. Martin used a survey approach to present the individual points of view "to get a sense of where those students were and then he would extend upon that," Martha explained. "We had students who were interested in trying to develop themselves as critics, so he organized a course [that was] a natural emanation from what we were doing in general. I remember his pacing up and down in front of the Commons building while the students went in, typed away, and filed their criticisms with him with a deadline the same night." Each wrote about every campus event. Martin admitted that his early attempts at teaching dance history and criticism (later named the first such coursework ever taught in an American university) were problematic: "There was nothing to go on and while I knew something about it, I didn't know enough to give a six-weeks' course off the top of my head. So I spent all my time in the library reference room and found things I had never heard of before. . . . I was one step ahead of them, but it was one step." Recalling that the course was scheduled first thing in the morning, his students could not stay awake. (Rescheduled the next year right after lunch, he said it was "the same thing!")[10]

Martha and John also commandeered a group of students for a "prodigious project" of a historical chart of dance and the related arts, which they would edit. Working as a committee, out of the library, the outcome was pages of parallel columns listing the development of dance within the context of social history and the other arts. Mimeographed copies made available for sale soon became valuable commodities for those returning to their college teaching.

Having an important critic such as Martin in their midst drew mixed reactions from the artists. José Limón, for one, would later recall the "irrepressible excitement" that mixed with the tension of occasionally finding himself at a table in the dining room with Martin among others such as Graham and Horst: "Martin is one of the few men who have frightened me. . . . He was the maker and unmaker of reputations. At his Olympian pleasure, or caprice, as it sometimes seemed to us dancers, you rose or fell. . . . As the hawk is to the rodent and the typhoon to the navigator, so was this man to us."[11] His presence, along with Louis Horst's, pressed artists such as Limón into a subliminal drive to succeed—without doubt, a carefully planned strategy by the directors. They would continue to invite the most uncompromising professional critics of the day, hospitably offering them a place to stay alongside artists and their companies. By reporting on activities at Bennington through their writing, they succeeded in bringing the experiment to national attention. In turn, the artists became acutely aware of the need to produce their best work. It was this tenacious forethought on Martha and Mary Jo's part that helped give Bennington its quick ascent to the vanguard of the arts world.

More important, Martha went to extraordinary lengths to ensure that the artists' abilities were undeterred. Attending to their every whim, Bennington would be her training ground for creating situations where artists quickly grew to rely on her. At Bennington College, and in other institutions for years to come, it would be Martha who literally brokered these dancers' future projects, as well as a good portion of their annual income.

Martha cannily set the tone by giving herself the most rigorous teaching schedule of any of them. In her dance composition course, her formal assignments were a crowded array of forms, using rounds, two- and three-part forms, canons, and theme and variations, with studies in dimension, level changes, direction, focus, as well as mixed, accumulative, and resultant rhythms. During one workshop performance her students performed sets of variations labeled "staccato-legato, sustained, cumulative rhythm, understatement and restatement" and "percussive movement, canon, dynamics, and succession." Another was set in a jazz medium. Insistent on teaching from every possible angle, Martha's classes offered a potpourri of problems to solve that must have proved daunting to students who had not even known what the word "choreography" meant before their encounter with "Miss Hill."

The notion that composition for dance could actually be taught had only recently been tested. Martha herself had been one of the first to teach principles of dance composition, beginning at NYU. Only Louis Horst had preceded her, at the Neighborhood Playhouse teaching his "Pre-classic Dance Forms" composition course to actors in 1929. College physical education departments such as Barnard included the making of dances as part of their modern dance courses, but formal training in this area was just beginning. "The whole idea of teaching composition is probably one of the landmark activities of the Bennington School of the Dance," Norman Lloyd said. "Until then no one ever took classes in dance composition. Somehow you declared yourself a choreographer. Bennington gave people the idea that dance composition can be taught [and that is what] perpetuates the art, and provides the literature." He added, "At that time it was *unwritten* literature!"

But it was Martha Hill's "Techniques" course on teaching methods designed to unify and "hold the school together," that was most needed at this point. As Hill explained:

> Physical education people who took daily classes with Graham and with Holm would say, "Martha [Graham] says this, and Hanya says this. . . . Martha says contraction and release. Well, release has as much contraction in a muscle as a contraction." I'd say, "Martha is using contraction in its dramatic sense as steel contracts in cold; you pull yourself together in a contraction. Sure, muscles are being used, but she doesn't mean the contraction of muscles. She is using words metaphorically, not literally in their physiological sense." I taught from principle, more analytically. The purpose of those fundamentals was to try to allay some of the fears and the confusion of people studying in several methods of work.

"I was in touch with everything that was going on," Martha admitted. "I made it my concern to figure out what every choreographer was doing. I'd seen all the concerts of everybody so I knew what they were doing." In the studio:

> instead of teaching, say, a Graham back fall, I would say, "Let us see all the ways a body can go to the floor and out of the floor." I always taught more or less from basic principles of space, time, force—the amount of force, of parts of the body. I would "discover" things that I thought would lead someplace. I felt I was the common denominator that tried to explain the language used by the artists which was frequently metaphorical and therefore highly descriptive, but not translatable into terms that some of the students knew in, say, a scientific context or other professional contexts.[12]

A surviving eight-minute silent film, shot in the summer of 1934 and labeled "Martha Hill Technique demonstrated by the students of the Bennington School of the Dance," gives an intriguing view of Hill and her students. In it a large group of women, dressed in light and dark leotard-tunics, moves in complementary swinging patterns on different levels. The first ensemble, standing in parallel position, swings down and up, then side into back falls, and hinges. In canon form the second group performs a slow side fall initiated from a contraction, repeating this in a progression lower and lower to their knees into a back fall. Another sequence shot from the ground shows a succession of leaps across the sky.

A very slender Hill with her light hair now tightly bound in a low bun, demonstrates slow, pressing arm gestures while changing lunges from side to side;

she then performs swings for the group (not unlike the phrase she demonstrated in the earlier NYU film). Remarkably disciplined, the group follows Hill's combination of phrases with eurythmic accuracy. The choreography shows Martha's interest in group motion, as the women perform a stepping pattern into lunges, bouncing with each step, with swinging arms, in lines of five, creating wavelike choreographic patterns. A final clip of film shows a group of skirt-clad women performing half-turn jumps. A soloist in a white dress repeats the pattern, echoed by the group with fists hitting thighs, the carriage and gestures very reminiscent of the movement in Graham's *Heretic*. But this time it was Martha Hill leading her dancing group to near martyrdom.[13]

At the end of the Bennington session, Graham, Humphrey, and Weidman gave "lecture-discussions on the modern dance" and performed repertory work in recitals that took place in the 150-seat "College Theatre" in the Commons Building. Norman recalled Graham's solo recital with Horst at the keyboard, "The first time seeing Martha Graham at Bennington was a great thrill. [It] gave you a sense of how great this art was and how fresh, how different— [giving] as a kind of benchmark against which you measured subsequent things. There have been very few subsequent things like that."

Humphrey and Weidman offered a series of solos and duets accompanied by pianists Pauline Lawrence and Vivian Fine, that included *Rudepoema, Counterpoint No.2*, and *Two Ecstatic Themes*. Hanya's contribution was a lecture-demonstration on the "modern German dance," which the *Bennington Banner* felt was consistent with the character of the school, "young in its first year," emphasizing "form and technique . . . as the groundwork for further and more ambitious compositions."[14] Other events that summer included a piano concert by Gregory Tucker,[15] and a "Demonstration Dance Lesson" presented by guest teacher Marge H'Doubler who showed motion picture clips of her dancers at the University of Wisconsin.

H'Doubler had traveled east while on her honeymoon, arriving a week after marrying Wayne Claxton. Thirteen years younger, Claxton was an art educator who stressed "art as a way of life" and had models at the University of Wisconsin dance to give his students "a kinesthetic awareness of the human body."[16] It is generally acknowledged that Marge until this point had had several very close relationships with other women: when she announced her intentions that August, her current companion became hysterical and "took to her bed for two weeks." The anticipation of Marge's visit at Bennington had more to do with catching a glance at the newly married couple then the content of her lecture.

Although that first summer of performance activities were modest in scale, these artists quickly saw the potential for their companies in residence on a college campus. The school provided studio space and covered production costs. City-weary artists had the unusual opportunity to work with their dancers for long, uninterrupted stretches of rehearsal. They were quick to recognize the significance of the project. Shelly was the first to comment: "These years brought dance from the gymnasium to the studio and theater. Something new was happening and people began to sit up and take notice."

Without question, the personal cost was great to Martha as a dancer who cherished opportunities to perform and create her own work. As the "Big Four" and others under her sponsorship grew in fame, her own chances diminished. As the one in charge, Martha became the facilitator rather than a competitor, and her own artistic ability often went unacknowledged by the others on campus. If, at first, the lack of parental trust had crippled her confidence, the omnipresence of her new artist-leaders meant that her own talent was ignored even further. Perhaps it was her suppressed ambition that drove the field into directions few had imagined.

Still, the end of the summer brought this group into a tightly commandeered unit that would endure for generations to follow. Living together in neutral territory certainly helped solidify their common mission. Within the boundaries of Bennington's pristine campus, they discovered that they actually cared for one another as individuals.

But what really changed the dance scene was that Martha Hill pressed these artists to build distinct technical styles that could be replicated in their own studios, not only by assistants but also by the students hungry for teaching materials. Here began the establishment of a sturdier art form upon which repertory could grow, unprecedented in the field and uniquely American in content.

Martha was aware that she was living in a time when warring forces were spreading throughout Europe. Hanya had to leave Bennington temporarily for a long journey to Germany. Her mission: to "rescue" her fifteen-year-old son Klaus before he was drafted into Hitler's Youth Corps.[17] How she would manage this, nobody knew. "We were heartsick with worry," Martha explained, "but we believed that Hanya would have the cunning and willpower to make it happen . . . and she did it."

On her return to New York City, Martha's income was secure enough to allow a move to her own small apartment at 85 Perry Street in the Village, where she would live for the next two years. Although she maintained a close relationship with Mary Jo, Martha at thirty-four finally was able to afford her own living quarters.

PART III

Private Lives and Common Goals

Martha and Mary Jo continued their campaign to make the Bennington experiment an ongoing success. Their advance letter to potential students for the 1935 session of the School of Dance boasted thirty faculty members with students coming "from every section of the country to share common interests of work and social life." The school offered very much the same program of study as the summer before, but this time all of the artists and their companies would come for a six-week stretch. In Mary Jo's view, what changed was the wide range of ability among students, and the "irresistible push for more opportunity to create and perform on the part of the artists. These changes came because the two originators had unwittingly opened a floodgate and a waiting tide had swept in."

In this "very generous climate," Hill and Leigh pulled together a more tightly organized advisory board for the School of the Dance, designed to act in "co-operation" with Bennington College and its permanent staff. The summer school formally became an autonomous unit to the college with a special board of trustees to oversee it. Approval for four more summer sessions would soon be granted. Academics John J. Coss, professor of philosophy and director of Columbia University's summer session and trustee of Bennington; Jay B. Nash from New York University; Dorothy Lawton, director of the Music Library of the New York Public Library—all proved to be loyal advisory board members and believers in the program. To guarantee harmonious endorsement for codirectors Hill and Shelly, Graham, Holm, Horst, Humphrey, Martin, and Weidman sat on the board as well. Martha counseled the artists that they were all important to the success of the unit, well aware of the host of conflicts among them.

The new "modern dance" proclaimed the importance of individual creativity, but there was concern that this very emphasis could be their downfall. The summer venture's greatness, Martha believed, would lie in bringing these factions together as a unit. The artists were rapidly emerging as leaders in the field in their separate and sometimes competitive lives in New York City; nonetheless, their connection with Bennington now bolstered their reputations and contributed to an increased number of dates on the "gymnasium circuit."

In the summer of 1935, it would be Martha's job to magnify their individual strengths and to unify them under the Bennington banner. The board had approved the general operating scheme for that summer with funds to be made available for costuming, composers, musicians, set designers, and construction fees. Each member of the "Big Four" was to be featured on consecutive summers. "Bennington never asked for ownership. It was there as a catalyst for the whole movement; it had no archival intentions," Hill later told Sali Ann Kriegsman. "Bennington was not interested in any way in tying up rights to productions. The reason for the Bennington School of the Dance was to help a new movement in the art and there was not a thought of putting anything in the way of the artist's making the best use of what [was] produced in the summer."[1]

Hill had earlier clarified her vision of Bennington, spelling out a five-year plan to the board in a move toward stability: a kind of "Salzburg of America." For the 1935 summer, Graham was to have a sizable budget for her workshop, with money for a composer and extra dancers. Doris and Charles were to receive the most support in 1936, with Hanya Holm's work featured in 1937. The summer of 1938 would be the culmination of the sequence, backing the production of new works by all four artists. Hill told the board that she planned to encourage the choreographers' collaboration with playwrights, poets, composers, and visual artists to create an atmosphere akin to a "Congress of the Arts." She reminded them that it would continue to be Bennington's responsibility to provide a place to stay and excellent food in a worry-free atmosphere.

Six of the twelve white clapboard cottages that housed students were allotted to the school. Living rooms were stripped to provide studios. The main dining room of the newly built Commons and old structures bearing the placenames of another day had to be used: the Carriage Barn, the Brooder, and the Chicken Coop became studio spaces. Performance space was another problem. According to Mary Jo, "The only theater, top floor of the Commons and an afterthought when the building was put up, betrayed its original function as an attic. Improvisation devised the workspaces. Inspiration was to fill them." "That little theater upstairs is historic," Becca Stickney, another colleague and fellow Cricket Hill resident marveled, "It was small but very deep, and so hot in the summer up there I don't know why some of these dancers didn't kill themselves because there was no wing space!"[2]

Shelly wrote about that summer, "We had the great good fortune in the presence of a person not even listed among the dance faculty. His name was Arch Lauterer." Lauterer, a designer from the Cleveland Playhouse, became one of Bennington's first theater professors in 1933. Called in as technical designer, he had, according to Hill, created a "very exciting stage" for the little theater in the Commons Building, after several other attempts at creative solutions. His first was to hastily transform (Shelly's words were "magnificently devised") the loft area above the dining hall (and beneath the bell tower) into a stage with barely enough acceptable dance space to accommodate solos and small group works. With unraked seating for less than 150 in the audience, the small theater would become a recital hall, as well as a studio for rehearsals and classes—all-important to Francis Fergusson, appointed head of drama in the winter of 1934. (Fergusson would soon became Lauterer's nemesis, calling the Commons theater at first sight, the school's "scandalously inadequate attic.")[3] Lauterer also transformed the carriage barn into a studio with mirrors and varnished floors.

The mimeographed handout for the 1935 summer program at Bennington contained few changes from the 1934 one except that the hairdressing shop was closed, greens fees of $1.50 were charged at the country club, and dressing for class was to take place in one's own room, with strict attention to costume regulations (no doubt to ward off earlier criticisms by Bennington's natives). The student handout sheet declared, "Tunics must be worn by all students over leotards at all times outside of studios." To further the efficiency of the Lost and Found, assigned numbers sewn to the inside top front edge of each piece of dancewear were required. All were small inconveniences for the delighted arrivals.

At final count 108 students were registered—many returning for a second year. Additions to the curriculum were made. A "workshop" program enlisting twenty-four others was set up to augment the artists' companies for Humphrey and Weidman to make large ensemble premieres possible. As an introduction to theater techniques, Martin's wife, Louise, taught a new course, "Basics of Dramatic Movement" (which Horst privately counseled dancers to avoid), and technical director Jane Ogborn taught "Stagecraft for Dancers." Martha and Mary Jo gave a series of sessions for teachers on the nature and function of dance. Martha taught sections of introductory and advanced composition as well.

Significantly, the summer school at Bennington (a women's college until 1969) would become a place that championed male dancers in an open environment for sexual freedom (and diversity) for both sexes. It was John Martin, as a prominent journalist, who was the loudest voice in raising the status and image of men in dance. Ruth St. Denis now followed her own "spiritual" path in dance. Once separated from St. Denis, Shawn had established his own summer school for dance, Jacob's Pillow in Lee, Massachusetts—one that featured a range of "ethnic" dance styles as well as his own teachings. Less than a decade earlier Denishawn's dancers had broken away to begin their own concertizing. Although Shawn had little interest in "modern" explorations and the creation of a personal movement style, his company Ted Shawn and his Men Dancers now maintained an active touring program across the country.[4]

Theater on Broadway also had its share of dancing men such as Fred Astaire as debonair role models, although few actually ventured into the dance concert field. After a year and a half as a chorus dancer in the Broadway musical *As Thousands Cheer,* José Limón began his first Bennington summer in 1935. Although somewhat shaky technically, he soon became one of the most promising male dancers on campus. As Weidman's assistant, José's masculine appearance immediately caught everyone's attention, but the young dancer only remembered an "irrepressible excitement that, along with sweat, saturated the atmosphere at the college."[5]

In planning for the 1935 summer of expanded residencies, Martha Hill seemed to be the only one confident that everyone would get along despite the crunch for studio space, students, and attention. She reasoned, "Doris and Charles and Martha, as well as Pauline, had grown up in the Denishawn Company together. They were like brothers and sisters. Martha and Charles had danced together in New York City's extravagant Lewisohn productions as partners. They were grown-up, intelligent artists, interested in what was happening to the art in the period. Why would there be problems?" In reality, her rationale was more based on her pact with her closest allies, Martha Graham and Louis Horst, who promised to help to make things work out. "Everybody expected there to be fisticuffs, but the only tensions were between the disciples," Hill confirmed. But Mary Jo remembered that they used to laugh about there being a Graham tree, a Humphrey-Weidman tree, and a Holm tree where people congregated after dinner. Yet Martha believed that "the leaders and the artists themselves were not clannish at all."

But if the directors did not perceive any tension among the "Big Four" privately, these artists thought differently. Although Holm, as an outsider, was the most willing to be collegial, her experiences the previous summer had been less than cordial. She recalled being snubbed in the dining room by Louis Horst and commented on "an awful lot of really green jealousy."[6] Invited in 1935 for a two-week teaching stint, she elected to take a leave of absence, and replaced herself with Tina Flade, who claimed to be "the youngest dancer of Mary Wigman's first famous group."[7] Doris still mistrusted the competitive situation, feeling that she always had to protect her own interests.

No matter their backgrounds, however, students thrived in the fertile environment. One thirty-five-year-old, Helen Mandel Levy, with only two weeks of previous training, relished the opportunity to study dance with these moderns. Leaving a husband in Philadelphia and her child at camp, she plunged into a summer of intense study, filling pages in a three-ring binder with meticulous notations on each of the seven courses she took. The vivacious, green-eyed brunette who began a lifelong friendship with Doris Humphrey that summer, described lessons of "harmony" and "discord" in weight shifts, lunges, turns, and walking patterns under Flade's tutelage. She explained that the class used percussion instruments (as did the modern dance that "originated in Germany") with Hindemith's set of four drums placed in a semicircle and Wigman's Gretsch drum needed to master the appropriate drumming techniques.

But the bulk of Levy's notes are crammed with information that shows the scope of Martha Hill's technique class: combinations of contractions, spirals, stretches, swings, and "rotations" in patterns at various tempi. She also describes myriad approaches in design and form from Martha's dance composition course. One page contains her teacher's warning against the use of improvised methods: "Better to compose by being disciplined. Teachers should set a problem, not tell pupils to 'listen to music and express themselves.'"[8]

A reviewer for *American Dancer* noted, "the spirit of Bennington is one of extreme absorption in all sorts of problems posed as relating to the dance. The teachers are dedicated, with a zeal amounting to consecration, to applying the clinical microscope and scalpel, in order that the eyes of the students may see the palpitating entrails of the arts which peasants called dancing." But he also observed that Martha's form-packed directives for her students pressed them into studies in space, focus, level, dimension, time, tempo, cumulative rhythms, changes in speed, and sequential forms of canon, round, theme and variations, as well as sonata and cycle forms. The critic complained about these strict lessons saying, "Research and experimentation is one thing and teaching dancing is another." He pronounced Martha Hill's composition class demonstration "a grimly theoretical approach to the dance."[9]

By now, each artist had his or her own teaching approach for creating dances. Ruth felt that

> Doris tended to be a builder in composition class. She tried to get them to use it and make something of it, presenting the material . . . and solving the problem. . . . Every once in a while I wished she would deviate a little bit for the thing that she wanted them to do, [saying] this doesn't solve the problem; this isn't it; this doesn't speak to the problem that you were supposed to speak to. She didn't do that too much. Louis had the body and the inside, whereas Doris was very much concerned with the body in space—always had the large space to teach in. She tried to analyze what she did [for steps] when she taught composition.

The variety of events offered that summer of 1935 was remarkable, reflecting the effervescent optimism of fellow artists in New York City. Roosevelt's Works Progress Administration, or WPA, had begun its eight-year run, bolstering employment for "publicly useful" work that included concert performance. At Bennington, among the usual presentations of student showcases, music concerts, demonstrations, and lecture-discussions, were the first stirrings for the use of dance as a political weapon. Jacques Barzun delivered a lecture "Culture and Revolution"; and George Beiswanger, "The Social Implications of the Contemporary Dance." Members of the New Dance League (having recently changed its name from Workers Dance League) presented "An Evening of Revolutionary Dance." Most of these choreographers were from Graham's company, with works by Jane Dudley, Sophie Maslow, and Anna Sokolow standouts in a performance given at the College Theatre on 28 July.

Martha's encouragement was more support of Graham dancers already in residence than sympathy for the politics being advanced.[10] She and Mary Jo sided with Louis Horst's perspective that the use of dance for political statements meant aesthetic betrayal.

Teddy Wiesner remembered that during this period Martha and Mary Jo were always under great pressure in handling day-to-day operations. Along with student problems were production ones. Arch's wife, Helen Lauterer, was hired to run the costume shop, but in short order, the situation proved impossible: "Each artist had a favorite seamstress in New York and when it was clear that Helen's little sewing room up in the roof of the Commons wasn't adequate and very hot, these seamstresses were brought to campus to get the costumes made."[11] Creating work at Bennington soon placed further demands on each dance artist as well, with "the nature of the contest" in Humphrey's words, now playing for higher stakes. One of the most recent challenges was that both Doris and Charles were now interested in developing works for larger ensembles; keeping a large group of dancers together, however, was an additional burden.

Graham still commanded the most attention as a solo artist on the series of programs at the College Theatre, although Tina Flade's solo concert and John Martin's lecture "The Ancient Art of Modern Dance" were enthusiastically received as well. But the highest praise among students went to the August presentation by the Humphrey–Weidman Dance Company. With repertory that included Humphrey's 1929 *Life of the Bee* (based on Maurice Maeterlinck's 1901 study of bees and created as a paradigm of human social activity) the highlight of Doris's offering was undoubtedly her *New Dance: Variations and Conclusion* (which would become the last section of her *New Dance Trilogy* the following summer).[12] As usual, it was the devoted Pauline Lawrence who designed Humphrey's costumes, with Eleanor King describing the indispensable Pauline as "prescient, intuitive; she could nag, she insisted, and always aesthetically she was right."[13] Local carpenters were hired to construct the cubes that made up the set pieces envisioned by Humphrey for her *New Dance,* like the ones that she had used when setting the piece in Manhattan before the Bennington summer began. In keeping with his determination that for true collaboration, music should be written for dance, Horst had suggested that his former teacher and good friend Wallingford Riegger write the commissioned score. Doris described the dance as an "affirmation from disorganization to organization," constructed in "broken form" that stated main themes with elaborations following. Riegger's powerfully rhythmic score for four hands at the piano was up to the task.

According to Humphrey biographer, Selma Jeanne Cohen, Riegger never knew that Doris had choreographed some of the movement using Roy Harris's *When Johnny Comes Marching Home,* as a substructure. Riegger's own working method seemed equally casual. After he viewed the dance (in silence) he wrote melodic lines and gave them over to Ruth and Norman asking them to "write my kind of chords for this." The result became a touchstone for its strength as a dance score.[14] For Doris, the dance represented "the world as it should be, where each person has a clear and harmonious relationship to his fellow beings." The work could also serve as a wish for change in the Bennington atmosphere, which, she confessed, "never appeals to me because it takes on the nature of a contest and is highly disturbing to my peace of mind."[15]

Declared by Martin in his *New York Times* review after its premiere as "one of the most exciting pieces in the modern repertoire," *New Dance* was the first landmark work produced at Bennington under Hill's direction. To José, *New Dance* was her "choreographic ode to the nobility of the human spirit." (It was also one that showed off his much improved technique.)[16] That Martin preferred Humphrey's choreography to Graham's and favored her in his reviews, would soon become clear when his take of Graham's *Panorama* hit the stands a few weeks later.

Martha Hill had created the perfect situation where artists could reap the publicity—if not necessarily the rewards—from having critics on campus: from now on pressmen, Martin and Horst (as editor of *Dance Observer*) were on hand to review every important event on campus. Later, novice critic Walter Terry of the *New York Herald Tribune* and the seasoned Margaret Lloyd of the Boston *Christian Science Monitor* (who praised *New Dance* as "the first pure example of the abstract symphonic ballet") would follow their lead. Recognition for dance at Bennington soon paralleled that of music festivals such as Tanglewood. Even the students began to enjoy the numbers of "newspaper boys" that began to appear on campus, wanting dancers out on the green for movies and newspaper photo shoots.

Bennington's artists began to realize the significance of their work as part of a larger vision. In her unpublished papers from that period, Doris reflected on the "great difference between modern dance as it is presented today and . . . as little as five or six years ago" leaving a "period of barrenness" for a "new theatrical form." The most striking changes that took place were in length, and the complexity of forms: instead of a number of five-minute recital pieces, Doris and Charles were now composing "long ballets, consecutive in idea," and as comments by "two dancers on contemporary life" in the "theater of movement rather than words."[17] All seemed to possess a grander sense of mission and direction not only for their own futures, but for the field of dance—the very mission that Martha Hill had been advocating.

Unexpectedly, the new workshop program, in Shelly's words, "belied its modest title by exploding into such dancing that the small college theatre clearly could not contain it. Somewhere a theatre of adequate dimensions had to be found." The issue of an adequate performing space had quickly become critical to the success of the school for both students and faculty. In time, it would become a major stumbling block for the six-week enterprise. The arrangement for this season's performances was that students generally previewed the first evening, with the second open as a public performance, according to Mary Jo. If the inadequacy of the Commons theater had been demonstrated earlier, this time it was "overwhelming" and amounted to "a mass assault" on the limited facilities. Bennington had caught the public's attention as a center for innovative dance performances, drawing curious patrons of the arts from miles around.

If Humphrey and the others willingly performed in the little Commons facility, space was not workable for the dance project that Graham now conceived. Her *Panorama* was to have commissioned decor in the form of mobiles designed and constructed by sculptor Alexander Calder (or "Sandy" as everyone called him).

Despite a flurry of outdoor campus activities such as master classes, filming, and lecture-demonstrations on the great lawn in front of the Commons, attempts to encourage Graham to consider using the same expanse for the performances of her new work failed. Graham later admitted to a certain amount of naïveté as she prepared for her upcoming venture: "In those days we were all very elementary and fearful of nothing—because we had nothing to be fearful of."[18]

As Sandy Calder began to assemble bits and pieces of his construction—brought in from his studio in Roxbury, Massachusetts, to Bennington in his 1930 LaSalle nine-seater touring car along with his French sheepdog, Feathers—Graham grew more and more apprehensive. When she first met Calder through their mutual friend Noguchi, he had been experimenting with "things with a little motion, some with more motion." Lincoln Kirstein and ballet patron Eddie Warburg had also suggested a collaborative venture with Calder to Martha Graham. The notion of group effort was exciting many artists during this time.

Calder's first motor-driven creation was dubbed *Mobile* by Marcel Duchamp in 1931. "In addition to something that moves, in French it also means motive," the sculptor explained.[19] This time, rather than using small electric motors, or cranks, he had the idea that dancers might generate the movement of his pieces, and he was anxious to try out the idea. For the time being, the affable Sandy continued on his own out of Graham's way, instead, presenting small wire pins to delighted dancers when they came by to see what he was creating.

Arch remained dissatisfied with the little theater's audience capacity and the floor-level seating. Mary Jo cheerily agreed that the little theater was "obviously out of the question" for the new "cycle" and an alternative had to be found. Weeks before the fourth event of the season, she reported in her unpublished memoir, "everyone involved with staging the series was less delighted at the pace of things than anxious about how to cope with it."

One imaginative setting that Arch came up with was for a tent to be erected beside the library. "Off went Arch to find one. A dull brown army tent? Not for Arch," Mary Jo recalled. Somewhere on Long Island, he came upon his conception of a proper tent, "not only capacious, but gaily red and white striped" that had been discarded as a shelter for some part of a racetrack." He bought it, and had it carted to Vermont. By this time, Martha Biehle as "custodian of the bluest of blue-sky budgets ever devised," was only slightly concerned. "More was to come—a platform for dancing since that couldn't be done on bare ground: a cable for electrical connections, since dancing called for light. The platform and the cable both materialized. Suffice to report that the tent came and was erected in a prophetic wind. Only the wind continued unconquered." Arch's answer was to have his two technical assistants—one already a veteran at assisting Arch, and the other, "known to be brave"—actually live in the tent so that he could handle it like a ship in full sail, slacking or tightening ropes as the wind dictated. "It never blew down. It just leaked. Clearly, even to the undauntable Arch, it was no home for a Festival," Mary Jo explained. "Installation of the theatre in the Armory was another matter, and meant completely redesigning its interior." Carrying forward stagecraft ideas of Adolph Appia's "living light," Arch now at least had a solid structure where he could control the lighting in tandem with the movement.

Graham had less than six weeks with her workshop group to set *Panorama* while waiting for Lloyd's new score and Calder's floor plans for the Armory's interior that would accommodate his three-tiered set to be used in one of the sections. Twelve members of Martha Graham's dance group "in residence" for the full six weeks, greatly added to the caliber of dancing on campus—and to the anxiety of the twenty-four students cast to dance alongside them.

Among the workshop dancers was Muriel Stuart, a teacher at the School of American Ballet. "Intensely curious" about the happenings at Bennington, it was Lincoln Kirstein who enrolled Stuart in the workshop as a "spy," according to writer Don McDonagh. The job was more difficult than she may have suspected. "To keep the punishment at an acceptable level, [ballet dancer Stuart] eventually had to affix soft pads to the soles of her feet," Teddy Wiesner remembered.[20]

Teddy had taken over Martha's NYU Sloatsburg job in 1934, but gave it up to become one of the "perennials" at Bennington, where that summer she was also cast in Graham's big group piece. To her, rehearsals seemed like "hours and hours of running in place on this wooden floor in a hot and humid tent that blew down halfway through the summer. We would be just exhausted, and we'd get so stiff and sore. At night we'd go back to the dormitory and sit and soak our feet in boric acid water, put lanolin on them, and wear socks to bed to get them to heal faster." She recalled that Graham's technique was very new to anybody that came from outside of New York City, and many in her large cast had not done anything like it before. "Most of us didn't have the stretch needed for Graham's movement, but we were all fascinated with it. Graham did talk about *Panorama* to some extent but she wasn't terribly explicit [about] the quality and style of what she wanted." Still, the dancers did come away with something they never forgot. "Martha was always very intense, and if things didn't go right she'd get very angry, and there's nothing more exciting than to see Martha Graham angry!"

Teddy blamed Graham's frustrations on her lack of experience working with such a large (and technically limited) group. "We were pretty rushed, and at the end we had to keep relearning because she would change things up to three or four days before the performances. We counted like mad and just had to be careful it didn't show." Years later at a gathering of dancers that had been in the original piece, few recalled very much about the actual movement, except "the running in place" that was a constant, and that their two-piece costumes created by Helen Lauterer consisted of pongee skirts over trunks and a bra top with short sleeves. "It seemed very daring to have a bare middle," Teddy recalled.[21]

To the young team of accompanists who eked out a living playing for Martha's classes at NYU, Bennington offered an incredible opportunity. Norman and Ruth Lloyd arrived on the scene with great anticipation: Norman to teach three courses a day and to do some accompanying, and Ruth to play for classes "all the time." Norman had not expected to take on a new role as composer; originally, Horst was to write the score for Graham's *Panorama*. He recalled that "sometime in the first week Louis said—it certainly wasn't put as a question—something to me about writing a work for Graham." Norman's response was ecstatic: "Working with Graham was a frightening experience. You are dealing with a monumental life force when you're involved with Graham. Regardless of anything, you don't say no to Martha Graham. There was no mention of fee. There *was* no fee. This was what you were there for." He admitted that he hadn't really done that much writing: "So in my spare time I had to teach a whole new subject to me." In trepidation, he agreed, knowing that he had four weeks to write a forty-minute work. As the dance was being choreographed each day, Lloyd worked to keep up with Graham. Ruth recalled that every day about four-thirty, Norman "would come home and sit in a hot tub to try and relax, because he still had eight or ten hours to go."

To make matters worse, Bennington's winter piano faculty was very guarded about the use of their instruments, and very distrustful of anybody in the dance. Norman continued, "I wasn't allowed to use any of the pianos in any of the studios; I had to go from living room to living room in the dormitories [looking for] uprights. I just went from pillar to post. It was miserable."

The first section that Graham choreographed was "a virtuoso, very fast kind of a witches' dance for Anna Sokolow and Anita Alverez—in an asymmetrical rhythmic pattern. Graham did that dance first. I just looked at the dance and got the quality, character of the dance. Then I would come with a little notebook and we would figure out the number of counts and the length of phrases as they came along. Then I would go back to whatever living room lounge piano I could find, and write something that would fit. Actually I took her melodic inflection for the witches' dance depending on how she counted it, for the momentum of the accent."

Norman always acknowledged Louis Horst as the force behind his career, and after this summer of trials by fire, the two men would remain friends for the rest of their lives, thoroughly enjoying each other's ribald sense of humor. Bonding like father and son, whenever possible their conversations avoided all reference to dance in deference to baseball. But when in need of mentoring, Norman admitted, he would go to Louis and say, "I'm stuck," and "Louis would say something that would unblock me so I could run back and write some more." By now they were among a free-flowing group of musicians that included Otto Luening, Greg Tucker, and Riegger who played poker and made terrible puns at lunchtime, calling themselves "The Hoosick Tunnel Marching Society."

Norman described the music he wrote for *Panorama*'s "Calder section" as "avant-garde, if we can think of it that way." He admitted, "I just ran out of ideas. I didn't know what to do with it and Louis said, 'Why don't we just repeat it?' So one measure would be flute and bass clarinet and then that would be repeated then with oboe and clarinet. One measure repeated over and over again, a kind of Erik Satie repetition in and out, and orchestrated with tones wide apart." Surmising that more complicated music would have been distracting, Norman explained, "It was a perfect avant-garde thing to have done because you were seeing dancers and seeing the huge beautiful discs of Calder's mobiles."

The composer confessed,

It was a mad scramble. When you're involved in something like this, all you want to do is get through with it and hope nobody falls down! . . . I learned another important thing from Graham that time. I took a piece in and played it, and she put her chin down and said, "No, I don't think that's right. There's something you have to learn and that is when to throw something away or put it aside when a thing isn't right." That was very important. That was postgraduate work in music composition.

Fellow composer Alex North (then working and living with Anna), was asked to help orchestrate Norman's piano sketches. According to Norman, however, Alex and Ruth would go off and play tennis instead. "I suddenly realized the night before this little orchestra came on campus, that the whole last scene hadn't been copied," he recalled, "so I stayed up the whole night writing out parts."

The dancers were disappointed that when they moved into the Armory, they couldn't do much with the mobiles. Calder also envisioned a huge lightning bolt that would go across the stage between the first and second parts. What resulted, Norman said, was a huge wooden machine "that never quite worked" and "was scrapped. It would have been a fine idea."[22]

The work spread over the Armory with performing on the floor and the bleachers in addition to the stage—all framed by a proscenium arch. "There were so many things to look at," Ruth Lloyd recalled. "With thirty-six dancers stationed at different positions, they had more space than the audience." But from Norman's view as conductor the work was a shambles. "The second night the trumpet player got lost, missed his cue, and left out a whole long solo. For twenty measures or so all we heard was this sort of noodling accompaniment. The dancers were going by count anyhow because they had almost no rehearsal with the orchestra." He conceded, "Musically I wasn't too happy about it, any more than Graham was too happy about the dance. With more time, and more experience, the results might have been better."

Norman added philosophically that dance at that time was declaring its independence from music. "I felt that [Martha] needed music, but the music should be secondary. It was very much in discussion how independent dance could be. The only way you can assert your independence is to make dance number one and make everything else subservient to that." Asked if he saw this as a collaborative effort, Norman Lloyd answered, "Not especially. This was purely a Graham opus."

Arch's redesign for the Armory posed an entirely new set of issues for Mary Jo as the administrator in charge of practical matters, including coverage under the liability policy taken out for audience protection. Bleachers designed to rise from floor to balcony, on which folding chairs could be placed had been built in advance and assembled in the off-campus building. Another problem occurred with the realization that the college policy covered only the campus. She explained, "A proper insurance company official appeared late in the afternoon preceding the first performance, crawled under the unlikely structure with notebook and pencil and emerged to announce the amount of 'mobile weight' it would support." She recalled a custom peculiar to the Bennington years that first appeared in August 1935: "A new form of applause developed—the beating of heels on the floor—[that] could later prove to be something of a hazard. Since nothing was likely to stop it, it would just have to be counted as part of the mobile weight."

Mary Jo dealt with other near catastrophes, "In all the summers of dancing at the Armory, violent thunderstorms accompanied by on-and-off deluges of rain never failed to make their appearance. Lights flickered. The overloaded area designated as a parking lot turned to muck. For this first event only one performance had been scheduled until advance demand necessitated announcing a second one." Martha and Mary Jo kept things going, cheerily observing "no one ever seemed to mind" when things went awry.

There were two performances added "by demand" for Martha Graham and her group, scheduled on the last weekend of the season, August 14 and 15. Presented with the first ensemble work in which she did not dance, Graham's 1934 *Celebration* and her solos *Sarabande* and *Frontier* were performed before the climatic premiere *Panorama*. (*Frontier*—originally the first section of *Perspectives*—had first been shown at the Guild Theatre the previous April with a

Noguchi set and a Horst score. Along with her 1930 *Lamentation* to music by Kodály, both quickly became signature solos that would secure her reputation as the most exciting dance artist of her time.)[23] Ruth Lloyd believed that the success of Graham's dances "had a great deal to do with the kind of music she danced to. Louis weaned her away from nineteenth-century romantic music and the sound of strings because Louis considered the use of strings as too romantic." For these works, Horst accompanied with his usual vitality, treating the piano more as a percussive instrument, than a melodic one.[24]

But it was with *Panorama* that an astounded audience knew history was being made. The audience for Graham's two evenings numbered more than a thousand, where "demand still exceeded capacity, even though the weather was its characteristic self. Flanked by a royal band of strong-arm helpers [they] literally drove the excess audience back out into the rain," according to Shelly. Yet possibly the most dramatic event of the summer took place between Graham and Martin the morning after the premiere. Martin gave *Panorama* an unenthusiastic review, calling the work "cerebral" and fraught with problems. When news of the *Times* piece hit Bennington, all silently watched as Graham entered the dining hall. José reported that Graham went straight to Martin and said, "Thank you very much! If I never see you again it will be much too soon."

By the end of the season, whether the artists liked it or not, more critics had come from every direction, including the *Boston Daily Eagle,* the *Christian Science Monitor,* and other New England papers, and from magazines such as *Theatre Arts Monthly* and *Newsweek.* Martha Hill's disdain for "yellow journalism" was obvious to the writers wooed into the Bennington circle. She had little use for gossip, probably because her own interpersonal skills relied so heavily on confidentiality. Still, she respected their words in print, whether positive or not. Outside appraisals were healthy for the field, Martha and Mary Jo knew.

Other artists on campus took the criticism in stride as well. Norman recalled that *Panorama* was also bitterly reviewed in the left-wing press because the work "didn't come out for solidarity forever or the typical slogan." To him Graham's statement was purely American, which is what was so appealing. "Graham was always just that one step or so ahead."

Martha Hill credited Mary Jo for her "knack for keeping colleagues and students on track and focused, and she was a confident curriculum adviser." From Mary Jo's perspective, however, her administrative job had more to do with mob control: "Throughout the session, visitors kept turning up—musicians, writers, people from the theater, educators, and just plain interested spectators. This tide—like the tide of students and audience—swelled by the season. The real aficionados began early to plan vacations to coincide with performances. And so, after the close of the second session, as after the first, the planners had to do some replanning." Thinking back, the Lloyds believed that the 1935 festival had put Bennington College "on the map." And at that point in their careers, "the college [gave] the kind of support which we never found in any of the other institutions. Bennington was a real love affair."

That fall of 1935, Mary Jo took on a commitment at the University of Chicago as associate professor in charge of student activities. (The next year she became chairman of the women's division of the Department of Physical Education.) Despite the move, Mary Jo's alliance to Martha remained strong, and the two were in communication throughout the academic year. By her own admission, Martha scribbled ideas on notes for Mary Jo to refine, and others to type. In Martha's words, Mary Jo was "a natural speechwriter, good with words." Unlike Mary Jo, Martha had an aversion to speechmaking that she would never get over. Even consenting to delivering occasional introductions and acknowledgments would aggravate her ulcers. "Writing was never Martha's strong suit," Belitt explained. "Martha Hill mustered the whole force of her being and said to Mary Jo: 'You write it up!'"

In a unusual "meeting of minds" event sponsored by the Elmhirst Committee of the college and the school of the dance, Mary Jo and Martha's daylong Forum on the Modern Dance took place on the last day of the summer session. As if to clarify and distill the meaning of modern dance, once and for all, eleven panel members (Graham, Hill, Horst, Humphrey, Lauterer, Lloyd, Martin, Nancy McKnight, Jane Ogborn, Shelly, and Weidman) took part, with Professor Eduard C. Lindeman acting as discussion leader. The Elmhirsts attended, along with a number of staff, students, and visitors for what must have been a historic moment at the college. Leading questions such as "What are the major distinctions to be made between modern dancing and conventional or classic dancing?" and "How is one to conceive of the role or function of the modern dance in modern society, particularly in American society?" brought forth such defining statements as: "the modern dance . . . represents a point of view rather than a system"; "the modern dance belongs to its period: it emerges as an expression of something vital in the life of the times"; and "the modern dance may be conceived in passion but executed in wisdom." These thoughts fill a nine-page document that summarizes the seriousness (and in an eerie way, the conclusiveness) of the discussions that transpired.[25]

Martha's carefully penned statement for the 1935–36 Bennington catalogue drew upon the Forum on the Modern Dance to explain the meaning and purpose of modern dance as fundamentally a communal art. However this in no way precedes development of individual styles, but rather provides opportunity for the individual to build her own point of view soundly and truly. The point of view is contemporary, dynamic, and non-dogmatic. The aim is to develop a discriminating and selective taste in art through experience and analysis . . . since the dance is so immediate an art . . . it is necessary that students have direct contact with different approaches represented by outstanding artists in the field.[26]

This credo, drawn out so deliberately with her colleagues would be Martha's from then on.

1. *Grace and Grant Hill, 1897. Courtesy of the Martha Hill Archives*

2. *Grace Martha Hill, 1904. Courtesy of the Martha Hill Archives*

3. *The Hill family at East Palestine Ohio home.* Left to right, *Katherine, Grant, Gene, Grace, Martha (with Rosebud, her doll), c. 1908. Courtesy of the Martha Hill Archives*

4. *Martha with brother Gene, c. 1910. Courtesy of the Martha Hill Archives*

5. *High school basketball team, 1915.*
Martha, fourth from left. *Courtesy of*
the East Palestine Memorial Library.

6. *"The Columbia" showboat.*
Courtesy of the Martha Hill Archives

7. *High school graduation portrait, 1918.*
Courtesy of the Martha Hill Archives

8. *Swedish gymnastics, Battle Creek Normal School of Physical Education, c. 1919. Courtesy of the Martha Hill Archives*

9. *Martha Hill, 1921. Courtesy of the Martha Hill Archives*

10. *Mary Jo Shelly, Kellogg School of Physical Education, c. 1921. Courtesy of the Martha Hill Archives*

11. *Dancers at Kansas State Teachers College, 1924.*
Courtesy of Fort Hays State University.

12. *Martha Hill dancing, Kansas State Teachers College, 1924.*
Courtesy of the Martha Hill Archives

13. *Martha Graham's* Primitive Mysteries, *c. 1931. Photo: Edward Moeller*

14–17. *Martha Hill and her technique class, NYU Graduate Dance Camp at Lake Sebago, Sloatsburg, N.Y, 1931. Courtesy of the Martha Hill Archives*

18. *Faculty and students, Bennington School of the Dance, 1934.*
First row, fifth from left: Louis Horst and Max, Martha Graham, Mary Jo Shelly, Gregory Tucker, Martha Hill, Ruth Lloyd, Bessie Schönberg, Norman Lloyd,
Martha Biehle (secretary), Dorothy Bird, May O'Donnell. Directly behind Hill, Helen Priest Rogers.

19-20. *Martha Hill dancing at Bennington, c. 1935.*
Courtesy of the Martha Hill Archives

21. *Betty Bloomer Ford in attitude, Martha Hill seated at center right, 1936.*
Photo: Thomas Bouchard, © *Diane Bouchard*

22. *Martha Hill, c. 1936. Courtesy of the Martha Hill Archives*

23. *Martha Hill, Bennington, 1936. Photo: Thomas Bouchard, © Diane Bouchard*

24. *Doris Humphrey in* With My Red Fires, *Bennington, 1936. Photo: Barbara Morgan*

26. *Arch Lauterer, 1937.*
Photo: Barbara Morgan

25. *Hanya Holm's* Trend, *Bennington, 1937. Photo: Barbara Morgan*

27. *Charles Weidman and José Limón, c. 1930's.*
Courtesy of the Juilliard School Archives

28. *Martha Graham and Doris Humphrey, Bennington School of the Dance at Mills College Mills, 1939. Photo: Ralph Jester. Courtesy of the Martha Hill Archives*

29. *Doris Humphrey with drum teaching at Mills, 1939. Photo: Thomas Bouchard, © Diane Bouchard*

The idea that female dancers must maintain their independence if they are to have a career in the profession is still prevalent among dancers today. It was a notion that began most dramatically with Isadora Duncan, who had many lovers and bore two children, before marrying poet Sergei Esenin. Accounts indicate that after a bad marriage, Loie Fuller's intimates were women. At thirty-six, St. Denis married Ted Shawn, a homosexual, in a "white marriage" for public view, although she herself often enjoyed the company of younger males. At thirty-six, Doris Humphrey married Leo Woodford, yet still remained independent.

Louis Horst continued to bellow against marriage as the ruination of artists. Although he and Graham remained devoted friends, they each moved on to other romantic involvements. After Graham's passionate affair with California artist Carlos Dyer during the summer of 1937, Horst "became attached" to the young, diminutive Graham company dancer, Nina Fonaroff.

Martha Hill, too, enjoyed the unfettered position of a single woman as intrigues continued among her colleagues. Martha, like other female dance professionals, reduced the men in her life to supporting players. Preoccupied with her career, Martha claimed to be too busy running from one place to another for more than an occasional tryst with a man—until she met Lefty.

When Thurston Jynkins Davies—or Lefty, as everyone called him—met Martha, he was the youngest college president in America. Born 7 December 1893, in Knoxville, Tennessee, he was the son of a Presbyterian minister. It would have pleased Martha's mother, had she known, that Davies came from a prominent family of ministers, and that Colorado College, where he became president, was founded for students drawn from evangelical churches. As a child growing up in Philadelphia, he attended the William Penn Charter School and went on to Princeton University. In many ways he resembled one of his undergraduate friends, F. Scott Fitzgerald: the Colorado College *Nugget* described the pair as possessing "enormous charm, good looks, perception, initiative." A classics major, after graduation from Princeton in 1916, Lefty joined the U.S. Marine Corps, fought in World War I, and received the Croix de Guerre, a Silver Star, and two Purple Hearts. "At war's end, Davies found himself pursued by precisely the same brand of personal devils that has destroyed the interpreter of the Jazz age," the Colorado College account of its presidents would later report.[1] Nonetheless, as a war hero, Lefty quickly found work as master at the Gilman Country School in Roland Park, Maryland, and then headmaster at the Nicols School in Buffalo, New York.

Shortly after his marriage in 1929, Lefty had convinced his wife Joyce to invest her inheritance in stocks. The unfortunate result would forever taint his marriage: Lefty could never quite get over the feeling that he was responsible for their financial downfall. Nor could his self-pitying and depressed wife. He returned to work at his alma mater after his two daughters were born, and for a time, family life in Princeton, New Jersey, seemed idyllic, with faculty parties and football games the major social events of their lives. Lefty was soon well regarded on campus and given more and more administrative responsibilities in positions more entrepreneurial than academic; he was employed in the alumni program and became the coordinator of the Princeton athletic program. He became president of Colorado College in 1934.

His wife Joyce was at her best when they first moved to Colorado, their daughter Judy remembered. "There she enjoyed being a college president's wife, and was a good one, making friends with faculty wives, phoning them often, leading a quite social life. She was then a pretty woman—slender and active." But once in Colorado, "family troubles in spades" multiplied, as Joyce's mental and physical health deteriorated. "By nature, she was quite nervous and a worrier—with plenty of justification. Though she did not complain at all, anyone could see that she was sad," Judy wrote in a family history for her children.[2]

Gregarious and ever-active Davies built a reputation for enticing donors to reach into their pockets, while gaining the trust of his faculty. Since becoming president, he had reinstated a summer session where he hoped to add dance, as Bennington had done so successfully.[3]

Now the president needed professional advice for a new dance program he wanted to put into place at Colorado College. Martha explained, "Being a schoolmaster, he always asked questions. He didn't like the watered-down kind of ballet that was going on." Lefty first consulted with friend Edith Isaacs, a highly respected figure in the theater world. "She said, 'Go to two people. John Martin and Martha Hill.' And [its] being a man's world, he went to John first, who said to him, 'The person you really need to talk to is Martha Hill.' So, 'thrown at him twice,' Lefty headed off to find me at New York University."

Martha remembered her first view of the handsome man on an unseasonably warm afternoon at the beginning of the spring semester of 1936. He was standing in the corridor, surrounded by a gaggle of young women outside the dance studio where she had just finished teaching. After introducing himself, he asked, "May I have a few moments to speak with you, Miss Hill?" Charmed, Martha replied, "Of course!" Observing his beautifully tailored woolen tweed overcoat and considering the heat, she added, "I share my office with several others. It's a closet, really. Good only for ripening bananas! My apartment is nearby. It will be quieter there." Later, she mused, "I don't know how I had the courage to say that!" They were attracted to each other at first sight. A passionate affair began that day that would change everything for Martha. "After that, the president of Colorado College continued to need advice!" At thirty-six, she had found the love of her life.

Friends observed a sudden change in Martha. Ruth remembered, "After that we all knew that Lefty was Martha's new love." Lefty cut an exciting figure, with an athletic build, auburn hair, and sun-dashed freckles, his roguish smile exuded confidence and goodwill. Martha was swept away by his ability to mix authority with charm—characteristics that many admired in her own personality.

Lefty's winning manner belied the sensitive core of a music lover. He had a natural singing voice (like Martha's father) and she adored the combination. "Being pure Welshman, Lefty was always interested in music." And she found in him an uncanny resemblance to her brother Gene in character and presence: striking in appearance, charming socially, and full of world-shaking ideas, with a glint of mischievousness in his eyes.

Because Lefty was a married man in a prominent position, their relationship would soon become a complex tangle of passion, secrecy, and need. Already caught up in a difficult marriage, Lefty had two teenage daughters to raise. For Martha, the situation was simpler: for the first time in her life she had fallen desperately in love.

Communication between the couple by mail and telephone continued to be discreet. Back in Colorado, Lefty dictated a letter to his secretary that arrived at New York University days after their first meeting. Could Martha possibly come to his college to help him evaluate the dance situation within the next few weeks? Arrangements to stay at the Antlers Hotel would, of course, be provided. Perhaps she might teach a master class during her visit. To all of this, she telegrammed yes.

Within two weeks Martha joined Lefty on campus for all intents and purposes as a guest consultant and, so far as Bennington was concerned, to recruit for the next summer. In the midst of pro forma meetings at Colorado College to assess its dance situation, administrators found Martha full of enthusiastic, forward-looking ideas and good sense.

Taken by the beauty of the quiet resort town, nestled at the base of Pike's Peak and Cheyenne Mountain, Martha was entranced when Lefty drove her through the picturesque red rock formations in the Garden of the Gods. He then escorted her to the illustrious Broadmoor Hotel for an intimate dinner. There he confessed the dilemma of his marriage situation and his attraction to her.

While in Colorado Springs, Martha observed that the town was publicized as the "Newport of the Rockies." Wanting to help his effort to advance the arts at Colorado College, Martha suggested to Lefty that joining forces with the town's Fine Arts Center, with its share of wealthy patrons, might also bring money into the college itself. A quick call guaranteed that Martha Graham would add a performance date at the end of April for Colorado Springs as part of her first transcontinental solo tour. This would be the first performance of modern dance in the area. When the event finally took place, the audience (made up of a good many of the college's faculty and staff, who were given tickets by President Davies) found the performance nearly incomprehensible. Martha's next recommendation—a performance by Holm and her newly established company—was perhaps a better bet for demystifying the new art of modern dance, she told Lefty. When Hanya's company appeared later in 1936, all were greatly relieved.[4]

Hill, Horst, and Graham had what we might today call alternative lifestyles, with the most important ingredient being independence. But, if each rejected the notion of marriage, in fact, all had personal (and legal) reasons for not marrying their lovers. Graham understood Hill's dilemma; she herself had been frustrated over the years with Horst, who refused to divorce his wife Betty. She consoled Hill over Lefty's marital status. Still, the long-distance relationship suited Martha. Some wondered if she kept up an unrelenting pace to replace what her life with Lefty could be. Yet they were doubtful that she would give up her own career for his. Clearly, Mary Jo's presence was part of the equation. "But during those first years Lefty and Martha somehow didn't quite make it all the way as a couple," Ruth Lloyd felt. "It was a very delicate situation." She remembered Martha expressing the pain of their separation. "We worried about the relationship." In contrast, Ruth and Norman were the ideal young married couple to those around them. They exuded happiness and the seeming beauty of a monogamous relationship. If Martha and Lefty intended to marry, the Colorado law of a seven-year wait before a spouse could be legally divorced from an institutionalized partner stopped them. "Of course he couldn't get a divorce because she was in an institution," Martha's friends surmised.

"I suppose if you're not married, you have to make a production. You can't be like a teenager. We knew Martha was very attached to Lefty and we only hoped that he would be good to her. If you're fortunate you find a mate early in life. But Martha had to keep on being her own private person while flirting with somebody, or loving them."[5] In Martha's environment among dancers there had been limited opportunities for heterosexual relationships; now at midlife, she had found intimacy with the man who would become the main focus of her personal life.

Shelly commented on the lack of male students in dance, a topic of concern for everyone in an art form predominantly made up of women. "This situation, like the whole composition of the school, mirrored the state of affairs in modern dance as a whole in this period." Taking on the challenge of training men, a new course feature for the upcoming summer at Bennington was to be Weidman's "Men's Workshop," in which he planned to develop his new work, *Quest*. The idea followed on the trustees' recent approval of "drama fellows" to supply men for Bennington's theater productions, setting precedent for paid actors and dancers on campus.

On her way back to New York City that spring, always on the lookout for new talent, Martha "discovered" Bill Bales at the Carnegie Institute of Technology at the University of Pittsburgh, where she "dragged him from under a piano" and recommended him to the Humphrey-Weidman School. Weidman had instructed Martha, "If you find any boys, send them to us." A follow-up letter from Weidman offering a scholarship "opened Pandora's box," according to Bales, for an important career in dance. Weidman invited the young dancer to Bennington for the summer of 1936, after which he was kept on "the inside track" for twenty-eight years, once he got there.[6]

Another to be asked to participate as a choreographer at Bennington (and distressed by the political and social upheaval on the home front and abroad) was Anna Sokolow who had become a prominent dance activist, returning as guest artist with the New Dance League. A member of Graham's group and assistant to Horst at the Neighborhood Playhouse, Sokolow now emerged as a gifted choreographer; according to Horst, she became his "second-best" student (Graham being his first). With Alex North, she spent time in Russia in 1934 and, according to her biographer, Larry Warren, when she returned, her passion for Soviet causes had "cooled considerably. . . . It took Anna many years to absorb the sobering new insights about the revolutionary country that was so idealized in her circle at home."[7]

In Manhattan, with the New Dance League Recital of Soloists the previous December, Anna had presented her *American Dance Hall* and *Speaker*.[8] By April 1936 she was featured with the Dance Unit at the YM-YWHA's Ninety-second Street Kaufmann Auditorium in *Opening Dance, Ballad (in a Popular Style), Four Little Salon Pieces, Inquisition '36,* and *Suite of Soviet Songs* (later, *Four Soviet Songs*). "While Anna had certain tendencies, she was never a complete left-wing Communist-dominated dancer, ever, and not a political dancer.

But she was a leader in social comment, generally," Norman believed. "Martha, Doris, and Charles were always being wooed by the Left, and received reviews in the left-wing press, although *Panorama* was panned by the left wing. A year or two later Americanism became part of the party line—the united front," he recalled.

Martha had championed Anna's "rebellious spirit" since their days dancing together with Graham. It was a quality that most defined Anna's work throughout their long association.[9] Martha Hill, too, had participated enthusiastically in a "common interest" group as a member of the First National Dance Congress and Festival, a joint effort to form one national unit by the New Dance League and the Dancers Association that was held 18–25 May 1936. Panels included "Dance in a Changing World," with Mura Dehn and Lee Strasberg taking part; and "Economic Status of Dancers, " with Frances Hawkins (now Graham's manager) and Tamiris speaking. The festival's performances were held at the Kaufmann Theatre of the Ninety-second Street YMHA, a place under William Kolodney's direction that soon became an important center of dance activity.[10] The array of performers featured many left-wingers. But Martha shrewdly sidestepped taking a position herself; following Horst's lead, she stayed clear of political statements or arguments generated by the central movers of the events.

In the ballet world, Russia's companies—once heralded as the primary source of the best ballet, aesthetically and technically—were now stifled by Stalin's recent decree that only social realism would be tolerated in the arts. Shifts of power were beginning to be felt. As Russians migrated into larger geographic circles, ideas of starting new ventures (as Diaghilev had done in Paris) were spreading to England and America.

One man to make a profound difference for ballet in America, would also, however vicariously, strongly influence Martha Hill's achievements in dance: Lincoln Kirstein. A Harvard graduate, he was independently wealthy, thanks to his father's partnership in Boston's Filene's Department Stores. Enamored by impresario Serge Diaghilev's Ballet Russes while visiting in Europe, Kirstein was determined to emulate that ballet world in America. He first met George Balanchine in Paris at a rehearsal of the choreographer's Les Ballets 1933. Trained as a dancer at the Imperial School, Balanchine left Russia in 1924, and had worked as a choreographer and ballet master for Ballets Russes from 1925 to 1929. Following the company to London for its final performances, Kirstein invited Balanchine to the United States where he could "proceed, with new ideas and young dancers." "He believes the future of ballet lies in America as do I," Kirstein wrote to a fellow Harvardite, trusted friend, and potential patron, Chick Austin, then the director of the Wadsworth Atheneum in Hartford, Connecticut.[11]

In the early thirties, Kirstein, with a group of Harvard friends (including Edward M. M. Walberg, also from a world of privilege), had already become an influential force in the art world. The two men had created the Harvard Society for Contemporary Art, a precursor to the Museum of Modern Art in New York, and had enjoyed the ballet when they traveled to Europe. Just out of college in 1933, Kirstein began publishing books and articles in quick succession on the visual arts including dance.[12] Kirstein served as one of photographer Walker Evans's "primary supporters," bringing his work to the attention of the world at large.[13] But it was most definitely Kirstein's unflagging patronage of George Balanchine for the next fifty years that would change the history of ballet in America.

After a disappointing false start in establishing a school in Hartford, Balanchine recognized almost immediately that the town was too small. Local dance teachers who didn't want the competition of a tuition-free school under the auspices of a museum, quickly made charges to the press against the "Bolsheviks." To placate the public, the ballet team explained that the school would not compete with other dancing schools, calling theirs a "cathedral of ballet" rather than a dancing school, to the chagrin of the locals. Balanchine, his business manager, Vladimir Dimitriew, and Kirstein made a hasty retreat back to New York.[14]

If humiliated by the experience, without further fanfare, Kirstein with Walberg as chief patron, worked to open the American School of Ballet in January 1934. It would take several configurations of ballet companies, however, before Kirstein managed to establish the New York City Ballet exclusively for Balanchine in 1948. For a new American Ballet Company, during the months of 1934 Balanchine staged his *Mozartiana* and *Dreams* with music by George Antheil (both revivals of works from his Ballets 1933) and created a new piece, *Serenade*, to music by Tchaikovsky for special performances for patrons, the first for Walburg's twenty-sixth birthday at Woodlands, the White Plains Walburg estate. A temporary hiatus of Balanchine's endeavors with Kirstein came, when Balanchine became very ill with tuberculosis, and then, as he made his own career, beginning with the 1936 Broadway production *On Your Toes* and also working in Hollywood for the next five years. The ever-idealistic Kirstein went on to establish an American company without him, called Ballet Caravan.

When Lincoln Kirstein asked Martha Hill for an opportunity to debut his company at Bennington, she agreed, insisting to Shelly that inclusion of his latest venture would broaden the scope of the program. Already known for his relentless energy and a man of extremes, Kirstein was, after all, a person with increasing power on the dance scene and could be an important asset.[15] Mary Jo, who guarded Martha's career as her most loyal friend, thought presenting Kirstein's company at Bennington was a mistake. She complained to Martha that she was holding on to her early love of ballet, from which she professed to be finally free. Martha pointed out that even if the vocabulary remained balletic, Kirstein's new effort might ferret out choreography that championed a healthier American spirit and perhaps serve as a counterbalance to the angst and browbeating of the leftist voices. In this first departure from Mary Jo's purer goals for dance education, Martha believed that a potentially important association might prove valuable. Reluctantly, Mary Jo gave in, while sensing the deep waters that would plague her more naive companion.

Mary Jo's dislike of ballet was obvious. She saw the new dance as "a point of view" rather than a system like ballet, one that strongly tied creative work with technical facility. She mentioned in a *Dance Observer* article in 1935, "The ballet period in education, in retrospect, did little service either to art or to education."[16] Ever-optimistic, Martha felt differently.

Hill's generosity in inviting Ballet Caravan to Bennington for the upcoming summer season brought Martha face-to-face with Kirstein. Her way of holding her own in male-dominated social, political, and educational realms was contrary to Kirstein's, as was her philosophical position, and financial and social means. Martha's middle-class midwestern upbringing was very different from his, yet they maintained similar positions as aesthetic overseers in a fledgling, temporal, and often chaotic field of dance. In 1936, Martha welcomed his broader view of the dance world and considered their professional friendship a distinct plus at this point in her career.

In many ways, the two were very much alike: both recognized genius in others, and placed themselves in unconditional service to the dance aesthetic they believed in. For Martha, it was her egalitarian faith in a circle of artists that would develop an indigenous new art form. For Kirstein, it was his certainty in proclaiming the future of American ballet "Balanchine" style. A saga of wits between them would play itself out in the following years.

Few could have predicted that for dance-lover Lincoln Kirstein, Ballet Caravan was a preliminary exercise before the eventual founding of New York City Ballet for his own creative "servant," George Balanchine. Nor could anyone imagine, perhaps save Mary Jo Shelly, that Hill and Kirstein, both so enamored with Graham's work, would later collide full-force in a power struggle at Lincoln Center.

As contemporaries, Hill and Kirstein held similar ambitions. Both relished the challenge of the "endless struggle involving artistic and institutional diplomacy, intrigue, and proselytizing . . . manipulat[ing] often inimical forces in the world of art and in society at large," as Kirstein's biographer Nicholas Jenkins, wrote. He added, "He was a promulgator of order who was fascinated and energized by the ubiquity of disorder."[17] Despite very different methods, both Hill and Kirstein fit that description, and the two would remain important competitors on the dance scene throughout their lives.

But during this period Hill and Kirstein shared simpler dreams for dance in America. Martha had quickly become the young champion of dancers and choreographers in a culture that provided no subsidy or provision for its artists and an ill-informed public from which to draw advocates. Her position as director of dance at Bennington gave an opportunity to connect various factions and styles of dance under one roof. She believed in democratic sharing, and by gaining trust she unified individuals to create a stronghold at Bennington. If Shelly was the one who kept the head count, it was Martha Hill who orchestrated "equality and parity" among the artists at Bennington, Norman Lloyd confirmed. "She was very aware and wanted to present things on an equal basis [which included] bringing in people from the outside with the idea that Bennington should present the whole picture of modern dance in America."

A further push for the encouragement of Ballet Caravan came from Martha Graham. Graham herself recalled her somewhat stormy first meeting with Kirstein in a theater lobby, "He said, 'I admire your dance.' I replied, 'Well, that isn't what you recently wrote. You called me the goddess who belched and I have never forgotten that.' He said, 'But that was before I knew you.' I said, 'You don't know me now.' And walked away. And that was that."[18] But ever in search of personal advantage from any quarter, Graham's opinion softened soon after, when Kirstein was at work on an article for Merle Armitage's *Martha Graham* (1937). While with Armitage, one of Graham's most ardent supporters, Kirstein is quoted as saying, "For her to come out of Denishawn was like a leghorn chicken giving birth to an eagle."[19] Kirstein also joined with Graham in boycotting Germany's 1936 Summer Olympic Games, when she rejected Hitler's propaganda chief Joseph Goebbels's invitation to perform at the opening ceremony.

The two had also exchanged extraordinary personal correspondence over affairs of the heart. Their correspondence at this time expressed great respect for each other. Her letters to him were filled with romance, admitting, "Through Carlos [Dyer] I saw what life could express—dignity and beauty, humanness, humor, dedication, spirituality, sensuality of a divine nature, responsibility." And more directly, "the ineffable gift to another of one's own ecstasy"; she further revealed, "Sometimes, just for an instant I have wanted to be a man—just to know one thing—the majesty of the seed—but in so doing I should lose the woman's sense—the holiness, the tenderness for the seed." She ended the letter with "I want the Sun—and so do you."[20]

Beyond these confidential conversations, Kirstein's ardor for Graham and her work, and for her genius as a dancer, would remain firm throughout her life. In his eyes, she was the single important modern dancer of the century. Occasionally Graham made suggestions to move Kirstein away from European ballet concepts. "In this I am the renegade 'modern,'" she apologized in a letter to him, continuing,

> What is known as "modern" dance, or contemporary dance is of immense value, in that it has related again man's adventure to our present scale. It never lives except in affect—but it can be the means of cleansing the eye and of freeing the body. . . . If it is pure it must dramatize its purity to be seen. That is to me what being theatrical means. The ballet began to dramatize its own theatrically, instead of the purity from which it issues. America needs dance—clear, broad, deep. A dancer's morality is his attitude toward his body. He keeps faith with certain natural laws.

In another letter to Kirstein, Graham wrote, "I hope you don't mind me leaning against you sometimes while I think aloud."[21]

Martha Hill, too, "wanted the Sun" at this point in her life. Hearing that President Davies was coming to Bennington "to study the summer school," Ruth recalled, "We hoped that Martha and Lefty would get together, relax, then see what happened. This was very important to her. And because Bennington gave us a sense of there being space, it was possible for him to come and not be examined. The two could be more or less private, because it *was* Bennington." Ruth remembered that when Lefty arrived, Martha had never been so radiant. Evenings of drinking at their favorite bar in Hoosatonic Falls increased. "Alcohol was always a problem for him, though I think Martha helped him control that somewhat," Ruth observed. Others found him rather full of himself, an egocentric sort, and wondered where the relationship might lead.

Another visitor that spring was her brother Gene. The stunning appearance of a "very handsome" officer in full uniform drew instant attention when he entered the Commons dining room for breakfast. Stories flew about how he stood on a chair to put his trousers on, to keep the creases wrinkle-free. As Martha proudly introduced him to her colleagues, they were intrigued by Gene's suave manner, noticing his engraved initials on the sterling silver flask he drew discreetly from his officer's jacket from time to time. That summer offered a rare glimpse of Martha's personal life.

In contrast, while Martha's own family background remained a near mystery, others openly discussed their early home lives; Graham regularly brought her mother to stay on campus. Doris wrote daily to her mother and father. Charles would often refer to his growing up in Nebraska, making referential works such as *And Daddy Was a Fireman* and *On My Mother's Side* throughout his career. José would harp on his domineering father and the misfortunes of his beloved but oppressed mother. Everyone was elated to see Hanya, a single parent, and her son, Klaus, as they romped with a pet goat and enjoyed impromptu soccer games with Louis's dachshund running interference on the lawn. (Only President Leigh suffered from the annoying complaints of non-animal lovers.)

This collegial atmosphere at Bennington delighted Martha and Mary Jo; the mix of events created a festive atmosphere, with every one involved and excited. A true festival should be open to all constituents and present many points of view, they insisted. All events were open to the public. "Every kind of difference did exist. Bennington summers aimed at exactly this realism," Mary Jo wrote unreservedly, adding that it was the "common concert—modern dance, that unified the group" bringing it together physically and holding it together psychologically. Proof of this was the presentation of Martin's lecture "The American Dance." It served as the "glue" for two solo "retrospective" recitals by Graham, and Holm's first major concerts with her Wigman School group. All admitted that Kirstein's Ballet Caravan, and lecture as well as the New Dance League performances encouraged spirited discussions and provided a rich tapestry of dance.

Beyond the school's success, Hill and Shelly had achieved a more utopian accomplishment at Bennington: a democratic environment for artists with common goals had become a reality very much in tune with the progressive ideas of the times. That summer's work would set a precedent for later projects. "No one cared about differences in economic status any more than they did about the other kinds of distinctions among the student body. Attitudes colored by regional and professional interests, a range in ability from beginner to established artist, a wide age span, divergent and often controversial social and political points of view—these strong contrasts within the school community gave it its unique quality," Mary Jo wrote in 1957.

As their own good work was honored, both began to consider the prospect of personal happiness beyond the dance community. Mary Jo sought friendships with other women; Martha passionately yearned for a long-term relationship with Lefty. Until these desires were resolved, their full energy went into their passion for dance with gusto and little regret.

Of the 102 students from twenty-nine different institutions on the 1936 summer roster, 17 percent were returning for the second time. Seven were veterans of all three sessions. In what would be one of the hottest summers of the century, there were 147 "mouths to feed" including the faculty and staff, according to Mary Jo.

Graham, Holm, Humphrey, and Weidman taught technique in two-week blocks, but the summer's focus was to be on the Humphrey-Weidman Company. Among the new faces in Weidman's workshop program were four male students in addition to the six men from his group that included Bales, Limón, and William Matons. Humphrey chose twenty-four students for her parallel "women's workshop," to be combined with ten from her concert group, including Katherine Litz, Beatrice Seckler, and Sybil Shearer.

That summer four students were also enrolled into the new program in choreography directed by Hill and Horst; joined by Martin, they jokingly called themselves the "Committee for Auditions." Ruth ("Rusty") Bloomer from the University of Michigan and Marian Van Tuyl from the University of Chicago were among those accepted. (Both would figure importantly in Martha's dance life later on.) The "unqualified" applicants were shuffled off to the general program.

Horst inaugurated a program in music composition for the dance for the 1936 session that included Norman's course geared at developing dance accompanists, "Music Accompaniment," and his own "Music Composition." For fledgling composers, this expansion "reflected the "growing aspects of the modern dance as a whole," Mary Jo felt. With the school's organization tightened considerably since the first session, students now were expected to work more deeply as creative artists, as well as in dance technique.

Surprisingly, as festival publicity person Frances Hawkins predicted, Ballet Caravan, with a collection of ballets based on popular American themes, added to the eclectic mix of dance offerings without much commotion.[1] "Modern Dance may be said to have launched Ballet Caravan," Kirstein later wrote.[2] For this endeavor, he assembled two concert programs for performances in the College Theatre "at the very center of the bitterly anti-ballet, 'modern-dance' school in Bennington, Vermont."[3] The ballets, performed by a company of twelve on 17 July 1936 were Lew Christensen's *Encounter* (to Mozart) and Eugene Loring's *Harlequin for President* (to Scarlatti), offered along with ballet classic divertissements. On the second night, *Promenade* (to music by Ravel and choreography by William Dollar) and *Pocahontas* (by Christensen, to music by Elliott Carter) were premiered, again followed by a series of divertissements.

Martha heartily enjoyed being with Lincoln throughout his week's stay, amused as she watched him nervously pin unfinished costumes and fuss over last-minute staging problems. While on campus Kirstein delivered a lecture on classic ballet that he had given earlier at Martin's New School series. A demonstration followed by William Dollar to a polite, if somewhat disgruntled audience of students (who later made their dislike for the affectations of the ballet idiom known to the administrators). Along with the lecture series, the addition of concerts by the New Dance League, one of Manhattan's leftist hotbeds for social action, confirmed that Martha Hill was a genius at incorporating the main trends and temper of the times at Bennington.

One of the overarching concerns affecting the attitudes and beliefs of a great many Americans—including these artists working in the mid-1930s—was the rising conflict between communist and fascist parties in Europe. Louis explained, "We were all a little pink against Franco."[4]

Limón recalled Wallingford Riegger knocking on the studio door one morning in August 1936 to say the radio has just announced that a junta of generals has launched an attack on Spain, from Morocco. "Carefree innocence was ended," José believed.[5] His response was to begin a solo, *Danza de la Muerte,* that would premiere the next summer.

For this third season of Bennington's Summer School of the Dance, the term "Festival" appeared for the first time "out loud in print," Mary Jo exclaimed. "'The Festival Series of Concerts' got its new name and was increased from five events to nine." Beginning on 13 August 1936, the series would belong to the Humphrey-Weidman Company and its delivery of nine stunning programs of modern dance.

The workshops produced Weidman's *Quest* to Norman Lloyd's score and Humphrey's completed trilogy, *Theatre Piece, New Dance,* and *With My Red Fires,* to music by Riegger, where in Shelly's words, "the whole brilliant drama was complete." In the process, however, the six-week deadline created as much tension as it did elation at performance time.

When Humphrey contemplated her Bennington project, William Blake's poetry had been her source of inspiration. On the way to Bennington for the summer, she wrote "Moralists point the finger," and "Scandalmongers laugh and leave them."[6] According to an early press release, Doris was "considering the central theme of brotherhood through the force of love in its romantic, possessive and destructive aspects." It added Blake's words, "When thought is closed in caves then love shall show its roots in deepest Hell."[7]

The idea of composing a dance on romantic love was even criticized by her own dancers as a "taboo" dance theme, according to Walter Terry. Doris responded that, "love can be both creative and destructive, and this is destructive love in which creative love wins. And they think I'm getting decadent."[8] One has to suspect that these ideas were drawn from her dealings with a domineering mother, mixed with ongoing emotional entanglements among Charles, José, and Pauline in her personal life. Martha Hill's difficult position in her affair with a married man was also very much on her mind.

Ruth Lloyd recalled that in preparation for the Armory performances, "Doris worked during the daytime, Charles worked at night. We all worked like mad." Ruth was slated to play for *With My Red Fires* and Norman to conduct. In contrast to the music Horst recommended for Graham's work, Doris's musical preferences leaned toward the melodic. "She was not a great advocate of dissonance. [With] no apologies for what she liked, Doris was very much her own person—always aiming at perfection."

But the effect of Doris's *With My Red Fires* and *Theatre Piece* was the nearest thing to a real symphonic composition in dance the Lloyds had ever known. Boasting forty-five dancers in addition to Humphrey and Weidman, it was the largest cast for any Bennington production. Doris's approach was more akin to composing a big symphony "like Beethoven's *Eroica*." They felt that people were swept off their feet by the exciting piece. "It was abstract with all kinds of crazy little realistic touches particularly in Charles's out-and-out pantomime sections." But to dancer José Limón, "the destructive power of possessive love was the central motif," and he was thrilled when the work was "received clamorously" by audiences and critics alike.[9]

As accompanist in Charles's technique classes, Norman was also his resident composer. "It was just an automatic thing anytime Charles did anything. It was part of my duties." Again, overwhelmed during "such a hysterical period," Norman had very little memory other than just putting notes on paper: "just a string of episodic material . . . Charles would do the dance—just spin movement out, the way a spider spins a web, almost like a natural thing, and make these long dances."

Nobody had any idea of how long *Quest* was until a day or two before the performance. A press release, cobbled together by Mary Jo and Martha, noted that the work would be "a choreographic pantomime dealing with the difficulties faced by the artist in contemporary life." But the choreographic process seemed a farce to its composer: "A lot of it [was] just filling up space and time with sound." Ruth quipped, "It was a piece about which you could say there are some very good sections."

John Martin wrote in his newly released book, *America Dancing*: "Actually, Charles Weidman is only at the beginning of his best period. . . . His art is utterly understated; there has been nobody in the dance before him to pattern after, and certainly there is nobody even remotely him in the dance today."[10]

If Martin continued his warm regard for Weidman, others who worked with him, including Doris, were finding him increasingly difficult, and their patience was beginning to wear thin. But of all among the faculty and dancers at Bennington, it was Charles who was the most fun-loving and the most openly homosexual. *Quest* struck a heartrending chord for those that saw it, at a time when many began to separate out and label sexual preferences. Shelly wrote, "It is doubtful if anyone who was in the Armory that evening has forgotten the event."[11] Martha would later praise Charles as a man of "theatrical knowledge" and "a man of courage in his art and in his life."[12]

Although there was a compelling drive "to do new things . . . not to record the old," according to Nona Schurman, Bennington's dancers continued to attract photographers to the site.[13] Thomas Bouchard became the "official" photographer that summer of 1936, brought on board "to supply the demands of the media," according to Mary Jo, at a time when the recording of images for posterity was a moot point.[14]

In a makeshift arrangement, Tom developed his negatives in a dormitory bathroom, and he soon found his work admired by a number of photo-eager, if penniless, subjects. Delighting in the "heroic period" of this crowd, Tom fell into easy comradeship among the musicians and artists on campus. Accustomed to capturing action with his lens, Bouchard "stalked" with his camera, capturing the dancers unaware, unstaged, and raw. On the lookout for a subject, he stopped Martha Hill as she was crossing the tennis courts after a long day of teaching, and asked if she would spend a few moments improvising so that he could shoot some film of her. Intrigued by the interplay of late afternoon shadows mingling with the white lines on the court, Martha filled the space with expansive lunges and outstretched arms. Bouchard photographed her experiments with tilts and extensions on the bleachers nearby, before she rushed off back to Cricket Hill to change for dinner. Bouchard's less than a dozen shots of Martha would become not only the most stunning photographs of her dancing at that time, but the only images captured by a professional that exist today.[15]

Bouchard had begun to photograph in the 1920s, the silent film era, when he had a studio on Hollywood and Vine (once taking shots of Denishawn's *Spirit of the Sea* dancers on a beach in California). Edgar Varèse had introduced him to Martha Graham, and Bouchard found modern dance a natural subject when he photographed Dance Repertory Theater's 1930–31 season.

Having moved his studio to Fortieth Street and Fifth Avenue in Manhattan in 1932, he sometimes photographed Martha Hill's students at NYU.

Doris had hired Bouchard to photograph *New Dance* and her Matriarch solo from *With My Red Fires* so that she would have prints for her upcoming fall tour on the ever-expanding "gymnasium circuit." Tom used the stagelights for a photo shoot after an Armory performance. Mary Jo related that a privileged few remained afterward to watch Bouchard photograph the production. By the early hours of the morning the exhausted company was dismissed. Only Doris remained, "standing like a vengeful arrow at the top of the central structure of Arch's stage. . . . The printed picture exists. So does the one the watchers saw of a great composer, a great work, and a great woman."

As a prelude to the Armory's evening shows, critics were also invited to a two-hour demonstration of student compositions in dance and music on Saturday morning, 15 August, in the College Theatre. Chosen "democratically, by student vote," the Saturday showings seemed "endless" to some. The section of intermediate and advanced choreography students under Martha Hill's direction, with Bessie assisting, presented a less rigid group of studies then those offered during the previous season, with theme and variation configurations based on jazz idioms such as the blues, waltz, and fox-trot.

The second section of the program for Horst's classes showed the clearly defined studies in "preclassic" forms in modern style (along with occasional authentic ones), as well as "ism" studies from his "Modern Forms in relation to the Other Arts" course.[16] The highlights of this showing included Van Tuyl's *Public Rejoicing* and Bloomer's *American Rustic*—both Americana studies. Larger studies, again by Bloomer, Van Tuyl (clearly the standout talents of the season) and others were presented as well, set to scores by Jean Williams, Beatrice Hellebrandt, and Esther Williamson.[17]

Even with the school population and interested Bennington locals guaranteeing a good turnout, the records show that of five hundred seats (seat price $1.10), the auditorium never had more than 350 paying guests. Shelly counted the total audience for the summer as exceeding three thousand. But critics, led by Horst and Martin, and excited concertgoers had spread the word: Bennington would soon become a hot spot for vacationers looking for enlightenment in their White Mountain travels.

In the midst of the school's success, stood Martha Hill, the force that held it all together while providing in her own teaching, the *Brooklyn Eagle* reported that August, "a point of equilibrium."[18] The 1936 session had run as smoothly as the last. Martha and Mary Jo proudly presented their report to the college trustees, saying that the Bennington Summer School of the Dance stood as "an astonishingly mild manifesto for a veritable revolution." As a "self-supporting and non-profit enterprise," they had educated audiences, and suitably used the college facilities during the summer recess at moderate cost to the students.

The budget figures for 1936 showed their scrupulous monitoring of the account books, managing a profit of nearly $15,000.[19] Martha and Mary Jo quietly delighted over their Bennington achievement when they returned to the urban pace of their university jobs. The hills of Vermont had become their summer Valhalla, with this sleepy New England place now a harbor for the people and the ideals they most treasured. Those ideals had also been sown in dance communities throughout the United States.

For the 1936–37 academic year, as the country rallied from the depths of economic depression, Bennington College bravely held to its progressive stance. A "trial" major in dance was announced in its second catalogue, with drama and music departments also seceding from the school's arts division. Solo and group work in choreography, and instruction in lighting and stage design were added to the college curriculum. Study in New York City's dance studios was encouraged during the winter's field and research period with Martha conveniently counseling students at her NYU office.[20] Participation in the intensive work of the Bennington Summer School of the Dance was highly recommended for dance majors, as they were now required to "develop skill and understanding as choreographer, performer and critic."[21] Now accustomed to her packed workweek, Martha passed the time on the long train journeys with paperwork, class planning, and much-needed catnaps. The hire of a second dance person at Bennington greatly eased Martha's workload.

Back in Manhattan in January 1937 Martha moved into a sunny, spacious studio apartment in an industrial building at 8 West Thirteenth Street with large floor-to-ceiling windows. It was an address she would keep for the next fifteen years. The loft had a Pullman kitchen "that only Martha could fit into," her student Hortense Lieberthal (Zera), known as "Hortie," recalled. (She remembered fondly that Martha gave her the keys to the place to use as a "honeymoon suite" after her city hall marriage to fellow NYU student Max Zera.)[22] Another student turned colleague, Hazel Johnson, stayed there for the weekend on occasion. At first, when she went to New York City for special concerts she stayed in a hotel in the East Twenties; when Martha found that out, however, she told her the area wasn't safe, and she was welcome to stay with her. Hazel remembered curtained-off sleeping quarters and the Southwest decor full of Indian rugs and Kachinas. "I thought it was so exotic. Always the first to sleep, I usually got the bed," she mused, "and I don't even remember saying thank-you!"

Mary Jo now focused on her job as part of the physical education department at the University of Chicago. Although she had little success in expanding the dance offerings there, Mary Jo continued to dedicate her summers to Bennington, a willing worker for the cause. When she arrived for the summer, Mary Jo was handed more and more "drone" work with each expanding project, and Martha settled into the role of the "artistic" director at Bennington with greater authority. "Mary Jo was obviously a very self-assured person. That was her pose, anyway," Ruth remarked years later, adding "she was not successful in making the kind of life she wanted . . . without men."[23] Others noticed that Mary Jo's easygoing nature had become more sardonic; they sensed her discomfort now that Martha was involved with Lefty. Some wondered if the ever more demanding Martha was taking advantage of Mary Jo's loyalty.

Buoyed by their unprecedented accomplishment at Bennington, Martha had an even more ambitious plan in mind: to create "a broader and more permanent" center to be called "The American School of the Dance," this time to be located in New York City. Among Martha's papers are theater rental flyers and letters about possible real estate properties as well as a 1936 School of American Ballet catalogue, perhaps kept as a structural model. Martha reasoned, Why not the same for modern dance?

Martha again enlisted Mary Jo's help and launched into the most expansive proposal of her career—one that sought to "solidify the whole field into one unit" and "carry on education in the dance" with "the services of experts for an impartial cross-section of the art." To seek funding, they drafted a proposed board of directors; the impressive array of advocates for the new "American School of the Dance" included Roosevelt's WPA advocate, Hallie Flanagan. Martha shopped for rental property with real estate agents, sending off comments to Mary Jo about each location.

But the women soon realized that, while Balanchine's and Kirstein's American School of Ballet had resources to secure their ballet enterprise, their only means of support rested on college administrators who had no intention of giving more than verbal approval for such an endeavor. Martha had won over the converted in concept, but her failure to attract outside funding put an end to her scheme. Mary Jo conceded, "For the American form of dance struggling for recognition, no one ever contemplated giving half a cent." The project was abandoned.

A steady flow of other commitments kept Martha busy. Already on the "board of auditions" to choose dancers for modern dance concerts sponsored by the New School of Social Research, she also took part in roundtable discussions that replaced the more formal speeches of previous years and alternated with recitals each week. All the while, her ardent love for Lefty stayed strong, keeping their time together during furtive weekend escapes most precious.

PART IV

The Late Thirties

In 1931, the Hill family had returned to the house in Salem built and rented out before they moved to Missouri. "It was a big, nice-looking house," Bill reminisced, "and it was where I grew up before going off to Case and then Hiram College. Martha wanted me to come to New York City to Pratt for engineering. I wish now that I had." As her brothers were growing up, Martha sent checks for their birthdays and at Christmas time. She was a generous older sister from a distance who saw that they went off to camp each summer with "blankets and everything. As far as I'm concerned, she was very unselfish."

Her brother Gene, mainly schooled in Missouri, attended the University of Missouri for a year before receiving an appointment to West Point. Bill confessed, "I really don't know but he got it somehow. I'm sure it was through Dad and a few other people. He was fairly bright, but he never really grew up. He bought his uniforms at Brooks Brothers. They were very expensive. Dad got the bills."

After graduating from West Point, on 12 June 1930, Gene was appointed second lieutenant in the Coast Artillery Corps. While stationed at Fort Sheridan in Chicago, he met Betty Phelps, the daughter of a "very wealthy family." They married in 1931, just before Gene was transferred to the Philippines. There he honed his skills in heavy artillery coastal defense under General MacArthur. Martha corresponded with her brother and new sister-in-law, wishing them well with cheery notes of encouragement and sending an excited telegram of congratulations to Betty who had returned home to have her baby daughter in October 1935. Discharged from the army in 1936, Gene moved back with his family to Highland Park, Chicago, where a son, David, was born early in 1937.

Although Gene seldom communicated with his own family, they were increasingly distressed by his unscrupulous behavior. "He apparently owed some officers money. I know they tried to nick Dad for it," Bill recalled. "He was a scam artist, always coming up with schemes to make a fortune with a habit of writing bad checks. Martha had trouble with him. She'd write him a check, and he'd upgrade it, adding zeros to the amount. He then wrote checks from an East Palestine bank where there wasn't any account. That's where he got in trouble and the law caught up to him. We didn't know this was going on. Back home, the sheriff knocked on our door to find his whereabouts. We were good friends of the chief and he came around and said, 'Do you know where your son is?'

They caught him in New York and put him in jail. It didn't go too well with him." Gene once again ordered a suit from his cell for his trial. "This time when Martha got the bill, she called to say, 'Can you imagine? Ordering a Brooks Brothers suit from a jail cell?'"[1]

In a desperate move, once released on bail, Gene had arranged a clandestine escape to China, where he had been hired by supporters of Chiang Kai-shek as a heavy artillery expert for guerrilla combat forces against the Japanese. He made his way to a ship in San Diego, California, but, as Bill remembered, "The law and the military caught up to him and he decided this was the end of the road. That was it." Imprisoned once more, he managed to slip a cyanide pill in his mouth, dying instantly. "That's what it says on his death certificate. Died of cyanide poisoning," Bill tersely recalled.[2]

Martha received the devastating news of Gene's suicide four days later, 20 November 1937. She carried on numbly. Hortie remembered that Martha entered the classroom at New York University and said that her brother was dead. She was feeling down, Martha said, but teaching was the best solace she knew of. The class began and the subject was never mentioned again.[3] But others sensed her grief. Ben Belitt said, "Martha knew dark things and that's why she wasn't afraid of the dark."

Not wanting to draw public attention to their shame and despondency, Grace and Grant placed an obituary notice in the East Palestine paper the following week. Martha tucked the clipping and a collection of Gene's letters and photographs into the cedar chest next to her bed. "When his remains came, they were buried in the family's cemetery plot next to Katherine. That was it. Nothing else was done about it. No service. Just a headstone there," Bill recalled, adding, "It was particularly sad for Mother, losing Katherine, and then losing Gene. I think Gene was closer to Mother than Martha or I. But she wasn't verbal about it." Gene's in-laws insisted that their daughter and their young grandchildren sever all ties with the Hill family. Grace and Grant never saw their grandchildren again. "Betty died shortly after Gene killed himself," Bill related years later, "I was told, 'broken heart.' The Phelps adopted the kids and changed their names from Hill to Phelps. Take it for what it's worth. That's all I know."

Martha was soothed by her telephone conversations and correspondence with Lefty, this time, ostensibly to help him shape a summer dance program for Colorado. She suggested that he hire "a good person who lived in the area" for his faculty. After talking to Hanya, Hill recommended Martha Wilcox for the position. Wilcox (who ran a studio in Denver and had studied with Holm at Perry-Mansfield in 1933), along with Harriet Roeder (also from Colorado), was encouraged by President Davies to study at Bennington the following summer. Once there, they were among the students selected to perform in Holm's *Trend*. Ever watchful for dedicated followers to fill the ranks as assistants, the chosen ones did a great deal of the teaching for their mentors. Both students filled the bill. At the same time, Lefty's search for recruits gave him another reason to visit Martha at Bennington.

Hill slated Hanya Holm as the major choreographer for the summer session of 1937. Martha was impressed that Hanya had started a school with technique as well as percussion and anatomy classes, and also by her "remarkable intelligence as artist, scientist, educator."[4] But she worried that Holm was having "a hard time because of the anti-German feeling in the East"—a dicey situation more than likely fueled on campus by Louis Horst. When Lefty complained to Martha that at Bennington, "you have all the stars," she suggested that Hanya might be just the "star" Colorado Springs needed.[5] The choreographer's work was more accessible to the "uninitiated," she told him—a correct assessment, considering the enthusiastic response Holm had received from her recent concert there.

In residence at Bennington for the full session and teaching the first four weeks, Hanya's task was to integrate students into a major new work for the festival through the workshop program. This time, Humphrey, Weidman, and Graham were slated to teach modern technique for only two weeks each.

When Martha asked Hortie to become her teaching assistant at Bennington, she was thrilled and would be at Martha's side in the classroom for the next six summers. Bessie Schönberg, now holding a job at Briarcliff Junior College, also followed Martha to Bennington each summer, after teaching part-time at Bennington during the academic year of 1934–35. Others, who had been on the Bennington summer faculty since its establishment, were delighted with their annual experiences. For Norman, "Every summer was quite different. Each had its own character." He added with pleasure, "And [the students] began to get younger and younger!"

The school's more finely tuned scheduling combined camaraderie with purpose. "We ate every meal in the faculty dining room and so it was natural we'd start conversations at breakfast, and continue at lunch and at dinner. We'd go for a drink in the evening and talk, and we'd have parties," Martha recalled. Eve Gentry (née Henrietta Greenhood), working with Hanya that summer, recalled her first experience there as a dancer: "Suddenly I had a family. And for the first time I wasn't worried about what to eat and where to sleep. All of us did what we loved most. As dancers we had the same needs, passion, and desires." She added philosophically, "Nothing else gave its support for the momentum for a future modern dance more than Bennington."[6]

Others remembered a very fluid kind of social situation that summer. After meals, everyone sat on the green, mixing together with Louis, Martha, and their dachshunds, along with Hanya and Doris with their sons in tow. A piano was often moved onto the Commons veranda where the Lloyds conducted impromptu sing-alongs and Louis played an occasional ragtime. Over time, tensions among the various groups seemed to have dissolved as their common mission for a modern dance became more secure. As Martha explained it, "To help a new movement in the art, no one thought of putting anything in the way of the work. In any pioneer period this is a perfectly natural move. Every one worked as a family in the art."[7]

The situation in Europe continued to dominate conversations. Reports of the brutality of the Spanish civil war and rising dictatorships circulated daily. But it was fascism that represented the darkest threat to these artists, who valued free expression above all else. Indeed, Limón later wrote in his memoir, "The Bennington summers became a way of life."[8] And he might have added, a great escape from the grim realities of a threatened peace. But they were not the only topics of conversation, for during this period, the two Marthas often confided in each other about their love lives. Graham had met Lefty earlier in Colorado and found him as charming as Hill described him. With Mary Jo in Chicago, it was now Graham who lent a sympathetic ear to Hill's outpouring of feelings about her relationship with Davies, while consoling her over the loss of her brother.

Graham was working out ideas for a new solo, *Immediate Tragedy: Dance of Dedication,* with a score being written by Henry Cowell (who had been recently imprisoned at Alcatraz on charges of child molestation).[9] Kirstein would call the finished work "a keystone masterpiece of the same powerful wave-length as the concatenation of energies operating throughout the world today."[10] Without doubt, world events determined the outer shape of the work, but one can also assume that its content was also drawn from the grief from her friends' suffering. Of those, Martha Hill's was the most immediate and the most devastating; Henry Cowell's, a close second.[11]

The first dance festival event on 30 July 1937 presented Martha Graham in concert, featuring the premieres of two solos, *Opening Dance* to a new score by Norman Lloyd and *Immediate Tragedy: Dance of Dedication.*[12] Although, Martin (and even Lloyd) considered the first work "less notable," he saw the second as "a picture of fortitude, especially woman's fortitude; of the acceptance of a challenge with a kind of passionate self-containment."[13] Limón viewed Graham's premiere, *Immediate Tragedy* effusively as "the apogee of all her works. For me it was a supreme experience, if not *the* supreme experience, of dance."[14]

The Lloyds agreed that Graham's *Immediate Tragedy*—although "definitely anti-Franco" like Humphrey's—was created from the standpoint of the individual.[15] As well as writing original music for *Opening Dance,* Norman was in charge of "fitting" Cowell's score to the dance. Norman was amazed to find that Cowell had devised an "elastic form" for his "somber and sparse" score. Although composer and choreographer had decided beforehand on the mood, tempo, and meter of the piece, Cowell didn't know the timing of each section. "With two basic phrases to be played by oboe and clarinet" and "each phrase existing in two-, three-, or eight-measure versions," Norman claimed that the whole arrangement process "took about an hour. The total effect was complete unity—as though dancer and composer had been in the closest communication."[16]

Surprisingly, Hill's own impressions were dramatically different. *Immediate Tragedy* was a dance she chose to forget. Instead it was Graham's *Opening Dance* that she remembered as her favorite years later, perhaps an indication of her optimism. Choreographed as a curtain-raiser to Norman's dancey rhythmic score, it was a beginning of new things and a life-inspiring statement. Martha Hill responded to these two works as gifts intrinsically related to her own life. That she would dismiss the dark experience of one and remember the positive spirit of another would be symbolic of the way she moved through her life. It was the key to her personal survival.

For the second offering of the Dance Festival at the Armory on 12 August, Norman had also written sections of the original score for José's equally dire view in his *Danza de la Muerte.* It was presented on the same program as Sokolow's work for ten woman (with a cast including Hortie and Betty Bloomer [Ford]). The Sokolow work was titled *Façade-Esposizione Italiana* (subtitled *Spectacle, Belle Arti, Giovanezza, Phantasmagoria*), and set to Alex North's score.[17] Anna confirmed the beauty of the Bennington experience as a fellow in 1937. "I was told you could do anything you want. Nobody censored you there. You could do what you pleased." Although she performed works already premiered in Manhattan, Bennington was a place that recognized the "deep value" of the work she was doing. "The fellowship gave me the strength to go on and to do what I believed in."[18] Also on this concert, choreographer Esther Junger presented equally intense, if less political, works including her *Dance to the People.* Meaning and content had become critical to modern dance.

The last two concerts of the Bennington Festival Series belonged to Hanya Holm. On each, her concert group of eleven women performed four works from her repertory (with two to scores by Riegger and one by Cowell) followed by the second half of the program with her hotly anticipated new work, *Trend,* which featured an additional twenty-two student dancers. Hanya danced with her group in *Festive Rhythm* and, in an unusual move, performed a solo in *Trend,* "The Gates Are Desolate." Unfortunately, Graham and Humphrey had reputations as consummate solo artists, and by comparison, Hanya did not project a commanding presence on stage, according to Ben Belitt, who had recently arrived on the Bennington campus.

Nonetheless, this major ensemble work by Holm would be considered her finest effort for the rest of her long life as a dance artist. She explained that her ideas had traveled a long path of development before they took shape; she even asked advice of theologian Paul Tillich in preparation for the work. She insisted "everything [be] determined by organic development, rather than intellectual decision," with "a continuous change of weight, of volume, of linear and dimensional values."[19]

Trend's momentous success was in no small part due to resident composer Wallingford Riegger, who struggled to give Holm a completed score in five sections to be played by Hanya's regular musician, Harvey Pollins. As performance neared, music director Norman Lloyd had to scramble to get parts to the eight other musicians who had consented to play it. For "dramatic effect" and a more futuristic ending, Holm made a bold move to end the piece with a recording of Edgard Varèse's *Ionization,* marking one of the first uses of amplified, recorded sound for dance.[20]

Viewers who saw *Trend* were overwhelmed by the grand scale of the work. As in the previous summer, the significant shift to longer and larger works at Bennington produced collaborative ventures as innovative, some said, as Diaghilev's Ballets Russes decades before. Everything about the production was ostentatious in style, beginning with the program description: "*Trend* is a picture of the processes of man's survival when the usages of living have lost their meaning and he has fallen into routine patterns of conformity. Though in this direction of decadence lie only catastrophe and ultimate annihilation, there emerges out of the ordeal itself a recognition of the common purposes of man and the conscious unity of life."

Overall, however, it was not elaborate sets and costumes but Arch Lauterer's uncluttered and austere stage concepts that made Bennington productions unique. Although Lauterer himself had taken another leave from Bennington to continue studying the Bauhaus and its connection to theater architecture, he left his assistant Gerard Gentile to follow his design and lighting plot for the Armory. Arch's absence most likely accounts for the added time between productions to make the task easier for his replacement.

The success of the season was proclaimed by the 1937 August-September issue of *Dance Observer* dedicated to Bennington's activities (as it had been the previous August). This time, however, students from Martin's dance criticism course wrote most of its reviews. "This is our contribution to a school which serves a most important function in the dance world," the editorial proclaimed.[21]

In their final report to the trustees at Bennington, Martha and Mary Jo named the college "the outstanding single agency for promoting the growth of the dance as an art in America," thanks to the "calibre and representativeness of both faculty and student body." This "new art in America promises to have a history of popular support and lay participation unique in the history of the arts in this country." The report pronounced the fulfillment of a utopian dream, more successful than any one could have predicted, and credited the school for "giving to a new and still struggling art a center which publicly identifies it as an independent art. The fact that this center is the common enterprise of a number of individual artists and other leaders in the field and that it has maintained its collective and non-partisan character through four intensive sessions give especial importance to its existence."[22]

After the Bennington summer, Martha returned to Manhattan with a renewed sense of mission. The dance scene had become richer and more expansive, and she had become central to its activities. Her reputation was confirmed in Martin's 1936 book, *America Dancing*. In a chapter dedicated to "The Bennington Group," he called Martha Hill "a key figure in the art." In it he states, "She could have made a successful career as a dancer . . . for she has a definite flair for movement and an exceptional gift for composition, but education is her paramount interest, and for it she is uniquely equipped. She combines to a remarkable degree the intuitiveness of the artist with the keen mind of the scientist, and out of the combination has come an analysis of movement and of the processes of composition . . . to revolutionize the methods of dance education in the colleges."[23] If in less than three years, Martha had risen to a position of high authority, her own reaction was mixed. Although flattered by Martin's words, she also recognized the compliant position the critic had determined for her as an educator. Earlier, with the Bennington offer in hand, when she asked Martha Graham for advice about whether to take the job or not, her reply was that it would give Hill an opportunity to create her own choreography (as Graham's Eastman School of Music position had served her in 1926). Now, duty-bound to the service of others, that possibility seemed more and more remote.

Possessing an easy ability to take charge when called upon, Martha Hill had refined her ability to project a selfless, democratic persona. Intelligence and reasonableness strengthened her every effort. The vibrancy in the tone of her voice with its clean midwestern diction had a way of capturing the attention of any group (no doubt, an attribute perfected through years of commanding technique classes). Martha's upstanding manner exuded friendliness and projected an image of the one "in the know" without a trace of ulterior motive: the causes Martha championed were for the common good after all. If opportunities seemed to fall into Martha's hands, in fact, she aggressively sought ways to facilitate those opportunities, herself central to every plan. Those closest to her knew that Martha meticulously outlined a course of action and positioned herself within it. They also understood the necessity of maintaining sturdy alliances with confidantes.

One such instance was in autumn 1937, when Martha enthusiastically joined the planning committee for one of Lincoln Kirstein's brainstorms: *Dance International, 1900–1937*. Having unsuccessfully tried in 1932 to establish a theater devoted to the arts (in Manhattan's Rockefeller Center), this time Kirstein spearheaded an ambitious two-month stretch of dance events. Beginning on 2 November, the events included fifteen informal afternoons at the Rainbow Room presenting dancers from forty countries, along with special art exhibits and film showings at the Museum of Modern Art. The main features were evenings of dance at the Center Theatre, with a ballet program (and Ballet Caravan participating) and, on closing night, 2 January 1938, "An Evening of Modern Dance" with St. Denis, Graham, Humphrey, Holm, Tamiris, and Weidman appearing with their groups.

Kirstein had earlier been invited by Horst to join the editorial board of *Dance Observer*. In its new policy statement in the October 1937 issue, the magazine vowed to bridge all dance forms and report on ballet and folk dance as well as modern dance. But Martha and Louis began to question Kirstein's motives after "ill-tempered remarks" (by his own admission) in a November 1937 article, "The Ballet: Sad but Hopeful" in which he fiercely attacked Fokine.[24] His outspoken "The Ballet: Tyranny and Blackmail" followed in December's issue. Colleagues on the editorial board were alarmed when Kirstein turned against John Martin for his outright espousal for the "new modern dance."[25]

Kirstein's relationship with Horst as the periodical's editor-in-chief quickly soured: "I . . . was forced to resign as ballet-critic from the *Dance Observer,* an anti-ballet monthly, because I had written an attack on Martin, which they refused to print."[26] Kirstein told his colleagues that although his "bread and butter luckily didn't depend on it," he intended to continue stating his opinions in print. (He moved on to write for *The Nation* and by 1940 had established his own journal, *Dance Index.*)[27]

After a busy fall at Bennington with Graham giving a concert in November, regular student demonstrations, and work on theater productions, Martha made plans for a sabbatical leave for the spring of 1938.[28] Limón, who had been in residence the previous spring, agreed to replace her for the semester. In preparation, he visited the campus in the midst of her frenzied schedule. Prepared to find himself in "enemy territory surrounded by the pampered female progeny of the rich," José was very quickly "disabused" of his "ignorance." He found the students intelligent and capable. In this "academy, laboratory, atelier, forum, and theater rolled into one, the school was a boldly innovative venture in preparing an elite, in the finest and fullest sense of that word, to enter and grace human society." He continued, "There was an excitement, a turmoil even, in the way the intellectual, cultural, and political state of the world was examined and discussed."[29]

Students instantly adored the Mexican Adonis before them in the classroom and he gained quick entry into the Cricket Hill clique as well. Becca Stickney recalled, "We all had great affection for each other. The core group was Martha, Ben and myself, and Ann Douglas, Mary Jo, and Pauline Lawrence and [each] took [his or her] own maverick route." She noted that although Ben and José were living in a safe community: "They and others were sort of secretive, but none of [their sexual preferences] was revealed in any of their actions." If she found José standoffish among the women, she added as an afterthought, "I'm not sure I would have known enough at that time to have recognized as a possibility that Martha and Mary Jo were [lovers]. But they were awfully good friends. In my day you didn't think a thought like that."

During his second semester stay José saw what few others from the summer festival perceived: Martha was a choreographer of excellent, if undervalued ability. He witnessed firsthand Martha's indefatigable dedication as "handmaiden to the art of dance" as she sometimes called herself. A production of Sophocles' *Elektra* was being mounted that was a collaborative effort: Bennington theater professor Francis Fergusson directed the speech; Martha, the gesture and choreography; and Lauterer, the "inspired" settings and lighting. José later wrote, "The result was a superbly stylized work of compelling power."[30] Even so, Martha's creative work was now almost totally set aside for college activities. She soon resigned herself to the idea.

In the spring of 1938, Lefty Davies led an effort "to advance the arts" in Colorado Springs by continuing to urge his college to join forces with the town's Fine Arts Center. The result was the creation of the Conference on the Fine Arts as an annual event. He had more and more need for "consultation" with Martha. In the fall of 1937 his conveniently timed business trips to Manhattan coincided with Martha's Bennington-free weekends. It was during her sabbatical semester that their casual romance developed into an ardent, if still secret, commitment.

Martha seemed always to be "looking down the tracks" for new places to spread the word. The idea of staying in one place geographically, and now intellectually, never interested her. While others would make one college their permanent base of influence—such as H'Doubler at the University of Wisconsin, and Bessie Schönberg at Sarah Lawrence—Martha moved from place to place with surprising ease.

At thirty-seven, Hill's passion for dance had transferred from personal ambition as a performer into dance as a cause beyond her own career. Yet the same drive that had brought her to New York City to seek out Graham now fed her desire to take responsibility. In a field well populated by egocentrics and free spirits, her mission was heartily embraced. Here was a woman who could be relied upon to consider the larger view and to confront the realities of the profession head-on. Notably, she was determined to champion those she deemed most deserving. If the combination of these factors elevated her from "good to great" as a leader, it also prompted a love of power and manipulation. In the studio she had learned to choreograph dancers' actions. Now the stakes had expanded, and she was in a position to orchestrate the direction of American dance. Ever the achiever, in a few short years Martha had consolidated the efforts of individuals into a solid movement now reaching for national identity.

Like Balanchine, who had declared, "But first a school," Martha saw Bennington's summer program as central to the future of modern dance. The story of the fifth session, as the "culmination of a plan" is "best told by reciting its highlights." Shelly wrote,

> Within the curriculum, two significant changes appeared among other refinements. A change of title from "Workshop Program" to "Professional Program," meant more than a change of words. Those who met the requirement for any one of the four groups within this program had to satisfy the most stringent demands . . . as full apprentice members of a concert group, not as students of a workshop.[1]

The second change was the addition of a program in stage design for dance (team-taught by Hill and Lauterer) that, in Shelly's words, "marked an evolution in the art of modern dance. . . . Action, accompaniment, setting—all had to be of a piece. Dance as true theatre was thus recognized." She added, "On the score of production, the 1938 session amounted to nothing less than sheer daring."

As a Bennington faculty member in drama and "designer of the dance theatre in the Vermont State Armory," Arch continued to be pivotal. Back from his studies in Germany and more enthusiastic than ever, he forged ahead with his aspirations of integrating light, sets, action, and sound. The fourth summer of performances would mark, if not quite an evolution in the art as he saw it, then a giant step forward in legitimizing production values as integral to theater art. He made light "dance with the dancers" by studiously mapping out the floor plan. He plotted light cues to the structural contour of the choreography and then, working with shafts of light, forced the viewer's gaze up and around.

The 1938 summer's pace was close to overwhelming for Hill and Shelly, with problems multiplying as the volume of activities unfolded. The competition was most intense among the four choreographers, each having earned a solid national reputation since Bennington's first year. As planned, all were on campus for the full six-week session to teach the 148 enrolled students and create "culminating" works for the festival.

In the studio, student dancer Anna Halprin was quick to observe that this high degree of professionalism could also have a "dehumanizing" effect. "My models were personalities and their points of view. . . . Our focus was on the teacher, and we were set up like mannequins in space and danced in the form of a military flank. And yet the movements were exciting, daring and physically exhilarating. It was all so new, fresh and revolutionary. The place was alive and vital with the energy of our leaders."[2]

The overall budget had jumped to more than $41,000. Although the total cost to students had risen over five years from $190 to $255, so had the size of salaries, with pay raises to $900 for Graham, and $600 each for Hanya, Doris, and Charles. This season, the finances were divided between artists and their companies to be augmented by a varying number of apprentices.

To develop new choreographers, it was Martha's idea to give special fellowship students the same opportunities that professionals had during the festival week. Those selected were Eleanor King (who had shown choreographic promise as a member of the Humphrey-Weidman company) and Louise Kloepper, from Holm's group of women—an exquisite dancer revered in the classroom but morbidly frightened when actually performing on stage. The third was Horst's choice, Marian Van Tuyl, who had proven herself a promising choreographer the summer before.

Under Martha's charge, the young artists planned a program of six short pieces with casts drawn from students in the general program. As King reset a solo suite for five dancers, she confessed that it was Martha who was the "fairy godmother" who "waved the wand," allowing her to use traditional music that was "very unorthodox at the time." Less ambitious works made the fellows' activities more manageable and produced a bumper crop of collaborations between composers and choreographers that summer. John Colman, Norman, and Esther Williamson were responsible for arranging King's music; Harvey Pollins and Gregory Tucker wrote original scores for Kloepper.[3] Tucker, assigned as composer for Van Tuyl's new work, was "on the button all the time." Marian felt "privileged," she said, "a word that describes my feeling for the whole experience."[4]

Martha arranged for a special session in which the entire faculty offered their expertise to the fellows in a long discussion about meaning and movement. Marian worried about the dreariness of a section she had created. Horst consoled her, saying, "In any dance there are some slower parts." And Graham advised, "What you do is not so important as how you do it."[5]

But it would be featured works by the "Big Four" that set off the frenzied demand for studios and pianos. Ever mindful of their reputations, all four had begun to work out materials in Manhattan months in advance of the cumulative events at Bennington. The results were Hanya's *Dance of Work and Play* to a score by Norman Lloyd and her *Dance Sonata* to music by Harrison Kerr; composer Vivian Fine collaborated with Weidman for *Opus 51*; and Ray Green with Graham for *American Document*. Humphrey opted to use Bach's *Passacaglia in C Minor* scored for two pianos instead of commissioning a score. Humphrey's use of Bach and the Kerr score marked a return to earlier methods of choreographing to existing music—to Horst's discomfort.[6]

True to form, whiz kid Norman Lloyd saw his collaboration with Hanya as high adventure. Although happily surprised after his first experience with Graham, the composer had to admit that almost any other project would be easier. "Holm really composed in the sense of putting the work together," he explained, crediting her Dalcroze background for her more organized choreographic method. "She had everything mapped out for *Dance of Work and Play* when I went to see it. Hanya had it all planned, laid out, structured," even handing him a rhythmic score in musical notation of each dancer's different rhythms. "So all I had to do was remember the feel of the dance. It was like doing a film score." By this time she had been influenced by her American colleagues, and imbued her dances with a sense of structure "which the Wigman dances didn't have," he observed. For Hanya's solo section "she just very slowly, silently, glided around, [wanting] the effect of being alone at midnight. So I wrote a very sparse four-hand piano piece, with one person playing and the other just tapping a pencil on a chair, like a clock ticking to suggest that kind of stillness . . . different from the . . . things that Martha or Doris were doing."

Ruth Lloyd recalled *Dance for Work and Play* as having a great deal of "moving in space . . . with lots of skirts . . . a very pleasant set of dances—a happy piece." For Norman, however, it was Hanya's "Wigman approach" that was so distinctive. He admitted frankly that Hanya had been too busy with technical problems (as had Graham) to discuss aesthetic or philosophic things. "I have no idea what Hanya had in mind. . . . We didn't talk a great deal about what was meant. [It] was a dance that had music with it. I worked the two together and adjusted tempos [if it was] too fast or too slow, or needed a little bit of a ritard here or there." At the same time, composer Vivian Fine worked out her score for Weidman's *Opus 51*, one Ruth described as a piece different in concept from his usual dramatic style, in three parts with a middle solo section of "kinetic pantomime."

Of all the choreographers, it was Doris who proceeded most calmly, inflicting a minimum of emotional trauma in her merge of student dancers and company members in *Passacaglia in C Minor*. Instead, Barbara Beiswanger recalled, "We were delighted to see how Doris Humphrey composed that dance . . . [with] the company and apprentice group [of twelve] all working together, dancing actually ten hours a day for the six weeks." Only "those tall boxes that we had to climb up and come down on a particular beat," caused trepidation. "This was a very precarious skill to master," she confessed.[7]

Frustration with makeshift theater and rehearsal spaces on campus mounted. Each year it became increasingly difficult to book the Armory as the place was used primarily as an army reserve training center. According to Mary Jo, since 1936, agreement about use of the Armory, "while always approached with due caution, had been reached." This year the Vermont National Guard had a new schedule and a new mood prevailed during the customary negotiations. Despite "the already announced ambitious Festival, maybe the Armory would not be available at all, or at least in time," Mary Jo wrote. Even so, she realized, the school and especially the festival, had become big business for the small Vermont town: "a fact not to be ignored even if never admitted. If the impossible interval of three days for installation of the theatre and rehearsal in it would do, the place was again ours. One full rehearsal in the Armory of each performance would have to be enough."

All would be subject to space limitations and the pressures of staging a series of the festival's increased dimensions. The rehearsals for four companies and the Fellows group had to happen somewhere while the school also went on. Charles, "judged the sturdiest," drew the tent, once again set up next to the library. "The others made do, as they had before, with the spaces in the campus buildings and one off-campus, found by chance in an unused loft of uncertain stability. But it, like the tent, survived the period of preparation," Mary Jo reported.

Again, Martha shared living quarters at Cricket Hill with Graham and her mother visiting from California, and with Ben Belitt. "Martha [Graham] and her mother lived on the first floor and Ben and I were on the second." By then it was common knowledge that Erick Hawkins and Graham were lovers. Hill felt that choreographically Graham was also in love "with the idea of Erick as a beautiful male figure who could carry out ideas in a way that she had not been able to do with the woman's group." She recalled late-evening conversations over tea in the kitchen with Erick. "With his Harvard background of classics, he talked about Greek drama and Greek myths, and shared [our] passion about the American Indian experience, since Erick was born in Trinidad, Colorado, and knew much about Indian ritual."

"Erick would come in and make coffee in the morning and puree vegetables for Martha's diet. He was really very much part of Martha's life there," Hill remembered. More often than not, with Graham consumed by this love affair and the awesome task of creating an evening-length work for the festival, it was Martha Hill who tended to the needs of Mrs. Graham. She ushered her about, often settling her in the reading room of the library when the appreciative lady had had her fill of watching dance. If Hill was not concerned about Graham's infatuation with Erick, Teddy was "startled" by it. "Erick had a very balletic style still—he hadn't gotten out of his ballet at all—and he was doing choreography which wasn't very good." Otto Luening jokingly labeled him, "the torso," although others openly despised his "cavalier" attitude.[8]

Graham had been introduced to Erick months before when she went backstage after a Dance International concert to congratulate him on his first choreographic venture for Ballet Caravan—*Showpiece,* to a Robert McBride score. Sensing Graham's attraction to the handsome man, sixteen years her junior, Kirstein (who found the young dancer "stubborn" and his choreography "impossibly difficult")[9] "arranged" for Erick to study with Graham that spring to improve his choreographic skills. Some believed that Erick was Kirstein's "serpent," sent to sabotage her group.

By July, he was at Bennington with a "principal" role in her upcoming *American Document* and had recently become the first male dancer in Graham's company. "I was in seventh heaven because Martha gave me a lot of dancing to do. . . . I had the best suntan I've ever had in my life. The costume for me was shorts and a little jacket, and I didn't have to put any body makeup on. I have the feeling that was the first time—except for Ted Shawn—that anybody in modern dance ever did anything without a shirt on. I was very euphoric. . . . The most important aspect of Bennington was being around Martha, learning from her; that was a terrific privilege." (Here the original interview transcript reads, "I hope I didn't learn her egotism because it hasn't made her happy and it hasn't made anyone happy.") Erick continues, "If I didn't learn anything else from her, I learned courage."[10]

Other new dancers joining Graham's company that summer included Nina Fonaroff (Louis's love interest) and Jean Erdman, a student at Sarah Lawrence whom Martha Graham had discovered when guest-teaching there. Jean arrived on campus "the Monday after her weekend honeymoon," having just married her professor, Joseph Campbell. Her new husband was amazed at what he saw, saying that a technique class at Bennington was "beholding a revelation of the Mankind of the Future. . . . The spirit was transported beyond the reach of words. Movement, meaning, and feeling were identical; verbalization would have been insane. . . . I tell you, it was something."[11]

Audiences who arrived at Bennington enjoyed a constant flow of events. For Festival Week, 8–13 August, each of the three programs was given twice. Mary Jo counted heads and claimed full houses in attendance, boasting a list of visitors that included Betty Horst, Isamu Noguchi, and Lincoln Kirstein. She described the main events of the festival as the "culmination of the five-year plan as six successive evenings . . . accompanied by a classic version of the annual summer thunderstorm." Nonetheless, the audience members "filled every seat and beat their heels with good reason."

The festival also supplied a full roster of daily activities. The College Theatre and Arch's striped tent held free afternoon events, including the following lectures: dance historian Curt Sachs, "Dance and Music"; Martin, "Background of the American Dance"; Sachs, "Dance, Anthropology, History"; and Martin, "Isadora Duncan and the Modern Dance." Also included was "Program of Music for the Dance," moderated by Horst with nine other composers. The Commons also housed exhibits of dance photographs taken at Bennington by Thomas Bouchard and Barbara Morgan as well as displays of dance costumes by Wright and Ditson, and books on dance from the Kamin Bookshop (a favorite haven among dancers on Manhattan's West Fifty-third Street).

"One had to pay a dollar to get into the Armory, if one was lucky enough to get in," Mary Jo explained. The series opened with a performance by the Fellows, followed by two shared evenings with Holm and Humphrey on one, and Graham and Weidman on the other. Hanya Holm's *Dance Sonata* and *Dance for Work and Play* were both deemed successes. Martin claimed Humphrey's *Passacaglia in C Minor* was "a magnificent piece . . . richly and imaginatively wrought."[12] The architectural masterpiece, set for a cast of twelve dancers from their concert group and eleven students, with Doris and Charles as the soloists, exceeded everyone's expectations.

On the second program, Weidman's works were also well received. Ruth considered *Opus 51* an "absolute gem—just perfect. The dance sparked a kind of music that just took off unlike anything Vivian has ever written in her life. It was almost Schubertian." Having suffered the creation of *Quest,* Norman had to admit, "To me *Opus 51* was just crystal clear—delightful."

But it was Graham who received the most attention at the festival for her *American Document,* an epic overview of the social history of the United States, danced in minstrel form to a new score by Ray Green based on American folk rhythms. It would be Graham's first experimentation with character playing and the spoken word, and her first major work using a distinctly American theme. Hill recalled the excitement that *American Document* created. "A young actor read from American documents of different kinds. It was a very thrilling work with Martha feeling so strongly American, and using things from the Declaration of Independence, from American Indian leaders, and words from the Bible—all intensely American, using speech, movement, music. But *American Document* was badly reviewed because it was too strange. It had not settled in. We hadn't begun to think in terms of theater."

Many had a hard time accepting that Erick Hawkins was so overpoweringly

the standout performer of the work. But Hill appreciated the handsome dancer's native sense of movement and felt that this made him correct in the part.
Most important, Erick's presence in Graham's company marked "the beginning of men in dance." Erick added another point to the equation: "It was the
first time that [Graham] could dance like a woman because she had a man to
dance with."[13]

As profits that summer would fall far below expenses, some sacrifice had to
be made. "The impossibility of supplying orchestra accompaniment for such
an extensive number and variety of works was out of the question," Mary Jo
confirmed. For every other season, a small orchestra had been imported. Because of Horst's influence, Graham's orchestra, consisting of winds and percussion, flute and piano, determined the others' choices. The decision was
partly economic, Ruth explained, as five wind instruments make more sound
than five strings.

"Under the overall direction of Norman Lloyd," Mary Jo commented, "any
detriment to the effect of the six evenings on the audience went unobserved.
Even the critics who came in a phalanx to cover the event failed to take notice of
anything other than the breathtaking dancing that filled Arch Lauterer's theater."
Insiders, though, recalled Arch's use of many "fins for entrances and exits that allowed the stage to be flooded with dancers or suddenly removed." Martha remembered Edith Isaacs "being thrilled with the theater and what she saw there."

"What turned out to be the final festival held in the Armory added still another series of titles to the list of major compositions. Not all of them were repeated elsewhere in identical form but each was conserved in some form in
later works," Mary Jo wrote proudly. Agnes de Mille later asked Martha Hill
whether she recognized the significance of the time. Her reply was, "Once in a
while we all glimpsed it after a performance. Sometimes it came over you that
you were living in an historic period but most of the time we were too busy to
be aware."[14]

If elated over a triumphant summer session, Martha and Mary Jo were soon
returned to the realities of deficit spending and the strained situation developing with Bennington's administrators. The board had hoped to capitalize on
the success of dance to build a more diversified arts program, but now became
more cautious because of impending threats of a world war.

With the five-year plan at Bennington accomplished, Martha Hill was eager
to move on. In a brash move, she convinced the School of Dance board to vote
in favor of holding the 1939 session at Mills College in Oakland, California.
The invitation came out of the natural affinity between the two colleges, each
fostering dance in its own region. According to Hill, the moving spirit behind

the idea was Rosalind Cassidy, chair of its Department of Physical Education and director of the summer school at Mills. Cassidy had nurtured a growing West Coast reputation for modern dance; her participating artists included Hanya, Bonnie Bird, Tina Flade, and Lester Horton. Cassidy had just hired Bennington's own Marion Van Tuyl to serve as Mills's full-time dance instructor.

Hill explained, "Mills was a very important outpost of dance, early on. It was like a western sister-school to Bennington, in a way, and very important to the development of dance and all of the arts on the coast. We used economy of means because we didn't know how it would go." Just as with the first summer at Bennington, the shift to Mills "was like a feather in the wind; you put it up and see what happens. In talking to the artists, each was happier to gamble a few weeks than to sample six the first summer."

In preparation for the change of locales, the 1938 festival program printed a simple announcement: "By invitation of the trustees of Mills College, the 1939 session of the Bennington School of the Dance will be held at Mills College, Oakland, California. In accepting this invitation to hold a session in the West, the School will share in the significant development of the modern dance in another section of America."[15]

As administrative director, Mary Jo handled the transition with her usual efficiency (just as she would take on myriad other positions at Bennington through 1954). Although the invitation to Mills had been "formally blessed" by the trustees of both colleges, she acknowledged, "some plain and not so plain figuring about everything from working space to cost remained to be done." With Bennington's own board of directors obviously relieved, Mary Jo stoically reasoned, "After such a culmination of the original plan there had to come a new departure. Figuratively and literally that took place."

Martha's journey north from her frenzied job in Manhattan to her half-week at Bennington continued to be a pleasure. Housemate Becca Stickney recalled, "Martha would arrive in time for lunch with all of us from Cricket Hill. Ben would have made a big soup. Then we'd all disperse to do the afternoon's work. Sometimes Martha would inspect the huge refrigerator, and go through it— keeping us all from getting botulism. It really was a family at Cricket Hill." Belitt agreed, saying, "We not only ate together—we drank together. The whole thing was intoxicating. We relished each other's company. We were all a team. We went on picnics together—as divisions of a college—to this place and that, in a way that is unthinkable today. We let our hair down—[leaving] behind all of those mystiques that other people in authority employ to exploit and divide one another. At that time—I might as well put this exuberantly—things were wide open."

"Keeping the necessary economies in view," Mary Jo was the first to travel cross-country in the dead of winter by train on the *Yankee Clipper* and then the *Chief* out of Chicago "to collect the essential facts along with a major cold in the head which made the visitor from the East less than an impressive emissary." The president of Mills received her "cordially but at a discreet distance." Mary Jo wired back to Martha that the deal was struck.

"Economy forsaken, the traveler returned in better accommodations" to as far as Albuquerque, New Mexico, where Martha, now enjoying a semester sabbatical from Bennington, joined her. Having first stopped off for an impromptu weekend with Lefty in Colorado, she went on to join Mary Jo for several weeks of touring Indian country, visiting Santa Fe and pueblos in the area, buying Navaho rugs, relics, and red pottery, once again going through ideas for coauthoring a book.

Martha went west again at spring semester's end and did much of the setting up at Mills before the season began. En route, she stopped off in Denver, and Colorado Springs to spend time with Lefty. As usual, there was an "official capacity" to her visit to the campus. She "spoke, led groups in dance and taught at the Colorado Springs Conference on the Fine Arts led by Colorado College and the Colorado Springs Art Centre" the May 1939 *Bennington College Bulletin* reported.[16] Lefty's new son-in-law, Colorado senior Howard Dilts had recently married the president's youngest daughter Judy, and he was a student accompanist for Martha Wilcox, earning extra money playing for dance classes. He recalled playing for a student show and the pleasure of having Martha Hill as a guest "critic." Although he had no idea that Lefty and Martha were romantically involved, Howard did find his presence to welcome her unusual enough to recall the event years later.

When she had a spare moment, Martha now shopped in men's departments for special ties. They were gifts she could slip in her purse to give Lefty when they met—ones that he could enjoy wearing without suspicion as a daily reminder of the woman he loved.

The 1939 plan to transplant the entire Bennington summer dance operation to Mills College in Berkeley, California, had consumed Martha and Mary Jo's winter. Besides their brief sojourns, details were mainly worked out long-distance. It presented the kind of challenge that Martha always enjoyed.

"Rosalind Cassidy offered us a $20,000 budget," Martha remembered. A good portion of that figure would have to go for the faculty's and staff members' travel across the country. The festival would be sacrificed. "Partly to compensate for this curtailment but as much because it made sense, the curriculum was consolidated into three major programs; one each in dance, music, and stage design," Mary Jo reported.

Dancers attending Mills for the 1939 summer session studied with an "associate" in a single technique for the first three weeks, then took daily classes taught by Graham and Holm (splitting her summer with teaching at Colorado College for the first time), or Humphrey and Weidman for the final three weeks. The study of music and stage design could be augmented with elected academic courses from the ongoing Mills College summer offerings.

Shelly wrote that "by the same minor miracle by which the five previous [school] budgets had been balanced, so did this one." From 1 July to 11 August of the 170 enrolled, the great majority was made up of full-time students with the geographical base shifting to about half from the West, a quarter from the Midwest, and the rest from the East, South, and from outside the United States. The range in age, experience, and professional classification duplicated almost exactly the statistics from previous sessions at Bennington.

These facts indicated to the directors that the school, regardless of location, was meeting a need for intensive study of dance led by recognized authorities. Even so, the modified program was a disappointment to some. Helen Knight, one of Hill's NYU students who had followed her to Bennington, remembered Mills as "not quite as professional. I didn't think there was quite as much dedication that summer." Nonetheless, she did believe there was extraordinary talent on campus. Most particularly, Mercier Cunningham, Bonnie Bird's student from the Cornish School in Seattle, was a standout with his "tremendous ballet technique and intelligence."[1]

Hill too, remembered the first Experimental Production Workshop session: "When we met students for the first time we had them go across the stage any way they wanted, running, walking, skipping, whatever. This tall young man went across the stage and I nudged Arch and said, 'We have something there.' [Cunningham] had something in the turn of his head, almost Nijinsky-like."[2] Horst, too, recognized Cunningham's potential in his course on preclassic forms composition. "Martha [Graham] and I took one look at him and said, 'Wouldn't you like to come to New York?'"[3] Cunningham soon became the second male dancer to join Graham's company.

For the first time in almost a decade, Martha Hill did not teach technique classes, concentrating instead on team-teaching, investigating "the source of ideas for the art" in freewheeling workshop sessions. "Arch, who was a great genius, was like a mountain goat leaping from peak to peak," with students completely bewildered because "he wasn't taking time to spell it out," Martha explained. She acted as interpreter, "just as I often thought that Kir[k]patrick was always an interpreter of John Dewey. I would see practical ways to implement what Arch was doing so that it wouldn't remain as an idea but would become factual experience for the students"—perhaps a description of her role as a facilitator in every situation. "We'd do all kinds of experiments in time and space. Arch might be trying to make some point about perspective that would be very esoteric, whereas I could be very flat-footed," she admitted:

> I'd say, "Well, you understand what we mean by perspective . . .that a figure as it recedes from you becomes smaller, as it approaches you it becomes larger. And what Arch is trying to do in this project is build variations on that idea." Or he would play time against space, by setting up vertical poles on the stage, and, say, "start right stage with the first pole, and then the second would be very close, the next one would be a little further away, the next a little further away with these vertical demarcations gradually increasing in space." When dancers walked across that space, they would seem to be going faster or slower, dependent upon the line of demarcation.

Martha and Ben conducted a second section of the experimental course that focused on text and dance with Wallace Stevens's *Thirteen Ways of Looking at a Blackbird* supplying the point of departure. "Ben said, 'Let the blackbird equal anything you like, a single idea; for instance, one's imagination,'" Martha explained. She then "synthesized the whole thing" for the final workshop. (Always a great favorite with students and faculty alike, Ben had begun long conversations about the use of text with Graham, who, beginning with *American Document,* began to consider further possibilities in her own work.)

The move to Mills and the elimination of a festival for one summer had unexpected consequences. For Ruth and Norman, it was a relaxed time, like a vacation from Bennington. "Suddenly there was more leisure. Work went on only five instead of seven days a week. Evenings were free, and a new rapport developed among everyone—a chance to meet, talk, compare experiences, and enjoy the lovely California setting. We didn't do production so there was none of that hysteria or tension. In that sense, it was rather pleasant."

The summer in California seemed to calm Martha Hill as well, giving her an opportunity to try out a newly permed hairstyle with bangs that framed her face for a more carefree look. Forgoing her usual sophisticated tailored suits and stacked heels, in snapshots taken by her friends, she appeared confident and relaxed in bright print dresses and sandals. She would soon enjoy the attention and "prestige" as director of a project that to her delight had become "an open-sesame for people who were teaching in the forward-looking colleges."

The session coincided with the Golden Gate International Exposition, with its eye-opening display of Western American and Pacific culture. Taking the short trip across the Golden Gate Bridge into San Francisco, friends "moved as a group," piling into the fairgrounds for a Trader Vic's dinner and drinks at night. On weekends, they traveled down the peninsula to Carmel, Monterey, and Big Sur country. "A very different summer indeed, and a rewarding interval between the highly concentrated activity of the Bennington summers," Shelly confirmed.

Louis Horst was the first to admit that he was very happy at Mills. Besides giving him the opportunity to hear the Budapest String Quartet (also in residence at the college that summer), the trip west combined his teaching with his yearly pilgrimage to his early stamping grounds in San Francisco, where his wife Betty ran a dance studio. (From the early 1930s, Graham and Horst traveled together to California. Graham visited her mother in Santa Barbara, then reunited with Louis to spend time in Indian country before the October school openings. This time Graham would "go camping" with Hawkins.)

Again, the dance summer became a haven for photographers, with Bouchard shooting candids across campus for a week. Barbara Morgan was in town to arrange her traveling exhibit of dance photographs taken during Bennington's previous summer for the Women's San Francisco Convention and the National Society of Directors of Physical Education. While on campus, she concentrated on photographing Limón in the studio. Taken by his extraordinary physical presence, Morgan found him an ideal subject, and one of the few who took advantage of the empty studio space in the evenings.

But the big filming event of the summer occurred when Ralph Jester's entire professional camera crew took the place over, stopping the school "in its tracks" for two weeks.

Jester was "a very good friend" of Martha's who had been a sculptor on the first Bennington art department faculty; he was now a documentary film-maker in Hollywood. The result was a short film, *Young America Dances*. The final footage produced by Ampix Productions, gives a rare glimpse of classes, rehearsals, and social gatherings, succinctly documenting the session. Hortie's solo, developed in the experimental workshop, *Never Sign a Letter Mrs.* "was a highpoint, and gave comic balance to the rest of the film," Belitt recalled. (Hortie remembered laughing with Ben and Martha over *Emily Post's Etiquette* as she searched for inspiration in the library.)

Teddy remembered the "great excitement" of having a Hollywood film shot on campus. "My car was in it!" she exclaimed.[4] Helen Knight called the Jester film "tremendous, although there was a lot of pulling people out of classes. Some thought this was ridiculous and others, a great idea." Released commercially in art theaters across the United States, Helen admitted the she went to see it in Chicago—"ten times!"[5]

The film's aim was to boost the national image of dance in America. Although it pleased Martha and Mary Jo, who had worked assiduously to make it happen, it evidently displeased Bennington's administrators, who considered themselves the original supporters of this new art form.

Forgoing a festival failed to suppress the drive to produce new work. Three events took place. "As the result of the greatly increased number of daily visitors to watch work going on, an audience was generated for what were called 'demonstrations,'" Mary Jo noted. The first, where John Cage joined Lou Harrison for a concert of modern American percussion music, drew more than a hundred listeners. The San Francisco *Chronicle* considered this "beginning a movement with the reduction of dance accompaniment to simple, essential rhythms without melody,"[6] predicting the strong influence these two men would have. Announced as student demonstrations, Graham, Holm, Humphrey, and Weidman, each with "the most unostentatious of introductions, turned loose the students they had been teaching in what was officially described as exercises in dance technique. Again, a capacity audience from miles around saw unforgettable dancing," Mary Jo reported.

At season's end for a scaled-down event in Lesser Hall, the ambitious teaching assistants, Limón, with Ethel Butler, Kloepper, and Katherine Manning, managed to produce a concert on their own. Limón's completed *Danzas Mexicanas* to music by Lionel Nowak was a highlight of the session, for which Humphrey spent her extra time "molding" José's choreographic talents: "Charles and I try to help when he is obviously looking stunning but not saying anything," as he worked on his portraits of five kinds of Mexicans—the

Indian, the Spanish invader, the peon, the landowner, and the Revolutionary. As José was gaining more of Doris's attention, Charles was becoming more difficult to manage. She wrote to her husband, "I've at last made up my mind that [Charles] cannot be let alone to do just as he pleases, because he lacks judgment so it's hard on me to be the only one with sense, but I'll have to accept it [despite] his winning charm and 'irresistible humor.'"[7]

Ever the cheerleader, Mary Jo wrote that the performance "electrified" Lesser Hall with the "veterans of other summers set to beating their heels on the floor. The one and only session of the Bennington School of the Dance at Mills College ended, as it deserved to, in a wall-shaking burst of applause."

After packing their bags, Ruth, Norman, Hanya with Klaus, Hortie, Martha, Mary Jo, and Teddy went to Hollywood to see the rushes of Jester's film. Then, having hired several cars, the group drove across the desert to New Mexico, stopping first at the Canyon de Chelly in Arizona to see the Snake Dance. Ruth and Norman referred to their "pilgrimage out west" as a "romantic thing." It was "related in part to Graham's and Louis's [ideals]" which, in turn, had been influenced by the writings of Indian enthusiast Mary Austin, and her idea "of the place determining something about the person or about a social culture, and the sense of space." Ruth continued, "Here was dance in its purest form for religious purposes completely in a closed involved community. Here was a kind of totality of their interests." Norman added, "an intertwining."

Arriving by train, Louis joined the entourage for the Intertribal Ceremonials at Gallup, New Mexico. "When we got to Gallup the people in charge of arranging the [ceremonials] recognized him and asked if he'd serve as a judge. The Indians from Oklahoma "had struck oil, and drove up in Cadillacs with costumes that looked as though they had come out of Brooks costumers. As a judge, Louis was telling the Indians whether they were authentic or not, because he knew more about the history of what they were doing than they did," Norman fondly remembered. After a shopping spree with everyone buying pots and rugs with what they had saved from their Mills paychecks, they piled onto the train heading to Chicago. (Once onboard, their exuberant mood changed to solemnity with the announcement that the Germans had invaded Poland.) Martha left the group when the train stopped in Denver, once again spending precious time in a rendezvous with Lefty.

Much had changed when Martha returned to the Vermont campus after that summer away. Leigh's eight-year contract would soon end—an arrangement that he himself had put into place, believing that no president should be in power for a longer duration. During his tenure Leigh had encouraged Martha to advocate the spread of the Bennington model to other locations. According to Norman, "The idea was that five years later we would move to some-place in the Midwest but the war interfered with all of this. You can't go on re-peating a formula forever, so it seemed like a legitimate thing." But with dance at Mills, and the inactivity on the Vermont campus, the theater and music people at Bennington rallied to create a more inclusive summer session in the arts, with closer connections to the winter school.

Having lost her edge as the central figure, Martha learned the importance of continuity, and keeping lines of communication strong, lessons she later put to good use. Other problems loomed large at Bennington. Taking a sabbatical in September 1939, Leigh appointed Lewis Jones as acting president. Letting it be known that he was looking for another position, Leigh headed off to Bard College as an "academic doctor" for "a very sick institution." Bennington itself had not received accreditation on the grounds that it had not proved that its grad-uates were "adequately prepared for further schooling." This news further de-pressed Leigh, who felt that he had done his best for Bennington.[8]

In 1940, back from Chicago, Mary Jo took charge as administrative director of Bennington's newly established School of the Arts. Programs now included music and drama, salvaging at least part of Martha's original plan. A new $90,000 theater, designed by Arch, was projected for completion in 1940–41, with dance, drama, and theater design workshops, but it never found a donor. Still, the trustees, impressed by the wild popularity of the past summers' activ-ities, voted to create a festival for all the arts. The decision had been made for dance to be a part of the new plan, but no longer the centerpiece. In retrospect, the 1938 summer session had nearly overwhelmed the campus's capacities.

Concerned that she had made an error of judgment with the Mills move, Martha was now faced with a less than enthusiastic return to the fold. She had learned to "never bite the hand that feeds," an expression that crept into her ad-vice to others, and she accepted the outcome. Friends noticed that her forth-rightness was more subdued, more conservative, shying away from controversy. For the duration, she would hold on to what she was offered, without a fight. Martha knew when to back off and when to opt for the "one who did it best." Be-litt observed, "The other half of Martha's magic was to stand for whatever re-mained to be known in the idiom in which she was master." Nevertheless, she would find herself in an increasingly uncomfortable position over the next years.

In the fall of 1939 José returned to a shared half-week schedule at Benning-ton, and found Martha at work on an adaptation of Hart Crane's poem *The Bridge*.[9] Lauterer, now drama chairman with Fergusson on sabbatical, launched the project that now consumed the arts scene at the college. The poem was "a kind of metaphor for art itself," Hart's biographer Clive Fisher wrote, "since every work of art marked a union between imagination and creation—and it remained a national epic in his mind because 'America herself was born of a fusion of European imagination and enterprise which made her singular among nations.'"[10] If Martha and her Village compatriots sought as impassionedly as Hart a fusion of the "heroic tongues" of a young America, the production concept remained Arch Lauterer's brainstorm, Martha recalled. "[Arch] loved that poem. . . . He designed the set. We started work in September—cast it, had a speaking chorus, a singing chorus, solo speakers, solo dancers, an orchestra, an original score. We had a wonderful student cast, too—Carol Channing was in it. Anybody who had ever known Hart Crane or ever written about him attended the performance[s]. They came from all over. People were so moved, tears streamed down their faces."[11] José called the work "rich and rewarding experience" with "devices and capacities" that were "entirely revolutionary."[12] It was the work that most impressed Ben Belitt over time, and he recalled in wonder, "What a paradox that Martha should move the words of Hart Crane's *Bridge* and [take] the challenge of Twentieth Century poetry in the end! Then, word-of-mouth was made one with the dance: articulation became total."

That spring, when José joined the more lucrative Broadway scene, performing in *Keep off the Grass,* Bill Bales took over his teaching at Bennington. The show's choreographer, George Balanchine, had, in the last few years, built a striking reputation in theater and film. But beginning with Balanchine's first command, "You go in center and do modern dance," confirmed José's disenchantment with Broadway and, no doubt, the choreographer. José longed for "the imagination and boldness" he had witnessed in *The Bridge* with "no need to think of box-office appeal," and he vowed to avoid future involvement on Broadway at all costs.[13] He opted to leave the show for California and a summer commitment to teach at Mills.

In the ballet realm, American Ballet Theatre, established in 1940, boldly entered the concert scene and, with a competitive ballet company at his heels, Kirstein again renewed his desire to establish a company of his own. With the establishment of these bigger, more visible companies, and an influx of talented Russian-trained teachers, the great divide between modern and ballet was now more pronounced.[14]

In the few short years since *Ballet Caravan* had debuted at Bennington, Kirstein had categorically devalued every emerging modern dancer on the scene except Martha Graham. He admitted,

I have long been suspect as an enemy of the "modern" or "concert" dance, and with a single exception [Graham] still vigorously am. I have always found to hate in most of it a persistent, arbitrary, priggish and doctrinaire avoidance of theatrical elements, a refusal to accept the tradition [of] classic dance as a basic theatrical instrument. I have been irritated by its prejudiced rejection of the form of ballet as a decadent hangover of feudalism. I do not think that a mere desire to dance is enough to make a dancer, or that six weeks at Bennington is a blanket diploma towards a professional stage-career.[15]

Years later, Kirstein is quoted as saying that his method was "behaving as if something were true even if it wasn't, and using as a kind of target or magnet a notion that if you could imagine a situation as if it were true, as if we had a theatre, as if there were a ballet company." It was a tactic that worked for generations to come—and one that Martha used with as much determination.[16]

The horror of the Nazi invasions distressed everyone in that troubled spring of 1940. In odd juxtaposition, the rising anxiety prompted educational institutions to recruit students more fervently than ever in an effort to bolster the dire economic situation that was forecast. As a result, during Bennington's winter break, Martha was asked to team up with Norman Lloyd to give lecture-demonstrations in Maryland and Pennsylvania under the auspices of the Association of American Colleges. Hazel, a Latin and music major at Webster College, went to one of their "teach-ins" at Hood College, Maryland at the suggestion of a professor who summered at Bennington. "Martha Hill and Norman Lloyd opened a whole new world for me. I felt as if I had never breathed before. It was magic. I don't think my feet quite touched the ground!" After expressing her interest in the summer music for dance program at Bennington, "Martha and Norman got me a full scholarship. My dad, who was a railroader, got me a pass, and my uncle gave me $25 for my birthday, so that set me up for the summer."

Once at Bennington, Hazel observed that "Martha and Mary Jo were the vanguard of progressive women [as] feminists. Although they didn't think of themselves as that, they were. They had things to do. They wanted to do them, and they had to figure out how to get them done. In their own way they were pioneers. If both were very bright and extremely competent, it was Martha with the ideas and Mary Jo who could see what had to be done. That's why they worked so well together."[17] Although Knight agreed with this assessment, she added, "Mary Jo was different as night and day from Martha."[18]

Even though Hazel knew of Martha's liaison with Lefty, she could see that the two women were very close. "There was great deal of talk that there was more than that. I think maybe it was true, and there wasn't anything wrong with it. They were expanding the bounds of what is permissible, and I think they were expanding the bounds there too. I always just took it for granted that they were lovers. But it never made any difference to me, and they never said a word about it. Not a word was spoken about it to anyone. It was just that you took it for granted, or you didn't, but ideas of feminism and lesbianism were clearly in the air," she explained. "I don't, to this day, have any evidence one way or the other. Sub rosa 'under the roses' I guess you'd call it. You knew it, but you never said anything about it."

The new summer plan at Bennington for 1940 placed dance as one of the four divisions of the School of the Arts in a six-week session format. The final week would again be devoted to the festival of performances. The revised configuration placed Mary Jo as administrative director; Martha, director of dance; Otto Luening, director of music; Francis Fergusson, again director of drama; and Lauterer, director of theater design. Although necessarily scaled down, figures proved that dance was far and away the dominant component, with eighty-seven students registered in dance compared to sixteen in music, twelve in drama, and four in theater design.

Hanya directed a master course in dance, with three teaching associates covering for her so that she could also take on a residency at Colorado College. Graham's group was the one resident producing company, with Ethel Butler teaching Graham technique. Charles and Doris were on a leave of absence that summer. Ballet and dance notation were added to the curriculum, although neither proved to be particularly popular with the students. Among the younger members who had recently joined Graham's company, however, most obligingly took Erick's ballet class, wanting to improve their line and elevation. Many observed striking changes in the technical demands of Martha's new choreography, and could see Erick's influence. If jumps and fuller, ankle-length skirts had entered into her once-sacred dark woolens period with the 1934 group work *Celebration* and her 1935 solo *Frontier,* Graham was now producing what she began to call "ballets."[19]

For Norman, the School of the Arts format spelled the demise of a dance theater that might have become, using Mary Jo's and Martha's earlier terminology, "a matrix art." "Up to this point, Bennington had become a gathering place for poets, musicians, painters, everybody—and you were getting these dance forms, as in *American Document.* It was this pushing out into new areas of theater, and looking at dance as a kind of total theater." In Norman's view, the development of the School of the Arts had the opposite effect, "fragmenting, whereas before this, you had dance as the matrix art, to which everything else contributed." In his opinion, the concept "weakened it . . . really came to an end. I think it's too bad it happened, because something else was on the verge of happening to bring together the arts." Both Martha and Doris had worked toward this new kind of theatrical form, he maintained, "towards some kind of a total theater [that was] one of the things that made Bennington distinctive, maybe for the first time in this country."[20]

Critic Don McDonagh later agreed that the Bennington idea had been "killed," with its earlier "free and easy interplay . . . lost and never regained."[21] Others were alarmed by the aesthetic shift that seemed to have blossomed that summer, all the more evident because Graham was the only resident choreographer for the season and the only other full-fledged dance presentation was, unfortunately, Erick Hawkins's recital.[22]

On 13 July, Hawkins presented three solos; *Liberty Tree* with music by Ralph Gilbert, *Insubstantial Pageant* to a Lehman Engel score, and *Yankee Bluebritches* to one by Hunter Johnson. They were his first choreographic ventures since his *Show Piece* for Ballet Caravan three years earlier. All received lackluster responses, although Kirstein—on campus for a lecture series "on theatrical dancing"—and Graham did their best to encourage him.

Kirstein and Graham, swiftly emerging as giants in the field, now corresponded regularly, something others never would have suspected. Later, in a 1941 letter from Graham to Kirstein as "Fellow-Pioneer," she wrote,

> Lincoln—we must stand—you and I—separately and perhaps together. . . .
> I have not yet the realism that lies behind the eyes—not in the outer lines of things. And you are not clear yet, either. But greater than all else is a deep inner primal power—in the body of the dance here. . . . You see I believe in you—and I believe in the bodies of my dancers and your dancers.[23]

Despite the lack of full-fledged dance festival offerings in 1940, the campus was still a center of dance activity. Hill, Lauterer, and Lloyd undertook an experimental production course to nurture more advanced choreographers. Six showcases featured works by students, and many of Graham's dancers were encouraged to choreograph under Horst's tutelage. The nine women in residence with Graham included Ethel Butler, Erdman, Nelle Fisher, and Fonaroff, who along with Sophie Maslow and Jane Dudley were also developing new materials for Horst's lecture-demonstrations that had become a popular asset to the company in New York City and on tour.[24]

A lively topic of conversation was how long the already portly Louis, who had gained a considerable amount of weight over the last few years, would be able to continue to reside in Buckminster Fuller's experimental Dymaxion House.[25] Placed next to the library where Arch's tent had been, using the unique structure's tiny bathroom and triangular shower had become a struggle for Horst. "At the time, he weighed about three hundred pounds and could not get himself out. Louis hated being constrained in any way. He was very frightened, with good reason, because it took a couple of people to pull him out," Graham recalled.[26] Also, every time there was a thunderstorm, the two Marthas would fret about his safety in the metal-framed abode. By midsummer, they convinced him to move into regular quarters, and the house was given over as a play area for faculty children.[27]

Despite limited resources, "there were some very good things that came about during the war years at Bennington," Norman had to admit. Hill's view was more philosophical than most. "Mainly from the influence of those years at Bennington, the teaching field was completely changed. People knew more about music by the 1940s. They were more experimental-minded about what they attempted to choreograph. They were more interested in collaborations."

Lauterer once again tried to improve the very deep stage of the 150-seat College Theatre, but he could do nothing to change the problem of no wing space to accommodate entrances and exits. Still, for the festival's opening night of Fergusson's drama department production, *The King and the Duke: A Melodramatic Farce from "Huckleberry Finn,"* the *Bennington Banner* reporter seemed more taken by the presence of important figures in the audience, noting the arrivals of Kirstein, musicians Roy Harris and Quincy Porter, and cohead of the Neighborhood Playhouse, Rita Wallace Morgenthau (whose daughter Jean was in Bennington's class of 1938).

John Martin commented politely in the *New York Times* on Martha Hill's choreography for *The King and the Duke,* "But the production as a whole was stuffy and academic."[28] Obliged to work collegially with Fergusson, now a "division" head of drama, Martha took the dismal reviews stoically. Others singled out Martha's choreographic talents. Ben was one of them, kindly calling her "as venturesome a catalyst and choreographer as the legendary divas whom she shepherded." But the placement of the work as an opening-night affair with its unwieldy cast of thirty-two, drawn from drama students who were mostly amateurs (as were its eleven musicians in the pit), was a mistake. To make matters worse, the work continued to be paired on alternate nights with Graham's full program of sterling works, *El Penitente, Every Soul Is a Circus: A Satire* (having premiered in New York City in December 1939), and *Letter to the World.* There was no contest between the two events.

Of Graham's two premieres at Bennington on 11 August 1940, *El Penitente* was a trio for herself, Erick, and Merce, in the form of a southwestern morality play—a ritual of sin, penance, and redemption. Horst's rhythmically tight score for the work gave precision and definite contrast between sections for the sturdy composition. For the first time, Graham used handheld props: an apple, a penitent's rope, and a wooden cross with a banner attached that doubled as a curtain.

But it was the second piece, *Letter to the World* that most closely aligned itself to traditional theater. Arch Lauterer's realistic set pieces of a bench, and a worktable emblematic of Emily Dickinson's "cloistered life" stunningly reversed the trend established by Noguchi's and Calder's earlier work for Graham. Edythe Gilfond's more traditional period costumes (with shoes rather than the now customary and symbolic bare feet) were matched by the use of dialogue. Louis found Hunter Johnson's score problematic, and he insisted on cuts throughout, as he made an all-out effort to salvage the work.[29]

Graham, playing the role of Emily Dickinson as the "one who dances," first worked with an actress, Margaret Meredith, playing her counterpart of the "one who speaks." (Hill's relationship to Graham comes to mind here.) Dissatisfied because as Meredith spoke at one side of the stage, she took the attention away from her dancing, Graham asked dancer Jean Erdman, who had studied acting, to stand in her place. The choreographer, not wanting to be upstaged, then integrated the lines with shifts in action to defuse the focus on the voice as a dominant component. "The difficulty of integrating dance, solo and group, with spoken word when the adherent is the psyche is considerable," *Dance Observer* critic Elizabeth McCausland commented in a review a month later.[30]

"I'm Nobody! Who are you? Are you Nobody too?" soon were playfully parroted on campus that summer, occasionally prompting more serious discussions about the interdisciplinary notions of the School of the Arts format. Dance should be able to integrate the arts, and *Letter to the World* would prove that, some commented. Others (including Merce Cunningham who felt increasingly uncomfortable in his role-playing in *Letter*) began to construct notions of their own against that idea, believing in the power of dance for dance's sake.

Louis Horst's preaching against literal representation was well known.[31] Modern dance is "a revolt against emotional display," he told his students—and Graham, who had begun to ignore his advice. "Movement should express an idea, rather than actually portraying the idea itself. Put away the idea which gave birth to the movement but use the elements of the movement." As the grand old man on campus, he still commanded respect and solemn obedience; he remained the champion of the modern movement, with dance an independent art. Yet within that art, he advocated experimentation: "There is no beauty when there is no longer a newness and a fresh viewpoint to be gained."[32] But Graham's experiments ran contrary to Horst's instructions: parts were played by nine women and five men (including Erick and Merce) handling "roles" rather than dancing out abstract ideas in movement through time and space.

Graham's *El Penitente* received praise all around, but *Letter to the World* received harsh criticism, harshest from the *New York Times*. Once again, Graham was infuriated. It took her almost a half-century to forgive the critic, when she wrote, "John Martin was such a delight and holy terror in our lives. He had the ability to see things with a clear cold eye although sometimes his way of seeing was not always ours. This could be discouraging." Reminded of his review for *Letter to the World* (where he concluded, "best to let it sleep in the Vermont hills"), Graham conceded that Martin did press her "to look deeper. . . . He created a world of challenge for all dancers and he prodded us to see the truth and to present it as daringly as we could."[33]

The gas shortage became the "official" Bennington excuse for shutting down future festival activities. Granted, lack of fuel did curtail travel to Bennington (although neighboring Tanglewood and Jacob's Pillow were still able to draw large audiences). But more than likely, internal competition and hostility from the other departments were the main reasons for the eventual demise of the summers of dance. The mixed reaction of the somewhat bewildered critics (who had expected to see the likes of the 1938 dance festival) was a definite disappointment. And even though the theater and music faculty found the summer eventful, the manic pace in which the dancers thrived was definitely not for them.

At Bennington, Martha Hill continued to create movement "on deck that underlined the story." As the selfless utilitarian choreographer, this was often more work than pleasure. Ever able to conceal her private thoughts, she took on assignments as they came along. "She was a woman of tremendous energy," Fergusson recalled when they worked together on the production of Gershwin's *Of Thee I Sing* and for sequences in *Blood Wedding* with Bales, composer Otto Luening, and Lauterer completing the team.[34] For Andre Obey's *Noah,* a participant remembered "tense" moments when Martha and Fergusson huddled together to get the right spring squat for the Monkey, the languor for the Cow, and the perfect nodding for the Sheep.[35]

Martha also staged productions at New York University on occasion: highlights were Norman Lloyd's adaptation of *Restless Land* and Alpenfels-Hill-Hussey's *Social Mores Reflected in Dance*. Martha had once dreamed of striking out on her own as an independent choreographer, but that desire had disappeared and she found some satisfaction through her involvement as the movement specialist in these collaborations. Again, she took a subservient role to others, willingly drafted into one project after another.

Martha's life seemed to be at a temporary lull. Now approaching her forties, she pondered the probable direction of her life as a single woman in a relationship that offered little prospect of children of her own. Martha desperately needed a change of pace.

PART V

The Forties

The effects of war raging in Europe dramatically changed the lives of Americans at home, bringing out the best and the worst in its citizens. The threat of a world war brought about the hoarding of black-market items such as sugar and silk stockings. Heated debates between the isolationists insisting on neutrality and the increasing numbers of Americans believing that war was inevitable escalated with each report of soldiers killed in battle. Despite the distressing climate, Martha recalled her own daily pattern: "I was very busy and very happy being busy!" In truth, however, for Martha the next years would prove difficult and be the least productive of her long career.

Having taken graduate courses from time to time, Martha completed her own master's degree at New York University in 1941. (Black dance artist Pearl Primus was among the graduate students who received her degree at the same time.) Martha's thesis was titled "An Analysis of Accompaniment for the Dance." The topic indicates her continuing interest in the interconnectedness of music and dance. While doing the coursework she served "as a kind of guinea pig," developing a master's program in dance for Bennington at the same time she designed a master's degree in dance education at NYU.

Meanwhile, on José's brief return to Manhattan he found his life in a "shambles." Limón had quarreled with his mentors and the atmosphere at the studio had become impossible. Returning to San Francisco and convinced that the West would hold "a golden future," he began to work on a duet program with the stunning ex-Graham dancer, May O'Donnell; he even moved into the studio she shared with her husband Ray Green and Gertrude Shurr. Subject to the draft as a Mexican alien, and classified as 1-A, he read the daily headlines with dismay, knowing that it was just a matter of time before he would be called to serve in the army.

In New York City, hoping to "say goodbye to the very long and exhausting tours," Doris and Charles—both presenting some of the finest works of their careers—had renovated a space as a studio theater at 108 West Sixteenth Street. "We are going to have a home to play in," Humphrey announced. With an entrance next to a brightly lit Chinese laundry, one pleased reviewer remarked that Pauline Lawrence had "taken a leaf out of the notebook of the Museum of Modern Art" in her design of the space. Pauline's superhuman abilities as jack-of-all-trades not only produced the company's elegant costumes, but her "clever" lighting, using Lauterer's system of strong light concentrated in one direction against subdued general lighting brought out sculptural values.[1]

Martha, with Mary Jo in town for the holidays, excitedly joined the company's opening-night performance the day after Christmas, and afterward invited the cast and friends to her loft to celebrate. Hazel remembered that such parties would always get noisy and shrill when they were all together.

During the spring months, as news at the war front worsened, the pair did their usual summer planning. Financial calculations grew more troubling. Martha related, "We were not money-minded in those days. You didn't wear your union card on your chest. It was a period of new things happening. You didn't think about it." The ever-practical Mary Jo, however, continued to watch Bennington's budget sheets carefully. "Between 1934 and 1940, although roughly only half a million dollars came into and went out to the exchequer, costs were always met, surpluses, if any, were minuscule." Lack of interest among outside funders continued to frustrate them: "Only the people who were there and the Colleges—Bennington for all but one year, Mills for the 1939 season—gave everything they had to give." For Mary Jo, "the gift more than sufficed."

Although scaled down in scope, three major styles in technique were offered in Bennington's summer of 1941 (now cloned into the June–July third semester). The Martha Graham Technique, the Hanya Holm Technique, and the Humphrey-Weidman Technique would be taught, the catalogue announced. This time, Humphrey and Weidman would be handling a master course for advanced students, as well as a repertory course—the first at Bennington—where Weidman's *Lynchtown* and Humphrey's *The Shakers* would be coached. Erick consented to labeling his course "Ballet for Modern Dancers." Bill Bales geared up for a new one in "Tap Technique" and Martha took on "Advanced Dance Composition" along with coteaching "Experimental Production" with Arch and Norman.

Having spent the previous summer in the "Brooder—a building attached to the Chicken Coop with a lot of bugs," Ruth, Norman, and their year-old son now returned to "a regular faculty house" greatly diminishing their carefree summer lifestyle. Although they managed live-in help, having a child on campus was the exception rather than the rule. When Hanya and Doris brought their sons to Vermont, they were usually shepherded off to camp for most of the duration. Louis's thoughts about children were by now legend; Hill, Graham, Shelly, and the others were doting "aunts" and "uncles"—yet certainly not eager babysitters.

Harriet Roeder, who had danced in Holm's *Trend* and was now in her company, took on the responsibility of teaching for her at Bennington. Meanwhile, Hanya worked with Lefty Davies to establish a full summer dance program under her direction in Colorado Springs. In that position for another forty-two years, Hanya built a stronghold for summer dance training in the West—a job that might have suited Martha, except for the proximity of Lefty's family. But the locale was perfect for Hanya. With full authority in Colorado Springs, her living quarters less communal, and free from the unwritten "anti-child" clause she sensed at Bennington, she began a summer residency of her own devising.[2]

When in Manhattan, Martha honed her skills at folk dance, becoming a regular attendee at folk dance expert May Gadd's English Folk Dance Society Association sessions at Columbia. Martha had long used square dancing to bring NYU men into her realm at Friday night socials. Now, as part of the war effort, she organized a number of square dances for servicemen through a course at NYU held at the Seamen's House (then located at the foot of Twentieth Street), often bringing along her female students. She also assisted Gadd (who proclaimed "Service men like country dancing!" as she served as program consultant with the U.S. Army and Navy departments), at other USO clubs.[3]

Martha once again carried over her love of American folk dancing to Bennington and planned evenings of "squares" complete with local fiddlers. Student Beth Olson Mitchell first sighted Martha in the Carriage Barn looking wonderful, dancing with posies stuck into her topknotted hair. For the Lloyds, their "extracurricular square dance orchestra" was the joy of the 1941 summer.

Arch Lauterer (who had left his wife Helen in 1937 for a student he married in 1939) continued to play an important part in shaping Bennington's productions. Always searching for new performing spaces, he had long had his eye on the little town's General Theatre, now the local movie house. In earlier years, it had been the Vermont stop for professional touring circuits routed to Montreal. Preparations were made for the college to present a Molière-Mozart double bill of the *School for Wives* and Mozart's *The Impresario* there. With incidental dances set by Martha Hill, the shows played to an enthusiastic local press. Originally it was to run "between showings of the feature picture on the first two Sundays and Mondays in August," according to a *Bennington Bulletin*. But the plan proved to be too much of a strain on the staff and the dates were changed to the two weeks after the dance festival was completed.

Compared to the major efforts of the Humphrey-Weidman and the Graham companies on campus, little attention went to a midsummer premiere of Hawkins's *In Time of Armament,* a "very romantic duet" he performed with Jean Erdman in a program shared with Jane Dudley. Workshops for student pieces were presented on the last Wednesday and Friday evenings of the session, along with works by Bales and Fonaroff. Also featured was a dance-drama based on Lauterer's scheme for *The Swallow Book* (by Ernst Toller) with Martha Hill's movement and Norman's music. Of the three elements in the work, the dancing part seems to have suffered the most from lack of space and, as with Graham's first attempts in *Letter,* critics complained that the dance-drama's intentionally static speaker produced a sense of monotony.

That summer, Henry Cowell appeared on campus to everyone's delight, participating in a concert of contemporary music where he played his "Piano Works," and percussion in a Lou Harrison piece. In a review of Bennington's music events for *Dance Observer,* Cowell remarked that if the music was "less splashy than that of the dance . . . it was no less significant, no less creative."[4] But in fact, Louis Horst spent a good amount of July more preoccupied with Joe DiMaggio's hitting streak (ending at fifty-six games) for the Yankees on the radio and in the papers.

Mary Jo's notion of a combined arts festival featuring "more significant work indicative of the seriousness of the times" influenced the look of the festival's major offerings. Although the number of works-in-progress was reduced to two and presented on alternate evenings beginning on 9 August, remarkably, the programs ran for ten straight performances to capacity audiences.

The first premiere was Humphrey's *Decade: A Biography of Modern Dance from 1930 to 1940,* with "scenes" by Weidman and music arranged by Lionel Nowak. Integrating students from her repertory work into the piece, the two-hour-long Humphrey-Weidman offering with eleven company members and six apprentices, was a choreographic retrospective of materials drawn from dances created for Humphrey-Weidman over the last ten years. Her effort to collaborate with playwright William Saroyan had fallen through, and she turned instead to the idea of "the struggle of pioneer art in a world geared to profit. We ought to be able to do that with feeling!" she wrote to her mother, Julia.[5] A total of nineteen scenes included excerpts from works as early as *Circular Descent* and *Water Study,* sections of *With My Red Fires,* and Weidman's *Ringside* and *The Happy Hypocrite.* Although Martha Hill felt a twinge of nostalgia in viewing this work, she wholeheartedly agreed with Margaret Lloyd of the *Christian Science Monitor* that no matter how "endearing. . . . This is no time for pioneers to be looking back."[6]

The second premiere, Graham's farcical *Punch and the Judy* to a score for two pianos by Robert McBride and set pieces by Lauterer, was by far the most successful, delighting Margaret Lloyd, who later called it a "sparkling domestic comedy" and the best "hit of the season."[7] Bennington's dance experiments now seemed "closer to real theater," critic Robert Horan believed, labeling the works "serious comedies."[8] Without doubt, this aesthetic shift had been strongly influenced by Bennington's change of focus toward interdisciplinary projects.

When the session was over, Bennington School of the Arts "moved off its hill top," in Martha's words, taking *The King and the Duke* to the First Green Mountain Festival of the Arts in Middlebury (organized to celebrate Vermont's sesquicentennial). Martin provided a lecture, Graham presented *Every Soul is a Circus,* and three works were offered by the Humphrey-Weidman Company.

The good turnout for the final concerts meant salaries were paid after all. The 1941 summer produced income of more than $30,000, leaving a deficit of more than four thousand dollars. (When it looked as though enrollment would not cover faculty salaries, it was Horst who was the first to relinquish his. And Martha had always considered her summer salary something extra to draw upon in case of emergency.) Although the dance component managed to come out even, the others did not, and the project faced a deficit "bound by the college"—in those days, hard circumstances to justify for the president and his board.

As her schedule veered away from the studio toward graduate work and student advising, Martha only occasionally donned leotards in Vermont. Her dancing was now pared down to less frequent movement demonstrations mixed with more and more verbal instructions. Still, her sophisticated demeanor radiated authority while the best in her classes demonstrated. One Bennington student was most impressed not by the dancing Martha, but by the one "briskly arriving from New York, moving with such style and energy and organization, an inconceivable and improbable combination of a Geisha and a Grant Wood with an aura of glamour."[9] Others believed that she was a "great teacher," recalling that Martha expressed "a kind of universal love and acceptance for every student which created an atmosphere conducive to growth and helped them reach their maximum potential."[10]

Another perspective comes from political economist Peter F. Drucker. He recognized John Dewey's influence on her teaching at Bennington, but nonetheless found Martha

> totally different from all of the other master teachers. All of them . . . focused on teaching. Martha Hill focused on learning. . . . And I don't think that any other of those wonderful Bennington teachers of the 1940's had remotely the impact that [she] did. They had devoted, excited, inspired students. Martha Hill had motivated learners. . . . Martha changed her students' lives. Yes, she was a great dance teacher. But even more, she was

uniquely what the word "pedagogue" originally meant—the leader, the motivator, the grower, the builder—and the only one I have been blessed to know in my eighty years of teacher-watching and my more than seventy years of teaching myself.[11]

Hazel, who would be in residence as a full-time musician at Bennington for the next five years, offered the sharp perspective of a dance accompanist trained to observe every move. She said of Martha: "I never saw her tired, I never saw her mopey. She was always up. The only thing is that she'd come up from New York City, every once in a while, 'in a high wind.' On edge. She wanted everything done yesterday. She'd tear into things and never slow down. This was the only mood I ever saw her in."

During this time, Martha's one strong family tie was with her brother Bill. He had joined the Air Force in 1941 after graduating from college in Ohio. First trained at Fort Riley as one of the last of the cavalry recruits, he then became an aviation cadet. (He already had a pilot's license.) In Arkansas "they washed me out for dangerous flying habits," and he was put on leave. "They didn't know what to do with me," he confessed. "Martha said, 'Why don't you come to New York for a while?' So I stayed with Martha in New York. I had an impacted wisdom tooth, so her dentist took care of that. Mary Jo and Martha took me out to a nightspot in Greenwich Village. Here I was in uniform—a private, with nothing on my sleeve. Some guy came up to me and said, 'Can I dance with you?' Mary Jo said, 'You don't want to dance with him!' Did she tell him off!"

But the sweetest "on leave" memory Bill had was while visiting Bennington. (Ben remembered that they were all very amused with Bill's happy-go-lucky manner.) On one occasion Martha arranged a fishing trip for him with composer Greg Tucker. "I got fishing gear out of the PX," Bill recalled, "and we visited his friend the artist, Norman Rockwell, who lived on a stream. Rockwell said, 'Why don't you boys try for trout out there?' We didn't catch many, but the experience was spectacular. Mary Jo lent me her car, and I got to see some of Vermont."

That same Model T Ford was also seen with Martha Graham behind the wheel driving around campus and to town. With no license and no fear, Martha Hill, who never dared drive herself, lived in terror of the trips, Graham reported. "When I took other teachers for a drive, she would say, "Pray! With Martha driving, that could be the end of the history of modern dance.""[12]

Martha Hill's enthusiasm for her work was now more and more centered on each semester's new group of potential dancers. In the fall of 1941 Ethel Winter came on the scene: "I wanted to dance and there were very few places where you could get a degree in those days." She remembered her first encounter with Martha when signing up for classes. "Martha came from a small town, so she understood when I admitted, 'I don't know what modern dance is.' She was very comforting and helpful in terms of adjustment, because I was petrified."[13]

Ethel recalled a seminar held at Mary Jo's and Martha's Franklin apartment:

It was a way of getting acquainted with the upperclassmen in the dance department. I remember Mary Jo's sense of humor. [Dancer Mark Ryder called it "acerbic."] Martha had all these pictures with numbers on them and we tried to identify who the dancer was. I wasn't very good at it, but you'd be surprised how quickly you can learn.

Martha would come up every Thursday night for a workshop where we showed our studies for criticism. Every week you had to get up and perform. We took composition all the way along, working independently under one faculty member's direction. Upperclassmen showed their dances even if they only added thirty seconds to it. The important thing was that we got up on stage and did it.

The young dancer remembered Martha's Saturday technique classes as "very different from Bales's and not quite as codified as the Graham technique. She did simpler things. She gave us swings and falls—more Humphrey, in a sense. She gave us a sense of breath and her use of space was really wonderful. She did all kinds of variations with lifts and turns, rhythmic changes and exploratory things." Of the handful of other Bennington dance majors that were Ethel's classmates, Dorothea Douglas, Beth Olson Mitchell, Pat Nanon, Carol Corbin-Newman, and Joan Skinner would all go on to exemplary careers in dance. All were dazzled by this sophisticated New Yorker with so many connections to the professional world in the arts.

Martha's two jobs would soon come into rare proximity with the help of the ever-obliging YM–YWHA's Dance Center program. Horst presided over two college demonstration events in the Kaufmann Recital Hall. The second, on 10 May 1942, would present Martha's students from New York University's Dance Club, which he was quick to point out, stressed "improvizational" [sic] and "recreational elements in their single weekly session." Martha's Bennington students, joining Sarah Lawrence's, fared better and were "aiming for a more nearly professional standard in artistic result, with more emphasis upon their finished compositions."[14] That occasion at the Y would be replicated every spring under Martha's direction through 1949.

By the end of 1941, everyone's lives had changed dramatically; the United States was now at war with Germany, Italy, and Japan. The day after Japan's attack on Pearl Harbor, 7 December 1941, forces were quickly mobilized. Women were urgently needed in the workforce, and "Rosie the Riveter" posters hung alongside the ones of Uncle Sam pointing his finger with the caption "I want YOU!" War bond drives were at a pitch. WPA ration books for commodities such as gas, rubber, leather, and metal further restricted travel. Food restrictions were placed on meat, butter, and sugar, and shortages sent Americans to their "victory gardens" to plant corn, tomatoes, and potatoes to preserve for the winter months. Families began to raise chickens for Sunday dinner in their otherwise meatless week.

Lefty now combined his work as college president with running the reserve corps training program for the North American Air Defense command and its Combat Operations Center at the new Camp Carson in Colorado Springs. Soon after, he took a leave of absence from the college and headed to Washington as a Marine lieutenant colonel to direct the "V-12" Marine Corps Reserve officer training program for American colleges and universities (serving from 1942 to 1945).

Before leaving Colorado, President Davies gave his seal of approval to the Fine Arts Center's 1942 symposia "War and the Arts" (for which Martha arranged José's participation). Limón also presented a concert of solos and duets (with new partner Helen Ellis) as part of the Modern Dance Concert for Colorado College's summer session.

Martha found herself fighting her own private war for the survival of dance under the new mandates of President Lewis at Bennington. She urged both Lefty and Mary Jo to write strong, if out-of-place statements, to justify the importance of the arts. In April 1942, Lefty was quoted in the *American Dancer* as saying that he believed the arts "can and should be aids to national morale. In promoting activities that help to stabilize people emotionally, we are directly aiding the maintenance of morale and thereby helping the war effort."[15]

That same month Mary Jo, as administrator of an "American institution" felt it necessary to "take stock of its resources for national service" in defense of plans for the upcoming summer. She had recently held together the president's office after Leigh's departure and during the installation of a new Bennington president. (Leigh went on to become the director of the Foreign Broadcasting Intelligence Service, and served on the Federal Communications Commission during the war.) Still, Mary Jo had time to write for *Dance Observer* that the summer session would carry forward the enterprise in the arts "begun in the peaceful summer of 1934" along with two new divisions, government and economics; science would also be added to the curriculum. She recounted the ground plan of dance study at Bennington, adding, "This comprehensive scheme has always seemed good. Now it seems imperative. . . . For the arts to meet the demands of war means a heightening and intensification of effort . . . the art must tap as deeply as possible, all that the dance offers. . . . The task, which Bennington has set for itself, is continuance of the essential services it can perform to American culture. This has always been the first consideration as it will be this summer."[16]

In a striking turn of events during this period, Pauline Lawrence, ever loyal to Doris over the years, now determined that she wanted to marry José, transferring her great gifts at organization to fortify his career. She insisted that she would never love anyone else so deeply. Perhaps more in a desire for security then an act of passion on José's part, a marriage agreement was struck. After a simple ceremony in San Francisco in October 1941, Pauline returned to New York City to life as usual, fulfilling a Humphrey-Weidman tour commitment. José lingered on the Pacific Northwest coast, working on a friend's chicken farm in between concert dates with May O'Donnell, and then taking on a teaching commitment at Colorado State Teachers College in Greeley for the spring. Drafted into the Entertainment Section of the Special Services Division of the Army, he was forced into "sober re-evaluation" of his chosen profession: "We out-Minskied Minsky. . . . I was a good soldier and I followed my orders. But I did a great deal of thinking." After his stint in the army, José complained that the "low standing of dance with the general public was due to the scatter-brained puerilities" of musical comedy dancing.[17] After his tour of duty, José rejoined the Humphrey-Weidman company in preparation for their all-Bach program, this time treated "no longer as a disciple but as an equal."[18] José's solo *Chaconne* premiered at the Studio Theatre at the end of December 1942. With an accompanying violinist playing Bach downstage left, *Dance Observer* critic George Beiswanger called the work "extraordinary," with "the most magnificent dancing he has ever done and in his most firm, released and brilliant composing."[19] Now married, he resolved to be unperturbed by Charles's newest romantic interest, dancer Peter Hamilton, who was now in the company.

Although officially still at Bennington College as "director-designer," Arch headed to Colorado College in the summer of 1942 to produce a "theatre dance," *Namesake,* with Holm choreographing and Roy Harris commissioned to write the score. In it Holm had each of the dancers not only speak, but gave them the "opportunity to project a personality" onstage (no doubt a precursor to her later work with Broadway musicals). Again, Graham's *Letter to the World* was credited as an influence. According to Lauterer, "movement rather than speech [was] its principal means of expression . . . a new expression of theatre in America."[20] (By the next spring, however, Holm had eliminated Lauterer's text.)

Belitt explained, "The war effort hit us all very hard. Institutional decisions often beget changes of precedents, as well as presidents: you get something different." With the presidency of Lewis Jones, the whole pattern changed. And the pattern that emerged was a war pattern. Ben continued,

> The word "basic" began to resonate. What we did with students was a clue of things to come. For example, Bennington in 1942 had turned into a *farm*: that was precedent carried to the institutional extremes. We were all in it. We had good reason to show "patriotism and civic virtue" as a college and a nation "at the ready." Instead of doing things that were un-basic, or flamboyant, do the *small* thing! Plant a seed! Spray it! Cultivate it! Cook and bake it! That was very fundamental, and though the pressure on Jones was intense, it seemed to us a very positive adventure: to carry the word "basic" as the keyword to a curriculum at war with banality. My own response as a citizen of thirty was finally: "I want *out* of here!"[21]

"That last summer of 1942, it never occurred to us that we could be asked not to continue," Martha reminisced. Yet even as signs of a "sinking ship" were acutely visible to the faculty, excited students continued to pour into the North Bennington station, ready to study dance. With a much-reduced budget and little support from the administration (save the attention she received from Mary Jo), Martha did her best to keep up a good front. In truth, things were falling apart.

Nona Schurman, who took over as teacher for Humphrey and Weidman (who were holding their own summer intensive course on West Sixteenth Street), lamented, "The war swallowed up most of the ambitions of my generation. From 1942 on it was just a matter of keeping the wolf from the door."[22]

When Martha's assistant, Bessie Schönberg, asked for a sick leave, it was Hortie Leiberthal who was called in as her replacement for the summer faculty. Among the thinning ranks remained the stalwart Louis Horst and Norman Lloyd. Martha Graham came with Erick at her side, using the summer residency as profitably as she had in previous years. Again, Erick taught ballet technique.

Along with beginning composition, Martha now taught two new courses designed to please the college's cry for relevance and patriotism. "Dance and Music Recreation" cotaught with Norman Lloyd and "American Country Dancing" were new configurations of American folk dancing that she had long enjoyed as an extracurricular activity. Louis's "Americana" study for his modern dance forms composition course (added as he worked with Martha on *Frontier* in 1935) had forecast this trend.

Revealing the American spirit through its folk idiom would soon become an overarching theme in the dance field. Dancing as a symbol of national identity suddenly became as jingoistic as it had been for centuries in other countries. Agnes de Mille premiered *Rodeo* with American Ballet Theatre in the fall of 1942, for which *Billy the Kid* and other ballets by Lew Christiansen for Ballet Caravan had prepared the way. In 1944, Graham moved with full force into her Americana period with *Appalachian Spring* set to Copland's commissioned score. All of these ballets remain the most significant examples of the period.

Although distressed that the war had "put an end to monies spent on production," Martha would not give up. "I would never be interested in anything where performance wasn't the end product," she insisted.[23] Limited circumstances notwithstanding, a variety of works were performed in the College Theatre for feedback both from those on campus and from interested outsiders. Graham took advantage of the time with her company to rework *American Document* and presented the result on 9 August. Less illustrious offerings included a program of dances by Jane Dudley, Sophie Maslow, and Bill Bales with dancers from the Graham company (including Pearl Lack [later Lang]), followed the next evening by Eve Gentry and Nona Schurman with their students.

Dance educators now understood that by this eighth summer at Bennington, Martha had succeeded in establishing the direct opposite of H'Doubler's aims for the field. Although Marge H'Doubler had again been invited to Bennington in 1938 for a lecture on her recently published *Dance: A Creative Art Experience*—the title itself commenting on Dewey's earlier *Art as Experience*—H'Doubler had firmly established herself as a leading dance aesthetician. The University of Wisconsin had become the "other" college for the study of dance.

The book that most significantly represented Martha Hill's point of view—although one of pictures, and not theories—was Barbara Morgan's extraordinary collection of photographs of Martha Graham and her company. *Martha Graham: Sixteen Dances in Photographs,* with a foreword by Graham, offers an extraordinary collection of photographs (now classic images), a brief statement of purpose by Morgan, a "choreographic record" by Louis Horst, and a statement by George Beiswanger that most captured the sentiment of the Bennington group: "The dance-poet—the 'maker'—stands complete. . . . Dancers speak through their dances: the artist *is* the work."[24] For Martha Hill this was the truest example of Dewey's philosophy. Graham (who seldom looked back and despised the idea of revivals of her work) struggled with words for a reprint of Morgan's book in 1980: "The only record of a dancer's art lies in the other arts. . . . Photographs . . . reveal facts of feature, bodily contour, and some secret of [the dancer's] power. . . . There is a complete focus upon a given instant." And, she insists, "The art of dance exists in the instant of execution."[25]

That July, Ted Shawn had joyfully taken up the banner for his new theater at Jacob's Pillow in Lee, Massachusetts, presenting a festival of dance of his own.[26] Ironically, each year Lauterer's plans for a new theater would resurface, and each year Mary Jo would look for funding to support it, never with any luck.

Although working with little institutional support, Martha had always been assured that even under the most modest circumstances, performers who wanted to show their work were welcome to do so. She encouraged three of Graham's most promising dancers, Cunningham, Erdman, and Fonaroff. Refining their own pieces, the three young choreographers presented a concert in the College Theatre on 1 August. It began with *Seeds of Brightness,* to Norman Lloyd's score and jointly choreographed by Cunningham and Erdman, as was the second. John Cage's music for *Credo in Us* was for radio bits and piano—struck inside and out—and a percussion ensemble that included kitchen pots and pans, a work that marked the beginning of Cage's lifelong association with Merce. Gregory Tucker wrote the score for their third duet *Ad Lib.* Each created a solo. Merce's *Renaissance Testimonials* had an original score by Maxwell Powers and Jean Erdman's *The Transformations of Medusa* featured music for the dance by Horst. Another of his scores was lovingly set to Nina's charming, detailed solo, *Little Theodolina,* with her *Cafe Chantant—Five A.M.* and her *Hoofer on a Fiver* completing the program. The content of this one concert gave a glimmer of the direction dance would take in the ensuing years.[27] Erdman worked on her own explorations into the realm of psychology and myth as her dance career gained prominence in the 1940s; Fonaroff chose a more subtle, humanistic approach; and Cunningham rejected the personal for a purer dance with dancing for its own sake.

Throughout the next decade, arguments raged over concepts of form and content. Even so, the strongest influence at this point on these young choreographers and composers was still Horst. He insisted that their work satisfy the condition of linking new music with new dance, and the concept had come of age with Graham continuing to produce works exclusively to new scores. (Only Erick Hawkins and Cunningham with John Cage would continue the idea with conviction. The difference in the end, however, was that Cage and Cunningham were completely opposed to the idea of a carefully wrought marriage of sound and motion, arguing that dance and sound were separate entities, needing only to exist at the same time.)

At the 1942 summer's end, the *Dance Observer* reported, "Plans and expectations not withstanding Bennington turned out to be primarily a school of the dance—very much as usual!"[28] But the little magazine also printed an editorial by Private Gervase Butler that expressed what these artists were thinking: "This war is an invasion of the mind, of the spirit, with every wicked genius in the world united in the axis effort to crush out all the human values that mean civilization."[29]

Having enjoyed in a period of optimism seldom enjoyed by groups of artists in the modern world, Bennington's program was now faltering. Rising capitalism, economic power brokering, and financial realities set in. Becca Stickney remembered:

> There was a big debt and Martha had to take that on personally. I remember Mary Jo Shelly saying to Martha, "You're got to stop dragging a dead horse!" Mary Jo was really letting her have it, telling her, "You've got to get rid of this thing. It isn't worth it. It isn't going to work." Some of us got together and we raised funds for Martha to help clear up this debt. Officially, we were told the reason the festival did not return to Bennington was that our theater was inadequate.[30]

But the sad truth—that Bennington administrators were just not behind the project—was now clear to everyone, including Martha.

By 1943, the horrors of war permeated every aspect of life in the United States. The government had transferred more than 100,000 Japanese-Americans from the West Coast to inland detention camps. Despite reports, few believed that the Nazis were gassing thousands of Jews a day in concentration camps. (More were horrified at the news that 487 had died in a fire in Boston's Coconut Grove nightclub, trapped by doors that opened inward.) Coffee was now added to the growing list of rationed goods.

That summer at Bennington, Hortie said to Teddy, "Did you know that they are going to take women in the Navy? Will you apply with me? 'Sure, I'll do it.' So we went into town and filled out applications. We had a cursory physical exam and mailed them in." Teddy remembered the day Mary Jo was called away from the dining room to answer a long-distance call from prizefighter Gene Tunney, the head of training for the men of the navy. He wanted Mary Jo to take over for the women. "She kept saying no, and he kept calling." When he came up to Bennington in person, Mary Jo finally agreed to do it.

Armed with her ability to administrate a dance camp, Mary Jo packed her bags, and put her best effort into creating a woman's militia. As a lieutenant commander in the Women's Naval Reserve in charge of Physical Training and Drill, she was among the first dozen commissioned women in the WAVES (Women Accepted for Volunteer Emergency Services). Within a month Mary Jo became assistant to Mildred McFee as director of training of the navy, in charge of the education programs and the expansion of the WAVES' training. (She saw to it that Teddy, too, rose to become a lieutenant commander, and director of emplacement for the WAVES in San Diego.)[1] Helen Knight, who also had signed up, recalled her arrival at the University of Wisconsin where a girls' dormitory was given over to the WAVES: "Mary Jo said, 'The next time I see you, you will be in Enid, Oklahoma . . . putting little Wavelettes to bed and getting them up in the morning.' 'No way,' I answered: 'I gave the Navy a song and dance and joined the American Red Cross [instead].'"[2]

Thinking back to the fall of 1943, Hazel said, "I know Martha missed Mary Jo. I didn't realize until then how much of the organization work Mary Jo had done at Bennington." It was clear to her that when Mary Jo, "a very calm, organized, and matter-of-fact, very attractive woman moved out of the picture, everything was left to Martha. And Martha was always dreaming up ideas, getting people together to do this and do that. I could see that was her métier."

Martha herself explained, "I wasn't by nature the kind to put on a uniform, but I did want to help with the war effort." That spring she traveled to New Orleans to address the 1942 convention of the American Association for Health, Physical Education, and Recreation on the war's implications for dance. She told her audience, "Fighting a modern war is not done just with the body. Physical fitness is too narrow a conception. The 'X' factor in war, call it morale or what you will, takes a great many forms and applies equally to the civilian, the defense worker, and the soldier." She goes on, "In this connection it would be foolish to ignore such an old, deeply rooted, and anciently useful medium as dancing, which has served people before in times of stress and can again in this critical time of ours."[3]

Helen Tamiris stopped the show as "Porterhouse Lucy" when she toured neighborhood theaters with the American Theater Wing's production of *It's Up To You*; in contrast, Martha withdrew behind her academic profile.[4] But she did fulfill a request from the U.S. Office of Education to write the dance section for the manual, *Physical Fitness through Physical Education for the Victory Corps*. "They even gave me an artist to sketch for the project. It was to contain simple movement that might help in hospital rehabilitation programs."

Eager to contribute, Martha created dance exercises "with skips and slides as well as things for the least able," but soon hit a snag. "We can't use the word 'dance,'" the editor told her. Martha replied, "Let's call it 'rhythmic activities.'" The editor was still adamant: "We can't use 'rhythmic activities.' Rhythm is definitely out. Moving in rhythm with another? This is not a subject to be discussed in mixed company." Finally Martha came up with "locomotor and axial gymnastics." Years later, relating this story, Martha added, "What strides we've made!" noting with some satisfaction that at least in the manual's glossary they had not eliminated the problematic words.[5]

Martha continued her trek each week to Bennington and back, joining Bill Bales (classified 4-F "for a bad knee, or ear, or something") and her gang of Cricket Hill cohorts—minus Ben, who, in Martha's words, "was directing traffic badly for the army." (Lincoln Kirstein had also joined the army, distinguishing himself as a chauffeur for General George S. Patton, and then supervising the recovery of a large collection of art looted by the Nazis and stored in the Steinberg Salt Mine.)

"Even the determination of Shelly and Hill could not prevent . . . the austerities of World War II from making the Bennington summer school impractical," Jack Anderson wrote, giving closure to the Bennington era.[6] With no oil for heat on campus for the winter of 1943, Bennington's students, staff, and faculty were told that the college must close down in the winter, further extending the spring semester into the summer months. Martha soon found herself jockeying a drastically reorganized school year to accommodate the longer winter break. Overall, the change played to Martha's advantage, with students coming into Manhattan to study at professional studios.[7]

Ethel remembered the winter of 1943. "I came to New York City, and lived at the Three Arts Club on Eighty-sixth Street with three or four others, and went to the Graham Studio and to ballet classes with one of the old Russians. We were on our own, other than informing Martha what we were doing as our work."[8] Martha Hill had gently nudged Graham to focus on the talented Bennington girl. "Martha [had] steered me to it," Ethel confessed, during the previous Graham-Horst June residency in 1942. The next summer, 1943, needing a temporary replacement for Pearl Lang (then in *Carousel* on Broadway), Graham cast Ethel for a *Circus* performance at Bennington. "[Martha Hill] was good at making things happen."[9] Another observed that Martha "determined one's mettle then directed it for the common good," a practice that amazed many and frustrated a few others.[10]

The change in calendar was, for Martha, another way to keep Graham and Horst "in residence" during the spring-summer college sessions of 1943 to 1945. Ever resourceful, she placed an ad in *Dance Observer* for the "new artist in residence plan," accepting "a limited number of special students" to work with Graham as the resident artist with her company, and Horst, as visiting lecturer.[11]

With this reduced program, other faculty members found work on other campuses, where little of Hill's kid-glove handling existed. At Sarah Lawrence, both Bessie and Norman enjoyed the friendship of the college's new president, William Schuman, and the three inaugurated an eight-week summer session titled "Workshop in Production."[12] Though their program would be short-lived, Martha was relieved that both had found positions.

Now a full-time faculty member at Colorado College, by the spring of 1943 Arch Lauterer was designing "under service club conditions" for Camp Carlson performances and working with Martha Wilcox at the Colorado Springs Fine Arts Center theater. Again, Lefty had taken Martha Hill's advice for the hiring. Graham warned Arch that one "cannot go into the catacombs entirely of any College," while admitting that her "beastly pride" was hurt by his backing away from further collaborations with her.[13] Arch responded to Graham, saying the "bitter truth [is that] teaching is the best means of earning a livilihood [*sic*] that I have."[14]

Despite hardships, Graham appreciated the peaceful quality of living on the Bennington campus, the undivided time to think and work. Graham's letter to Lauterer alludes to her state of well-being: "The sun has come up and the wind is high. I'm going to walk to North Bennington to try to get some meat."[15] For Horst, continuing his summer residencies at Bennington meant a time to relax with those he loved the most, doing what he loved the most—including listening to ticker-tape radio broadcasts of the New York Yankees when they played the Boston Red Sox. Both also greatly appreciated being served three meals a day and escaping from the oppressive heat of their tiny Manhattan studio apartments.

Having found money from the college the previous summer to commission collaboration for Graham with Hunter Johnson, for 1943 Hill again finagled the creation of one more exemplary work with set and props by Lauterer. (She had also managed to bring Graham dancers Dudley and Maslow to the campus, where they rehearsed with Bales for their own upcoming concerts as well.) The result was *Deaths and Entrances,* shown in a "private preview" at Bennington in mid-July. Performed in practice clothes, the work that began with a libretto based on Emily Dickinson's words grew to contain such scenes as "The Little Tippler," "Blue Seas," "The Ancestress," "March," and "New England Funeral." Viewers, if somewhat mystified at the direction Graham's work was taking, agreed that *Death* was perpetually "engrossing to watch."

The one full production of the summer was Arch Lauterer's adaptation of Carl Sandburg's *The People, Yes!* a combination of speech, dance, and music. When Arch returned to campus with the project, Martha and Bill composed the dances, and Gregory Tucker wrote the music under Catharine Osgood's direction. In Ben's view, this was Hill's most exciting work. (Another configuration of this piece would soon find its way into the Dudley-Maslow-Bales repertory.)

While on campus, Arch gave a special seminar. Other events included a discussion group, "Dance Today," led by Graham, and the usual rounds of student workshops and country dancing. *Dance Observer,* in its October issue reported that a special treat that summer had been the showing of "Mr. And Mrs. Simon Moselsio's Harmon Foundation" film of Graham in her landmark solo, *Lamentation.*[16]

Discreet weekends for Martha and Lefty on the New Jersey Shore continued during the war years—easier to arrange thanks to his commitments in Washington. Under the pretense of a visit to his sister in Philadelphia, Lefty would drive south down the White Horse Pike, picking up a box of Martha's favorite Tripician chocolate macaroons on his way. Having taken the train from New

York City, Martha would be waiting in Atlantic City. The two relished the surf and the shore dinners on the boardwalk, before returning to their favorite casino hotel filled with men on furlough and their sweethearts. Both needed an "R & R" almost as badly as those in the service. Parting became more and more difficult. Lefty returned to mounting responsibilities and the frenetic pace in Washington; Martha, to her increasingly staid life of teaching.[17]

As World War II continued, Martha kept in touch with her brother, Bill, who stayed stateside for various military duties. He wanted his girlfriend Mary Ann to call upon Martha when she first came to New York City to begin her WAVES training at Hunter College. She remembered, "I called Martha, and graciousness herself, she said she wanted to see me. I knocked on her door. Martha was wonderful. We talked and she took me to Longchamps on Fifth Avenue for dinner. Then she put me back on the subway."[18] Martha must have intuited the seriousness of the couple's relationship: Bill and Mary Ann were later married at Pensacola Naval Air Station in October 1944. Martha claimed that she was too involved in her teaching assignments to be present at the ceremony. In truth, she had never resolved her strained relationship with her parents: there is also no existing correspondence with them from these years.

While at Bennington, with Bill Bales handling most of the technique classes, Martha spent much of her time advising majors and overseeing their choreographic projects. In a December YMHA dance center concert, it would be Ethel's solo *Un Dolor Hoy* that was "the high spot of the day."[19] At NYU, as well, with a roster of guest teachers and assistants scheduled into the semester, Martha's main energies went into producing a strong generation of dance people, advising graduate students on their dissertations, and generating dance research.

On 8 May 1945 Americans celebrated the end of the war in Europe. By August 14, Japan had surrendered, ending World War II. Mary Jo's postwar responsibilities were to oversee the demobilization of the WAVES from their wartime strength of 85,000, earning her a citation from James V. Forrestal, secretary of the navy. Her position reverted to the reserves as a commander and she returned to civilian duties in Bennington's administration.

For Martha, the next years would be transitional and relatively calm. She seemed to fall into a kind of midlife crisis, anxious for change as she watched the last of the remaining Bennington colleagues find their own ways. One casualty of this period was the disbanding of the Humphrey-Weidman Company following Doris Humphrey's retirement as a dancer in 1945. Although seldom working as a soloist herself, Hanya Holm had actively concertized with her group from 1936 to 1944; after a short lull in her career, however, she turned to Broadway as choreographer, beginning in 1947 with *Bloomer Girl,* and then *Ballet Ballads* followed by *Kiss Me Kate.* Although continuing to choreograph such hit shows as *My Fair Lady* and *Camelot,* Holm's summers were still devoted to directing dance intensives at Colorado College. Graham remained the last of the "Big Four" to sustain a full-fledged company after the war years, with her own intensive four-week "June course" of "dance techniques and composition" running successfully at her 66 Fifth Avenue studio before what would be her last respite at Bennington in the summer of 1945.

The war had drastically altered the pattern of the lives of those Martha loved most. In contrast, hers had changed very little. Along with miscellaneous involvements, she continued to straddle jobs at two institutions. Martha's reputation as a leader in dance was now as firmly established as her willingness to serve in any capacity "for the good" of the art form.

World events had drawn the United States out of its earlier provincialism; artists across the country were mobilized to look at urban centers other than Manhattan as hubs for increased activity. For Martha, however, New York City remained the center of her universe and the place most able to emerge as the "dance capital" of the world—even though her personal life (except for her liaison with Lefty) had slumped into tedium.

Although some dance education professionals had applauded her earlier *Dance Observer* effort to encourage publication of dance materials, Martha was increasingly dismayed over their lack of interest in archiving dance.[20] History in the making must be documented not only by critics, she believed, but also by saving the artifacts of the art form such as programs, film, photographs, and oral interviews. Although the New York Public Library had long housed dance materials in their music division, librarian Genevieve Oswald had spoken to Martha about wanting to establish a separate dance archive: "one that is not attached to the other arts, where a scholar can use manuscripts, view films and prints, read clippings and letters in one place."[21]

Martha and Lefty's time together in New York City had always included drinks and dinner at the Princeton Club. It was there that Martha encouraged Lefty's clubmates to become involved in supporting worthy dance projects such as the establishment of the New York Public Library's dance collection. The head of the library, Carlton Sprague Smith, was a good friend of Lefty's (according to Martha, "Lefty was well known to Carlton as the moving spirit at Colorado College") and they saw him regularly at the club. After several arranged luncheons with Oswald, the New York Public Library Dance Collection was born in 1944 as a separate division of the research libraries.[22]

Dance had come of age in the fifteen years since Martha Hill performed on stage with Graham. Growing at a rate that no one could have predicted, by the spring of 1945, dance had become a legitimate performing art in many circles. Barbara Morgan's photographs of modern American dance were exhibited at the Museum of Modern Art in New York City. Among a growing array of advocates was Jean Erdman's husband, Joseph Campbell, who would go on to be considered a leading scholar on myth and ritual. While serving on the editorial board of *Dance Observer,* he wrote treatises on dance and on the "psychological effects of aesthetic form and the archetypes of myth and symbol."[23]

Three months later, the journal included an article by H'Doubler, "the Dean of American Dance Educators," in which she wrote, "Modern dance is a concept—a point of view and not a prescribed system." She continued, "Educational dance is a process not an end in itself. . . . The term Modern Dance should not be confused with the personalized dance manner of contemporary artist dancers." She closed with "Educational Dance should be the basic foundation for dance as an art. It is the beginning of art understanding with movement as the expressive medium."[24] Martha reacted unsympathetically to the article, reinforcing her own view that in the name of educational dance, the various training techniques of artists were, in fact, clearly defined; she dismissed the article as old-fashioned and self-serving. For her, H'Doubler's whole philosophy was wrongheaded: there should be no such thing as "educational dance." The best learning came directly from the best dancers and choreographers—those able to articulate the essence of the art form with the most authority.

When Lefty returned as president of Colorado College to head the school's seventy-fifth anniversary endowment campaign, Martha faced her own curtailed schedule with little hope of more than sporadic personal happiness. With no possibility of holding a full summer program at Bennington in 1946, she instead gave Doris Humphrey free rein to create and premiere works on campus: the results were *The Story of Mankind,* to a score by Lionel Nowak, and *Lament for Ignacio Sánchez Mejías* (with Limón as Mejías) to Norman Lloyd's music. After the residency, Martha, desperate for a change of pace, accepted a teaching position in August for a postsession at the University of California in Los Angeles. Traveling across the United States by train, she stopped in Ohio for a brief visit with her parents, and then in Colorado to view Hanya's dance program (and, of course, to see Lefty).

The couple had planned to meet again on her return trip, but a crisis suddenly intervened. Lefty's daughter, Judy, contracted poliomyelitis. She was first placed in isolation hospital quarters in Houston, then moved to "a warm springs place" near San Antonio, and then to a hospital in Galveston for another eight months. At each location, Judy's distraught father was by her side.

During this period, Lefty's personal life continued to fall apart. He had filed for a divorce, but Joyce had been diagnosed as a schizophrenic. In and out of institutions, she would neither give her consent nor remain stable long enough to undergo divorce proceedings. Because of the discouraging situation, Martha and Lefty continued to plan each rendezvous with extraordinary discretion. At Bennington, Becca Stickney recalled Lefty's occasional visits. "We liked Lefty. Lefty was very much in her life in the forties. He was familiar to us Cricket Hillers. Martha was a good drinker. Lefty was a better drinker. We all drank quite a lot in those days. . . . The favorite drink at the time was a manhattan, or worse, a dry martini."

Lefty had returned to Colorado College in 1946 to find that the college trustees "did not want him back, even though he was very popular with students and faculty, had raised money and increased the enrollment." His daughter Judy wrote, "The real reason—not generally known—was that [he] had become an alcoholic over the years. Back in those unenlightened days, that was nothing the trustees could handle as they might today."

Early in the fall of 1947 Lefty's last duties as president included attending a football team and presiding over the opening convocation, where he told his audience, "It is a tragic thing that people of the intellectual ability who attend a college like this do not take advantage of all that it has to offer. And if your lives in college can't be well-rounded, I for one don't know when they will be." It was a solemn statement to young students from a president engulfed in illness and tragedy—and about to be without a job.

Judy recorded sadly that her father's "crack-up forced him to leave the college—a cause of grief for the whole community"; she conceded, however, that "he drowned his sorrow in rye." The *Princeton Alumni Review* reported blithely that Lefty left the college on "a leave of absence" on 1 December 1947, "ill from a chest infection he apparently caught while watching the freshman football team beat the University of Colorado freshmen on an icy-cold, windy, November afternoon." But Judy knew that the school "had mixed reactions to both his earlier leaves of absence and his alcohol problem." Forced out by the trustees, Martha would become Lefty's link to recovery.[25]

Lefty came to New York City to be treated for his drinking problem. "He had long been pursued by precisely the same brand of personal devils that had destroyed the interpreter of the Jazz Age," Judy believed, referring to F. Scott Fitzgerald and his "lost generation."[26] Battling alcoholism, Lefty's health and stamina had deteriorated. Without employment, he was painfully depressed and disheartened. It was Martha who now became the saving grace of his life. Some suspected that it was precisely Lefty's "joie de vivre" and rebellion against discipline that had attracted Martha, so hungry for personal happiness, yet so unable to release these qualities in herself.

If Martha Hill, now in her late forties, was at the locus of a fast-developing dance scene, her friend and idol, Martha Graham had suddenly become a household name. With Graham's star turn as mystery guest for "Miss Hush" (chosen because of her sexy speaking voice, Graham believed), the dancer had slipped into homes across the country via a radio contest for the March of Dimes. For months, Americans tried to guess her identity as the jackpot rose. Graham had become a celebrity among highbrows too: the *New Yorker* profiled Graham in an article in the 27 December 1947 issue. Perhaps expecting a more exotic figure to interview, writer Angela Gibbs described Graham's somber, businesslike appearance, and poked fun at Horst's "corpulent" stature as her "Svengali."[27] Nonetheless, the article was cause for celebration that New Year's Eve at Martha Hill's loft. Louis and his dachshund, Spud, were the first to arrive through more than two feet of snow after what had been one of the worst snowstorms in New York's history. Martha Hill and Louis Horst felt victorious that night as Graham's "behind-the-scene" creators. For them, it was Graham who still symbolized the kind of modern dance in which they believed. But the greatest cause for celebration at that party was Lefty's solid presence at Martha Hill's side. They were together at last.

Hill, like Graham, understood the value of self-image and public presentation. The image of a "liberated" woman, Martha smoked cigarettes and sipped martinis as easily as she entered a room in smartly tailored clothing. Students continued to view her as the ultimate example of a confident, sophisticated woman; she was doubly admired for her ability to make things happen.

Interested in streamlining her own life, Martha began to break away from the idea of Bennington as a link to the modern dance world. Her job at New York University, if no longer inspiring, at least gave Martha security and a title: assistant professor of education and, in 1947–48, a full-time contract with a salary of three thousand dollars and initial support for a new summer dance center.

While in California in 1946, Martha had entertained the possibility of helping coordinate a future summer dance intensive there. Now, instead, she began to mull over the revival of a school for summer study and festival for dance on the East Coast. Bennington was no longer an option; its president, Jones, considered the arts superfluous to postwar needs. Instead, Martha was determined to reconstruct the Bennington model, this time under New York University's aegis. Adept at cultivating relationships, she contacted the dean of the School of Education, Jay Nash. On 22 November 1946 Martha wrote "The dance needs a rallying point, and needs it more urgently now than ever before. The Bennington School of the Dance was that. This letter and the thoughts behind it are full of winged things with the eggs still in embryo form but while we're thinking in these terms here is another such thought." The letter concluded, "The need is certainly now. I shall feel no peace until we are at work on a definite plan for the future."[28]

Nash replied enthusiastically five days later, reminding Martha that "it only takes only one follower to be a leader," and he would be her follower. He began a series of cryptic memos with "I believe the eggs are hatching. I expect by the summer of 1948 that we will have developed the wings and the claw. I am exceedingly anxious to push ahead with this with all possible vigor. The next step is a pattern of details with some reference to ultimate questions of space, faculty and budget."[29] Martha quickly responded to a letter from Deans Rosecrance, Nash, and Pichett with "Yes for 1947" and "No for 47," lists of pros and cons to begin a year ahead of time, adding notes such as "1. Need of the field. 2. Some other project may open. Rumor of summer arts project at Sarah Lawrence. We have good possibility of enrollment [but need more time] to assemble significant faculty. MG is going to Europe for the war dept., spring '47. Louis Horst is going to Mills. He is also an important person for our faculty. I am under contract to Bennington through July 12." She then lists the most critical problem: the need "to find adequate space to carry on such a project/to publicize/Housing problem in NYC." She concludes, "Yes on 1948."[30] With an initial go-ahead, Martha began her search for a location at New York University, checking out the recently acquired DeForest House on the north side of Washington Square as a possible "year-round dance center in New York."

Searching for an out-of-town campus location not more than an hour and a half away from New York, she inquired about Adelphi, Bard, and Briarcliff Colleges. By April 1947 she had also looked over the facilities at Vassar and then Connecticut College, on the recommendation of John Martin, who owned a summer home in Old Mystic nearby. Hill wrote back to Nash after a visit to New London, "I think Connecticut College is a better base, and geographic location, with more attractive living space, and equally good studio space, but a far superior theatre." She also suspected that she would have "more freedom and cooperation there" from the faculty and administration.[31]

Notable among things that had changed dramatically in the postwar world was the movement of women into higher echelon positions. One of those women was Connecticut College's president, Rosemary Park. As an administrator, Park believed that colleges should assume "the protection and assistance of the creative artist which was in earlier days the prerogative of kings. We are neither as generous or as demanding as the monarchs, but in pleasing us the artists please audiences of hundreds, not just the favored few."[32] Dance had brought prestige to the Bennington campus, and that same promise of success now intrigued the Connecticut administrator.

Many of Martha's early career accomplishments had relied on men in powerful positions, and she had taken the workings of "old boy clubs" in stride. Like Graham, she believed that the modern dance stood for "the freedom of women in America . . . as a moment of emancipation"; nonetheless, she paid especial attention to the important men in her life.[33] They included Kellogg, Leigh, Horst, Lefty Davies, and, now, Nash. With each of them, trust was the most significant quality of their relationship. For the first half of her life, Martha had found sanctuary among women. In the latter half, the shift from reliance on women to reliance on and preference for the company of men was gradual but definite. Her association with Rosemary Park in this light is an interesting one. Her male superiors at Bennington and New York University had given Hill carte blanche. The Connecticut College president, on the other hand, would steadfastly assert herself as the top of the administrative hierarchy over Hill for the summer dance sessions.

President Park, who began at the school as a German professor, had just taken on her new responsibility as head of Connecticut College. A lover of the arts, like Robert Leigh, she was convinced of the importance of preserving the merits of tradition "even though they may appear in untraditional guises." She admitted, "It is a long way from the construing of Latin roots, once the core of education, to the modern dance, but the society which prized the former has ceased to exist. If the devotion and discipline once formed in Latin grammar can be cultivated through Dance, virtue has not entirely passed from us."[34]

The president had already set up a Summer School of the Arts that ran in 1945 and 1946, organized by English department faculty member John F. Moore, with course offerings in music, graphic arts, poetry, and drama. The addition of dance would be most welcome, Park felt. At Martha Hill's recommendation, it was Bill Bales, with musician Betty Horner Walberg, that Park hired to teach a special summer course "to test the waters" for the feasibility of a full summer program of dance.[35] In the meantime, Martha, with Moore and Ruth Bloomer, worked with an administrative board drawn from both NYU and Connecticut College for a dance festival under the aegis of both schools. Their efforts were rewarded with a letter from Rosemary Park in December 1947, stating: "After considerable discussion with trustees and faculty members, I have decided that CC will cooperate with New York University in a summer school of the dance in the next summer subject to our mutual agreement on administrative details. Mr. Moore, Director of our Summer Session, could be assistant with you and Miss Shelly as directors of the School and I am sure that Miss Bloomer will wish to cooperate, too." She adds, "Hope New York University will give official sanction to this as we have done."[36]

Still not convinced, the trustees of New York University maintained that a new program should be closer to Washington Square, certainly in New York City or, at the very least, New York State. To placate her NYU colleagues, throughout the spring of 1947 Martha continued halfhearted attempts to seek out other possibilities, with letters asking for possible rental of space for a summer 1948 program at Brearley School, Miss Porter's School (whose principal suggested instead, the Master's School in Dobbs Ferry, New York), and Hunter College. None expressed interest. But with Park's firm backing, the plan for a reincarnation of the Bennington summer model on the Connecticut campus was now in motion, and New York University officials finally accepted the arrangement.

That first summer, in 1948, if modest in scope, would establish the summer dance program as the new place to study modern dance. It also promised a new location for an "American Dance Festival" where "distinguished examples of modern dance" could be seen onstage by new audiences and another generation of students.

Martha was determined to keep Mary Jo involved in her new project; as a loyal friend, Mary Jo consented, if in name only. Now romantically involved in a relationship with a fellow WAVE, the couple had recently purchased a summer cottage on Block Island off New London's shores and accessible by ferry. As Martha struggled to accept that a festival would have to be mounted without her, she understood that Mary Jo's involvement was elsewhere. Her position with the WAVES had given her life significance and dignity. Now in the public view, many strong women were assumed to be lesbians and Mary Jo was proudly one of them.

Although Mary Jo had been listed as an administrative director at equal pay to Martha's in the initial budget sheets, she soon bowed out of the position, only consenting to serve on the administrative board for the next three years. Mary Jo remained Martha's most trusted friend, yet at this point in their lives they rarely spent time together. Still, each had specified the other as an heir in their wills. Their shared cedar chest of family mementos, photographs, and personal treasures remained in Martha's Thirteenth Street apartment.

Now, with Mary Jo "in absentia," Rusty Bloomer became the "assistant administrative director representing Connecticut College," later taking John Moore's place after his sudden death that year. The "old girl" network was at play again. This time, it would be Bloomer as a full-time faculty member at Connecticut College from 1945 and the "elbow grease" of the operation, who agreed to serve Martha Hill. A New Englander, with a "straight-from-the-shoulder, matter-of-fact" personality, the redhead had been a student at Bennington's first summer session in 1934 and had received her degrees under Hill's tutelage at NYU.

Like Martha and Mary Jo, Rusty had been on the faculty of the University of Oregon, before going on to the University of Michigan and Denison College. She then joined the legions of Martha's ex-students placed strategically in "outpost positions" for what had now become an army of advocates for the cause. For Rusty, taking on the position meant complementing Martha's "missionary zeal." She never openly complained about a role subservient to Martha and complied with the demands of nearly everyone else on campus. With no ambitions as a performer or choreographer herself, Rusty became a competent administrator and a willing servant to the undertaking.

The Summer School for Dance resurfaced at Connecticut College for Women in 1948 with Martha at its helm. The newly configured concert series was now officially named "An American Dance Festival." Arrangements between the two schools were finally settled upon, with New York University collecting the tuition (leaving Martha responsible for all admissions and Hortie helping with mailing and odd jobs) and Connecticut College responsible for room and board, maintenance, and theater production fees. Based on calculations from her Bennington years, Martha told the board that she expected to break even—an overoptimistic promise that would prove very difficult to achieve in the postwar economy. The total salary outlay was calculated at $12,320. "Demonstration" expenses of $1,250 were added.[1]

Ever supportive of her Bennington colleagues, Martha worked to secure their commitments for the new venture in Connecticut. Writing to Arch Lauterer, now full-time at Mills College, she asked if he would consider returning to the East for the summer. His response was that, although he had schedule conflicts, he would be happy to help launch the festival productions and be in charge of the "Stagecraft Studio and Theatre Design." She also invited Ben, now back on the Bennington faculty after his stint in the service and a year abroad on a Guggenheim in 1945. Having just published a book of poetry, *The Fivefold Mesh,* and needing a break, Ben happily accepted the opportunity to teach a special workshop on poetry and dance.

Nearly a decade had passed since this collection of artists had worked together and Martha was careful to ask for any suggestions each returning dance artist might have. Having earned a reputation as a respected pedagogue and now overseeing a developing dance education program at the Ninety-second Street YM-YWHA, Doris Humphrey offered a number of ideas for changes in the curriculum design.

Humphrey wanted to see a seminar in dance education and a course in theater and costume design for dance implemented, as well as voice training combined with dance and music, "because in general, most dancers don't talk." She urged the creation of a seminar in lyric theater, musical resources for accompaniment other than piano and percussion, dance teaching material and methods for high school teachers, and a technique and style class for men only, "taught by a man." She questioned the proposed plan of offering eight technique sections and eleven composition courses: "It seems to me that's a questionable proportion. Do people really want to compose more than dance now? And isn't thirty [students] too many in a technique class?"[2] If all were sturdy ideas, most were beyond the scope of the budget. Martha opted instead for a program similar to the Bennington one, with cost-efficient large technique and repertory classes, combined with smaller composition courses to give students opportunities to perform and receive criticism for their own work. Performance showcases were "the way dancers learned," she insisted. Dancing, choreographing, and performing, as well as watching dancing were key to her educational formula: a balanced program gave equal emphasis to the art of dance in the studio and on the stage.

The most striking difference that Martha noted at Connecticut was release from the interarts power plays that over the last eight years had all but smothered her dance work at Bennington. For one thing, at Connecticut, no other arts faculty wanted equal participation: a fresh start meant that Martha could go back to the aim for dance as the matrix art that she had earlier plotted with Mary Jo. This time, free of the encumbrances of committees, Martha would make sure that *she* was the one to make the final decisions as chair of the advisory board and head of the school. But the Bennington model of collaborations between composers and choreographers began to fall by the wayside. With stronger musicians' unions, improved theater sound systems, and a wealth of new recordings now available to choreographers, the utopian model of creating a uniquely new piece would become more difficult to sustain despite the Bennington group's ongoing commitment to the idea in principle.

Martha wrote to Park in February 1948: "I am very happy and confident about the summer with Connecticut College sponsoring the School. I believe that we shall find the current plan even wiser than we know as time goes along."[3] With 119 students at final count,[4] the director had once again achieved the improbable, even mentioning to Walter Terry that she hoped that this might develop into a year-round center for dance training.[5]

Martha settled on campus in a well-appointed faculty house at the edge of Connecticut College's stately campus beautifully situated on a hilltop above New London's Thames River. The college's location, with the feel of the Bennington quadrille, immediately pleased arriving students and faculty on their arrival. Courses in composition, music, and notation were held in cleared-out living rooms of dormitories, with technique and repertory taught in five larger spaces in the school's physical education facilities (later to be replaced by the spacious Crozier-Williams student center complex that included four massive studios, a pool, and a cafeteria). And the summer program had full use of the well-equipped, "air-cooled" Frank Loomis Palmer auditorium. With a 1,330 seating capacity, it was definitely the main attraction for those choreographers who had struggled with Bennington's makeshift theaters.

As at Bennington, evening lectures and rehearsals and events were scheduled at an unending pace. Mark Ryder, who had been a student on the Bennington campus as well, found Connecticut College "a place that acknowledged the value of your activity" with "no worries." If "perhaps more cost-conscious . . . more institutional than Bennington," it was nonetheless "a very nice ivory tower."[6]

The three companies "in residence" slated to perform at Palmer at the end of the six-week session were Graham's, the newly formed José Limón and Company, and the Dudley-Maslow-Bales trio. Premieres were to be commissioned for works by Graham and Humphrey (making a piece for the Limón company).

The first major crisis of the summer for Hill occurred when Graham suddenly "refused to come," Hazel recalled. "Of course Martha Hill wanted to make a place for Martha. I think one of her main goals in starting these places was for Martha to make work. And she wouldn't come. Graham was not cooperative, to put it mildly, and Martha Hill was counting on her to get the school going. She was to be the luminary of the summer. And she just flatly said no. That was the only time I saw Martha Hill down," she recalled. "She didn't slow down any. She did things with energy, but I think she cried a lot about that." The compromise was that Graham would come up for performances but would not teach, and Hawkins was guaranteed a spot as choreographer on the festival, with Lauterer agreeing to take on his stage design.

That Martha Hill had worked closely with Graham without conflict over the years was in itself a remarkable achievement. Bill Carter, a dancer who worked with Graham several seasons later, explained that the choreographer displayed "an absolute, unbelievable opposition—great strength and power of love and generosity, and an ability to annihilate. These passions didn't show at the same time but consecutively."[7] Like Louis, however, Martha Hill accepted Graham's often difficult behavior because in their minds, whether "in the glooms," or completely unreasonable, she's "the only one there is."[8]

Pearl Lang, Ethel Winter, and Yuriko taught for Graham that summer while rehearsing for the company's new work. (By 1950, with Helen McGehee, they would join the ranks as Graham's most valued dancers and master teachers of Graham's distinctive and well-formulated technique and would continue to do so over the next decades.) The others teaching technique that summer included Bales, Dudley, and Limón, with musicians Ruth and Norman happily returning to the fold after two uninspired summer sessions at Sarah Lawrence.[9]

Because Doris was no longer willing or able to teach technique, it was José Limón that she wanted as her replacement, a move that would gradually diminish the Humphrey-Weidman stamp on technical methods taught on her behalf. José had assimilated the Humphrey-Weidman style, adding movement phrases of his own based on a penchant for using his newly coined "isolations" along with a more percussive attack.[10]

Two years earlier José had stated in an article for *Dance Observer,* "The kind of dance which interests me is that which strives to be adult. Solemn, tragic, austere dances." Totally opposite to Charles in temperament and ambition, José's view would play a strong role in the kind of work Martha Hill presented as modern dance in the future—one that gained in stature with José's "uncompromising attitude toward artistic values" but lost a good deal of its humor in the process.[11]

At an interview conducted in the sandwich shop, "Miss Hill . . . vigorously discussed the aims of the summer school, all the while stressing the difference between dance and other art forms. 'A student must see dance. It cannot be taught vicariously. Therefore this project has great value as a meeting place where visual exchange of ideas is possible.'"[12] That summer, assistants Patricia Birch, Stuart Hodes, Betty Jones, and Donald McKayle (all to become leaders in the field) worked together to produce a newsletter named *Dance Advance* after its first issue. The handout for students expressed the exhilaration of reclaiming a summer space for dance, complete with many of Bennington's original cast of characters.[13]

Norman noticed that some of the older faculty members had mellowed somewhat. Horst and Humphrey developed very different but complementary systems that perhaps did more to jump-start the art of choreography in the United States than any other influence. Now considered authorities, both taught principles of composition to hundreds of young dancers a year, advising, critiquing their work long after formal study finished, and creating performance opportunities for the most promising.[14]

"One of the nice things that happened at Connecticut College was the mutual respect of Louis and Doris in the teaching of composition," Norman observed. "Louis would always defer to Doris, or Doris to Louis. Here were these two people whose teachings could have negated each other, because they were both teaching composition but from very different approaches. But Louis knew what Doris had contributed in dance and appreciated it and Doris knew what Louis did." Ruth, who accompanied both, believed that "Doris tended to be a builder. She tried to get them to present the material, use it, and make something of it to solve the problem. Louis's approach was from the body, from the inside, whereas Doris was very much concerned with the body in space."

The nine-day American Dance Festival of concerts in the summer of 1948 presented an array of offerings with José Limón and Company in three of Humphrey's strongest works, *Day on Earth, Story of Mankind, Lament for Ignacio Sánchez Mejías,* a premiere, *Corybantic,* for five dancers (with José as "The Defender"), as well as his own solo *Chaconne in D Minor.* All were strong vehicles for José as a performing artist. But *Corybantic,* in Limón's words was "a heroic failure" and because the public obviously hated it, was "one of the cruel experiences" of his career.[15]

New London was predominately a blue-collar-worker and navy town, with neighboring summer colonies of vacationers along the shoreline and citizens not in the habit of supporting the arts. The college made attempts to target audiences from more affluent communities such as Stonington, Mystic, Old Lyme, and Essex, who nonetheless remained fairly ambivalent about supporting the new artistic venture "on the hill."[16]

Looking for a theme to contrast to other recent works, Humphrey chose to portray a battle of conflicting forces, playing with some of the same ideas as *With My Red Fires.* This time the ill-fated work was "based upon Greek rites of wild and destructive dances [that] by implication [were] meant to have current significance."[17] As Humphrey's first and only attempt at delving into the Greek themes that would become so important to Graham, it would be the first work that included young dancer Betty Jones (who also served as José's classroom assistant). Along with Pauline Koner (always billed as guest artist) Betty would become pivotal to the Limón company's future success.[18]

The Dudley-Maslow-Bales Trio Ensemble worked with dancers drawn from Manhattan's New Dance Group, where they taught. The Group was known for its round-the-clock class offerings and continuing leftist sympathies. The trio produced the most earthy, least esoteric programming of the series. Drawing themes from American folklore and social observations, their concert for Palmer included Maslow's *Folksay, Dust Bowl Ballads* (with folk singer Woody Guthrie accompanying), and Dudley's 1941 *Harmonica Breakdown* (to recorded music by Sonny Terry and Oh Red) among the most notable of the twelve short works. The trio could be counted on for much-needed comic relief. Bales's *The Lonely Ones,* inspired by William Steig's drawings, and Maslow's *Champion,* based on the Ring Lardner story, were definite crowd-pleasers for the otherwise bemused local audiences.

For a new festival making its mark, the technical mounting of Graham's large repertory programs under the direction of Henry Kurth and Arch Lauterer proved to be nothing short of monumental. Graham presented *Appalachian Spring, Dark Meadow, Hérodiade, Errand into the Maze, Cave of the Heart,* and *Night Journey*—a remarkable (and expensive) accomplishment by any standard. But it was her new *Wilderness Stair* (subtitled and later retitled *Diversion of Angels*), with a score by Norman Dello Joio that evoked the wildest enthusiasm of the festival. Revealing the pleasures of young love, the lyric work for six women and four men, was no doubt inspired by Graham's own love affair with Hawkins. It would be her first choreography in which she did not dance.

Wanting the look and feel of a desert for the new piece, Graham suggested to Dello Joio that the score should take as long to perform as it takes the sun to come up.[19] Noguchi's original set design, created to simulate the desert's horizon, included rocks to be slid upstage, which proved too unwieldy. (It soon became the set for Balanchine's 1948 ballet *Orpheus.*) Instead, Noguchi supplied a "stretched taut and cratered" gray background curtain for the Connecticut performances. It, too, was later abandoned.

The other premiere of the festival, postponed twice, finally made the boards for the last concert. It was Erick Hawkins's *The Strangler,* a "dance-drama" duet based on the Oedipus myth. Poor reviews poured in. One critic said the work possessed even less movement and more talk than his previous creations. Still others reviled the "bombastic" posturing and "confused" text drawn from Robert Fitzgerald's poetry. Actor Joseph Wiseman (who later married Graham dancer Pearl Lang) predicted a failure, even as he passed Graham in the wings: "All's well that ends!" he rasped to her, glad to be offstage.[20] Only Arch Lauterer's set received a good notice.

"Things had become more and more impossible with Erick around. People got so angry when he blossomed on the scene. He took over Graham's place and ruled the roost, and she kowtowed to him," Hazel recalled. "He was so airy. We're going to do this and that. No relation to reality—no relation to money, to anything—absolutely infuriating. And Graham was 'Yes, Erick. Yes, Erick,' and you wanted to kick her too." Those who had stood behind Graham as the ultimate independent woman were now completely disgusted: "You wanted to smack her [because she] let him use her money to put on his own idiotic dances. She couldn't have believed that he was a good dancer. He wasn't. She was living in her own fantasy and couldn't be coaxed out of it." If Martha Hill agreed on a personal level, she also knew that Erick had taken on a number of the managerial tasks for Graham, and was now in charge of productions, seeking out funding sources, and scheduling tour dates—jobs that Louis had performed in the past.

In turn, Erick sensed the general loathing that brewed around his every action. The emotionally charged situation was evident to everyone. But it was Louis Horst who complained the loudest. Louis was conducting the new Dello Joio score with an inexperienced orchestra at the dress rehearsal when Graham lost her patience with what she perceived as constant disruptions from the pit. She conferred with Erick, and then snapped, "Louis, this has got to stop!" Enraged, Louis officially quit his position as Graham's musical director after the last downbeat of their final performance at the festival.[21]

As friends, the two Marthas continued to share personal frustrations in an effort to work out the difficult circumstances with their respective lovers. Graham, who had been in this intense relationship for nearly as long as Hill had been with Lefty, fretted that Erick now wanted to share top billing with her. Hill ached to share living quarters with Lefty in Manhattan. Both now believed that marriage might remove the ambiguities of their lives.

Preoccupied with Lefty's on again, off again attempts at rehabilitation and continuing his job search, at the end of each day Martha would call him in Manhattan. Anxious about his drinking problem, she offered words of encouragement, half-wishing that she could be with him in Manhattan, half-wanting him to join her whenever he could. Aware of the situation, Hazel remarked, "I'm sure that was part of her 'black cloud' during that first summer at Connecticut College. But it was Graham's romantic saga—not Hill's better concealed one— that was gossiped about that summer. Hawkins was thirty-nine. Graham was fifty-four. Friends worried that both women were in foolhardy liaisons. For Graham's sake, Hill did her best to placate Erick's anger at being humiliated by the college's strict dormitory rules that forbade unmarried couples from sharing the same room on campus, but in his mind the situation further illustrated his subservient position. Erick was determined to marry. Graham told Hill that she "had to post her bond with society." She wanted to set the record straight, de Mille reported, adding devilishly, "But why? She never had before."[22]

For Horst too, the 1948 summer session was wracked with personal turmoil. Days after the last performance at Connecticut, Louis was the first to know of their plans. Graham slipped a note under his door saying that she and Erick were going to New Mexico, where they planned to marry. "Imagine! After all those years!" Louis exclaimed. "A note under the door!" They should have known better than to spoil things with marriage vows, Louis insisted. Within months, their relationship began to deteriorate: within two years, they no longer shared the apartment where they had lived discreetly for years.

A story that circulated afterward gives a sense that Connecticut College had not replaced the halcyon days of Bennington: Rosemary Park gave a dinner party for the faculty and said to Louis, "Mr. Horst, what a shame you have to go back to the heat of New York City." To that he replied, "Yes. I'll go back to my Eleventh Street apartment, open the window wide, look down the street to my left, then down the street to my right, and say, 'Thank God! No trees!'"[23]

Although this first festival in New London was deemed a success, there was a deficit of $6,500 at the end of the summer. Martha once again felt personally responsible. That fall, she quickly organized a fund-raiser with the help of Dr. Kolodney at the Ninety-second Street Y to recoup some of the losses. Satisfied with the effort, the administrators of the two schools agreed to continue their support. (Their faith would be rewarded: the next summer would see the birth of another classic modern work, *The Moor's Pavane*.)

As an advocate for dance on every front, Hill had influenced many of the other New York City arts organizations that had emerged on the scene. On the advisory commission and the executive committee of the city's Board of Education, she was part of the planning for a high school for the performing arts (HPA), the first of its kind in the country. In the fall of 1948, the school opened its doors on 120 West Forty-sixth Street with departments of music, drama, and dance. Of the 350 students, sixty were accepted as dance students with Hill, Graham, Martin, de Mille, and Kirstein on the advisory commission. Few of these advisers found time to be present at the auditions where frightened fourteen- and fifteen-year-olds followed dance orders with large numbers pinned to their leotards. But Martha was always there. Ever hungry to find young talent, once she discovered someone with a special gift for movement, she was expert at claiming him or her for the next generation. (One in that group of HPA's hopefuls was Rina Gluck, who became an important dancer for Israel's Bat Dor.)

In the ballet world, by the 1949–50 season, Balanchine's New York City Ballet had gained a significant following fostered by its previous three seasons at the City Center of Music and Drama (the New York City Center) at 131 West Fifty-fifth Street. Originally the Mecca Temple, the theater complex was taken over for nonpayment of taxes in 1943 by the City of New York. By Ballet Society's second (1947–48) season, Morton Baum, now chairing City Center's executive committee, by chance attended a company rehearsal where he discovered the nucleus for the Center's own company. It was Baum who suggested the name change from Ballet Society to the New York City Ballet. Kirstein had moved the entourage into the theater as a resident company as soon as it was renovated by the City of New York, and Balanchine began preparing for its fourth season the following spring. Popular prices spurring a new generation of ballet-goers encouraged Balanchine's choreographic outpouring for his beautifully trained dancers. Although in time his opinion would change, John Martin continued to write lukewarm reviews with little appreciation for the abstract quality of Balanchine's ballets, as he pressed on for a single, unified modern dance repertory company of dancers in which a number of gifted choreographers could create.

From her dancing days with Graham in Dance Repertory Theater in 1930 and 1931, Martha, too, believed in the strength of programming a number of choreographers on the same bill "in repertory." A festival format, as at Bennington and ADF at Connecticut College, served individual companies and their choreographers well—most important, it drew new audiences. By masterfully organizing these out-of-town programs, Martha had become a leading contributor to the repertory concept.

But in Manhattan, almost twenty years had passed since Dance Repertory Theater's historic attempt to present modern dance companies in repertory concerts. Now managing directors, publicist Isadora Bennett and cofounder of ABT Richard Pleasant were determined to match the New York City Ballet's box office success, by re-creating the modern repertory concept. Martha served as chairman of the advisory committee, made up of Norman Lloyd, Horst, and lighting designer Jean Rosenthal, for the newly coined New York City Dance Theatre series. Conferring with the "choreographer-sponsors" Valerie Bettis, Graham, and Holm (who was now enjoying unprecedented success as a Broadway choreographer), as well as with Humphrey, Limón, Maslow, Tamiris, and Weidman, the committee selected works. Performances, slated to end the day before Christmas, included twenty-five pieces by twelve choreographers.

Three days after another Bennington fund-raising concert at the Y under her direction that December, Martha Hill helped prepare for the onslaught of ten nights of history-making at City Center. The dance project featured works by three of the original "Big Four," with Limón the obvious shoo-in for Martha Graham. If the end result looked oddly similar to the previous summer's concerts at Palmer auditorium, this Manhattan version rightfully served as the culmination of a decade of growth in the field.

"It is a triumph that American dance is at last being recognized and given its rightful place among the other theatre arts, drama, opera and ballet which the City Center sponsors," the *Dance Observer* noted. For the reviewer, the initial season represented "a clear cross-section" in the inauguration of the repertory system, providing a place for revivals of modern classics, Humphrey's *Shakers,* Holm's *Ozark Suite,* and Weidman's *Atavisms,* among them. "American dance, now in its third generation, has finally reached its majority. And in so doing is reaching a new audience as well."[24] Walter Terry wrote that the season was "an enormously exciting one," and counseled "upon the future of this organization hinges the future of modern dance, of American contemporary dance itself, for the art has gone about as far as it can go through the isolated, separated activities of small groups and soloists, brilliant though most of them are. Consolidation of performing talent, of choreographic gifts and of repertory are essential if America's native dance is to equal (not rival) American ballet."[25] As optimistic as Martha, the codirectors, critics, and the participants were, City Center determined that there would be no subsequent seasons and the notion of sustaining a sister company to the New York City Ballet had vanished. It would take another fifteen years for the repertory concept to come forth on this scale again.

Graham had opted out of the series, a move that ultimately served her well. Instead of joining the other moderns, she embarked on an extensive "transcontinental" tour, giving forty-one concerts, mostly on college campuses, with another important tour scheduled for the next winter (1950). Without doubt, these tours and similar ones by other artists who had presented work at City Center, also contributed greatly to the rapid growth of modern dance throughout the United States.

Back in their academic world, Hill and Bales led a little group of ten students on their own grassroots tour of northeastern colleges during Bennington's nonresident term. In April, their students again appeared at the Y in a program with the Sarah Lawrence dance group.[26] Encouraging dance at both ends of the spectrum, Hill seemed to handle both with uncomplicated grace and equal ease. Though others might have developed loftier ambitions for themselves, Martha gladly served whatever was good for the cause of dance, wherever and whenever the opportunity arose.

To Martha's delight, in the winter of 1949, Lefty settled into an apartment of his own at 22 West Twelfth Street and by March landed a job that he relished. As educational director and executive assistant to the president at Town Hall, Inc., Davies handled the operations of the auditorium of the landmark theater on West Forty-third Street. A pioneer institution for adult education and a world-famous concert and lecture hall, its programming had begun to feature events in the field of international understanding.

Lefty now worked under George V. Denny, Jr. The two men soon allied themselves to create a dynamic team for progressive ideas. Martha explained, "Lefty, who was a very fine speaker himself, got involved in the radio program *America's Town Meeting of the Air*. He was really Denny's alternate. He spoke and introduced speakers on the air. It was very important."

Denny believed: "Absolutely the only force that can control the fearsome energy of the atom is man with his capacity to think. . . . In a world whose fate can be changed hourly by new political thinking, new scientific developments, small accidents, you must—to be equal to your responsibilities—inform yourself of what is happening in all fields, in all parts of the world!"[1] Lefty was responsible for general administration and supervision of Town Hall and dealt with the deeper financial struggles of the organization (that included neglected tax liabilities). For the brochure "A Modern Institution Functioning in the American Tradition" Lefty's words matched Denny's in tone and message: "In the heart of a 'cold' metropolis has grown up a warmly responsive American institution, dedicated to the objectives of individual and of social development . . . which today in their contemporary context require contemporary progressive techniques."[2]

Lefty was also responsible for an extensive lecture program that called itself a series of "international missions on a people-to-people basis," generating Town Hall's reputation as "national gathering place for the free exchange of ideas and public opinions."[3] His position would soon open recruitment possibilities for Martha as she learned through his connections of talented young dancers from Europe, Mexico, the Near and Far East, and later, Israel. As the objective of these projects was "to bring together citizens" of the world to the United States, Martha's own connections contributed significantly.

With Lefty now permanently residing in New York City, the separate pieces of her life were coming together at last. The pair enjoyed brisk walks together, marveling at the city's richly varied architecture. As they strolled the city blocks, they talked over the day's events. If Martha tried to analyze students' problems, Lefty, amazed at how involved she became with their personal lives, would warn that she was not their psychiatrist. Ethel Winter recalled that one of those walks led to an impromptu visit to her half-renovated brownstone on East Thirty-first Street "to see how things were going."

As plans for summer 1949 in Connecticut developed, the awkwardness of the two-college arrangement for the summer school of dance had become more apparent. NYU now recognized the undertaking as essentially Connecticut College's affair. At the same time, more summer dance study options at other institutions were following ADF's lead. Limón as well as Graham (who claimed hers to be in its sixteenth year of operation) advertised their own June intensive courses in Manhattan—courses designed primarily for college students, many drawn to New York City by earlier company appearances on their campuses.

Martha Hill worried in a note to her Connecticut College liaison, Rusty, that by June 9 only fifty-six applications had been received for the upcoming Connecticut session. Rusty dashed a note back to Martha, warning that they "could not run without 100" and suggesting that both supporting institutions might be willing to take a small deficit. Martha answered, "I'll try to impress New York University with the folly of trying to cut salaries (again) and staff, and impress them with their responsibility."[4] Fortunately, the final numbers of students reached an acceptable range. The summer began with ninety-three students, a faculty of twenty, eight additional staff members, and twenty-eight concert group members.[5] The administrative configuration this time was Rosemary Park and Martha Hill acting as cochairmen of the administrative board of the school, Martha and Rusty as cochairmen of the advisory board of the school, and Teddy Wiesner as administrative assistant.

Martha's correspondence to Rosemary and Rusty relayed her efforts to get lighting designer Jean Rosenthal at a "rock bottom" salary to replace Arch, who had committed to the summer session of dance at Mills. (She had also managed to arrange scholarships for three of the enrolled.)[6] Ben and Norman did not plan to return. Although these departures made the need to cut staff easier for Martha, the loss of two of her most gifted and fun-loving cohorts was a difficult reminder that the Bennington "esprit de corps" was a thing of the past.

That summer at ADF was stellar for José. His newly formed group, José Limón and Company, appeared for the first time at the American Dance Festival in New London. Still performing a good amount of Doris's repertory, José's company now included Letita Ide, Jones, and Koner, as well as the striking lean and blond Dutchman, Lucas Hoving, who had danced with Kurt Jooss.

Suffering from an increasingly painful arthritic hip, and having disbanded the Humphrey-Weidman Company (with Weidman now presenting his works with Peter Hamilton), Humphrey's new arrangement as artistic adviser to José meant that she had a ready group of dancers to choreograph on, without the burdens of running a company. To no one's surprise, however, the bulk of this work fell on the very same shoulders that it had in the old company. Pauline Limón continued to run the books, organize the tours, and design and construct the costumes for her husband.

One of Limón's two premieres at ADF, *The Moor's Pavane: Variations on the Theme of Othello*, astounded its audience with its greatness. John Martin exclaimed in his *Times* review, "the whole work is rich, dark, intense and utterly absorbing."[7] José's reputation was confirmed not only as "undoubtedly the leading male of the modern dance," but as a choreographer of stature.[8] Martha Hill now realized, as Martin had predicted all along, that José's work held great hope for the future of modern dance. After a full decade of slow choreographic development, under Doris's watchful eye, Limón now surpassed everyone's expectations.

Martha often hosted informal opening-night post-performance receptions for the artists, important visitors, and critics at her spacious New London apartment overlooking the Thames. Beth Olson Mitchell, who had completed an internship at Mills after Bennington, assisted Martha at Connecticut that year, acting as her gofer. "Because I had a car, it was my responsibility to shop for party foods and liquor," she recalled, happy to cope with the drudgework of the understaffed administrators.[9]

Usually the first person backstage after a performance, Martha uncharacteristically sent congratulations backstage by letter: "Saturday Night. José, Pauline and Doris, It was a magnificent concert tonight—what dancing and what a company! I am so happy you three made the struggle for the summer seem a small effort for so fine a thing. I send you my love, Martha." This time Lefty had arrived on campus for the performance. Uneasy with the effusive greenroom practice of greeting sweaty, half-naked dancers, as applause faded, Lefty quickly disappeared to get his car, in order to pull Martha away for their time alone. Sunday for the couple meant relaxing over Bloody Marys and a lobster brunch at New London's chic Lighthouse Inn. After Lefty's departure, however, and her return to the campus that afternoon, Martha was once more struck by the reality that *she* was the one responsible for everything. Bouts with ulcers steadily worsened over that difficult summer.

Louis Horst recalled that evening of *Pavane*'s premiere with unfettered emotion. After the work was over, with the moment of silence before a roaring response—always a signal of profound experience in the theater—the white-haired, 250 pounds–plus, slipped out of his twelfth-row aisle seat in Palmer auditorium. He trotted across campus to the coffeeshop to gather his thoughts for the review due by midnight for New London's evening edition of *The Day*. He was surprised when Doris sat at the table next to him. "You didn't stay to the end of the show either," Doris observed. He admitted, "I just couldn't. After *Moor's Pavane* I had to leave." "I felt the same way," she confessed. Louis added, "I know that work is your doing!" With a soft smile, she admitted, "Well, maybe three-fourths of it."[10]

Earlier, José had written of the general concern that American dance would disappear when its contemporary personalities retired from the stage. For him, the solution was to "submit to the direction of an experienced and proven artist. I think all our dancing would be of a higher caliber."[11] José had submitted and emerged victoriously.

But other moderns plotted careers on their own. One interesting newcomer to the ADF scene was Valerie Bettis, who arrived on campus with her company of actor-dancers. To many, Bettis's intensely emotional *Desperate Heart* epitomized the integration of poetry with dance. Her contribution to the festival included a stream-of consciousness adaptation of Faulkner's novel, *As I Lay Dying* and a new work, *Domino Furioso*, to words by John Malcolm Brinnin and music by Bernardo Segall, set on commedia dell'arte characters (a reccurring theme among choreographers). One critic called *Furioso* "one great big colorful mish-mash."[12]

An infinitely more successful work at the festival was Humphrey's *Invention*, "so finished and so beautifully performed at its opening that it left nothing to be desired. . . . It is a refreshing piece; fleet, fresh, wholesome, unencumbered by symbolism or story, uninhibited by décor or properties. It is a dance in space and in time, and a thoroughly satisfying experience."[13] Again, Humphrey proved the worthiest master of the series.

Martha remained enthusiastic about recording dance history in the making. That summer a film crew from the civilian affairs division of the army appeared on campus—a connection nudged along by Mary Jo. As they had with the similar filming event of *Young America Dances* at Mills ten years earlier, dancers delighted in the prospect of being immortalized on celluloid. This time the result was *Creative Leisure*, a film about the summer dance program at Connecticut College, produced and released "for public education use through the United States Office of Education." Herbert Kerkow produced the film; Norman Lloyd provided the background score. With little dialogue, it was designed to show the work of dancers "while others vacationed."[14] In it, the ever-present Horst plays for a bevy of young women gathered around the piano in their jersey skirts and midriff tops. Limón demonstrates short phrases from his repertory, replicated by groups of dancers across the living room's bare wooden floor, led by beauties Ruth Currier and Betty Jones. They are later seen onstage in excerpts from Humphrey's *Invention*, after a clip of Bill Bales warming up, and the charming Valerie Bettis and her company anxiously waiting their turn on the boards.[15]

Visitors wandering among students marveled at a curriculum more varied than at Bennington for the "energetic, inexhaustible and indomitable."[16] Only the absence of Martha Graham from this season's teaching faculty upset them. For Martha Hill, too, the disappointment was real. It would be the first summer school of dance she had overseen without Graham's day-to-day presence, contributing to an emotional separation from the project she had not experienced before. Her struggle with an increasingly fragile situation at NYU did not help.[17]

Audience turnout was disappointing, despite such attempts to encourage attendance as a community square dance and other public relations events. Predictably, money problems surfaced at the end of the 1949 season. In a note to Martha, Rusty summarized: "Artistically and educationally it has been a remarkable summer. Financially we again have not been successful, but the Festival has not lost nearly as much money this year."[18] At least, once again, Martha had established herself as a founding leader and dance educator. And now her influence spread into wider circles as the field of dance began to enter the cultural mainstream. With a more solid basis in academic settings, dance was finding broader audiences through the emergence of more periodicals and newspapers featuring reviews and articles on dance, along with a proliferation of local studios cropping up across the United States.

Martha was quoted in a *New York Times* article that winter: "The first attribute of life is action. To dance is to be intensely alive."[19] In other ways, the dance field had come of age, although ballet and modern dance contingents were still suspicious of each other. In a move for greater unity, Horst's *Dance Observer* now printed cover photographs of American Ballet Theatre stars. He wrote glowingly about Antony Tudor's new works, while others rhapsodized over Balanchine's exciting new company. Modern dance began to be recognized as an integral part of the theater scene.

By the 1950s, younger dancers had learned that, almost without exception, the most direct path to recognition was to study with proven artists in hopes of joining their companies. This rite of passage would continue throughout the Eisenhower years, only to be challenged a decade later—along with much else in the United States.

On 20 February 1950 Martha received word that her mother had died suddenly at seventy-two. "She dropped dead in the dining room just home from jury duty. Before that she was in good shape—no heart problems or anything," her daughter-in-law, Mary Ann Hill, said. She recalled that Martha did not go home for the funeral. Not surprised, Mary Ann sympathized, "I never felt very close to her, either." Bill explained, "It was Mother who was so against her dancing, not Father."[20]

After her mother's death, Martha found it easier to return to Ohio to be with Bill's family and her father. The next Thanksgiving, she traveled back to Salem for a visit. "Martha's personal life was a private matter, not talked about. If you didn't ask the question, you didn't get the answer," Bill explained. Prying into affairs of the heart was just not done in the Hill family. Mary Ann added, "They were very taciturn. You could sit in the parlor with them and no one would speak."

But both remembered Martha making a phone call; they inadvertently overheard "Honey," and something about him meeting her at the train station when she got back. Mary Ann remembered saying to Bill, "'Martha's got somebody in New York!' But she would never tell us anything. It was only then that we found out about Lefty."

Arrangements for the third New York University–Connecticut College Summer School of Dance in 1950 were temporarily halted with Rusty's sudden illness and hospital stay. President Park helped the deteriorating situation by making more of her regular staff available. For Martha, cutting expenses began with eliminating independent press agent Isadora Bennett. Martha wrote her that with "no money in the budget" she could not accept her "very kind offer of help." Connecticut College's staff would now take care of the publicity for the festival and school.[21] Working through NYU, Martha handled contracts for the faculty and staff while plotting the repertory offerings and the allocation of the production monies.

Unable to guarantee that classes would fill by the third season at Connecticut College, ads no longer named the artists-in-residence, saying simply that an "outstanding faculty of artists and educators" would be teaching. Chosen as the two dance companies in residence for the 1950 summer session at Connecticut College were again José Limón's with Doris as artistic director, and the Dudley-Maslow-Bales Trio. Among the five guest artists were Merce Cunningham, who presented four solos (including *Two Step* and *Root of the Unfocus*), and Pearl

Primus and her company, bringing black dance to the festival for the first time.[22] (Mary Wigman had been invited for a summer residence, but stalled because of visa problems; she accepted a teaching assignment in Switzerland instead.)[23]

Of the thirty-five dance works presented at the festival, five were new. José and Letitia Ide were called the "ideal cast" for his new work *The Exiles*. In the retelling of the Adam and Eve story, with music by Arnold Schönberg, they suggested "Michelangelo figures in motion in their long diagonal flight from up stage left to down stage right," Martha noted.[24] Limón also created a less successful series of solos, duets, and trios in *Concert*, with Simon Sadoff onstage at the keyboard, playing Bach preludes and fugues. If the form was well accepted on the ballet stage, here it seemed to have little impact. Jane Dudley premiered a group work, *Passional*, to music of Bartók, and Bales, a new solo, *Impromptu*, to an Erik Satie score. Sophie Maslow presented her completed *The Village I Knew* to its Tucker score.

Martha's final report claimed an audience of approximately eight thousand, with the last performance boasting the festival's first sold-out house. Critics from metropolitan papers of New York, Boston, Hartford, and Chicago covered the festival, along with periodicals and Louis's daily reviews for the local paper. Sixteen different radio interviews and discussions reached the airways as part of an audience education program. Of the seventy-nine students, twenty-three were from the United States and Israel, with five enrolled under the G.I. Bill. More than half were undergraduates from some thirty colleges and schools.[25]

A dramatic change in Martha's own career began with a phone call from William Schuman, president of the Juilliard School of Music in Manhattan. Hill was Schuman's choice as the person most able to design and direct a dance division for the music school. Recommended by Norman Lloyd[26] and seconded by Graham, Schuman had worked with Hill on a Y panel that encouraged music and dance collaborations. It was there that Schuman began conversations about the possibility of a dance component for the prominent conservatory on Morningside Heights. Martha remembered:

> Bill asked me, "What do you think about a dance department at Juilliard?" He wanted to make it professional, like the music school. I told him there wasn't such a thing in America. Dance has always been part of Physical Education or Art, or at a studio. . . . Bill was very open to new ideas and to collaboration among the arts—not at all a purist. It's that kind of openness that let things happen. And he believed that "education, as well as art," must "be of its own time."[27]

Schuman, who had become president of the Juilliard School of Music in 1945, acknowledged that "it took a lot of doing" to create the school's dance division. But he was determined that Juilliard would benefit because "dancers would be closer to music and get a better education in music, and the musicians would learn something about dance. . . . I thought it would be a tremendous contribution for the school to make." When he announced his plan, the school's board of directors expressed grave concern. Schuman gallantly responded, "Not only do I want a dance division, but someday a drama division! Don't worry, it will be short of establishing a medical school!"[28]

Coming from the faculty of Sarah Lawrence, the thirty-six-year-old composer took on Juilliard's somewhat stodgy conservatism full force. Years later, when asked why he wanted a dance division, Schuman responded:

> First, dance has always been very closely associated with music—handmaidens, as the phrase goes—and second, there was no conservatory of dance comparable to Juilliard in music. . . . I knew the dance view very well. . . . There was no sense of an entire field being studied and that's why I thought it would be a tremendous contribution for the school to make. . . . And that worked out very, very well.

The third reason behind Schuman's initiative was his belief in the need for close creative collaboration between the two arts.

Schuman's own composing experience began as collaborator with Antony Tudor for his psychological *Undertow* in 1945, and continued in his work with Martha Graham for her 1947 *Night Journey* and her 1950 *The Legend of Judith*.[29] The composer found that "contemporary dance theater demanded intelligence, versatility and technical range from its artists" and he saw dance as "a living example of an art that was continually renewing itself."[30] His own music suited dance, with its full polyphonic melodic lines, strong rhythms, and emotionally stirring triadic harmonies.

By February 1951, Martha Hill had a contract as head of the new Department of Dance at Juilliard with a starting salary of $7,000 along with a personal note from the delighted president. It said, "If official notes could permit the inclusion of thousands of lush adjectives, you would have a clearer idea of how I feel. See ya Monday, Affectionately, Bill."[31] That Monday they sealed the agreement over ice cream sodas at Schrafft's on lower Fifth Avenue.

PART VI

Dance within the Conservatory

Ready for a new challenge, Martha happily began to design a training ground for dancers at Juilliard. Bennington's public relations representative (who happened to be Mary Jo) reported Martha's leave of absence. That fall of 1951, Mary Jo also left Bennington to become a colonel in the Air Force; at this time the services were trying to increase their recruitment of women for the Korean emergency.

Although Martha had officially resigned from both Bennington and New York University effective 1 July 1951, separating herself from the summer festival activities would prove more difficult. After three years of modest support (that included some released teaching time for Hill), NYU administrators now used Martha's resignation as a reason to pull out of the ADF equation. Disregarding her earlier report of the "exhilarating and penetrating . . . profoundly rewarding experience," NYU board members saw no reason to stay in the project. As long as Martha was on the faculty, Jay Nash supported her every effort, but knowing that she would be resigning to take a job at Juilliard, he agreed that the school should withdraw its support. (Nash himself left NYU in 1953.)

Rosemary Park and Connecticut College gladly took on the entire summer project for 1951: the school was reaping more national acclaim than she, or her board of trustees, had ever imagined possible. With the hiring of an office assistant, Rusty's job was somewhat eased; yet it was Martha who remained irreplaceable. For the summer of 1951, the companies in residence were saddled with most of the teaching as well as festival performing. Bales, Dudley, Limón, and Maslow became the core faculty, each teaching in the studio during the day and rehearsing every night and weekend.

Limón's company now replaced Graham's as the major contributor to the festival performances. The novelty of the season was the return of Charles Weidman who presented a new solo, *A Song for You*. But the larger ensemble works were Limón's *Tonantzintla* (recently created while in residence at Bellas Artes in Mexico City,) and Humphrey's revival of *Passacaglia and Fugue in C Minor*, performed by her repertory class. Perhaps the most important contribution was Humphrey's creation of *Quartet No. 1. (Night Spell)*, set to music by Priaulx Rainer for dancers Currier, Hoving, Jones, and Limón.

As Juilliard's founding director of dance for the 1951–52 academic year, Martha entered into the most difficult period of her career. With the position came the opportunity to develop a curriculum that would set a standard for dance training in the United States, unencumbered by the standards of academic disciplines outside the performing arts.

Martha once mused about the problems of joining forces with a music school, with its demands for musical integrity and allegiance to classical repertory. It was a place where the choice of composers and scores needed official approval from the president with live musical performances always a necessity. Nonetheless, alignment with a music school appealed to her concept of training the complete dance artist.

Hill and Schuman agreed about the importance of institutional support for the arts: their life's work depended on it. They also knew that to achieve this at Juilliard, the new enterprise needed the best faculty of artist-teachers to be had. For modern, Graham, Humphrey, and Horst headed the list of "must-haves." Martha recalled:

> Bill said, "Whom would you want?" I said, "[Antony] Tudor for ballet, Martha for modern." . . . [This was] the first chance I got to do ballet and modern dance together. . . . The curriculum was conceived [from] what I had discovered in my own life of ballet, modern dance, music . . . I incorporated it all.[1]

Surprisingly, her vision for a new classicism in American dance meant training dancers in both ballet and modern dance idioms. The time for conflicting dance philosophies was over, she insisted. This combined training now became Hill's mantra for developing the complete dancer. Having lived through that argument at Bennington, Martha was firmly convinced that strong ballet technique was essential for a professional dancer.

"By the time I came to Juilliard, modern dance had pretty well established itself, but there was still great rivalry between ballet and modern dance. [B]ack then it was just assumed that they mixed about as well as oil and water," Martha explained.[2] She recalled harsh criticism with people saying, "It'll never work to put ballet and modern dance together under the same roof. They'll kill each other."[3] Muriel Topaz, a student that first year, remembered: "In those days if you were a modern dancer you didn't take ballet. You were supposed to hate ballet. I had my first ballet class ever in the world with Tudor!" (It would be Topaz—known as "Mickey"—who years later would take over Martha Hill's position at Juilliard.)[4] For June Dunbar, soon to join the Juilliard faculty, Martha was to create a "violently new" department bringing together dancers from various philosophical camps to teach at a conservatory in tandem: "Dance was enormously divided in those years. . . . It was a time when people were trying to develop turf, philosophically, in dance."[5]

With this new start, Martha wanted a broad mix of dance styles, with composition, dance notation, and music study interjected, and repertory the cohesive ingredient in the mix. Although the study of dance composition had grown in importance, virtually no training ground for ballet choreographers existed. Schuman concurred that from a musician's perspective, it was the ballet companies that traditionally performed with full orchestras—for which potential commissions might come to Juilliard composers and Juilliard instrumentalists.[6]

If Graham epitomized the high art of disciplined technique, it was Humphrey whose works exemplified the finest choreographic craftsmanship from a humanistic vantage point. Horst remained the acknowledged authority of dance composition training, respected for his principles of abstraction and his belief in collaborations between composers and choreographers. All three agreed to serve as master teachers at Juilliard.

Hiring Tudor was a calculated risk on Martha's part: Writer P. W. Manchester credits Tudor's ultimate success at teaching late starters to the fact that he was "never more than a barely adequate technician. The marvel is that his brain must have absorbed everything his body could never do, and this later made him a great teacher."[7]

At that time resident choreographer for the Metropolitan Opera Ballet, Tudor's strongest association since 1940 had been with American Ballet Theatre, where he had for years set works such as *Dim Lustre* in 1943 and his masterwork *Lilac Garden* (Jardin aux Lilas) under Lucia Chase's direction. He had established himself as the "king of the psychological ballet," more aligned with modern dance than with classical ballet. His works dealt with emotions of everyday life—in contrast to Balanchine, who saw ballet as the purist art in his plotless neoclassical style. The works of these two creative artists were, in critic Anna Kisselgoff's words, a "difference in mind set." She has quoted Balanchine as saying that they were "aesthetic opposites. . . . Tudor was very English, and City Ballet dancers did not fit into Oxfords or comfortable shoes. . . . It was a cruel but factual remark. Tudor's dancers . . . deal with the emotions of everyday life, while Balanchine saw ballet as artifice refined."[8] American Ballet Theatre was now widely recognized as a prestigious company committed to the production of ballet classics and a range of choreographers (including Tudor along with Americans Agnes de Mille and Eugene Loring) rather than a commitment to single choreographer, as in the case with Balanchine at the New York City Ballet.

By 1950, Tudor had also become the resident director of the Metropolitan Opera Ballet School and the Metropolitan Opera Ballet, both illustrious positions in the minds of Juilliard's administration—although in fact, after staging three operas for the 1950 season, it would be ten years before he choreographed for another two.[9] Biographer Donna Perlmutter astutely observed, "If he chose to exile himself from brand-name ballet . . . in fact, he was more attuned to modern dance, which, in its very genesis, dealt seriously—not commercially—with the subjects it addressed. Challenge, some would say a perverse challenge, characterized the Tudor career."[10] But Hill knew he was right for the job on hearing his lecture "Ballet Today" for the New York Dance Film Society in the spring of 1951. According to a *Dance Observer* article, Tudor stated that there should be a constant opening of doors by the teacher for the student, with the dancer conscious of contributing to the whole. These were also the very reasons that he worked so well in Hill's combined dance offering at Juilliard.

Additionally, Hill and Tudor advocated the Met's Enrico Cecchetti technical style as one that more comfortably suited an American ballet company. In the beginning, as the new director, Martha was subject to the "added disbelief . . . from the Russophiles. How could one base training in ballet on the British concept?"[11] She understood that its grounded pliés, soft flowing arms, and essential "Englishness" were dramatically different in quality from what was being taught by Russian counterparts. It was a gentler, more lyrical way of moving, much kinder to the body than the Russian style's sharper accents and angles, with the characteristic forced turn-out, fast footwork, and high leg extensions that dominated Balanchine's work. It was this difference in style that would make the decision to hire Tudor and his contingent an important—if continually confrontational—one for the future of dance at Juilliard.

Kirstein, himself encouraging a mixed repertory for the young New York City Ballet company, had recommended Tudor's *Time Table* for its 1949 season. Indeed, in 1951—the year Martha was pulling together her Juilliard faculty—he not only contracted Tudor to stage *Lilac Garden* for the New York City Ballet, he also commissioned him to create two new works for the company. The unspectacular results were *Lady of the Camellias* in 1951 and *La Gloire* in 1952. (Tudor's works were soon dropped from NYCB's repertory, however he would later return to stage *Dim Lustre* for the company in 1964.)[12] Even if Kirstein's initial enthusiasm was dampened, Tudor's work for NYCB did attract the daily press; for Hill and Schuman, the choreographer was a perfect addition for Juilliard's new dance division. To Louis Horst, as critic for his militantly modern *Dance Observer*, Tudor was a genius. Martha Graham and Tudor saw eye-to-eye and openly praised each other's work. (Limón, in contrast, barely tolerated Tudor: once on the faculty, the two grew to dislike each other silently and intensely.)[13]

Tudor's colleague at the Met school, Margaret Craske, also joined the first dance faculty. A leading Cecchetti authority who had danced with Diaghilev, Craske was Tudor's most important teacher in London. A frumpy, no-nonsense Englishwoman, Craske taught exacting Cecchetti adagios and combinations "by the book," having come to New York in 1946 to become ballet mistress of American Ballet Theatre. Shortly after, she joined the Metropolitan Opera Ballet School faculty. The charming Alfredo Corvino, also drawn from the Metropolitan after a career with Kurt Jooss's touring company and Ballet Russes de Monte Carlo, offered students the security of solid lesson plans. Later arrivals joining the ballet teaching team were Mattlyn Gavers, Audrey Keene, and Maggie Black. All taught ballet technique firmly rooted in exercises derived from Cecchetti's, with placement and purity of line essential.

With shaven head and sharply chiseled features, Tudor taught class in white shirt and tie, trousers and street shoes. His lessons were filled with complex choreographic explorations and high challenges. Once a pattern of movements was established (Tudor hated the idea of "steps" and stringing together combinations), he played with difficult changes of direction and dynamics, then manipulated time signatures to develop mental acuity and speed—the antithesis of Balanchine's and Kirstein's belief that "steps stay."[14] Tudor's classes were full of mind games, mischief, and sometimes biting commentary. His longtime Juilliard pianist Betty Sawyer admitted that his cruelty was "extraordinary" but acknowledged that he could weigh her own "quivering insecurity" against her attributes to make a fair judgment. "He did the same with dancers. He tipped the balance by his love of knowledge and his human understanding." Tudor's subjects for study were often students who underwent his odd use of psychoanalysis. But beyond his idiosyncratic teaching style, it was Tudor's "sensitivity to musical structure and inner meaning" that made him an excellent choice for the dance faculty.[15] Sawyer points out that he was a choreographer who heard and understood music like a composer. And, unlike the many choreographers who use music homophonically (that is, steps matched to accompaniment), Tudor's approach was polyphonic, with his movement phrases as lines within a mainly contrapuntal texture. He never tried to mimic details; instead, he responded to the kinetic quality and expressive development of the details, their varying tensions and releases within phrases."[16]

Martha had also invited Agnes de Mille and Jerome Robbins (then assistant director at New York City Ballet) to join the first ballet faculty. Although he had expressed interest, to Martha's disappointment, Robbins never signed a contract. De Mille taught several master classes during the first year, but soon found herself too busy as a choreographer on Broadway to continue.

Graham and Humphrey, by then the acclaimed matriarchs of modern dance, would take responsibility for the modern component. If Martha still harbored the idea of Graham as central in her plan, Graham once again balked at the idea of actually participating fully herself, only agreeing to lend her name and her company to Juilliard's teaching roster. Her own school on East Sixty-third Street was her first priority. When the department opened, neither artist taught technique any longer. Instead Graham sent her company members, Helen McGehee, Ethel Winter, and occasionally Mary Hinkson and Bert Ross to teach. Humphrey taught advanced dance composition and oversaw the second style of modern study in the studio. (It was labeled "Humphrey-Limón" technique by the time José Limón officially joined the faculty with Betty Jones as his assistant in 1953.) Armed with these master teachers, what initially seemed like a utopian dream soon represented an educational choice for young dancers that would ignite college dance departments across the country—many of which were barely able to justify modern dance in their own curriculum.

In 1951 Juilliard's annual tuition was $650. Fifty-six students (forty-eight women and eight men) that Hill praised as "some of the best talents around" made up the first class with many drawn from Bennington, High School of the Performing Arts, and New York University. Muriel Topaz, who had been a student in education at NYU and taken classes in movement and folk dance with Martha, recalled: "I thought she was a character, but I was very enamored of her ideas." Martha encouraged her to take the first Juilliard dance entrance exam. "To this day I don't know how I ever got in." She confessed, "We were a very motley crew."

Martha's previous experience in undergraduate environments certainly helped as she designed a four-year program offering a diploma and a five-year B.S. degree. Both offered dance majors in ballet or modern (Graham or Humphrey-Limón) techniques. The unusually heavy dose of required courses for both degrees included thirty-six points of academic credit, daily ballet and modern classes, six semesters of dance composition, and eight semesters of dance notation (using Laban's theories and now labeled "Labanotation," it was taught by Ann Hutchinson, who joined the faculty during the first year). A hefty eight semesters of Literature and Materials in Music were required of Juilliard students in every discipline, along with annual jury exams and a senior pre-graduation exam.

Martha now faced an entirely different kind of student from those she had taught for years in liberal arts venues: ones who auditioned specifically because they aspired to careers in dance. Many had come from studio environments.

She admitted, "[During] the first year, I was very shocked because when I said they had to go to the [obligatory] Wednesday one o'clock concerts, students would say, 'Well, what do I get out of it?' They wanted to get into a show, or into a concert company the fastest way possible. They had no qualitative sense. They'd want to stretch and jump and do only that. I can remember being very depressed when they didn't want to take Literature and Materials of Music. So I had great public relations work inside and outside at Juilliard."[17]

For the dance department the most critical issue at first was the need for space; any sharing of facilities was not well met by other divisions. But for Martha, now able to combine her energies under one roof, there was no turning back. She had her master teachers, two large studios with sprung wooden floors (albeit shared with the orchestra and the opera theater departments), and access to a well-equipped stage in Manhattan. From the student's perspective, Muriel recalled, "The curriculum was laid out, so you didn't have a lot of choices. But in terms of integrating it into something, I felt I was on my own. Martha wasn't a nurturer, in the sense of hanging over you like a mother. If you were in trouble, you could go to her and get help. Other than that, she expected you to have a certain amount of maturity to take care of yourself."

By the second semester, Graham had warmed up to the idea of participation at Juilliard. In March 1952 she agreed to be a guest speaker at the Sixth American Symposium of the International Federation of Music, held at the school. In conjunction, Graham brought her company into the Juilliard Theater for a gala concert that April. If the symposium was billed as a fund-raiser for dance scholarships and celebrated the opening of the department, Graham herself reaped the benefit of a full symphony orchestra, and assistance from the National Council on the Arts. The result was her *Canticle for Innocent Comedians* in April 1952 to music by Thomas Ribbink.

As in the Bennington and Connecticut College programs, repertory was an important ingredient in Martha's educational mix, and arts planners were becoming more enthusiastic about the idea of a repertory theater for dance. Symphony orchestras worked efficiently with the repertory concept, Schuman maintained, "Why not dance?" With this in mind, Hill presented another round of "inaugural" concerts to orchestral works choreographed by Graham, Humphrey, Limón and Tudor in the fall of 1952.[18]

Graham's contribution was in a way, a kind of thank-you to Martha Hill. After the last performance, the two Marthas and Lefty shared a cab back to the East Side: Graham to East Sixty-third Street east of Third, and the couple, to Lefty's nearby apartment. On the way, Graham confessed that she had to "go about the business of getting her own house in order." She had accepted a significant offer of support from her former student, friend, patron, and member of the European banking family, Bethsabée de Rothschild, and now was determined to give her full energy to her own school and company. Appreciative of the income her company made through their teaching at Juilliard, Graham explained that her personal involvement would be in name only.

With Graham's earlier withdrawal from the daily activities at ADF in 1948, and now at Juilliard, Martha Hill once again realized that she could not rely on the power of a single figure—most particularly Graham, whose participation ran so hot and cold. Later she remarked that Graham's actions were for the best. "The more tightly a system is codified, the more straightjacketed a dancer becomes," Hill admitted, perhaps to cover the reality of losing Graham who had always been a linchpin for success. A broader, more eclectic approach for the training of professional dancers had become "wise."[19]

Under Hill's guard, the remaining "in-house" professionals flourished and produced some of their best work, ever thankful that they were earning their rent while espousing their personal manifestos. Martha had become paymaster, not only for their summer work, but year-round. Now that Graham had essentially defected, Limón would become the most significant benefactor.

First and foremost, Martha served as an advocate for the artists on her team. To Tudor, she gave carte blanche to any choreographic projects he wanted (or didn't want) to pursue. She also knew that Tudor's association with the Metropolitan Ballet School would serve Juilliard's more advanced ballet students well. In a free-flowing setup, a selected few were allowed to take the 11 A.M. professional classes with Tudor in the Opera House's gargantuan two-story open space, where wonderfully worn wooden floors made it one of the finest dance studios in all of Manhattan. It was this kind of informal arrangement that Martha had worked out for her Bennington students, and now continued to perfect for her Juilliard ones.

Leaves for professional reasons would be freely granted. Graham's dancers, too, worked their teaching schedules around touring and their availability. It was a freewheeling pact that worked so long as Martha at the helm was the ultimate authority: while protecting her artist-teachers' careers, she would never interfere with (or even observe) the actual goings-on during class time unless invited. "While cooking one can always substitute ingredients," Martha once told a houseguest. Her teachers at Juilliard, too, were interchangeable. Substitutes enhanced the work in the classroom as all were chosen from an inner circle of like-minded artists where mutual trust was key.

As Martha bowed to her artist faculty, however, some grumbling took place among the students. "We were so pinched for any kind of facility, that we were a little resentful that so much time went to the Limón company for their re-hearsals. But Martha saw her role as supporting the field. Students were part of that, but not the only part. And as twenty-year-olds we thought we should be the only thing she was concerned about," Muriel Topaz remembered about her student days at Juilliard.[20]

One young faculty member, Betty Jones, disagreed with Martha's eclectic approach of mixing technical styles. "Students should have one teacher and one direction," she told Martha, who listened, but stood her ground. At Juilliard she had opted for a balance where dancers "learned free-flow movement that traveled through space from Humphrey-Limón studies, bound and spiral and floor-based actions from Graham, and line from ballet."[21] In time, most students would find this broad spectrum of possibilities gave them a distinct advantage in the field. [22]

Martha's office off the lobby of the Juilliard Theater held (barely) her desk and one for her secretary, a filing cabinet, an easy chair and a coatrack for visitors. Still, the twelve-by-sixteen space was a bustling center for the entire dance department. Student helpers remembered the way Martha would exclaim, "A-a-a-a-a-ntony!" when he dropped by on his way to teach on the sixth floor. Horst's weekly visits were also causes to stop all office activities, predictably minutes before noon on his Wednesday teaching day. Depositing his coat and cap, he discussed materials being prepared for upcoming workshops, before trotting off to teach his class in group forms. Then it was on to the homey lunchroom or, on occasion, to the school's famed "One O'clock Concert," and then on to teach his courses in preclassic and modern dance forms before he returned to say goodbye.

A lunch break for Martha was taken less to eat than as an opportunity to share ideas with faculty members from other divisions, who enjoyed their conversation among the "dance people." The tensions of her new Juilliard job, with its long work hours and multiple problems, had contributed to her erratic eating patterns. She remembered to drink milk to neutralize the caffeine intake of the ever-present cup of coffee on her desk. She lunched in the cafeteria on a salad or piece of roast chicken. If Martha no longer danced, her exercise consisted of being "on the run," in the corridors, the studios, or off to meetings with administrators. If she did sit at her desk, it was usually to speak on the telephone—a favorite activity that increased significantly as the department grew. (Even so, she was scrupulous about her visits to her doctor and dentist, calling either without hesitation.)

Within the first two years, the division's success was firmly established, bolstered by the significant presence of the field's leading dance artists. Yet from the beginning, the department had its critics. The music faculty openly resented the use of the school's money and resources for anything other than music.

In the spring of 1952, *Collier's* magazine featured an article on Juilliard's new dance department. Titled "Song and Dance College," the writer related: "The school was founded to help talented people produce beautiful sounds, not hurdle through the air with arms and legs every which way."[23] The national attention paid off. Students were thrilled to see their pictures in the publication, although one admitted that they were not ready for public performances themselves. "It took a few years before we were up to it," Muriel, photographed for the article, recalled, "and Martha was not going to put something on the stage that didn't look right." Martha always looked toward the bigger picture: in response to another article on the dance department, Hill wrote to Schuman, "We are not only a 'first' but an 'only.' In other words, we have a monopoly.... Praise the Lord and pass the ammunition."[24]

Auditioning in the spring of 1952, Paul Taylor found Martha "an enthusiastic woman deeply committed to contemporary American dance." She soon became his "Rosetta Stone": "Her loud, clear voice easily transcended Juilliard's noisy halls, and being an authority on all types of dance matters, she knew exactly what she was shouting about." Describing her, Paul recalled, "a minor influence left over from Graham days was still noticeable in the way she wore her hair—a topknot which in her version had migrated off to the left, where it clung precariously, giving her a sprightly, humorous look."[25] A few years later, another student, Michael Uthoff, had a similar impression when he first met Martha in her office, comparing the hairdo to Olive Oyl's. But, he conceded, "when I walked out, I knew I had opened a door to the future, a door opened for me by a matriarch of dance.... I had found a mentor and left that room convinced in the purity and beauty of dance as never before."[26]

Among Taylor's other classmates were Nancy King (Zeckendorf), who went on to dance with the Metropolitan Opera; Carolyn Brown, who became a soloist and Merce Cunningham's partner, and Richard England, director for the second companies of ABT and the Joffrey Ballet. Few stayed long enough to graduate—a kink in the system that Martha never really worked out. If a solid dancing opportunity came along, she advised, one should take it. And many of them did. But Martha reveled in the anxious world of success-driven talents in this conservatory, where everyone was as obsessed with achievement as she had always been.

After a sixteen-year relationship as lovers, Martha and Lefty were married on the evening of 1 October 1952. One month after Lefty was finally granted a divorce, the ceremony took place in the Philadelphia home of Lefty's sister and his brother-in-law, Dr. Robert Gearhart, a Presbyterian minister who officiated.[1] Martha wore a simple but elegant dress and an orchid corsage. Lefty placed a white carnation in his lapel. The Lloyds attended, as did Letita (Tish) Evans, her husband, Paul Frank, and the Zeras.[2] Bill Hill was the only one there from Martha's family.

It was a rare occasion where Martha's "compartmentalized" lives merged briefly. Bill observed: "She led a triple life. She didn't bring them together. But here she had her former students, and Lefty, and then me." He remembered few details about the occasion years later, except that he had paid for the train to get there with the "meat money. We were struggling financially then." The marriage was a complete surprise to him and he was amazed when he saw the couple together for the first time.

"For Martha, Lefty could do no wrong," Bill's wife, Mary Ann said, adding that she could see that they "dearly loved each other and were very compatible. Martha thought the sun rose and set in Lefty. She absolutely adored that man, and it was so not typical for her. She was so feminist, but to turn around and bow down to a man—and that's what she did with Lefty—was such a switch for her." For the first time in anyone's memory, Martha would play the subservient role (not unlike the one her colleagues fretted about as they observed Graham's behavior with Hawkins).

Martha reveled in each moment spent in Lefty's company and some resented that the marriage curtailed her earlier openness among friends. After the marriage, they saw little of Martha socially. Few of her colleagues really interested Lefty, now caught up in an array of duties, having taken over George V. Denny's position as moderator and director of weekly forums and radio broadcasts of *America's Town Meetings of the Air*. Instead, Martha chose social occasions with her own friends selectively.

On her way to meet Lefty at Hortie and Max Zera's apartment for dinner one evening early in their marriage, Martha stopped to buy him slippers, insisting that he put them on when they arrived. Lefty had stubbed his toe coming out of the shower that morning, Martha explained, and she wanted to make him comfortable. Astounded at the lengths she went to please her new husband,

Hortie remarked, "Martha, you'll spoil it for the rest of us!" This was so contradictory to the Martha she knew.

The couple returned to live at Lefty's 332 East Fiftieth Street apartment, while scouting for a place of their own. By the spring, they settled on a Brooklyn Heights area that appealed to Martha as reminiscent of the Village of the 1930s. The spacious second-floor brownstone they found at 210 Columbia Heights had panoramic views of the New York City Harbor, spanning from the Statue of Liberty to the Brooklyn Bridge.

With the scant belongings of a divorcé, Lefty merged his collection of books with Martha's along their high-ceilinged walls, adding his favorite painting by Colorado College's art department head, Bodman Robinson, and starting a collection of old maps of Brooklyn Heights. A new mattress and a sofa bed for the living room (always a well-guarded secret) were their only purchases. Her eclectic assortment of southwestern furniture, Spanish American Bultos, retablos, and pottery sat comfortably with assorted varieties of cacti, needing little more then the sunlight from the massive Victorian windows. Neither wanted more than creature comforts, although the Swiss shower with circular jets that complemented their one-bedroom abode soon became an irreplaceable luxury. Watching the sun set over the Manhattan skyline from their veranda never ceased to delight the couple.

Martha Graham (by all accounts very similar to Lefty in temperament) expressed delight at their marriage, sending a wedding gift of an ancient clay lamb. The cherished Greek artifact was placed on the fireplace mantel to symbolize the peace the couple now shared.

The new Mrs. Davies would later encourage her new stepdaughter Judy to meet Graham after a performance while on tour in California. Her connection "with the Davies clan is deep & extensive," Martha told Judy. "She and Thurston Davies are as twins in age and she loves Lefty very much. I have known Martha Graham since (can you believe it?) 1926 or 1927! And I danced in her company 1929–31. Then we were always at Bennington together. . . . I've cooked Thanksgiving dinner for her—looked out for her mother—all the old associations."[3]

The couple arranged obligatory family gatherings that included cordial dinner parties with the Gearharts in Philadelphia on special occasions; they managed two short trips to Ohio to meet Martha's family before her father died. The first took place when Martha and Lefty drove to Orville. "It was the first time Dad, Mary Ann, and our two boys met Lefty," Bill remembered. They all journeyed to Ironton to visit Lefty's own homestead. Bill remembered, "We liked Lefty very much. He was a great guy. . . . The boys thought Lefty was wonderful. He knew how to get along with kids." After that, when Martha's brother and his family or Lefty's children came to town, Martha played the gracious hostess, shepherding them around town on various sightseeing adventures. (Later Bill's boys visited on their own. But Martha, Mary Ann remembered, "was not the mothering kind. She just taught them how to get around, set them loose on the subway, and that was it. . . . They loved it!")

At the same time that she worked to organize a new household, Martha faced an uphill battle to maintain a division whose position was precarious at best. Unable to draw on funds from Juilliard's endowment (set up exclusively for music), she was aware that the Rockefeller Foundation's Division of Humanities had just begun a new era of arts funding with a three-year grant to the New York City Ballet. Even though the times indicated dance was a growing art form, Juilliard's board of trustees could easily be swayed to eliminate dance by recognizing it as the financial burden that it was. Martha quickly learned to be careful what she asked for. Fortunate in having the full confidence of Schuman and her colleagues, she now had Lefty, a sophisticated mediator and politician, to guide her.

Lefty knew how decisions were made in the business world. He was constantly amazed at his new wife's tenacity, but distressed at the personal toll these events were taking on her. More often than not, he advised Martha to watch her step or to stay out of the fray. Lefty admitted to a certain amount of selfishness in wanting Martha's undivided attention after so many years apart. His own job at Town Hall now demanded mandatory photo shoots, meetings, and social occasions with foreign dignitaries. Lefty delighted in Martha's presence at these official functions when she could manage it.

In a few short years, Thurston Davies had exchanged his position as college president for one of increasing power at the center of Manhattan's political, social, and arts world. During this period of her life, Martha was torn between her duties to Juilliard and her desire to spend more time with Lefty. Increasingly she found herself deferring her responsibilities at Juilliard in favor of important events relating to his position. Fortunately, her involvement in Lefty's work not only broadened her view of the world, but also opened up new perspectives for dance.

For the first time in her life, Martha was part of a wider urban arena with some of the brightest minds in her generation outside of her dance circle. Programming for *America's Town Meetings of the Air* now dealt with critical issues, such as the cold war, internal national security, the defense buildup, political and military commitments abroad, and corruption and leftist infiltration of labor unions among its subjects. These topics and others such as "Is the Fair

Deal Destroying Individual Responsibility?" and "Are Women as Competent as Men in Business" brought Lefty into communication with leading figures of the day, including Norman Cousins, Gerald R. Ford (then a congressman from Michigan), and Adlai Stevenson. Other projects Lefty designed under the auspices of Town Hall were now linked to New York City politicians and agencies as well as national and international ones.

In Lefty's role as emissary, meetings with Senate and House members and President Eisenhower in Washington were common. His plans now included developing a "short course" titled "The Presidency in Moments of Crisis," with the possibility of former presidents Herbert Hoover opening the series and Harry S. Truman closing it. Other events on Lefty's calendar ran the gamut, from meetings with executives from the Ford Foundation, Voice of America, and the Arabian American Oil Company to representatives from the State Department and the United States Information Agency. More and more often Martha was called upon to host special cocktail parties in Brooklyn Heights for groups of lecturers, such as those who were part of a thirteen-week radio series to make "the outside world aware of the interest of American people in Asia."[4]

No doubt at Martha's urging, Lefty managed to program several dance lectures into Town Hall's calendar. In January 1953, following a new Friends of Music series with Paul Hindemith, Darius Milhaud, and Igor Stravinsky conducting, Agnes de Mille gave a lecture, "The World of Ballet." By November, after a Frank Lloyd Wright lecture, Graham gave one, titled "What the Dance Means to Me."[5] Lefty's wife was not only an asset and charming presence at public affairs; she was also a confidante of considerable wisdom who knew how to make things happen. She clearly delighted in her role as Mrs. Thurston Davies.

The dance department at Juilliard was now building a reputation not only for training dancers but also for producing choreography strongly linked to the school's philosophy of sponsoring new contemporary music. Beginning in December 1952, with six performances in the Juilliard Concert Hall, Limón's company presented *The Moor's Pavane* to music by Henry Purcell, and *The Visitation* and *The Exiles* (both to Arnold Schönberg scores) as well as his 1949 *La Malinche* to Norman Lloyd's score. The program also included *El Grito*, a work Limón had created while in residence at Mexico's Palacio de Bellas Artes the year before, to a score by Silvestre Revueltas.[6]

Heartened that dance had become a credible sister art to music, the next month, Martha encouraged student musicians into the dance studio "to do it, to see it, and to talk and read about it."[7] She now taught elective movement sessions for musicians: George McGeary was one piano major who wandered into her class, beginning a lifelong enthusiasm for dance.

In May 1953, the first official public presentation of Juilliard's dance students was set up in lecture-demonstration format. (The cast included Richard Englund, Muriel Topaz, and Paul Taylor.) Tudor's "Let's Be Basic" was paired with Humphrey's "What Dances Are Made Of." Tudor also produced his modest *Exercise Piece* to a string quartet by Arriaga y Balzola. To complete the program, Humphrey staged "Desert Gods," a section from her *Song of the West* to music by Roy Harris.

Limón's company next took the Juilliard stage in January 1954, when the choreographer premiered his *Ode to the Dance* (to a Samuel Barber score) along with Humphrey's *Ruins and Visions*, a new work based on a Stephen Spender poem (and set to Britten's *String Quartets Nos. 1 and 2*). *Dance Observer* called it "an uneven but fascinating work. Its eight scenes, partly realistic, partly imagined, run fluidly into each other and the whole texture is handled with enormous technical facility."[8] (A work of compelling intrigue to Limón, he regretted not being able to revive it over the next years.) Pauline Koner (who always insisted on being billed as guest artist with the company and now demanded the inclusion of a work of her own) danced her *Cassandra* to Copland's "Piano Variations." These concerts drew attention and money into the dance scholarship fund and proved Limón's eagerness to become a part of the department's modern wing.

The next weekend of concerts, with the Juilliard Orchestra and Humphrey as artistic director and guest choreographer, included an extraordinary collection of Doris's choreography with Limón's company dancing her more recent successes *Ritmo Jondo* (Surinach, 1953) and *Night Spell* (Rainier, 1951), along with *Day on Earth* (Copland, 1947), her *Lament for Ignacio Sánchez Mejías* (Lloyd, 1945), and a revival of *Variations and Conclusion* from *New Dance*. Although Humphrey's works were flawlessly danced and produced, she now, as Hering wrote for *Dance Magazine*, devoted her efforts to developing a new company for young dancers "untouched by long years of working alone in a studio and untouched by the bitterness of the frustrated performer."[9] Consequently, her position became respectfully but oddly superseded by Limón's imposing presence onstage, where he virtually claimed ownership of her momentous work. From now on, Limón was to become a key player in Martha's close-knit faculty.

Although educating Juilliard's dance students seemed overshadowed by Martha's more arduous effort to serve the performance field, she knew that academic rigor was essential, even in this conservatory. The minutes (a formality soon abandoned) of a 1954 dance faculty meeting noted some worrying about the exclusion of "dance history and criticism," with the suggestion that Edwin Denby, the prosaic, well-respected dance writer, might come and lecture every other week. Brought in to lecture for several classes, he quickly realized that teaching was not for him. By default, Martha herself became the dance history instructor.[10]

In the next few years Martha found a way to introduce scientific movement study into the curriculum. She did this by bringing in Dr. Lulu Sweigard (her old friend from Teachers College and faculty colleague at New York University from 1931 to 1943) to teach a course titled "Posture and Body Mechanics." Based on theories by Mabel Elsworth Todd that had been a part of Martha's and her early training, Sweigard added her own practice of mental imagery for deep muscle relaxation in what she called "rest position." Many took advantage of Sweigard's "hands-on" pressure point therapy as they lay on long tables. It was an opportunity for students to gain a better understanding of kinesiology and a way to rid the muscular (if not the emotional) stress from the dancer's body—and to nap without guilt after a day of grueling physical torture for some.[11]

In June 1954 Martha and Lefty managed to get away on a much-needed vacation. He preferred cruises on luxury ships to remote places, more for their ability to isolate Martha from the telephone than anything else. It was Martha's secretary from Juilliard who delightedly saw them off on a cruise to Mexico. Her letters flowed to the Maria Cristina Hotel in Mexico City where the couple settled for several weeks, sightseeing, museum-going, and shopping in the bustling city. In them, she tried to make her reports "as unbusinesslike and holidayfied as possible," knowing full well that any information not passed on would cause havoc in the office later on.[12] (Martha's meticulous attention to detail in every scrap of correspondence was by then notorious to anyone working under her command. None dared to take responsibility for any action, no matter how trivial, without her direction.) The next month the couple journeyed to Ohio for a brief visit. It would be the last time Martha saw her aging father.

Never politically active before, Martha now shared Lefty's outrage with the government's McCarthy hearings and the subsequent blacklisting of suspected communist left-wingers. That July of 1954, *America's Town Hall of the Air* reached more than 275 radio stations of the ABC network with "The Army-McCarthy Hearings: Intention and Effect." As part of the broadcast, Lefty maintained as neutral a profile as possible, but his position was well known among their friends. Particularly distressing was the questioning of tap dancer Paul Draper (whom Martha considered the finest tap artist of the time) and his stage partner, musician Larry Adler. Another close friend under investigation was the actress and founding member of the Actors' Studio, Kim Hunter (whose role as Stella in Tennessee Williams's *A Streetcar Named Desire* had created a sensation on Broadway). The couple made a point of continuing these friendships, welcoming them at weekend parties and special occasions whenever possible during that period.[13]

Martha's support was still key to the project at Connecticut College and her word important to major decisions; by the summer of 1954, however, her presence on campus was minimal, only arriving in New London for the last weekend of festival activities. She wrote to Rusty, "I shall be up for the festival Aug. 17–18 and Lefty will be there for as much of it as possible—dependent on Town Hall duties. The Lloyds will know our arrival times."[14] While maintaining her formal position as director "in absentia," the well-disciplined colleagues under her supervision carried on without complaint.

That 1954 season the summer school managed to show a profit. Connecticut College Summer School of the Dance was now financially in the black.[15] With the assistance of a Rockefeller Grant for $13,400—others would come to the aid of modern dance through 1961 and again at a critical point in 1965—it had been possible to award the first American Dance Festival commission of $1,500 to José Limón as "a gesture of friendship to one who has contributed so much to the school."[16] The result was *The Traitor* to Gunther Schuller's music. The all-male piece based on the betrayal of Christ was an immediate success. His mentor Humphrey's *Felipe el Loco* to classic guitar music was a work created for Limón as the flamenco dancer Felix Fernández. The work was disappointing; it received little attention and was never recorded or revived.

Juilliard dance students, having gained professional connections as well as a diploma, now began to chart their careers by taking college teaching positions as Hill had done, sometimes replacing colleagues she had recommended decades earlier. Some found outlets to begin choreographing or established companies of their own, both ballet and modern. Martha's ever-widening network grew as some of the international students returned to their native countries. But the transition from studio to stage for a dancer was a struggle at best and she agreed with Doris Humphrey that an intermediate step should be created for those aspiring to join dance professional companies.

Forging ahead, Martha asked Schuman for help in creating a resident "semi-professional" dance company at Juilliard, with Humphrey the obvious choice as artistic director. Establishing an organization in dance parallel to the Juilliard Opera Theater and the Juilliard Orchestra appealed to Schuman. It would also be an enterprising move for Doris Humphrey who, although receiving the 1954 Capezio Award as choreographer, was now without a company of her own.[17] Limón might have been involved, but his company was on a highly successful tour under the State Department's arrangement with the American National Theater and Academy (ANTA, established in 1935 by Congress to generate the presentation of theatrical productions and stimulate public interest in theater). ANTA was the administrative agent for the new International Exchange Program in the Performing Arts.[18]

It was no coincidence that from ANTA's 1954 contract with the State Department (as a precursor under President Eisenhower to the U.S. government's establishment of the National Endowment for the Arts) until the end of its existence in 1962, Martha Hill was a mainstay of its "panel of experts." Emily Coleman of *Newsweek* and Terry were the only others who served monthly on the unpaid committee for the full eight years. Kirstein was on the panel through January 1960 and Lucia Chase through the summer of 1960—a situation John Martin considered "phony" and self-serving, as both of their companies were applicants for grants.[19] Their replacements were Bill Bales and Kolodney from the Y, most likely at Martha's suggestion. Doris Humphrey served until her death in 1958, Bethsebée de Rothschild from 1955 to 1957, and Agnes de Mille from 1958 to 1962, among others. Undoubtedly, Hill used this powerful position to further support of Graham and Limón, primarily.

For the new company that materialized as Juilliard Dance Theater, sixteen dancers were culled from open auditions. Young professionals—among them, Jeff Duncan, Lola Huth, Don Redlich, and Joyce Trisler—signed contracts allowing small per diems when touring, and the opportunity to work with major choreographers as well as take courses within the extension division of the school. Although the company's operation was run out of the dance department's office, it was designed to run independently. Major blocks of space were given over for evening rehearsals three times a week throughout the semester in the school's largest studio, room 610. Humphrey expressed her appreciation for Juilliard's subsidy "with money for production, orchestra, and the rest—a situation unheard of in the modern dance."[20] JDT, as it was coined, however, offered little advantage to the school's student body; once more, Martha had to contend with regular division students who resented the company's preferential treatment. (To soften the blow, by 1957 a few were selected to join the company.)

In the spring of 1955, Schuman and Hill had their first repertory company on the boards of the Juilliard Theater for JDT's first public performances, featuring Sokolow's *La Primavera*, Humphrey's new *The Rock and the Spring*, and a revival of her 1928 *Life of the Bee*. A subsidized training ground for dancers had been initiated and a mainstream "repertory" concept was now in play.

Fortified with a repertory company at her disposal, a tight alliance of colleagues at Juilliard, and a friendly press, Martha geared up to face the most influential cultural power brokers of the period.

Plans for Lincoln Square, 1955–1956

The American dance scene of the 1950s faced a critical moment with the beginning of public and private support for the art form. The proposal of the Lincoln Center complex—America's first major cultural center—and the choices made during this decade would influence the direction of dance for years to come. Throughout, Martha played a significant role in positioning dance at Juilliard and in the arts. Of all of the considerable challenges that Martha faced, placing modern, or now more often called contemporary concert dance, within Lincoln Center was the greatest.

If Martha shared the general postwar disenchantment, she kept those thoughts in check and hoped for the best. In the fivefold increase of ballet companies and the just-released Ford study of the country's performing arts organizations and institutions, she saw progress.

Experience had taught Martha how to build support in a difficult situation. She knew the value of having a "foot in the door" with or without financial support, and avoided any situation that might arouse controversy until she had a tactical plan in place. Then she would win battles repeatedly for the next twenty years.

It was Kirstein, as managing director and a board member of City Center, whose power was based with those who had money. He now fought ceaselessly to claim the exclusive rights to a theater for the New York City Ballet in the new complex. (He would later add his determination to acquire the planned Juilliard dance facility for NYCB's School of American Ballet, believing from private conversations with the duplicitous Peter Mennin that the space would soon be theirs for the asking.) In the words of his biographer, "Kirstein laid down his life for classical ballet—hustling, animating, inspiring, bullying, dreaming in the service of his great cause," surviving "real and constant anxiety, three nervous breakdowns, bankruptcies, etc." in the "co-creation" with Balanchine of the City Ballet and its affiliated School of American Ballet.[1]

Martin L. Sokol, writing about the New York City Opera, recognized that as early as 1953 "ugly politics and power plays" had entered Lincoln Center's creation.[2] The first organization to be invited into the center was the New York City Ballet to the exclusion of the other performing units who did not "reckon" with Kirstein, he believed. Although Charles M. Spofford is regarded as the "original moving force for Lincoln Center,"[3] a memorandum from Lincoln Kirstein to City Center's Morris and Baum two years earlier had already envisioned "a new building . . . the ideal site would be central; a block, or indeed two blocks. . . . Also included would be the School of American Ballet, which would pay annual rent; possibly to the Juilliard School on a similar basis."[4] Despite evidence that Kirstein was a prime mover behind the Lincoln Square initiative, Sokol praised him for never losing his artistic integrity or sense of honor, though "volatile, impulsive," and "occasionally less than diplomatic"— all characteristics well known to Martha Hill.[5]

The initial exploratory meeting for what would become Lincoln Center was called at the invitation of John D. Rockefeller (JDR) III, widely known as head of the nation's first family of wealth and power. On 25 October 1955, six men concerned about the future of the performing arts in New York City came together. Joining JDR at a private luncheon at the Century Association, the exclusive men's club on West Forty-third Street, were representatives from the Metropolitan Opera Association, Charles M. Spofford, chairman of its executive committee, and Anthony A. Bliss, its president. Also attending were two representatives of the New York Philharmonic-Symphony Society: Floyd Blair, its chairman, and Arthur A. Houghton, Jr., its president; architect Wallace K. Harrison was also present.

JDR III's meeting was called on the heels of the city's urban renewal program under the chairmanship of Robert Moses and Mayor Robert Wagner. Seven days later, JDR III's son David, called Robert Moses into his office to ask the favor of a "rub out" of a narrow street to allow Chase to squeeze an enormous building into Lower Manhattan.[6] By early 1955, they had determined that an eighteen-block area north of Columbus Circle between Sixty-second and Seventieth Streets on the West Side of Manhattan should be redeveloped (although the project was not officially announced by Moses until 29 October 1956). Moses had asked his old friend, architect Harrison, what he thought of a site west of Broadway between Sixty-third and Sixty-fourth Streets for an opera house. Harrison then went to Charles M. Spofford, who in turn moved to win approval from the Metropolitan's "New House" committee and its full board.

For years, JDR III had been a close ally of Robert Moses and had promised to do most of the fund-raising for the commissioner's Lincoln Center project. With JDR III's associate and secretary, Edgar B. Young, in tow, Moses was then brought into the discussions.[7] These men also held separate meetings about a possible arts center with Rockefeller Foundation officers and with Schuman and Mark Schubart, dean of Juilliard, followed by a meeting with Henry Heald, president of New York University. After the initial gathering at the Century Club, Rockefeller "felt strongly" that their small group should be enlarged to bring in other leaders "with a variety of experience and judgment." Both Devereux C. Josephs (chairman of New York Life Insurance, overseer of Harvard University, and trustee of the New York Public Library and the Metropolitan Museum of Art) and Robert E. Blum (vice president of Abraham & Straus department store, president of the Brooklyn Institute of Arts and Sciences, and longtime friend of Moses) agreed to join the group. At a second meeting they elected JDR III chairman.[8]

JDR III then invited Lincoln Kirstein to join the group. Kirstein was by then well known among the wealthiest and most powerful arts patrons as someone "utterly devoted to the art of the dance and, in particular, to the New York City Ballet . . . an idealist and a perfectionist." With "personal knowledge about the arts he [was able to] render opinions that the business and legal members of the group could not supply."[9]

By 1955, Martha began to feel the ramifications of being associated with one of the leading arts institutions in America. Now it was not just the emergence of modern dance that was important to her, but the development of a comprehensive training program within Juilliard's dance curriculum. She told Connecticut College Summer School of the Dance students of "the revolutionary wave" initiated by the work of Graham, Humphrey, and Weidman, as well as Wigman's innovations in Germany in the 1920s: "Anti-ballet at first, the movement gained artistic security, [and in turn] influenced the older style (witness Tudor, Loring, de Mille and Robbins), and now no longer needs to negate ballet."[10] An early champion of new dance forms, Martha now began publicly to shift her support toward a more traditional, ballet-driven approach to dance training—surprisingly close to Kirstein's view.

Martha had always consciously worked to distance herself from controversy, but by 1956 she was increasingly entangled in the complex situation among the potential constituents and arts leaders of Lincoln Square. As Juilliard's dance head, she found herself in a significant power struggle, with Kirstein as a constant agitator. (Those who knew him realized that Kirstein was subject to bipolar mood swings.)[11] At a time in her life when she was least interested in confrontation, Martha was to begin an unrelenting David and Goliath scenario.

Kirstein never suspected that ultimately his most arduous opponent would be Martha Hill. He believed that if you repeat something long enough, it becomes the truth, and he took it upon himself to do the repeating. It was a technique Martha herself had applied for years—one that she and Kirstein would play out to the bitter end.

The committee's "search" for a dance constituent proved to be a "more intractable problem" than any had anticipated. In 1956, the exploratory committee had expected the New York City Ballet to join. But as a part of the City

Center of Music and Drama, the company was not an independent institution. "Early in the fight Kirstein used more direct tactics," and the battle for control of the State Theater was "waged on many fronts."[12] Without question, it was Kirstein's determination to claim a theater for NYCB apart from its mother organization that influenced the final outcome.

Kirstein continued to proselytize for "a single American Ballet company"; ruthless in his disregard of other dance institutions, he considered Hill's dance division a mild threat that could easily be disposed of at the right time.[13] In a letter dated 10 November 1956 to his committee, he attacked the quality of the dancing at the Metropolitan Opera's own ballet school where "there are many mothers who ignorantly think that entrance into the school guarantees their daughter's career on the great stage of the Met." He then degrades the ballet school by referring to its "rather (sub-)subsistence level." [14]

If with this denigration Kirstein had effectively eliminated the Metropolitan Opera Ballet from inclusion at Lincoln Square; his next contenders, however, would be more difficult to eliminate. Once aware of a potential coup in favor of Balanchine's company, directors Lucia Chase and Oliver Smith of American Ballet Theatre asked the committee to be included in their discussions.[15] To Chase's credit, she continued to hound the committee, alerting others, including Martha Hill, of the situation. (Another venture fighting for attention was Rebecca Harkness's new ballet company with Robert Joffrey at her side.) Now faced with a "constituent status" issue, with the Metropolitan and the Philharmonic insisting on "only one institution sponsoring each art" policy, ABT's request created a bothersome state of "uncertainty" for committee members.

On 13 December 1956, Kirstein began an outright attack on Julliard's dance division. His first weapon was an eighteen-section memorandum to Young on the educational facilities in the Lincoln Square Project: "since it seems likely that the Juilliard School of Music will be the chosen instrument to head the educational services of the development." He advised, "It may be well to analyze those services other than the musical instruction." He first dismissed Juilliard's opera theater wing for its "severe restriction of the taste of the administrative personnel and the lack-lustre quality of [its] over-all direction and performance." His typed memo then set the stage for the dance division's demise: "The Juillard [sic] formed a Department of the Dance, under the direction of Miss Martha Hill, some five years ago. Since 1936, Miss Hill has been in charge of the Bennington (Vermont) School of the Modern (free-form, concert, idiosyncratic) dance and has been associated with the Modern Dancers: Martha Graham, Doris Humphries [sic], Charles Weidman, and the musical accompanist, Luis [sic] Horst." He goes on to explain, "During the decade 1935–1945 some interesting, individualistic and highly esoteric special work was created by the dancers, under the general administration of Miss Hill who is extremely energetic, capable and intelligent. But the Modern Dance declined with the disappearance of its chief protagonists. A second generation of dancers of star caliber never appeared. Miss Hill accommodated the remnants of the Bennington staff at Juillard [sic]. William Schumann [sic] had composed ballets for Martha Graham, is interested in theater, and for a variety of reasons, legitimate in themselves, but inoperative in practice, adopted Miss Hill's suggestions for a dance-division."[16]

In this unsigned document where he refers to himself in third person, Kirstein demonstrates his adept means of persuasion. The committee, made up primarily of businessmen with little personal knowledge of dance, were prepared to take this widely respected theater- and art-world man at his word. His comments then narrow to one of Balanchine's chief competitors: " The Juillrad [sic] Dance Division, recognizing the need for an extension into the fifties of the classic theatrical traditional dance (ballet) engaged Antony Tudor, a British born ex-dancer and choreographer of repute, who himself was nearest in philosophy to the free-form idiosyncratic modern-type dance."[17]

Kirstein had rightly pointed out that the technical level of the division's college-age students, particularly in ballet, was far below standard; this would be a constant challenge to the ballet faculty. In the first years of the department, Martha had cleverly focused the attention in public performances on faculty members, and then on the Juilliard Dance Theater, keeping direct criticism of the department's students to a minimum. Within the school's confines, she relied on Horst's work with student choreographers to give sophistication to informal workshop presentations and Juilliard's "one o'clock concert" series, with ballet seldom on the programs.

Tudor was a thorn in Kirstein's side, Martha knew, not only because of his brilliance as a choreographer (that some believed exceeded Balanchine's) but because of his continued association with the Metropolitan Opera Ballet and American Ballet Theatre. Kirstein reiterated Tudor's reputation for being very slow in creating new work and claimed that the choreographer could not deal with prescribed union time constraints—a red flag for the businessmen in the group.

Kirstein's letter then goes on to denounce the division's objectives, concluding, "The ballet students at the Juillard [sic] start too old to be well trained and are encumbered by a general-education program. . . . [T]he Juillard [sic] Dance Department has produced no dancer or choreographer of quality, and while the dance-division may make its way, it has no connection with any major ballet organization and no standing in the professional dance-education of the nation." [18] Given a chance to defend her position, Martha would certainly have named the outstanding first group of Juilliard dancers, who were already making their mark in the field. But she was never consulted.

Ironically, this volatile situation brewed during the most fulfilling time of Martha and Lefty's life together. Lefty's position at Town Hall was coming to a close. By August 1955, with attendance diminishing, costs rising, and the "undisputed competition of radio and television," the diversified program of speakers on "public affairs, civic, national and international, authors, critics in all fields of the arts" forged into its last year as a "free platform as a non-profit, non-sectarian, non-discriminatory organization devoted to adult education and to better citizenship." After 928 programs, *America's Town Hall of the Air* was broadcast for the last time. Lefty helped work out Town Hall's reorganization and new affiliation with New York University and accepted another position that would consume and delight the couple for the next few years. [19]

Although Martha had distanced herself from involvement in Connecticut College Summer School of the Dance, for the following four years she was listed as codirector (on leave). Rusty, as assistant professor of physical education, remained at the helm of the project—a frustrating situation for her at best. [20] Whatever the external administrative arrangement, Martha served as the most authorative voice. In writer Jack Anderson's words, she was "an arbiter of festival policies and aesthetics." [21]

After Rusty's death in April 1959, Jeanette Schlottmann (Roosevelt) was her replacement as a full-time dance instructor at the college and director of a summer school that had fast become a leading center for dance study. [22] Not wanting to disturb an operation that was running smoothly (and not willing to give up her powerful position), Martha continued as the school's de facto leader, agreeing to remain on the festival's board (which in her mind was "a communal enterprise" anyway), attending several meetings a year, communicating by phone, and only appearing for important events on campus.

Martha and Lefty both had well-filled month-at-a-glance calendars. Lefty's September 1956 notations show that most of their evenings were spent at social events connected to work. A rare weekend was spent at the Limón farm in New Jersey after a Princeton-Rutgers football game. He recorded frequent meetings with friends for drinks at the Princeton Club's Tiger Bar, and jotted down important dates for Martha as well. (A 3 September entry notes, "The Dance Office opens.")

In a letter to his daughter Judy, Lefty wrote how busy Martha was, arranging an upcoming CBS film shoot for "Let's Take a Trip" at Juilliard. He added,

"I have been commuting to Washington. We are both very happy about the way everything is developing." Martha often added a brief message at the end of his letters; this time she wrote, "I've just come over to the office & we're on our way to the United Nations."[23]

Lefty had begun to work as a consultant for the Port Authority; throughout the fall, his own hectic schedule included planning for a massive Brooklyn waterfront renovation.[24] At the same time, he won the position of head of the American Pavilion at the upcoming World's Fair in Brussels.

Lefty rushed into a flurry of conferences in Washington, D.C., and Brussels planning events. Over a period of fifteen days, after Monday-morning meetings at the Port Authority office, he helicoptered to La Guardia Airport for a plane to Washington. Although his job would complicate Martha's own work schedule, they both knew it was a chance of a lifetime. She would find a way to leave her own commitments behind, she promised him. But over his next two-and-a-half years on the job, Martha only managed to leave Juilliard for two successive spring terms.

That same September of 1956, her father, then living in the Mennonite Home for the Aged in Orville, Ohio, died at eighty-eight. Martha came home for the funeral, "forever grateful" to her brother and sister-in-law who had taken care of her parents for years.[25] The estate was settled among its heirs, Martha, Bill, and the Phelps children.

The 1955–1956 year was a strong one for the dance department at Juilliard. At season's end, as part of Juilliard's Fiftieth Anniversary Celebration and Festival of American Music series, Limón created his monumental *Variations on a Theme* (titled *There is a Time* in subsequent performances). Created with an elegant commissioned score for orchestra by Norman Dello Joio, the work was an immediate success.

Writing later about the work, Martha referred to its use of the "never ending, all-embracing, all inclusive circle . . . which is the central theme, to be varied in space and in the bodies of the dancers." Quoting a Robert Frost poem, she added, "We dance round in a ring and suppose / But the Secret sits in the middle and knows."[26] In a broader sense, when Martha wrote about *There is a Time*, she could have been speaking about her own life in dance. The dance embodied the kind she had long sought to champion.

With the revival of Humphrey's 1934 collaboration with Vivian Fine, *The Race of Life*, and the premiere of the choreographer's *Dawn in New York* to music by Hunter Johnson, the celebration program not only illustrated the music and dance collaborations that had begun at Bennington, but the maturing of concert dance as an art form in its own right.

In the fall semester of 1956, I was one of the starry-eyed first-year students. Although I had sailed confidently through the audition process the previous spring, the actual day of arrival was another matter. In line to register for courses—just as Ethel Winter had at Bennington—I met the woman who would convince me that I was in the right place.

Martha Hill focused on each person before her with the precision of an analyst. After the first few sentences, I knew that she was approachable and in charge. Later, Martha met my father Brydon Mansfield, a man desperately disorganized at his first visit to Juilliard. He said, "I have three questions. Who is Martha Hill? Has my daughter Janet finished her music placement exam? And can you tell me where the nearest men's room is?" She answered him with mercifully matched rapid-fire accuracy, "I am Martha Hill. Janet is on a tour of the building, and the men's room is down the corridor to the right!" My father never once doubted that his daughter was in safe hands for the next four years of college in the big city. Martha had the knack of memorizing a name by repeating it during a first encounter, and remembering it on the second, whether days, or years later. She never forgot meeting my father, the "charming" Mr. Mansfield, that day—an event they laughed about at my graduation.

Throughout those years I was seldom aware that Martha had any other life but the one I observed at Juilliard. I vaguely recalled Martha's trips to Brussels but they seemed incidental to her steady authority over my college career. How shocking now to count up the months that she was away!

But with the Brussels assignment, the couple's life had changed dramatically. Lefty flew to Paris and Brussels and back to Washington in December to discuss Ed Stone's designs for the American Pavilion, finally taking a leave of absence from the Port Authority to join the U.S. government project full-time in January.

By the new year of 1957, the *New York Times* formally announced that Dr. Thurston J. Davies was named as executive director of the Office of the U.S. Commissioner General to the Brussels World's Fair of 1958. Lefty's photograph accompanied the news article, captioned "Aide for Brussels Fair Named by U.S. Agency." The item stated that the position "reflected the importance attached by the U.S. Government to American participation in the Brussels Fair, the first world's fair to be held since N.Y.'s huge exhibition in 1939."[27] That summer Lefty's calling card claimed 244–246 Rue de la Loi as his address in Brussels, as he oversaw the building of the pavilion, reported by *Time* magazine to be "as wide as Rome's coliseum with plastic roof and honeycomb walls."[28]

Back home, the drama continued to unfold among the Lincoln Square committee members, as evidenced in their letters to Ed Young. Although Schuman was able to protect Martha from direct involvement with internal politics, he did ask her to articulate the division's philosophical mission in writing. In conversations with Graham, Horst, Humphrey, Limón, and Tudor, she worked to solidify the idea that the combination of ballet and modern idioms were not only complementary units of study, but necessary to each other in training future dancers. Humphrey and Limón were not enthusiastic, asking, "Why do we need ballet when we can do this on our own?" Both agreed to go along with Martha's plan but confessed that they were never happy about the decision.

Martha's vision of a dance art that went beyond a single style was diametrically opposed to Kirstein's. She had learned that the creation of an equal playing field was the best environment for emerging talent. Competition was not only completely American in character; it opened up broader possibilities for diversity.

PART VII

Between Two Worlds

Personal letters from Martha were always handwritten and brief, basically a whereabouts report. Her correspondence to family and friends was usually limited to postcards from her travels. A letter meant the inclusion of genuine news, as in one addressed to José at his new living quarters in the Hotel Ruxton, 50 West Seventy-second Street. "You probably saw the newspaper announcement of the ANTA meeting. There appears to be a somewhat different climate of opinion at headquarters in Washington in regard to choice of artists & groups for export which I'll tell you about when I see you in NL."[1] Kirstein had first been named adviser in 1954 to the State Department for ANTA's foreign tours and his strong influence on the panel was the issue here. But as Humphrey was also on the panel with Hill, Limón's company had sure support.

The summer of 1957 was one of the most relaxed of Martha's married life. Bill Hill brought his family to town for a week's vacation, and Martha organized family outings that included trips to the Bronx Zoo and the beach at Coney Island. But with the next project always on her mind, she wrote to José, "I've just had a wire from Chavez to phone him this coming Tuesday at 4 p.m. at the Barbizon Plaza Hotel which I shall do, and will hope to see him. Love to you and Pauline, Martha," adding, "Will see you next Friday! Hurrah!"[2]

Their correspondence reveals how much José relied upon Martha and her support of his career. She was one of the three women José depended upon, along with Doris and Pauline. For example, as he wrestled with possibilities for music to accompany his latest creation, *Blue Roses* (based on Tennessee Williams's *The Glass Menagerie*), it was Martha who negotiated with composers on Limón's behalf, this time getting an arrangement of composer Paul Bowles's themes for the August premiere at Palmer auditorium. As usual, it was Doris who advised José choreographically and Pauline who organized rehearsals, designed the costumes, and took care of all financial and practical matters.

In another letter to Pauline and José, in 1957, Martha gives a sense of her increasingly distant relationship with the Summer School of Dance (celebrating its tenth anniversary with Graham back on the festival performance roster). Time with Lefty, who was now preparing for a move to Brussels, and her recovery from a hellish year at Juilliard, had become priorities. In the letter, she discusses her plans to arrive in New London for the festival's opening, adding, "Lefty and I go to Atlantic City for some surf August 7–11 but otherwise I expect to be here and have time to do anything you might need." Then, in an unusual admission, Martha added, "I'm coming out of the Juilliard doldrums now. I had a bad case of Juilliard-induced allergy to paper work. So I've been being housewifely and flower-gardenish as the best antidote for that malady & Lefty says he's never seen me so relaxed. I miss you—and love you—and look forward to seeing you at Festival, Ever, Martha."[3]

When Martha returned to Juilliard's academic school year of 1957–58, the number of dance students had risen to 109: seventy-five regular and thirty-four enrolled as part-time students in the extension division. (This number included members of Juilliard Dance Theater who had the option of taking courses.) As Lefty had noted in his calendar, her first project of the school year was to superintend a CBS film crew when they arrived to shoot an episode of the children's television series *Let's Take a Trip*. The program featured a visit to the bustling Saturday Preparatory Division dance classes for children and to a Juilliard Dance Theater rehearsal conducted by Humphrey. Although she had managed a film shoot for Humphrey's *Ritmo Jondo* in the winter of 1954, this time the television crew's presence stirred interest in preserving all of the division's work on film. Martha made a plea to Schuman for money: "Every music concert is recorded for posterity at Juilliard, why not every dance concert?"[4] Receiving an annual stipend of $500 pegged for the task of filming each work presented at the major concerts of the year, Martha hired filmmaker Dwight Godwin and set aside a shooting day in the theater starting with that spring's performances.[5]

Throughout her career, Martha had learned to "hold her cards close to her chest"—an expression she sometimes used to describe others. Now at Juilliard every aspect of the division's functioning seemed to require her constant monitoring. In the fall of 1957, funding for a full-time administrative assistant was advanced; June Dunbar was hired to cover Martha's planned leave-of-absence for the spring semester. But June would soon discover that her boss was not about to allow others to make any decisions on her behalf, whether she was present or not.

For Dunbar, the transition was shaky at best. "Martha asked me to keep her chair warm. . . . I was a person who was very much involved in the day-to-day running of the department . . . being sure the grades got in, exams were scheduled . . . and all that sort of stuff." Once in the position, Vassar-educated Dunbar's statuesque presence and sophisticated demeanor immediately impressed Juilliard's administrators.

At first, Martha appreciated the opportunity to delegate responsibility, as Lefty had encouraged her to do. But before long, she began to suspect that June was vying for her job, and tensions arose. Bewildered, June confessed that it was "very, very difficult for me to work with Martha Hill, who is a strong-willed woman. She didn't recognize that some valid ideas concerning the Dance Division might come from other people. She was not a very generous collaborator in that respect and I felt that I was always being corrected or dismissed for not having her thought exactly, in duplicate form, on a parallel track. So, I began to feel quite frustrated."

Martha finally left her Juilliard post in Dunbar's hands on 19 November 1957, boarding the SS *United States* with Lefty and arriving in Brussels to prepare for the opening of the fair. June wrote, "I hope that your crossing was pleasant and festive, and that you had some time to relax before starting a busy schedule in Belgium," adding about the Juilliard schedule, "I certainly don't know how you manage to get through the day with such ease."[6]

Earlier, Limón had returned from a State Department tour in Europe fired with an idea for a dance that paid homage to the courage of the people in war-torn Poland. Martha and Bill Schuman had "endorsed the scheme," leaving June to undertake details of the *Missa Brevis* production involving orchestra, a chorus of sixteen, and Juilliard Dance Theater members supplementing his professional company, for a total of twenty-two dancers.[7] By the end of the semester, as her exhausted replacement, June enviously referred to Martha's reports of "French lessons and socializing" that included dinner with Queen Mother Elizabeth of Belgium.

In the meantime, with Martha Hill safely on her way to Europe and beyond earshot, Kirstein began to attack the dance department directly. He wrote to Young that beyond its teaching of ballet, he was sure that Schuman wanted "to continue the rather loose instruction in the Modern Dance which is the only thing his very much older students could be able to learn, and neither of these instructions could do a professional dance company of acrobatic virtuosi much good."[8] Further, the unsuccessful department's resources, in Kirstein's view, were "wastefully bungled."[9]

Throughout, Schuman refused to give way. Increasingly outspoken, he advocated "an educational premise of choice in a democratic society"—a position he had held from the beginning. Kirstein and Balanchine believed in ballet as a set vocabulary, he explained: "That's a perfectly legitimate view for any performing artist to have, but I never considered it legitimate for an educator to have. I think an educator has to have a much broader view." Reiterating Martha's beliefs (with rationales solidly grounded in progressive thought as well), he continued, "Whether or not [one] likes the materials has nothing to do with it. You have to present them, so there's a choice, unless you have a totalitarian approach to education. I've always believed that . . . in a democratic society art should be elite, in terms of the best, but the democratic side comes in the dissemination of the product of art, which should be available to everybody, and the study of art, which should be available to everybody."[10]

Although Bill Schuman regularly updated Martha on the latest political maneuvers over the new Lincoln Center project, distance allowed Martha to be removed from the controversy. She also had insider reports from an acquaintance, Dr. George Stoddard, a man known for fairness while dean of New York University.

Stoddard had been appointed chair of the exploratory committee on the dance for the project in January 1957.[11] The new committee included Young, dance critics Martin and Terry as consultants, a Mr. Knauth as "rapporteur," and Kirstein. Stoddard encountered "rigid opposition and fears of an artistic disaster" from this all-male contingent when he bravely (if naïvely) suggested, first to Lucia Chase and then to Kirstein, a possible merger of American Ballet Theatre and New York City Ballet.[12] Throughout the following months, Chase pressed for the inclusion of ABT and Stoddard tried again to find a corporate framework to accommodate both companies. Kirstein rejected the idea as ludicrous.

On 6 March 1957 Stoddard distributed a draft statement from the exploratory committee on the eventual place of dance in Lincoln Center. A month later, after weighing the strengths and weaknesses of each to determine which company "best met the criteria for inclusion in Lincoln Center" or whether a new one should be created, the committee concluded that the NYCB should be chosen. Encouraged, Kirstein proceeded to lay plans, but the decision was far from settled upon.

It took an additional two years for the various committees on dance for the Lincoln Center project to change the "principle of exclusivity" into "a doctrine of primacy." To move the situation forward, the thirteen-member Advisory Council on the Dance of Lincoln Center was formed to include Chase, Martha Graham, Kolodney of the Ninety-second Street Y, and Schuman. (Martha Hill was never invited to participate.) Its first meeting was assembled by JDR III in his office at 30 Rockefeller Plaza on 13 January 1958. Rockefeller's opening remarks emphasized the "importance of artistic and financial autonomy for each constituent unit." When he asked for opinions, several offered them candidly. "Mr. Fleischmann spoke enthusiastically in favor of the formation of one great Ballet Company in America," the minutes recorded. Chase added, "A home [was] essential to a Ballet Company if that Company was to rank with Europe's finest." Kolodney interjected that "since the American community already accepted Ballet, the Center Dance Constituent concept should embrace other

Dance forms which needed help for their growth and acceptance." Graham said she would welcome "a combined Dance organization that would afford contemporary dance the opportunity of working together with Ballet."

Schuman asked the hard question that others had avoided: Can a single company do the bidding of the various stylistic and choreographic demands made on it? Before the meeting adjourned, discussion centered around "a single company of sufficient size to serve ideally the specialized forms of the Contemporary Dance, the Classical Ballet and Modern Ballet."[13]

Another opportunity for modern dance to "make its break through to popular recognition" was about to fail, just as Marcia Siegal had described the earlier New York City Dance Theatre attempt in 1949.[14] Once again the concept of individualism at the core of modern dance became insurmountable. Yet a single ruling artistic director from the ballet idiom was not seen as a problem. If settling on the New York City Ballet had been a foregone conclusion to the men this committee was "advising," they were now hearing comments very different from those of Kirstein—who remained uncharacteristically quiet throughout the January 1958 meeting except to submit that the techniques of the ballet "had expanded and absorbed much from modern dance."

The group's next meeting on 11 February 1958 generated more intense discussions after the "in confidence" announcement of the appointment of Philip Johnson as architect of the new dance theater. (Soon after, the Avery Architecture and Fine Arts Library at Columbia displayed Johnson's model of the State Theater in its lobby.) Sensing that a theater for contemporary dance was never seriously considered part of the plan, Kolodney then asked for "flexibility of design of several of the other Lincoln Center auditoria." He then suggested "a 500 seat recital hall might be capable of staging a dance recital." Schuman took the opportunity to submit his idea for the creation of "an expanded co. of up to 150 dancers perhaps two years ahead of the completion of the Dance Theater for the field of contemporary dance." Graham pointed out that a ballet training foundation was important in the field of contemporary Dance. As if coached by Martha Hill for the occasion, Graham's uncharacteristic stance seemed to have made an impression. Ballet Theatre Foundation's directors continued to press for inclusion by asking that Lincoln Center's ballet facilities serve as a home for a new national ballet company. This idea was followed by discussion about whether a strong Lincoln Center Ballet Company would spell the extinction of the three existing ballet companies."[15] (Kirstein was obviously way ahead of this group in his own planning for NYCB's future.)

By 1959, W. McNeil Lowry's leadership for the Division of the Humanities and the Arts of the Ford Foundation provided a grant to Ballet Society for a survey of the teaching of ballet in America. Soon after, scholarship grants were in place for gifted dancers from all over the country to attend the School of the American Ballet—what Balanchine and Kirstein called "Mac's efforts to strengthen dance in the provinces."[16] Terry in the *Tribune* would label this "a scandal" and quote Hill as calling it "an unhealthy monopoly." The result would dramatically impact the future of American ballet with the establishment of satellite schools under NYCB's wing.[17]

The minutes for the next advisory council meeting make it clear that a home for American Ballet Theatre at Lincoln Center was not in the cards. Stoddard's "merger" efforts were gradually worn down by Kirstein's nonstop maneuvers, facts carefully concealed from the public. With no direct affirmation announced, Martin and Terry did not take the story to the press. When Martha Hill received the news, she told Schuman that the move was a travesty. Much preferring ABT as a company, Martha was never an advocate of the work of Balanchine or his New York City Ballet: she disliked what she considered Balanchine's lack of musicality, the exaggerated and fractured lines of the dancers, and, in her opinion, their unfeeling and cold performance style.

The subject now moved on to a school for dance at Lincoln Center. In a report to the advisory group, one paragraph sounded an alarm to Graham and her colleagues: "The committee believes that an active ballet school in direct association with the Constituent Unit of the Dance will be an important feature of Lincoln Center." It was also explicitly stated that when the advisory committee was dismantled, "arranging the coordination" with Juilliard's dance division "must eventually exist."[18]

Taking this as a positive sign, Bill Schuman wrote to Martha while in Brussels about possible relationships for a resident repertory company at the new center to be called the Lincoln Square Dance Theater. This center could potentially serve students and graduates as Juilliard Dance Theater had, he reasoned, especially as "Juilliard Dance Division already has this relationship with the Metropolitan Opera Company Ballet." But as he lobbied for a resident company somehow connected to Juilliard, Schuman soon realized that, for Kirstein's committee, theater designs were clearly referenced from a "ballet standpoint"; that is, a "sufficiently large" dance theater stage for sets and choreography with audience capacity matching Brooklyn Academy of Music's of 2,200.[19]

At one of the last sessions of the committee on training and education (again taking place while Martha was in Europe), Schuman gave a report on Juilliard's relations with the Lincoln Center Board. Because of the training requirements of a resident dance company, the Metropolitan Opera Ballet, and potentially the repertory drama group might work together with the newly formed Dance Department of the Juilliard School, "sharing of staff choreographers and integrating dance students." He visualized the Juilliard Dance Department "virtually as a Junior Performing Company."[20] The idea dismayed some on the committee as unrealistic, but both Hill and Schuman would return to it.

Early planning for Juilliard's move from Claremont Avenue as a constituent at Lincoln Square had begun in earnest by the spring of 1957—although at about the same time, Kirstein's "rather loose instruction in the Modern Dance" memo had circulated in Rockefeller's circle. Once Martha returned to the States she began to work with her dance faculty and architects Pietro Belluschi and Eduardo F. Catalano, who were commissioned to design the complex (in what is now labeled "Brutalist-style"). In the past, Martha had foreseen the demands of being associated with a leading arts institution. But creating a place for dance at Lincoln Center would be a challenge beyond imagination.

These early discussions with the architects determined the square feet needed for an estimated two studios, with the optimum established of forty-five by forty-five feet and thirty feet high. After two years, the number of studios had grown to six, with seven additional rooms for offices and dressing areas in the plans. Hill, Limón, and Tudor served as consultants with de Mille, Holm, and Jerome Robbins as advisers. Information was gathered from around the world, with the facilities of the Royal Danish, the Royal Ballet of London, and the Jooss School in Essen, Germany, as well as Wigman's studio in Berlin, examined. The group studied each set of revised blueprints. More toilets for visitors, staff, and faculty on the rehearsal floor were needed, as well as additional locker room space and a drying room for studio clothes, they determined.

Meanwhile, progress was being made with the actual building of Lincoln Center. Structures began to rise on the city blocks that bordered Broadway's drug-infested area (known as "Needle Park" by seasoned New Yorkers). When Robert Moses's Title I bill passed, slum clearance funds were quickly spent. Local community outcry escalated as the city condemned and relocated thousands of low-income tenants to the Bronx and Harlem. Once evacuated, rows of six-story tenements were leveled at breakneck speed and their evicted tenants relocated to the more than one hundred new housing projects rising on the fringes of the city.

With June Dunbar running the department, Juilliard Dance Theater once again presented outstanding repertory for its April 1958 concert series: Donald McKayle's *Out of the Chrysalis*, Sokolow's *Session '58*, and Humphrey's new *Descent into the Dream*. But it was Limón's completed ensemble work, *Missa Brevis*, that stood out, according to Louis Horst, with its "eloquent beauty and compassion and simple directness" that created "an aura of shining nobility that struck home with overwhelming power."[21] With the striking benefit of Juilliard's musicians for Kodály's vital score, *Missa Brevis* offered an incomparable experience. (Only American Dance Festival in New London was able to produce as fine a repertory series—although less and less with live music—in quality and scope. That summer, seven choreographers produced a range of works as avant-garde as Merce Cunningham's *Antic Meet* and as classic as Humphrey's 1929 *Life of the Bee* and her 1953 *Ritmo Jondo*.)

Among the ever-critical world of creative artists, modern dance still had its dissenters—evidenced when Anton Kodály expressed his displeasure with Limón's interpretation of his music. José recalled Martha Hill's behind-the-scenes role in placating the enraged composer after seeing Jac Venza's National Education Television film of the choreographer's *Missa Brevis* for the first time. Limón remembered that Kodály called the work

> ugly, the choreography crude, the dancing worse, the costumes terrible. Martha Hill, who had accompanied me to this painful encounter, explained that this was a dance idiom and style so indigenous to this country, and in consequence strange and jarring to one accustomed only to the European styles, that perhaps further experience and familiarity with contemporary dance styles would modify his opinion. After all, modern music had at first sounded crude and ugly. This she did with gentle tact and calm. Somewhat mollified . . . We parted in a cordial mood—he even conceded that parts of the dance were not too unprepossessing. They were interesting, even impressive.[22]

Of the two years and seven months of Lefty's tenure running the American Pavilion of the World's Fair, he calculated that Martha had been with him for this extraordinary time in his career for a total of twelve months. But while *Missa Brevis* was being created at Juilliard, and Kirstein and Schuman headed up their Rockefeller committees, Martha was organizing "at-home" entertainment arrangements with her housekeeper, delighting in the local food markets and relaxing at the corner café with the international edition of the *Herald Tribune*.

In the spring of 1958, as Helen Tamiris took up the banner for the inclusion of modern dance at Lincoln Center, June's letters to Martha dealt with Juilliard Dance Theater budgets, mentioning in passing that the *New York Times* reported the Sputnik II model was attracting about the same number of crowds as the fashion parade at the American pavilion, and that in thirty-six hours the fairgrounds were transformed from acres of construction materials into a magnificent park.[23] In correspondence with his daughters, Lefty regularly mentioned the couple's activities in the midst of a bevy of concerts, receptions, dinner parties, and special events. By May 1958, he was fully engaged in World's Fair activities, lunching with the Austrian Delegation at the Vatican, viewing Kabuki and fireworks at the Japanese pavilion opening, or marshaling Benny Goodman and his band for a week of performances.

The couple spent a four-day weekend in Paris that June, returning for an evening concert by Leontyne Price at the fair. Then they were back to an intense schedule of hosting throughout the summer. Their calendar was crammed with notations for dinner dates and cocktail parties, followed by events sponsored by the U.S. government such as the Harlem Globetrotters and a Byron Janis concert. When Hortie and Max Zera arrived, Martha delighted in bustling her friends from one event to another, seeing a production of *Wonderful Town*, American Ballet Theatre, and performances by the Bolshoi Ballet. When conductor Fred Prausnitz and Bill Schuman were on the scene for performances of the Juilliard Orchestra that month, Mr. and Mrs. Davies were there to welcome them.

Agnes de Mille came to the fair amid presentations of jazz concerts, the MIT Choral Society, and a Rosalyn Turich recital. Agnes observed that the American Pavilion "was the most popular in the whole fairgrounds, not because it was the most beautiful—and it was—but because it had two advantages: It had a big pool outside with a wide lip on which people could sit and put their feet in the water when they got tired, and it had the only free toilets on the grounds."[24] Agnes de Mille was not the only one to realize that Balanchine's New York City Ballet had not been invited to perform at the fair (an interesting omission in light of the ongoing controversy back in Manhattan). Instead, the Davies escorted de Mille to Jerome Robbins's *Ballets USA*, offering what the couple considered a perfect example of America's dance in its amalgam of ballet and modern.

At the end of July 1958 Martha and Lefty traveled to Amsterdam for a week of sightseeing and precious time together, taking a city boat trip, going to the flower markets, visiting the towns of Marken and Volendam, and enjoying an Aalameer boat trip. They visited the Rijksmuseum and the Rembrandt House and browsed in department stores. The couple then returned to a second month in Brussels and a schedule at the American Pavilion crammed with a whirlwind of concerts by pianists Ralph Kirkpatrick, John Browning, and the New York Woodwind Quintet. And they savored performances by the Moscow Circus and Moisseev's Dance Ensemble, all with the usual evening rounds of receptions and cocktail parties.

The couple continued to greet a constant stream of visitors to the fair before Martha headed back to New York on 9 September aboard the *Rotterdam*. After ten full months together, she left her husband in the capable hands of their housekeeper along with a list of instructions. Parting this time was more difficult: with the situation facing Martha at Juilliard she could not foresee a date of return.

Arriving in New York Harbor on 17 September 1958, she moved into temporary quarters at Brooklyn's Hotel Rossert, as renovations on the apartment at 210 were not yet completed. Exhausted, she contracted a bronchial infection that took several weeks to overcome.

Lefty's correspondence described his bustling schedule. "Who ever said the pace of this fair would slacken off, come Sept. 1 was crazy. We've had an extremely busy week & I just got back from the office," he wrote, detailing concerts, dinner parties, and briefing sessions. "I miss you and love you more all the time," and he added, "Have you any idea when you might return?"[25] It is a question Lefty asked Martha again and again in his letters.

Back home, Martha was quickly immersed in the battle for modern dance representation at Lincoln Center. Planning sessions were ongoing for Manhattan's new arts center at Lincoln Square as President Dwight D. Eisenhower, shovel in hand, "broke ground" at an official ceremony on 14 May 1959. Tudor had joined Martha in discussions with the Juilliard architects, asking for the "elimination of uniformity" for the dance studios, which should be equipped with state-of-the-art audio, filming, and video systems. Martha insisted on windows at least eight feet from the floor to allow for mirrors. Soon after, Limón participated, too, testing samples of the all-important "sprung" flooring and determining whether they should be covered with Balanchine's preferred flooring of gray "battleship" linoleum or the traditional choice of tung oil–treated maple. They chose wood. Their input into the wood-paneled Juilliard theater design with its gracious seating arrangement for a capacity of just over one thousand would result in what they agreed was the finest dance theater in the country. But even as the dance faculty was making architectural decisions at Juilliard, John D. Rockefeller III's committee was making more critical decisions about the future of the "dance theater" on the plaza—to the exclusion of the dance community.

Little by little, tension mounted as information about what would be known as Lincoln Center and the New York State Theater (originally named Theater for the Dance and Operetta), found its way to the New York press. Perhaps the fullest disclosure came from Horst's little *Dance Observer* journal. Its the first editorial on the subject, Arthur Todd's "Which Direction for Dance at Lincoln Center?" reported on "the most provocative dance news of the moment in America. . . . Just where American modern dance, other domestic ballet companies or the great foreign ballet organizations . . . could fit into all this is at the moment uncertain. This is but one of the many questions regarding the future of American dance at Lincoln Center that still remains to be answered."[1]

In *Dance Observer*'s November issue, it was writer Harry Bernstein's turn to speak of the "cumulative body of speculation" and the fate of dance in the proposed dance theater. "Is modern dance to be allowed only on sufferance and by way of the back door? . . . The future of modern dance in the United States may well be profoundly affected by the decisions and the provisions made for it at Lincoln Center."[2]

The ever-audacious Helen Tamiris had come forward as its champion with the same ardor that she had invested in the 1930 and 1931 Dance Repertory Theatre series. (If decades earlier she seemed to stand alone, ignored by her contemporaries, it was because, according to Hill, Tamiris was too busy with other ventures, including Broadway. When de Mille complained openly of her own exclusion, the reason was the same.) Tamiris and de Mille's commercial projects had earlier worked against the principled values of Hill's contingent, but now their political acumen and tenacious efforts were much appreciated.

This time, Tamiris prepared a statement for a permanent dance center. The resulting seventeen-page document quotes Margaret Lloyd of the *Christian Science Monitor*: "The American Modern Dance Theater is a long-held ideal, and the time is now ripe for its realization. . . . It would integrate the best of the fragmented units now practicing this native art into a composite whole." It also quotes Walter Terry's exclamation that "America's modern dance . . . has changed the course of the dance art itself not only through its tenets and technical innovations but also through the choreographic masterworks it has produced." He determined that "a 'living' repository in the form of a modern dance repertory company must be established." In the statement, Tamiris calls dance an art "in which the individuals change from generation to generation. The whole of the fine achievement of the Modern Dance, both past and future, needs support, a permanent plan and a center."[3]

Strong rallying for the cause took place during the next eight months, generating a proposal for a modern dance residency. Tamiris and her group submitted a three-year project proposal to the committee for a basic company of thirty-five dancers for $272,905. (A cover letter to Terry from Tamiris is signed "Thanks H," indicating that it was Terry who delivered the unsolicited document.) A future was first posited by an eight-page "statement of purpose" for "The American Modern Dance Theatre . . . to perform the works of the great modern choreographers."[4] The proposition caused the stir among the committee members that Tamiris had anticipated. A memorandum from Young to Stoddard and Allen responded to the document, handed to him in a luncheon conversation: "As I read it I find it indicative of a more widespread interest across the country and perhaps a stronger interest in Modern dance than I had realized existed."[5]

During the fall semester of 1958 at Juilliard, other problems had escalated. Doris had written that she was not able to return to Juilliard. "My doctor says, 'No work for a year' finding that what I thought was indigestion was really a hospital case, i.e. a major operation, exploratory, in which they found extensive inflammation, i.e. this must be reduced by various means if I am to survive, one of which is rest. Naturally this is an awful shock and hurts more than pain in my belly!" In fact, the exploratory revealed inoperable stomach cancer. Unbelievable by today's standards, this information was kept from her. Still, Doris understood the implications. "The doctor is going to allow me to finish my book at home, but he says, 'no rehearsals, no classes, no responsibility, no running around.' He gives me no promises about the future after a year. Only probably, 'yes.'"

Doris then suggested disbanding the Juilliard Dance Theater. "You and I both must put personal considerations aside and think realistically about the quality of survival of the JDT. It would be of no use to anybody to have it limp along or end up with a whimper. It's harder to say 'no' than 'yes!' . . . I think the whole idea of keeping the thing going without me is very chancy." She ends with, "June just brought the flowers. Bless you, Doris."[6]

Giving up the department's semiprofessional repertory company at this point would have consequences, Martha knew. With Bill Schuman's projected scheme, assignments made to choreographers, dates, and orchestra, and a student body of dancers still not strong enough technically to handle the scope of programming, Martha's decision was to keep JDT in place throughout the 1958–59 academic year. With José and his company inaugurating the State Department's International Exchange Program with a tour in South America and away for most of the semester, the director would have to find solutions—and diversions—to keep the student dancers working.

Martha cleverly used a "smoke and mirrors" technique to cover what appeared to be a department headed for disaster. Even Charles Weidman (who had silently become persona non grata, but now resurfaced as a recovering alcoholic) was invited to give a master class—one filled with zany stories and pantomime exercises that included picking strawberries. Yurek Lazowski was brought in for weekly character classes. His dozens of grand pliés into springing kicks at the barre rid anyone of the desire to become a Cossack dancer. Martha persuaded Tudor to teach a course in ballet arrangement, replacing Doris's important advanced composition course. June taught a class in improvisation—perhaps the first ever offered in a school where electronic music and jazz were still beneath the dignity of a "first-class" conservatory.[7] Jazz, of course, had been thriving for generations in the neighboring clubs of Harlem, but had no connection to the musicians in this ivory tower.

Martha continued to calm an increasingly disgruntled student body. One student, admittedly one of the most argumentative, remembered going into the dance office with complaints almost weekly. Each time, Martha listened solemnly before offering logical explanations. The student recalled, "Amazingly, I would come out in agreement with her point of view, totally satisfied with her answers."[8] Dance majors soon understood that Martha's letter of recommendation would be all-important to their careers. One, for example, read, "Her abilities and qualities are truly exceptional. She is a fine artist. She is a superior teacher. She has a great sense of responsibility. I have only the highest praise for her."[9] If convinced of a student's worth, Martha's approval generally remained in force throughout an entire career, leaving numbers of indebted recipients throughout the field freely admitting, "I owe my career to Martha Hill."

Lefty, still in Belgium, continued to host an array of American groups, including the San Francisco Actors Workshop, the Washington National Symphony, and the Juilliard String Quartet. On 1 October 1958 he wrote, "I hate not having our sixth anniversary together and miss you and love you more than ever." He followed this with a Western Union telegram (as he was fond of doing) to Martha at the Juilliard dance office to say "Happy Anniversary / wish we could celebrate together / six happiest years / all my love."[10] Lefty soon after lamented, "I love you my darling and we're neither of us quite normal, I think, when we're not together. Try not to work hard & hurry back as soon as you can." In his next letter he wrote, "Dearest. I'm here in Cologne for the weekend and return tomorrow. The city is nice and the cathedral wonderful, but the weather is *lousy*. Chilly, foggy, wet. I've walked miles and read a couple of good detective stories & I know it has been good for me to get away from the job for a couple of days. You left two months ago yesterday—by far the longest two of my life!" And in the next, "I miss you and want you and love you more than I can ever say. Lefty."[11]

By the third week of October in 1958, Lefty was anticipating farewell parties and closing ceremonies, and arranging the dismantling of exhibits. Questions of whether the Belgian government would take over the pavilion or whether he needed to supervise its demolition were on his mind. He wrote, "I have just come from a luncheon with the Burgomaster of Brussels to discuss demolition; at 3:30 PM, a ceremony for the award of a prize to the person who buys the 500,000th Hot Dog(!); a reception for a group of visiting dignitaries at the Embassy; a reception and speech to the Air Force Command Band. All this and office work too."[12]

He ends another letter with "I just don't feel alive without you. I love you & miss you & want you, Lefty." He remained depressed and worried "because I'm afraid you're getting very run-down & overworked. You sure ought to strike for a raise in salary," he jibed—a joke between them because Lefty considered her income pitifully low.

Again Lefty spoke of Martha's pending return, "I think we should just forget the whole thing for the weeks you're over here. I want to get to Malaga and relax!" By 11 November, Lefty responded to Martha's letter sent six days earlier, "I don't blame you for being discouraged about getting away—I am too because so far I can't get from your letters any real suggestion as to when you'll get away. I know what you're up against, of course, and I really see no way out of the dilemma. Right now I can't see the slightest reason to justify a trip back to New York on my part—much as I would love it."[13]

Despite Lefty's pleas for her return to Brussels, Martha could not get away from Juilliard until the Thanksgiving break. Fortunately, flying to Brussels on 25 November 1958, and again leaving June in charge of the Juilliard office, she was about to spend the most carefree two months of her life with Lefty. After several weeks of nonstop social events in Brussels, the couple flew to Paris.

Martha had written to one of her favorite recent Juilliard dance graduates, Jerry Bywaters, then studying with French mime Marcel Marceau in Paris, to ask if they could take her to lunch. The young woman remembered, "We worked out the date and time for us to meet at the American Embassy. After being away from Juilliard for a time, I longed to see her again and meet the man she had fallen in love with. And I longed to dine in a fine Paris restaurant; the meager size of my Fulbright stipend had so far precluded that."

Jerry recalled their meeting in the American Embassy's courtyard. "I spotted Miss Hill right away. At her side was a gentleman who looked just as distinguished as I had assumed he would. Miss Hill later confided that at first, she hadn't seen me coming." Originally from Texas, in a few short months Jerry had managed to transform herself into a reasonable facsimile of a Parisienne. "After exchanging greetings, we lunched in one of the finest restaurants I had ever been to. Miss Hill was radiant; she looked better than I had ever seen her. Lefty, too, was animated and seemed very, very happy. It was obvious just from looking at the two of them that they were very much in love. They held hands and couldn't stop looking at each other." Conversation ranged from Jerry's dance classes, performances, and impressions of Paris to "the latest news from Juilliard and from the fair in Brussels."[14]

From Paris, the couple flew to Madrid to begin three weeks of a much-anticipated vacation. They drove south to the warmer climate of Málaga and then sixty kilometers to the Marbella Club "for food, sleep and swimming" and a visit to the nearby resort town of Torremolinos as Lefty had planned.[15] A wise traveler, Martha carried a bare minimum satchel. They returned via Barcelona to Madrid, and then flew to Rome where they marveled at the city's treasures, the Vatican's vast collections of art, and the splendor of standing in the Coliseum. As first-time explorers in Italy, they traveled to Florence and Milan, where Martha was profoundly moved by the architectural glory and artistic perfection of Michelangelo's genius. But it was being with Lefty that would remain her most poignant memory of these excursions.

With Doris Humphrey's death in December 1958, the future of JDT was as problematic as the choreographer had predicted. By the first week of 1959, June was apologizing for the flurry of "urgent letters to you on your vacation," confessing that she really needed Martha to "advise and help." "I must admit that Doris' death has really left an awfully big gap," she wrote. The morale "seemed to have dived to an all time low now that Doris is not at the helm."[16] Worried that the dancers might resign (none were on contract), June reported to Martha that one dancer had already been replaced.[17]

To handle the situation, June arranged a meeting after a company showing of work-in-progress to stress the "vital importance" of upcoming performances at the YMHA, a tour scheduled for the Midwest, and the May series in the Juilliard Theater. June's detailed report to Martha notes that even conductor Fred Prausnitz had attended along with Helen Tamiris, who had been recently enlisted to create a work for the company.

Also at the showing was writer and dance historian Selma Jeanne Cohen, who had acted as Doris's personal secretary and liaison to the company while editing Humphrey's book on choreography.[18] Bringing a huge Whitman's Sampler, Selma Jeanne placed it on the piano. It was a Christmas gift to the company that Doris had asked her to deliver to the next rehearsal. (Guiltily, someone volunteered to open the chocolates during a rehearsal break. The five-pound box was empty by the end of the rehearsal.)

But it was Doris's husband Leo Woodford whose presence most alerted the dancers. They had never seen Leo before in the rehearsal hall: his arrival was the clearest indication that the loss of their artistic director had sounded the death knell for the future of JDT as well.[19]

Doris left no will, making the tangle of administrative problems more complicated. She did, however, leave a small trust set up to underwrite Juilliard Dance Theater tour expenses. "The fund is unable to be touched because evidently, it is in your name," June wrote to Martha. "Both Leo and Humphrey [her son, Charles Woodford, Jr.] asked that everyone who inquired about sending flowers to Doris send money instead to Juilliard for the use of JDT."[20]

Torn between her desire to stay with Lefty in Brussels and the real need to handle important decisions at Juilliard, Martha bowed to professional responsibilities. Much to Lefty's dismay, Martha flew back earlier than expected to begin the spring semester at Juilliard at the end of January. She found a department thankful for her return.

Although all praised June for her interim handling, it was Martha whose expertise was critically needed. She asked June to serve as her associate director, a position she held for the next ten years. But from then on, Martha had no intention of delegating important matters and June quickly saw no prospect of Martha's retiring anytime soon. "I didn't feel I had a future there, let's put it that way," she explained.[21] Others felt a tension in the air when the two women were in the office together. June confessed that she spent more hours in analysis to counter the psychological stress of the situation than she cared to recall. Even so, she would grow to appreciate Martha's special talents. "It was an exciting time because there were no other dance conservatories in the United States." She conceded that it was Martha's vision that "really did it."[22]

In Lefty's absence that winter, Martha added virtually every dance concert event in Manhattan to her already tight schedule, including the new ANTA series (presenting shared dance programs in a Broadway house not unlike the 1950 concert series at City Center). On a sadder occasion, she attended Robert Leigh's wife's funeral with Bennington colleagues at the Presbyterian Church in Manhattan.

At Juilliard, preparations for upcoming spring 1959 concerts were fraught with difficulties. Juilliard Dance Theater, at work on what was to be Humphrey's last choreographic project, *Brandenburg Concerto No. 4*, had only one section finished. Limón dancer Ruth Currier, who had served as Doris's assistant in the past years, had agreed to complete the piece using notes taken at Doris's bedside the previous fall, intertwined with movement themes from previous Humphrey works.

If Tamiris's earlier efforts had influenced Lincoln Center's board in any way, she would see little of its rewards as a choreographer. Martha, however, did show her appreciation: in line with Schuman's idea of developing repertory that might filter into a larger venue at Lincoln Center, she hired both Tamiris and Valerie Bettis as guest choreographers to create works for Juilliard Dance Theater's concerts. During rehearsals for Helen's ensemble work, *Dance for Walt Whitman* (to David Diamond's "Rounds for String Orchestra"), the choreographer had difficulty counting after the first few measures of the music and was soon lost in its persuasive canonic melody. Dancers entering after the first few measures relied on sight cues rather than counts, and never quite knew what they were doing—perhaps a clue to why Tamiris's talent as a choreographer was sometimes dismissed by her colleagues.[23]

Nonetheless, the joyous, nonstop full energy of the second performance was an unprecedented success, partly because the audience included Maya Plisetskaya and others from the Bolshoi, who had just finished their first historic

Metropolitan Opera House appearances in the United States. The other modern works—Bettis's *Closed Door*, Humphrey's *Lament for Ignacio Sánchez Mejías*, and Limón's *Missa Brevis*—were for them a strange new dance style, but Tamiris's *Dance* contained exactly the kind of pyrotechnics they appreciated. In typical Russian style, they clapped in rhythm every time dancer Jaime Rogers performed a spectacular series of split-leg jumps.[24] After the performance the Bolshoi dancers were invited backstage to meet the cast. It was an exhilarating moment for those who had recently witnessed the Bolshoi's astounding performances at the Met. All gathered around Martha as she spoke eloquently (through an interpreter) about dance as a universal language. It was a speech Martha had perfected in Brussels.

On 11 March 1959 Martha's calendar noted: "TJD arrives." (On his own calendar TJD laments their time apart with a jotted calculation, "2 yrs 7 mo" under his initials and "10 mo" under hers.)[25] Having performed his final duties in Brussels, Lefty returned to New York to become a member of the Port Authority Commission as a principal consultant to the Downtown–Lower Manhattan Association, Inc., to continue the development of the World Trade Center.

The couple soon returned to their stressful work schedules, with Martha directing the spring sequence of events at Juilliard, from dress rehearsals and public performances to exams for majors, graduate and alumni dinners, days of entrance exams, and commencement, before the doors of the dance office officially closed for the summer.

One of the most unusual happenings in Manhattan that spring of 1959 was a Lincoln Kirstein commission for NYCB: *Episodes*, cocreated by Balanchine and Graham to Anton Webern's orchestral works. It was symbolic of the ever-increasing divide between the ballet and modern contingents on the Lincoln Center dance scene. Of all the moderns, only Graham offered a significant threat to Kirstein's scheme of things. Perhaps he thought this infusion of modern dance into classic repertory might prove once and for all that the two forms did not mix. In Paul Taylor's words, by putting these two giants together Kirstein now "firmed up the firing line between the two camps."[26]

The work premiered at City Center with Graham herself playing Mary, Queen of Scots; in an odd switch, Paul Taylor, then in Graham's company, was "drafted" by Kirstein to perform in the Balanchine half. (Taylor describes Lincoln's appearance as "quite large, big boned, with a strong beaky nose and a less-than-marvelous dentist . . . camouflaging his sensitivity and shyness with bluster." He also noted, "Take a tall Diaghilev, an undersized Frankenstein monster, a masculine Madame Curie, scramble them all together, and you'll get a fair approximation of Lincoln on the rampage.")[27]

Agnes de Mille described the program's opening night; the audience rose when Martha appeared on the stage and again at the end. "Balanchine was rewarded with nothing like this for his part of the production. . . . At the conclusion of that first evening, "neither Kirstein or Balanchine came back to say a word. Not one. . . . It was unprecedented conduct."[28] After the eight scheduled performances of the season, Graham's part I of the project was dropped. But for the next two seasons, Taylor danced Balanchine's "fly in glass of milk" solo in the ballet segment to the delight of modern advocates (and the confusion of NYCB regulars) during successive runs.

After a relaxed July in Brooklyn Heights, Martha traveled to New London for the last week's festival events of 1959. The summer school (having dropped the *An* before American Dance Festival in 1949) removed the word *the* to the more concise Connecticut College School of Dance for the 1959 season. Thanks to Rosemary Park's fund-raising efforts, the beautiful campus now boasted the new air-conditioned Crozier-Williams center that had opened in the fall of 1957.

Although the festival concerts were billed as a tribute to Humphrey, ADF featured not only her work performed by Limón's company, but also two new pieces by Limón himself. His lugubrious new *Tenebrae 1914* was a dance-drama based on the unlikely dance material of the life of a World War I nurse (with a set by Ming Cho Lee to recommend it). The second, stronger work was a trio, *The Apostate*. Merce Cunningham and his company premiered *Rune* (using chance to determine the order of sections) with Robert Rauschenberg costumes: it was a dance described by Horst as a "pleasure to behold." [29]

Martha expressed overall enthusiasm about the quality, depth, and range of the offerings, but she was clearly more cautious in supporting Merce's work. It was Graham and Limón that audiences must see as American representatives, she later commented in a 1961 ANTA panel. Merce "needed a more sophisticated audience . . . not for South America, Africa, or Asia," areas then being served. (She also pressed for sending the best musical comedy and jazz as ambassadors to represent the country in this cold war period.)[30] But it was the Juilliard Dance Department to which Martha now gave her full attention. The result would be what many dance alumni now proclaim its "golden age."

PART VIII

The Sixties

Although lively discussions among Juilliard's faculty members were generally confined to dining-room conversations, strong opinions sometimes surfaced at end-of-the-year jury examinations. It was a time when the entire dance faculty came together for two to three days at hourly wages to evaluate each student's progress. Of course, a faculty made up primarily of artists presented its own difficulties: José once qualified his admiration of a student's study with the comment, "When I seethe with jealousy and wish the work was my own, I know the work is good."[1] Expectations ran high and, as might be expected, emotional outbursts were commonplace. Martha handled each situation with ease, often taking the opportunity to reconcile personal differences that had developed among faculty members.

Personal remarks to young aspiring artists—some already suffering from fragile self-esteem—if generally honest, were sometimes harsh. Dancer-choreographer Martha Clarke, whose brilliant career began as a founding member of the innovative company Pilobolus (she was later cofounder of Crowsnest), recalled one such end-of-the-year session where she performed a short, consciously awkward solo to a Bach piece for clavier and strings. The faculty members who had nurtured the composition thought that the work was superlative. José did not: "My dear, you are throwing dirty dish water at a monument." Clarke was somewhat appeased later that afternoon when Tudor stopped her in the hallway to say he thought the solo was interesting. She recovered enough to celebrate her "first artistic controversy with a bottle of champagne."[2] The next year, Martha Hill saw to it that Clarke was "protected" under Sokolow's choreographic wing, where her "strangeness" was amply appreciated. But Hill, too, was sometimes very blunt with her comments—a peculiarity that grew more pronounced over the years. She was capable of telling students that they weren't "Juilliard material" and should not return to the school.[3]

In the fall of 1959 at his entrance exam, Carl Wolz faced this formidable dance jury. The department's audition style was to seat the faculty behind a long table—Martha in the middle, ballet people on one side, modern on the other, with composition and notation teachers at the ends. All jotted notes on forms as students took brief classes in both ballet and modern styles, before performing a study of their own creation. At such occasions, Martha was at her best and most officious.

Carl's decision at age twenty-five to enter the dance profession was not unusual among Juilliard's recruits during this time—particularly among the males.

After a stint in the navy, Carl had received a degree at the University of Chicago and planned to become an architect. With a passing interest in dance, he had studied a little ballet and, on a lark, went to see the touring Doris Humphrey Dance Theatre perform. "I thought, 'Wow! This is great stuff.' While talking to company members, they said, 'Oh, do you dance? Why don't you come to NYC and audition?' So, I thought if Juilliard accepts me, I'd go into dance. If not, I'll continue with architecture." At the end of the brief solo that Wolz had prepared for Juilliard's entrance exam, he overheard someone whisper, "He's awfully old," and Martha's distinctive voice reply, "Well, there are other careers in dance besides performance." To his great surprise, "they took me." The event marked the beginning of a strong friendship that lasted for the rest of Martha's life.

From then on, Carl carefully watched Martha's office management style as a work-study student, "mostly typing names into her enormous address book to keep it up to date." He observed, "Martha was a very cool lady. She saw that life has problems and living is solving those problems. She met each day with a new fire to be put out—always very positive about things." He was always aware of Martha's constant struggle to keep the department afloat: at that point it was common knowledge in the dance office that the New York City Ballet contingent was an increasing threat to the future of the dance department. Yet, "she was never bitter. Martha just fought the next battle."[4]

Knowing of his interest in architecture, one of the assignments Martha gave to Carl was to care for the architectural drawings and blueprints that arrived periodically for the new Juilliard building at Lincoln Center. Carl observed that she never "dissed" anybody. "Not even Lincoln Kirstein, whom she felt was a difficult person. She always saw it as different opinions, something to be resolved. There were no airs. She was just Martha, out of the Midwest and with the great sophistication of living in New York. She was a hands-on person, always on the telephone, always visiting the studios, and during production, always out in the house talking about the staging, costumes, and the lighting. She was really interested in excellence not only in the artists that she brought together, but also in the students that she nurtured. Her total commitment to every aspect of the educational process was a model for me." It was a professional stance he would emulate with extraordinary success for years to come.

But Carl was soon to learn that the workings of the conservatory system had drawbacks. Rumors about romantic liaisons between mentors and their adoring students in the one-on-one music divisions were rampant. Many were fabricated, some were not. Although dancers generally studied with master teachers in groups, Martha knew that her division was not exempt from this. Students noticed that she chose to look the other way.[5] In fact, ethical issues seemed never to surface when it came to sex in the hallowed halls of Juilliard (before laws prohibiting harassment and discrimination). Horst liked to quote Nietzsche: "Whatever is done from love always occurs beyond good and evil." He also liked to quip, "We're one big family. One big, unhappy family."[6] Producing the artistic work was the ultimate aim. Personal lives had little to do with that.

One of the most enigmatic personalities at Juilliard was the much-admired Antony Tudor. Martha repeatedly urged Tudor to create "occasion" pieces for Juilliard's ballet students. In the fall of 1953, halfheartedly, he had consented to participate in Juilliard's Festival of British Music, creating *Elizabethan Dances and Music* in six sections, using four women and four men. Under Frederic Cohen's direction, Tudor also choreographed a masque, *Britannia Triumphans* (originally staged by Inigo Jones and William D'Avanant in 1637).[7]

Throughout the 1950s, interspersed with his Juilliard commitment, Tudor had created *Offenbach in the Underworld* for the Philadelphia Ballet Company (1954), *La Leyenda de José* in 1958 for the Teatro Colón in Buenos Aires, and *Hail and Farewell* for the Metropolitan Opera Ballet. During this period, Tudor also traveled extensively, setting ballets such as *Echoing of Trumpets* in Sweden for the Royal Swedish Ballet, and taking leaves to work with companies in Israel, Athens, Greece, London, and Japan (an association that began in 1954).[8] None of his recent choreography contained the special mark of genius heralded in his earlier masterpieces. Even so, Tudor often persuaded promising dancers he worked with to come to Juilliard to study with him (as Limón sometimes did). Martha usually came up with scholarship money and approved student visas.

The department's April 1960 concerts, presented by the newly named Juilliard Dance Ensemble (a replacement for the now defunct Juilliard Dance Theater), were the first ones performed completely by students without the cover of an in-house company of professionals. Tudor, named director of the "Ballet Evenings," choreographed a new work to Franz Schubert's "Octet in F Major." *A Choreographer Comments* was a witty series of short studies illustrating the components of ballet: "Jeté—a spring from one foot to another" was presented in one section; "587 Arabesques" and "Tour—A turn. 60 turns" in others. One section featured the striking German, Philippine (Pina) Bausch bouréeing in high heels. For "Pas de Chat: Step of the Cat," a dancer entered in full cat costume to illustrate a single step. Also presented were La Meri's *Four Seasons*, Helmut Kluge's setting of Raoul Feuillet's *Ballet de Neuf Danseurs* (1700), and a reworking of Louis Peçour's *L'Europe Galante* (1697). A trio by Gilbert Reed, *The Clowns* (with alumnus Bruce Marks in the cast), closed the bill. While each piece broadened the scope of the department's more classic offerings, all were clever repertory choices: none demanded strong pointe or precise ensemble work.

When Martha asked Tudor to revive his gentle 1953 *Little Improvisations* to Robert Schumann's *Kinderszenen* for that concert series, he cast the piece with two of the division's most promising black dancers, Mercedes Ellington and William Louther. Perfectly capturing the subtle nuances of childhood play—with only a bench and a piece of apple-green flannel as props—they cuddled a baby, romped in swordplay, and danced a mazurka, as if amusing themselves in an attic on a rainy day.[9] If a modest work, it was a serviceable one for Juilliard students, recast again and again for tours into the city schools. For the spring of 1962, Tudor surprised his audiences with an assemblage of pieces choreographed by ballet faculty members Black, Corvino, Fiorella Keane, and himself in *Gradus and Parnassum* set to a variety of scores. His "Dance Studies Less Orthodox," (Elliott Carter) featured a student in a gorilla suit. Tudor did not produce any other work for the department for the next nine years.

In truth, Tudor by his own admission, had lost the desire to choreograph. Whether artist's block or lack of inspiration, Tudor taught classical studies during class time, preferring to set Petipa excerpts rather than create his own. Now deeply involved in Zen Buddhism (by 1970 he was president of the First Zen Institute on East Thirteenth Street), Tudor's interest shifted to teaching the nuances of ballet: motivating the stretch of a tendu, defining the line, and exuding quality into a port-de-bras.

Working on complex combinations of pirouettes in Tudor's class were always an ordeal and he knew it. For one exercise he sat on a conductor's stool, took a cigarette package from his shirt pocket and placed it in his subject's right hand. Tudor then instructed the dancer to execute a double to the right, handing the pack back to him at its completion. The lesson miraculously brought clarity to the arm's "lead and follow through" action, and the "science" of turning. Partnering classes often ended with "finger" turns and a sequence from the "Rose adagio," with each woman proceeding down the line of cavaliers.[10] But "every combination he gave at the barre, every adagio in center work had originality, purpose and depth," biographer Perlmutter emphasized.[11]

For the summer of 1960, students and alumni from the dance department now represented Juilliard in the Spoleto Festival and made their way through to other important connections. Pina soon joined the Metropolitan Opera Ballet Company. Mabel Robinson, Sylvia Waters, and Dudley Williams would become dancers in Alvin Ailey's new company. (Ailey recalled that when he had been a young choreographer with the dream of starting his own company, Martha Hill had been a key influence.)[12] After eight years of existence, the department's reputation had developed considerably. Martha had created a stable and well-regarded dance contingent.

Nearby, Columbia's rising racial strife with the community was festering. Yet even though Juilliard sat on the edge of Harlem, its position seemed idyllic by comparison. Martha was ever a champion of minorities in a field that constantly dealt with its own prejudices. In fact, African American dancers were counted among the most valued performers in the department: Mary Hinkson, teaching Graham technique, was a strong presence in the department. At the same time other extraordinary black students, such as singer Shirley Verrett, were making their mark in the music division.

One of Martha's favorite dance students was Mercedes Ellington, the "Duke's" granddaughter. Mercedes recalled being invited to Sunday dinner in Brooklyn Heights, bringing along a boyfriend who was in the navy. "Martha thought that Lefty would enjoy talking to him about his experiences in the service," Mercedes remembered (and more than likely, she wanted to check up on whom Mercedes was dating). Just as Hortie Zera had discovered earlier, Mercedes recalled, "The whole time, I couldn't believe how loving they were together and what a different person Martha was from the one I knew at school. She was so kittenish and submissive!"[13]

But the couple's idyllic life was soon threatened. Lefty, a chain-smoker and a heavy drinker for years, was diagnosed with cancer of the esophagus that summer of 1960. Nonetheless, on 23 July, Lefty and Martha penned a cheerful letter to "Judy [his daughter], Howard & all Dilts": "My job is interesting and demanding and I've had to travel, particularly to Washington, quite a bit. How much longer it will last, I don't know, and it's certainly fortunate that I've been able to go on working so long" (subtly referring to his illness). "Martha is, thank the Lord, getting the best rest she's had in years & is doing prodigious jobs in the apartment, which is as spectacular as usual. . . . Lots of love to you all, Daddy." And in Martha's handwriting: "As TJ says, dear, I've been cleaning closets, dresser drawers, & all the jobs I don't have time for during the Juilliard rat race—our flower boxes are a joy—We may have some tomatoes before frost. Are any of the children garden minded? I've always hankered to garden in California where everything grows so luxuriantly. . . . We miss you & think of— Very much love, Martha."[14]

After surgery at Columbia-Presbyterian Hospital, Lefty was told that he had less than a year to live. Martha did her best to maintain a positive front, as each day she watched Lefty's physical decline. For a while Lefty was able to take a car service to his Manhattan office for short periods, but he soon reduced his schedule to consulting work handled from the apartment.

Before the 1960–61 school year started for Martha, Lefty had lost the ability to enjoy two of his passions: talking and eating. Unable to handle much more than a liquid diet, he was reduced to writing what he could not speak. But never lost was his love of Martha and his concern for her future. She must continue at Juilliard, he insisted. Reluctantly, Martha resumed her daily subway trip to Manhattan's West Side.

Uncharacteristically, she arrived around noon, with June covering any morning problems. Martha no longer attended late rehearsals. José and Bill Schuman rallied to her side, coming up with a major collaborative effort for the department that would consolidate her production worries, and take two semesters to complete. Enlisting a coterie of Juilliard composers (including Jacob Druckman, Norman Lloyd, Vincent Persichetti, and Robert Starer) to write variations on his theme, Schuman presented the hourlong score to Limón by the new year. José then created a large ensemble work to be performed with the Juilliard Orchestra. The momentous project was not only the highpoint of the spring season of 1961; it proved Schuman's commitment to dance at Juilliard at a time when Martha most needed his personal support.

Though not always so loyal to Juilliard as a home base, that winter Tudor also contributed to the production scene. Having taken on a weekly teaching stint in Philadelphia, he pleased Martha by giving the department's best ballet students an opportunity to perform in his arrangement of *Sleeping Beauty*, in concert with the Philadelphia Orchestra conducted by Eugene Ormandy.

After closing the dance office in June 1961, Martha busied herself with chores while Lefty slept and doted upon him when he was awake. Now that Lefty was housebound; friends respected the couple's desire to spend these last months together. Martha regularly telephoned Judy in California with updates on his condition. Although word spread discreetly in the dance community of Martha's troubles, Bill and Mary Ann never learned of Lefty's terminal illness.

Thurston Davies died at the Columbia-Presbyterian Medical Center on 13 August 1961. A *Times* obituary listed his survivors as "Martha, his two daughters, Mary Louise and Judy, eight grandchildren and a sister." His funeral was held three days later at the Central Presbyterian Church on Park Avenue and Sixty-fourth Street. The church was filled with Princeton classmates, friends, "and others he had known throughout his colorful life," Judy remembered. "Always a popular man—friendly and concerned for people and issues everywhere, like all of us, he had both weak spots and strength and courage. I remember him best for his great enthusiasm for life." Alongside uniformed members of the U.S. Marine Corps, twenty Princeton classmates of 1916 acted as honorary pallbearers. After the service, Martha and brother Bill accompanied Lefty's body to Pennsylvania Station and by train to Ironton, Ohio, where he was interred with a military service. After roots of ivy from Princeton's Nassau Hall were planted at Lefty's gravesite, Martha returned to New York with the trifold memorial flag packed in her luggage.

Soon after, Martha received a letter from Pearl Primus, now in Monroma, Liberia, West Africa. At the time, she was caring for her son Oniven, in bed with malaria; nonetheless, she sent prayers for Lefty.[15] Martha tucked the note among letters from Lefty and placed them in her chest of family keepsakes next to the flag, alongside a large envelope filled with his photographs.

Devastated, Martha secluded herself in the apartment. Jerry Bywaters, who paid yearly visits from Texas where she had returned to teach after Paris, was one of her first visitors. Martha told her of the numbers of telephone calls from friends and associates after Lefty's death. "All conveyed sympathy and concern." But there was only one call—from Martha Graham—that bolstered her spirits. Graham told her, "'Well, you found your soul mate and you had him for quite awhile; that's more than I ever had.'"[16]

A married life so full of rich experiences now gave way to a period of grieving for Martha. Returning to Juilliard, she was appreciative of colleagues who closely guarded her well-being. Friends encouraged her gradual emergence from deep depression that only alcohol seemed to alleviate. Learning to live again as a single person, she dwelt less on the past; more than ever, she lived vicariously through the young students around her. Remarkably, few of them had any idea of the pain Martha was going through, although some noticed that Martha drank more now. "I never saw her drunk," one friend said, "but I know she had a drinking problem after Lefty's death." Several others confirmed this observation.

Lefty's pension and stocks, combined with Martha's own Juilliard salary, left her secure enough to live modestly. As Martha reestablished a pattern of living from a decade before, her apartment remained her sanctuary. The same living-room sofa (that had prompted Lefty to warn her, "For God's sake, don't let anyone know that's a pull-out bed!") and their eclectic mix of furniture would remain exactly the same for years to come. Martha's Native American artifacts coexisted for another thirty-four years along with their collection of Delft tiles and quaint etchings of street scenes in Brussels the couple had purchased together. Lefty's Princeton yearbooks remained on the bookshelves: a model of the "Atomium" (the Brussels World's Fair's central attraction) stayed on a side table. Martha's pencil cacti grew to almost six feet. An aloe plant in a huge ceramic basin defied being moved.

For the first Thanksgiving after Lefty's death, Martha went to Ohio for the weekend to reconnect with her brother and his family. From then on she would return for the holiday when her schedule permitted. Although intimidated by her commanding voice, the children enjoyed her company. "But they called her 'Uncle Martha.' It was always Uncle Martha!" And because of the date's proximity to Martha's 1 December birthday, her sister-in-law always insisted on a party. "'I don't want to celebrate my birthday. I didn't do anything to deserve a celebration!' she'd complain. 'Just the fact that you're here for another year is cause for celebration!'" Mary Ann replied. Back in Ohio her pleas never worked, but when Martha said no to anyone else who dared suggest a celebration, they listened and obliged. In time, Martha's—like Graham's—exact age became more and more vague.[17]

Lefty's death forced Martha to take control of her life as a single woman once more. Now a situation was developing that would take all of her resourcefulness. Martha would soon find herself fighting for the future of contemporary dance with renewed energy.

Throughout this period, Martha received weekly reports on the latest developments from Bill Schuman, warning of trouble ahead. Lowry was at work giving "new legitimacy" to dance by wholeheartedly advocating Balanchine's New York City Ballet model. Although Graham, Hill, Horst, Limón, and Tudor remained in tight communication over the controversy, all avoided making any public statements.

In June 1961, as Kirstein bantered issues of cartels about, he pressed the board for studios within the Juilliard complex for his School of American Ballet. In response, Schuman wrote a letter (addressed to Young) to protect Hill's dance department. Refusing to view dance "from a narrow, or, certainly, a cultist point of view," Schuman further insisted: "The Center is on record with the dance world in the breadth of its conviction that not only ballet but the so-called modern dance must be included. In our program we will certainly wish to emphasize ballet training and to make certain that such training even within the confines of ballet is not limited to a single esthetic. Similarly, we would wish to have broad opportunities for study of other dance forms and techniques."[1] After a response from Young suggesting an "open mind," Schuman answered firmly, "The degree to which we will be able to cooperate with the professional dance company will depend largely on the persons who operated this company and their attitude."[2]

In the spring of 1962, with a major change of command, Bill Schuman was selected as the first chairman of Lincoln Center. Peter Mennin was hired to replace him as the new Juilliard president. The administrative shift would prove a mixed blessing for Martha and the world of dance.

Time magazine described Mennin as a "tall, elegant and reserved man with a dual reputation as composer, then as an educator.[3] The meticulously groomed six-footer with graying wavy hair and tidy mustache cut a dramatically different figure from the easygoing Schuman. The new president's image, complete with pin-striped double-breasted suits and silk rep ties, was also a contrast to his fellow composers—at least the ones the Juilliard faculty knew. At the end of his twenty-one years as president, the *Juilliard News Bulletin* would herald his fortitude for taking on the "extraordinary challenge of major decision-making in the transition from small scale conservatory in the shadow of Columbia University into the center spotlight of Mid-Manhattan at Lincoln Center."[4] But during those years, his lack of sympathy for modern dance was evident.

Martha distrusted Peter Mennin from the start, and for good reason. The new president's first move was to pressure Martha to drop ballet and retitle the department the "American Dance Division." (In fact, Mennin formally reported to the Juilliard board of meetings with Balanchine, and later Kirstein, in "exploratory discussions regarding the possible association" between the School of American Ballet and Juilliard as early as 25 March 1963.)[5] Suspecting that Mennin was acting in deference to Kirstein's plans to move the NYCB's School of American Ballet into Juilliard's dance quarters, Martha became more guarded in her communication with the administration, screening phone calls and scrutinizing interoffice memos for signs of subversion.

While Martha's goal was to educate a versatile performing artist, knowledgeable about all aspects of the dance field, Mennin's primary goal was for perfection onstage at any cost. Particularly critical of the level of the department's ballet work (whether he admitted it or not) his benchmark for excellence was the Balanchine model. It was a curse hanging over Martha's head for years to come: the dance department was simply not up to either Balanchine's standards or those of the Music Division in Mennin's view. Kirstein's intolerance "of overweight dancers with dirty feet"[6] seemed to have fired Mennin's memos as he commented about the "second-rate level" of training within the dance department that could no way match the "prestige and quality of Balanchine."[7]

When Mary Chudick became the dance department's secretary in 1962, Martha soon found an ally. Mary was sharp-witted and enthusiastic—a facsimile of Mary Jo Shelly in work ethic and stamina. A crackerjack office manager, she was the perfect foil for Martha's working style as a "people" person. Mary, who possessed excellent dictation and typing skills and had no particular interest in dance, found Martha to be a reasonable boss. Her last job had been as secretary for a businessman whom she likened to the Gestapo: "If I could work for him, I could work for anybody." As Martha's implacable "girl Friday," Mary became the organizational glue for the department in short order. Handling all paperwork with remarkable efficiency, she organized filing cabinets that became the heart of the office, archiving every piece of correspondence and newspaper clipping that Martha collected. June, as assistant director, was placed in a second office and determinedly kept reasonable hours, allowing Martha the freedom to gallivant the halls and stay through the evening hours of rehearsal and production. The overall result was possibly the tightest administrative operation that Juilliard would see for the next decade.

Although the creation of an American dance repertory company was credited as the brainchild of William Schuman in his effort to bring modern dance into Lincoln Center, the concept had long been Martha Hill's.[8] Discussions continued as the two sought ways to configure a new resident dance company to replace Juilliard Dance Theater. On her ever-present yellow legal pad, Martha outlined a scheme where, as head of the dance department, she would direct a dance theater company (presumably housed at the new State Theater and Juilliard's own opera-dance theater where the Metropolitan Ballet School might interact as a constituent). The company might have a board, she suggested, consisting of the president of Juilliard and members chosen from Lincoln Center and a dance advisory council, for an organization structured similarly to her earlier dream in 1937, and the model used by the American Dance Festival at Connecticut College.

This resident company would make possible the production of repertory in ballet and modern dance, as well as commission new works by guest artists for their own company members, augmented with Juilliard students. Although Martha's chart did not list names, it designated "artistic heads of Ballet and Modern dance at Juilliard." No doubt she had Limón and Tudor in mind.[9]

Martha's master plan drew a tentative timetable of completion dates of the Met, Juilliard, and the dance theater, with side notations such as "5 yr plan should be made," and "Will NYC audiences support a dance theater? Will resident co. tour USA?" and a query on the use of the theater during summer months for festivals. Her proposed list for the companies to have seasons consisted of the New York City Ballet, American Ballet Theatre, the Martha Graham and the José Limón companies, and the San Francisco Ballet. Martha drafted a monthly rehearsal and production calendar designed to accommodate other companies, as well as charts for how the Juilliard School might interrelate with the Lincoln Center theaters.[10]

The first official invitation to join the Lincoln Center as a constituent was extended to the New York City Ballet in December 1962 (under the guise of participating as part of New York's World's Fair). Outrage in dance circles was immediate. Martha now took a proactive stance, joining colleagues and the press in protest. Terry reported on the "emotion-charged situation" in the *Herald Tribune*. Kirstein accused Schuman of seeking absolute control of both the State Theater and the Vivian Beaumont Theater.

Armed with Martha's earlier suggestions, by May 1963 Schuman formally presented the idea of a dance repertory company structured organizationally "like that of an orchestra" to Lincoln Center's executive committee. Favorably impressed, the committee encouraged further development of the plan. (*Dance Magazine* reported that Schuman intended to ask for a three-year subsidy for the formation of a "small dance company with its own music ensemble to build a repertory of jazz, modern and ballet, giving new choreographers the opportunity to experiment.")[11]

With constituent development significantly delayed by the need for definite programming, the New York City Ballet's invitation to appear at the officially designated "New York State Theater" would be extended for a total of twenty weeks in each of the two years of the New York World's Fair of 1964 and 1965.[12] During this period, negotiations with City Center gradually shifted away from the question of its constituency status as a whole unit to NYCB's exclusive use in the theater. Immediately following the 23 April opening, planning was resumed to complete the constituency and booking arrangements for the State Theater in the year 1966 when the special World's Fair program would no longer be in effect.[13]

With modest hope for at least some recognition of other dance companies, José Limón was fast becoming the spokesman of the "modern" contingent, with Martha Hill behind him. Armed with appropriately large ensemble concert works ready to be performed, Limón was invited to present his company at the plaza as part of an "Introduction to Lincoln Center" series. The program was designed to serve as a preview before the official opening in April 1964 of the New York Philharmonic Hall (later renamed Avery Fisher Hall).[14] As a member of the Limón Company, I remember the anticipation of signing "temporary" AGMA (American Guild of Musical Artists) papers and receiving an actual paycheck backstage from Pauline Limón. It was a thrilling, if short-lived, experience to join the ranks of employed artists at Lincoln Center. The single evening gala on 7 January 1963 included *The Moor's Pavane* and *Missa Brevis* (with full chorus testing the hall's acoustics and giving the new organ its first public performance).[15] "Let us hope that the high standards that they have set will be maintained in the future," Hughes of the *Times* exclaimed—at that point, wishful thinking.

At Martha Graham's annual birthday celebration for José and Louis Horst on 12 January 1964, conversation focused on Lincoln Center. The social event would be Horst's last. Returning from teaching at the Neighborhood Playhouse a week later, he suffered a heart attack that proved fatal. *Dance Observer*—the little journal he had so faithfully edited from his apartment (and organized the layout on the top of his piano) for the past thirty years—printed its last issue that January. Graham had earlier written that she could not imagine what it would have been like if *Dance Observer* and Louis Horst "had been missing from our lives. We cannot be really objective about either of them; you never can be about the absolutely indispensable."[16]

For Martha Hill, Louis's death signaled the end of an era. Louis had given her steady support and encouragement for most of the last forty of his eighty years of life. Both had Martha Graham "in common." She was their idol—the one who "made it all worthwhile." For years they had confided in each other about how to handle Graham's "insincerities." They had repeated, "But who else is there?" Louis would say woefully to Martha Hill. "There is no one else."[17]

This troika of leaders all had the gift of longevity. (The two Marthas lived well into their nineties, outliving many of their contemporaries.) Like three business partners, they had built empires of their own devising, without capital, and for the most fleeting of commodities. In the dance world, Horst had been a "symbol of fixity" for these women (and many others, including myself). He had also been their touchstone to success.[18]

Adding fuel to the fire, in March 1965, the Rockefeller Brothers Fund (not coincidentally, having hired Norman Lloyd as an executive in 1962) produced a report on the future of theater, dance, and music in America. The Rockefeller Panel report, *The Performing Arts Problems and Prospects*, presented a sobering appraisal of dance in the United States, naming only one theater—Jacob's Pillow—devoted exclusively to the dance. It also noted that $3,000 to $3,500 was a year's average income for a professional dancer, with NYCB the first company in America to offer its dancers year-round employment in 1964.

The report named patrons Lucia Chase (for ABT), Lincoln Kirstein, Ruth Page in Chicago, and Jean Riddell, as well as two foundations under the names of Bethsabée de Rothschild and Rebekah Harkness, as having "all but carried American dance on their shoulders for the past thirty years." That is, until the Ford Foundation joined them in 1963 by announcing grants totaling $7,756,000 over ten years to "upgrade professional and training standards and build audiences in America." These grants, according to the Rockefeller study "understandably brought the whole dance field under new scrutiny."[19]

Lloyd's Rockefeller paper stressed the urgent need to support the permanent companies that did exist and showed potential for growth because

> the vitality of this art form, as of every other, depends as much upon the creation of new forms and contemporary expressions as upon the conservation of the heritage of the past. . . . In other words, modern dance needs as much encouragement as classical ballet. . . . [R]enewed efforts should be made to provide a permanent theatre in which several dance forms might be presented [to give] . . . an assurance of opportunities to create and perform.

Although encouraged by the Rockefeller report, Martha knew from experience that "foundations have made the excuse that the modern dancers can't cooperate" as "an easy out for people who don't really know."[20] Still, the controversy over Ford's show of favoritism countered by the Rockefeller study's factual boost, definitely moved the modern contingent into a more solid proactive stance.

Pressing forward, Schuman had convinced the Lincoln Center board that a modern dance federation might be given a chance as a kind of "living repository," and his efforts finally paid off. A modern repertory company called the American Dance Theatre sprang into existence when a grant of $70,000 suddenly came from the New York State Council on the Arts' New Projects Underwriting Fund for programming connected with the World's Fair. Again, Hill acted behind the scenes to make possible a connection with the Juilliard Dance Department. With the hiring of Limón as artistic director and Roger Englander as producer, she would continue to be an important behind-the-scenes adviser.

Limón assembled an eclectic pickup company, employing some of his own company dancers and a few required for the Sokolow casting. Unfortunately the new company's debut performances in November 1964 were organized as hastily as the dates were given. As might be expected, the work of Limón and his Juilliard colleagues dominated the repertory, taking the most prominent Saturday evening slot. The group of names did not escape attacks by *Times* reporter Allen Hughes, who had earlier complained that August's 1964 American Dance Festival had "focused attention on one set of dance people" in "some sort of perpetual wake" for Doris Humphrey.[21]

Privately expressing his own misgivings about the Lincoln Center project, Limón feared that smaller companies would be edged out. Facing an offer he couldn't refuse, however, José fought his personal discomfort with what he considered the center's commercial stance and plowed forward in the greatest challenge of his professional life. But neither he nor Hill, as his key adviser, read the warning signs of programming trouble from the previous summer (1964) at ADF in Connecticut.

Of the twenty-eight dancers chosen for this first series, more than half were drawn from Juilliard dance department rosters. One omission was noted loud and clear: Martha Graham was not involved.[22] Graham later explained her stance, "A long time ago, I decided that my place was front and center. That's where I chose to be, and that's where I remain."[23] She could think of no personal advantage in sharing her audiences or her reputation at this point in her career.

The first State Theater modern repertory "tryout" offered works created mainly by the department's faculty. Humphrey's *Lament for Ignacio Sánchez Mejías*, created in 1951, with a score by Norman Lloyd; Limón's *A Choreographic Offering*, to music by J.S. Bach (and dedicated to Humphrey); and Sokolow's *The Question*, set to a Charles Ives score—were all works that had been rehearsed and performed earlier at the school. Added to this was an opener choreographed by Donald McKayle, who represented an emerging group of talented black choreographers.

At the beginning of the run, seats were nearly filled and the press was encouraging. Gradually audiences thinned and less than stellar critical reviews rolled in. P. W. Manchester advised in the *Christian Science Monitor* that Lincoln Center's directors should first come to grips with the dual problem of establishing a single capable performing group and learning how to present programming to "bring American modern to a general dance audience instead of keeping it within the bounds of colleges and the limited stages of a few auditoriums." She went on, "A pity that the one new work, McKayle's *Workout*, should have been so trivial." *Choreographic Offering* had premiered at ADF the summer before, and Sokolow's *The Question* had been created earlier for Juilliard, she noted, conceding that Limón had "performed wonders in welding a company of this caliber in so short a time."[24]

Authorized by the board to give advice, Schuman pressed to keep American Dance Theatre alive, with the perhaps exaggerated argument that there were an additional forty professional dance companies in the country needing support. But the board, now more guarded then ever in the development of new operations, firmly refused to give any financial assistance for a spring season of modern dance.

But when dates opened up at the State Theater, a second series of performances materialized for the American Dance Theatre. Knowing that NYCB had all but won exclusive rights to the State Theater, and sensing that he was not up to the task, Limón's responses to the press began to take a pessimistic tone.

José now characterized the modern dance as "experimental and not a popular art," perhaps alluding to his programming of Merce Cunningham and Company into the second season in March 1965. Since their shared weekend of concerts at ADF in the summer of 1958, the two men acknowledged the uneasy balance of their aesthetic positions. In Limón dancer Michael Hollander's words, the two currents in dance were "passing in opposite directions: José drifting somewhat nostalgically from the 20th century back in time; Merce venturing ahead, beyond the familiar pale of current practice."[25] Their artistic paths would not cross again until ADT's 1965 series.

If Hill and Limón had reservations about Cunningham's work over the years, both wanted avant-garde trends to be included in the repertory mix at Lincoln Center, and Merce was still "family." Still, they were distressed when *Winterbranch* received scathing criticism just as it had at ADF's Palmer auditorium the previous summer when Merce's dance "in the dark" to a score by

LaMonte Young was reported to ricochet sound at decibels higher then safe for the human ear. Leonard Harris in the *New York World Telegram* voted the by now infamous score as the "most likely to empty a theater," but added, "I wouldn't have missed it for the world. . . . Take your earplugs and dark glasses. But go."[26] Once more, a mixed press helped prove Kirstein's point to the board that modern dance was unsubstantial at its core, and not worthy of entry into the high art of dance alongside ballet.

For critic Douglas Watt of the *Daily News*, Alwin Nikolais's *Imago* provided "the most excitement" for this seven-day American Dance Theatre "conglomerate . . . for assorted modern dance groups." Humphrey's *Passacaglia* was called a "rather dull study" in contrast.[27] But Hughes of the *Times* argued that the work was "unequivocally modern dance." Except for that classic, "the fortunes of the American Dance Theatre took a sharp downward turn," he stated, "with a program that did no credit to modern dance in America."[28]

Newsweek's aptly titled article "Thorn[y] Evangelists" commented crustily, "The stubborn dream of a permanent repertory company for modern dance refuses to die. . . . It was ironic that after so many indigent years, modern dancers had money enough—but too little time. Of the 101 dancers who performed last week, only 30, hastily recruited and intensively rehearsed, belonged to what was called the ADT. They dubbed themselves, after the endless rehearsals, the '10 cents a dance' company." The article dismissed the entire modern dance movement as unworthy of Lincoln Center, complaining that "too often discipline has hardened into discipleship" and concluding, "The weakest modern dance is often a consequence of the medium's greatest strength—freedom." And in the ultimate put-down to Limón, the writer comments, "If that dream comes true, the ADT will also need an artistic administrator capable of an intelligent, ruthless selectivity."[29]

During these events, it was Martha Hill with whom Limón kept intense counsel. A note to her dated 26 April 1965 suggested "cross[ing] our fingers for your discreet and Machiavellian dinner."[30] Together they created lists of supporters to be recommended for the dance council that included Gertrude Macy, John Martin, and Rosemary Park (Connecticut College's new president), Charles Shain, Ben Sommers in an effort to keep the modern company operating—to no avail. ADT had troublesome practical problems as well. Limón was not a businessman—his wife Pauline was known to dole out his daily five-dollar spending money at the beginning of each day—and American Dance Theatre under his artistic direction folded as hastily as it was set up.

On 15 June 1965, Bill Schuman released another memo in a final attempt to keep American Dance Theatre alive under Juilliard's wing, stating that Limón was now to become artistic director of such a company and serve as head of education in modern American dance at Juilliard. Hill's title would be changed to "administrative head."[31] But prospects for funding began to dim at the same time (as did Schuman's confidence in Limón), and JDR III began asking Schuman to scale back his "impresario function" as the Lincoln Center board would not be able to find resources for unbudgeted future programs—specifically this one.[32]

In a reflective piece for the *Times*, Clive Barnes revisited what had *not* happened at Lincoln Center, and why. Writing in the "happy atmosphere" of Connecticut College's "cradle of the American dance" (where by its nineteenth summer its number of premieres had risen to ninety-six to become a "shop window" of the art), he found himself wondering, "Whatever happened to the ADT?" He then harped on the idea that "modern dancers, sturdy independents to the death, seem to have a natural antipathy to large organizations. Then again they are frightened of losing their individual sovereignty."[33] His argument folded neatly into Kirstein's position.

Tom deGaetani (technical director at Juilliard before taking a similar post Lincoln Center) was one of many who blamed the rise of commercialism for the loss of a place for modern dance on the plaza. (By now the New York City Ballet enterprise had established a firm marketing plan that was the envy of its competitors.) That Lincoln Center "has fallen flat on its face as an independent developer and producer of artistry is incontestable," he wrote for *Dance Magazine*, adding, "One need only look at its initial efforts in drama and modern dance to see how bad the Big Boys really can be."[34]

Contrasts and Conflicts, 1965–1968

While a monolithic headquarters for the arts was being built at Lincoln Center, a counterculture was rapidly surfacing. Don McDonagh later wrote in his book *The Rise and Fall and Rise of Modern Dance*, "If anything has characterized the dance revolution of the 1960's, it has been freedom—the freedom to move in new and unaccustomed ways in places that have been excluded from conventional theater dance."[1]

Over time, the word "modern" continued to be exchanged for "contemporary"—more and more influenced by European trends—to indicate a wider, more encompassing range of dance styles. With a mounting sense that the label "modern" was too limiting, dance writers and historians sought to describe what they perceived as a postmodernist trend (later canonized by Sally Banes's 1980 book *Terpsichore in Sneakers*) more in line with developments in the other arts.

Although sympathetic to new ideas, Martha Hill worried that the modern dance philosophy of individuality she had championed so ardently in the 1930s was fast dissipating into trendy choreographic look-alikes. The undercurrent of change now catching critical attention seldom found its way into Julliard's domain, where enthusiasm for what was happening downtown was confined to discussions in dance composition classes and among faculty members during coffee breaks.

In training dancers, Martha saw the distinct advantage of ballet (with its reliance on the repetition of codified steps, pointe work, and traditional partnering) for developing line, strength, and clarity. At the same time, studying the well-established styles of Graham and Limón in modern dance offered rigorous torso work, the use of gesture, weight, flow, and rhythmic nuance. From her perspective, training in both forms still complemented each other, combining the tenets of discipline with the possibility of individualism. She welcomed the overlapping of techniques of ballet and modern as a natural evolution within both forms. Robbins and Tudor were creating modern ballets, after all. And even Graham now referred to her works as "contemporary ballets."

At the height of its commercial power, the Graham Company filled the Mark Hellinger Theater on Broadway during a three-week season in 1965. With this rise in company status came an increasing number of dance students to Graham's Center of Contemporary Dance on East Sixty-third Street—even if the artist's own life was spiraling out of control. One student remembered

Miss Graham in a rare appearance when Graham interrupted a class "to hurl philosophical exhortations and wounding comments at us, mocking our lack of passion and our flabby muscles." Disheartened, this student moved on to study "meandering paths of abstraction, chance, and Zen philosophy at the less oppressive Cunningham studio."[2]

Other centers for modern dance making their mark included Alwin Nikolais's school on Henry Street, the well-established midtown New Dance Group, and a good number of independent studios in Manhattan that offered study options. Many aspiring dancers from a growing number of colleges offering courses in dance continued to fortify their studies with summer sessions at the American Dance Festival in Connecticut. Ballet studios proliferated. But in a unique twist, the Juilliard Dance Department was the single place where all of its dancers were expected to be proficient in both modern and ballet techniques.

Just as the 1930s revolutionaries at Bennington had, increasing numbers of young dancers both inside and outside Juilliard, now wanted to choreograph their own ideas. Giving independent concerts at the once popular 92nd Street Y's Kaufmann auditorium (with its newly instituted audition procedures and increased rental fees) had become passé. Fledgling choreographers now looked for opportunities to showcase their work in more cooperative settings, such as Jeff Duncan's egalitarian Dance Theater Workshop on West Twentieth Street. And they sought out such locations as gymnasiums and church halls as possible performance spaces. Sponsored series producing group concerts began to crop up in out-of-the-way theaters connected to institutions: the YMCA's Clark Center, the New School (with its Choreoconcerts), and Barnard College's Dance Uptown.[3] Although most were shoestring operations, these maverick venues were drawing enthusiastic attention by the press.

In these less restricted havens, a growing disregard for classical training and "serious" music was evident: the use of a wide range of accompaniment ran the gamut from popular mixes on collage tapes and sound effects, to electronic manipulations. All were the polar opposite of what acoustic repertory stood for at Juilliard.

Prompting some—Martha included—to notice the emergence of a "me" generation in dance, potential choreographers found themselves in a more relaxed environment, free from judgment (except by their peers). Granted, the events at these venues were underrehearsed and loosely staged, publicized mainly by word of mouth and posters tacked around town. Even so they inspired movement experimentation that was very much a part of an emerging social and political front. Along with free dance listings in the *Village Voice*, writer Jill Johnston's wacky articles drew a cadre of young people looking for free performances to experience a new thing called "performance art."

At the nucleus of this phenomenon in dance was a group of dancers studying at the Cunningham studio including Lucinda Childs, Steve Paxton (a former student at Juilliard), and Yvonne Rainer. Wanting to make their own work, these dancers were encouraged by John Cage (himself having given composition workshops for dancers at Merce's studio in the early 1950s) to study with musician Robert Ellis Dunn. In Dunn's words, artists should strive for the "rejection of artifice and illusion." Having served as Horst's pianist in his composition classes, and "out of anger" over the master teacher's outdated approaches, Dunn (then married to Judith Dunn, a dancer in Merce's company) agreed to run sessions for his first handful of inquisitive students. In the ten to twelve workshop sessions that Dunn taught four times from 1960 to 1962, he borrowed Cage's theories of structure, introducing chance, play, and the use of everyday movement, sometimes illuminated by Erik Satie scores.

For these like-minded dancers anxious to experiment, Dunn's cool "anything goes" teaching style was the freeing incentive they needed to disengage themselves from expressionist traditions.[4] These were ideas also advocated by their painter friends, including Robert Rauschenberg, who declared in 1959, "A canvas is never empty." Their play with perception and assemblage of the ordinary drew heavily from notions that the Black Mountain College's experimental artists-in-residence—Cunningham and Cage among them—spearheaded in the 1950s. Conveniently, the ecclesiastic space used as a performing area at Judson Church on Washington Square (owing to the dwindling numbers of churchgoers, the church was now "dedicated to serving the needs of the city") was offered to a group of dance experimenters. The assistant pastor was Al Carmines whose own performances (such as his musical *Christmas Rappings*) set the mood of the place, while the no-dressing-room situation promoted an easy, unisex, dancing-in-sweats look.

In 1965, Yvonne Rainer had come forth with her "No" manifesto that many saw as "an aesthetics of denial." Welcomed into the avant-garde artist scene, casual costuming became de rigueur: leotards and tights were out. "No gel" white lighting was another way to achieve a less pretentious look. Bows were eliminated. And with no prescribed theater seating arrangement or price of admission, the new generation of dance enthusiasts felt comfortable at last.

As "outsider" groups multiplied, so did an uncomfortable feeling toward the Juilliard and Balanchine training models as staunchly elitist. Within the decade, if having a dance degree from Juilliard meant an "in" with Manhattan's major companies, it meant sure expulsion from sponsorship in places to show new work—Dance Theater Workshop, later under David White's direction, among them.

In contrast, dancers in the cloistered studios of Juilliard on Claremont Avenue continued to put in long hours beyond daily training of evening and weekend repertory rehearsals. Social life (if any) amounted to pizza at Tony's on Broadway or chance meetings at the Laundromat.

Having refined the department's curriculum during its first fifteen years, Martha was all the more convinced that the discipline of ballet and modern must remain at the core of a dancer's regime. Despite the positive effect of the many graduates entering the field, whether a dance department would ever take residency in the new Juilliard building remained a question.

The previous fall (1964), Peter Mennin and Bill Schuman had exchanged a round of letters about an intended press release that Mennin described as "a general understanding . . . regarding future association" of Juilliard and the School of American Ballet. (In the various meetings "the association of the two schools was always kept separate from the subject of the NYCB," Mennin had insisted.) Schuman countered, "Dear Pete, In connection with any announcement; postpone: I agree with the implication in your letter that the subject of dance education at Juilliard and the subject of the NYCB at L.C. are separate ones. . . . Why don't we consider, then, that the educational aspect is the sole responsibility of Juilliard, as the prime constituent for education?"[5] Once again, Schuman saved the dance department from Mennin's attempt to dispose of it.

According to future Juilliard president Joseph Polisi, Mennin firmly expected a "future plan for dance education at Juilliard to be squarely based on the presence of the School of American Ballet [SAB] with Balanchine in charge. The current dance division of the school would be eliminated, although a hazy proviso continued to linger in which modern dance instruction might be integrated into the dance curriculum in the distant future."[6]

Mennin had earlier been hedging his bets with a strategy to intertwine the Juilliard Dance Division and the failed American Dance Theatre. Now, the dance department's demise was, in fact, all but a done deal when Kirstein, Balanchine, and Mennin signed an agreement between SAB and Juilliard in late June 1965. Without consulting with Martha, Mennin avoided the consequences of making his plan known as he tinkered with the notion of a "Division of Modern Dance."[7] Meanwhile, he doubled his efforts to press Hill into retirement (no doubt to make the transition easier) before fully embracing a commitment with the School of American Ballet as the exclusive dance component at Juilliard.

The truth was that the last remaining holdout for any dance on the plaza beside Balanchine's was Juilliard's (now officially titled) Dance Division in

Martha's hands. With Hill sturdily at the helm, taking over all of the dance studios originally designated for her department would prove to be more difficult for Balanchine's contingent than Kirstein and Mennin had imagined.

That October of 1965, Hill and apprehensive dance faculty members (the author among them) were called into a music classroom on Juilliard's fifth floor for the meeting. One of the first to arrive, Martha was smartly dressed in a scarlet woolen plaid suit with her trademark matching velvet ribbon securing her hair. She settled into the one professor's chair. As the faculty entered, they arranged themselves at the writing desks lined up to face a giant blackboard etched with musical staves. Mennin rushed in, apologizing profusely for the odd dislocation of the meeting away from his office. (One could only suspect that it gave him the opportunity to come and leave expediently.) After a flurry of introductions and without a gentlemanly seating arrangement for him in the room, he worked to assume a casual stance. Finally leaning against the concert grand piano, document in hand, he said, "I am here to give you important news about the dance at Juilliard. There will be a national press conference shortly, and I want you to be the first to have this information."

The School of American Ballet would be integrated into the expanding Juilliard framework as an independent unit, collaborating actively with the school's performing activities, he explained. If that was a major announcement for the stunned faculty (less so for Martha who had been struggling with the situation for months), further consternation ensued when he announced that plans were "under consideration for the establishment of a Division of Modern American Dance at Juilliard, which would provide training in the various idioms of contemporary dance." The group went from sheer disbelief to hot anger. Colleagues turned toward Martha in alarm, finding it hard to believe that the years of integrating ballet and modern into the curriculum would now fall apart. Someone said, "There must be some recourse!" And another, "What can we do about this, Martha?" "We'll ride the tide. Things will work out," was her answer. She would find a way.

Back in her office, Martha sent a flurry of memos to Mennin requesting word changes to the press release, asking to remove the "under consideration" clause, and the term "modern." The president approved neither, and the original statement was released. When the news appeared in print, the *Times* added a clarifying note to the published release that "many people had been under the impression that such a division did exist, in fact, if not in name. The dance department . . . offers both classical and modern training."[8]

As the formidable financial risk of the move into a thirty million–dollar building daunted Juilliard administrators, another year slipped by before questions about the dance department's future were again officially raised by Mennin. If the inclusion of dance at Juilliard was no longer questioned, the kind of dance had become a sore topic. Among the powerful men in Mennin's circle, it was McNeil Lowry, bolstered by his position as head of the Ford Foundation, who gave Balanchine and Kirstein a strong negotiating edge for a takeover of Juilliard's dance quarters.

Mennin had met with Lowry in October 1965 and Schuman reported to JDR III about another "fruitful meeting" where all "agreed to develop a more formal basis for cooperation; rep theater and the school." Lowry later admitted that he sympathized with "Pete" because he was stuck with "all that crappy . . . modern dance that Martha Hill had brought down from Bennington and had found a home in Juilliard" with its ballet offering "all very, very skimpy and undeveloped."[9] With this attitude at play, now any hope of dance at Lincoln Center in any form other than Balanchine's would rely on the ingenuity of Martha Hill and Schuman in their combined positions of power.

Under fire, Hill worked to present the highest caliber in programming possible for her increasingly capable dancers, although still cautious about presenting ballet repertory. Dance activities on Claremont Avenue continued at full pace in preparation for the February 1965 student performances, with two superlative works by Anna Sokolow: *Ballade* (with Ze'eva Cohen and Dennis Nahat in the cast); and *Odes* for a cast of twenty-three, set to music by Edgard Varèse. Also featured were Doris Humphrey's 1953 classic *Ritmo Jondo* to Carlos Surinach's score and Limón's *Variations on a Theme by Paganini* (Brahms), works perfectly suited for the gifted young dancers in the cast. The department continued to gain stamina in its May 1966 concerts, with Sokolow as resident choreographer, creating *Night* for seventeen dancers to a Luciano Berio score, and Limón conbtributing his masterwork, "There Is a Time." (During this period, Limón was heavily invested in a large forty-five-minute work—in silence, barring a few incidental sounds—that he titled *The Winged* for an August premiere at ADF.)

As Martha's old stomping ground, Greenwich Village, was championing a new set of dance rebels (now actively opposing the Vietnam War), she too was raising social consciousness for the contemporary dance field. For Martha, Anna Sokolow's terse dramatic works were the perfect means for enticing young students to be their most intensely physical and most acutely aware of their place in society. Creating a total of twenty-eight new works and setting dozens of revivals, Anna created choreography that took a hard look at the times. Anna had become, in a sense, Martha Hill's choreographic alter ego.

Many, including Jerome Robbins, revered Sokolow's genius as a choreographer. (His own explorations at his American Theater Laboratory from 1966 to 1968 explored world theater idioms, effectively giving him a retreat from NYCB.) Martha saw to it that Anna received a paycheck for what she did best and made sure that her works were meticulously produced in the Juilliard Theater. Throughout Anna's stormy bouts with mental illness, Martha's allegiance remained firm. Cleverly, Martha eliminated any pedagogical conflicts by enlisting Anna only to work with dancers as a choreographer, never as a classroom teacher.

Students auditioning for each new Sokolow project were given the option of dropping out if they couldn't handle Anna's difficult ways. A tyrant in the rehearsal hall, Sokolow's working methods were legend among those she terrorized. "When she wanted my sternum up she made a little fist and punched me right in the back, exclaiming, 'There you go!'" one student recalled. But Anna's hard-edged dance statements were in perfect sync with Martha's personal viewpoint, and she saw to it that Anna, her friend from the Bennington years, maintained a well-respected position in dance.

Showing the heightened capacities of students trained equally in ballet and modern, the next season's April 1967 concerts included a revival of Tudor's *Lilac Garden*. A definite coup, Hill's personal victory was in convincing Tudor to once more bring his work to the Juilliard stage (a task perhaps made easier by the recent success of his *Shadowplay* for England's Royal Ballet). His lead dancers Sue Knapp, Robert LaPone, and Janet Sumner proved an excellent cast for one of the most sophisticated and difficult works in the contemporary ballet repertory. "Barnes wrote that we were too young for the roles," Janet recalled, "but we savored the opportunity, and Tudor seemed pleased with us."[10] Martha knew the value of presenting classic gems, and this ballet was one of the finest.

Hill also convinced Graham that the Dance Department had a superb cast for *Diversion of Angels*: the heat was on to prove that Juilliard could produce dancers as high in quality as its musicians, and this careful selection of repertory paid off. In his *Times* review, Clive Barnes noted "no shortage of enterprise," and the dancers' "exceptional discipline," marveling at Hill's repertory choices.[11] And there were two world premieres: Anna Sokolow's *Memories*, set to a jazzy score by Teo Macero, and Limón's tormented dance macabre, *MacAber's Dance*, set to a Druckman score and utilizing twenty-six dancers. Terry's *World Journal Tribune* review ended with "a closing bravo to one of American's major dance figures, Martha Hill, who heads Juilliard's dance department and who produced this important evening of dance."[12]

That spring of 1967, while at work as adviser on the script for the film *Four*

Pioneers (a documentary shown to young dancers in universities for years to come), Martha also submitted a ten-year plan (projecting the modest yearly amount of $209,100) to show Mennin how cost-effective her department could be. Not impressed, Mennin responded by warning that the "burdens placed on Juilliard regarding the Div. of Drama and Dance in the immediate future are awesome."[13] Money, Martha knew, was the bottom line: the American School of Ballet had it. The dance division did not.

By the school year 1967–68, with the reputation of the department growing, and the concert hall filling for dance events, Mennin found himself caught by the public's enthusiasm for Juilliard's special brand of dance. He had to "justify his awkward decision to the profession, the general public and the Lincoln Center leadership," according to Polisi.[14] Trying a subtler process of elimination, he placed a cap on the number of dance students admitted, reducing the total number of students in the department to seventy students. More than half were foreign students: seventeen from Israel, ten from Japan (six recruited by Tudor during his stay there), three from Australia, three from Chile, and four from France. The Preparatory Division's dance classes for children on Saturdays that had flourished for more than a decade were to be eliminated with the move, as was the extension division that had regularly admitted up to fifteen part-time "special studies" dance students. (This had been one of Hill's ways to enlist talented pre-professionals who even with scholarships could not afford tuition fees.)

In reaction to Hill's stubborn refusal to drop ballet from the curriculum, Mennin continued to hound her about the imminent elimination of the dance department. A sequence of memos from Peter Mennin's office included one that warned of the "clear possibility that dance training at Juilliard may not be continued beyond the school year of 1968–69."[15]

To strengthen her case, Martha then issued a statement to serve as a handout describing the department's philosophical goals. She was aided in composing the statement by Juilliard's press person, Vera Michaelson, who had volunteered her services in defense of Hill's position. What made the Juilliard dance plan unique, the statement affirmed, "is its scope [and] . . . its linking with performance under the supervision of outstanding choreographers representing the various dance forms." Michaelson noted, "Although a proud believer in the importance of modern dance as perhaps the profoundest and most original expression of America in the arts, Miss Hill herself had begun her training in ballet, and she knew that dance could not be confined to any one technique."[16]

Paradoxically, no one questioned Martha's early training learned within the physical education gymnasiums of Kellogg and fortified with Chalif and Vestoff manuals. Although recognized as a leading educator of America's new modern dance, Martha was now actually refusing to accept that banner for one with a broader mission. Thanks to their training in ballet as well as modern, Juilliard's dancers were not only dancing in the Graham, Alvin Ailey, and Limón companies; they had joined the Metropolitan Opera Ballet, American Ballet Theatre, and the newly established Joffrey and Harkness companies.

Despite his often churlish and difficult ways, Antony Tudor, as the Metropolitan Opera–connected ballet master, was still at the center of Martha's enterprise. Her reason for supporting him was apparent: Tudor was her trump card, the one person who could keep Kirstein's ever-gnawing influence at bay. Tudor's hold on the ballet world was still significant and his expertise as a master teacher and head of the ballet faculty could not be faulted.

Modern companies that Martha Hill championed, such as those of Ailey, Graham, and the up-and-coming Paul Taylor, were now able to offer a limited number of workweeks for their dancers. Funding prospects for touring and funding of dance projects from the newly created National Foundation of the Arts and Humanities (passed by Congress in 1966) and from the now established New York State Council on the Arts sent huge numbers of potential dance applicants scurrying for nonprofit status and more formal organizational arrangements. Regional ballet companies emerging across the United States also created attractive options, to Hill's delight. A 1968 Ford Foundation study documented a dramatic rise of at least twenty-five modern dance companies in New York City alone; words such as "explosion" and "proliferation" now peppered news articles. All evidenced a vibrant growth pattern for the art form. Yet Martha worried that the direction of modern dance was dangerously close to falling into cultish, idiosyncratic hands. Oddly, some of Lincoln Center's planners seemed to have more confidence in the future of American modern dance than Martha.

The saga continued. One of the many memos from Dean Waldrop enclosed a drafted memorandum with an additional phrase of "as now constituted" to Mennin's original wording about the future of the department. With the acuity of a lawyer, Martha responded, "You have asked for my comments and they follow." Point by point, she admonishes "self-contradictory" language, and argues that the term "Modern American Dance" should be defined. As for her division, it continued to represent a broader aesthetic.[17] This time, the corrections were incorporated, yet dance students were informed that the latest prediction was that the division might not be continued beyond 1970–71.

Martha's resistance to an obstructive administration would eventually pay off, but it would take years rather than months to resolve the department's position. Sylvia Yamada, an incoming student who had studied with Carl Wolz in Hawaii, recalled, "They told us from day one 'it's likely that you won't graduate.'" She and her other classmates took the information in stride: "I don't think we were in it for the degree. Actually, the degree wasn't that important."[18]

Once again, Martha rallied for support among her associates. Bill Bales, who took charge of Bennington's dance department after Hill's departure, had left in 1966 to create a dance program at the new Purchase College, of the State University of New York. He wrote to Mennin, "The heart of the Juilliard training program is the integration of ballet and modern dance techniques. If one of these styles is eliminated, the concept disintegrates. American dance takes a giant step backwards, and Juilliard renounces its leadership in innovative performing arts education in the United States. I urge you to re-consider any action that would willfully harm your distinguished Dance Department."[19]

But perhaps the most significant voices of protest were from the Juilliard dance students themselves. Dancers Gary Masters and Risa Steinberg both worked as student assistants in the dance office and knew the situation firsthand. Taking the lead, they organized a student committee and started with a letter-writing campaign, saying, "We believe it is not too late to save the Dance Department in its present form (including the major in ballet), if action is taken immediately." They phoned the press, "stating the facts"; using Martha's huge address book as a resource, they asked for letters of support to be forwarded to Mennin and Mayor Lindsay. Martha sidestepped actually advising them, saying she didn't want it to become personal—knowing full well that she would be fired outright. Expressing her frustration at not being able to do anything herself, Martha knew that Mary Chudick would help where needed. "We were so angry and devastated that we worked fast in a whirlwind of energy," Risa remembered, "We realized that if we didn't do something, all of a sudden it was going to be over."[20] Printing three thousand copies of protest letters, Juilliard dancers passed them out in front of the State Theater each evening. To any letter of support that came to her, Martha wrote a fervent thank-you note.

By now it was public knowledge that dance at Juilliard was in trouble. Preparing for the worst-case scenario, Martha called a faculty meeting to express her fear that the department's demise seemed imminent. The continuation of their work at Juilliard had been a year-to-year proposition, and now she encouraged each to consider other teaching offers. Not one left.

Once the press picked up the story, several well-timed articles came out attacking Mennin's plan for the department's elimination. Douglas Turnbaugh's scathing 20 May 1968 feature article in *New York*, titled "Good Guys vs. Bad Guys at Lincoln Center," made the situation plain. "The achievement of the Juilliard Dance Department is one of the most impressive in dance history." He praised it "as a model for the successful incorporation of a professional dance division in an academic setting," adding, "It looks like the ground has been sold from under the feet of the Juilliard Dance Department. The dance studios in the new Juilliard have already been allocated to the School of the American Ballet. Who else?"

The harangue continued:

A special building, a Dance Theatre, loomed on the horizon in the Lincoln Center complex. This theatre was to establish Dance among its less ephemeral peers in the Arts. The pioneers . . . had struggled without surcease through the great cultural wilderness. They enriched it as they passed, sowing the seeds for the Arts Centers now in turbulent bloom from coast to coast. Respite and recognition finally shimmered on the horizon—an oasis marked by the vigorous waterspout of the Revson Fountain in Lincoln Center Plaza came in view. No mirage: the building was there. . . . But the pioneers surviving the trek arrived to find the territory already staked out by George Balanchine, the culture baron of the dance world who never wasted any time on the wilderness trail. . . . While his school is called the School of *American* Ballet, his company the New York City Ballet, and his dancing ground the New York State Theater, these city, state, and federal appellations do not at all mean that the range and diversity of American dance is represented at Lincoln Center. On the contrary, ballet is the only form of dance represented, and only one kind of ballet at that.

Martha could not have been happier with Turnbaugh's praise of her department as "a singular instance of what can be created by dedicated artists working within a climate favorable to their most diverse techniques and aesthetic impulses. This tenderly nurtured growth is probably going to be torn out by the roots. . . . Fortunately artists have a sense of their own worth, and these frightful back-room strategies of disposal cannot destroy their talent, however much it wounds their self-esteem. Rather, it is the cultural life of New York City that is enfeebled and diminished by such perverse exclusions from our Performing Arts Center."[1]

Turnbaugh again came to Martha's defense in a sequel article on 15 July 1968: "Another Round to the Bad Guys." Robert Sabin also wrote a searing article for the July 1968 issue of *Dance Magazine* titled "Juilliard on the Crossroads": "All this leaves observers horrified. It creates the monopoly of a single Russian ballet–derived dance style at Lincoln Center."[2] Dancers and critics alike were aghast that the Kirstein-Balanchine enterprise was about to become the sole dance presence in residence at Lincoln Center.

Adding fuel to the fire, Robert Commaday's "The Squeeze-Out at the Juilliard" for the *San Francisco Chronicle* offered a fierce attack on "what can happen when a group of producing companies goes to bed with a cultural center." Pointing the finger directly at Kirstein, "accused by many as trying to control all dance in Lincoln Center," the writer suggested that Hill's department might move in toto to San Francisco where it would be better appreciated. Commaday attached a copy of the article in a letter to Martha saying, "Enclosed is my blow for freedom, peace, and happy dancers."[3] She answered, "The whole future has been hanging in the balance ever since you were here. Your extra fine article helped tremendously in this 'stay of execution' or reprieve, I know. Nothing like a strong voice from the Pacific Coast to make the power of public opinion loom large and real." She continued, "Fighting for our lives has prevented my observing the amenities [of a timely response]. I have felt grateful to you but have been working on the situation overtime."[4]

Without question, these public disclosures infuriated Juilliard's administrators and created a hornet's nest for Lincoln Center's board. Having already provided convincing arguments against his major competitors and secured Lincoln Center's commitment to the New York City Ballet, Kirstein now focused on the elimination of Juilliard's dance department.

Funding for Juilliard's own dance and drama components were problematic; as a private music school, its major endowment was directed toward musical activities. Having convinced the school's trustees of the importance of supporting the dance department in 1951, Schuman had held the school responsible for that commitment. For him, the new addition of a drama division was another issue. As it was what the Lincoln Center board had wanted in the first place, he felt they should take some responsibility for funding it.[5]

Throughout Juilliard's negotiations with Lincoln Center, it was clear that the move from Claremont Avenue would increase maintenance costs sevenfold. The dance department ran modestly on a $100,000 budget with a yearly deficit of $20,000. Martha knew how to keep costs down but, by her own admission, she was never good at fund-raising. In contrast, New York City Ballet's financial and political support was now expanded with an upstate New York summer home for the company in Saratoga, created as a "sign of friendship with Kirstein" by (now) Governor Nelson Rockefeller.[6]

To make matters worse from Martha's point of view, Bill Schuman had officially resigned as president of Lincoln Center, after locking horns with JDR III, who had accused him of being financially irresponsible. Having lost its most trusted ally, the future of the department looked bleak. Yet with stunning resilience, Martha conjured up another plan. As a last recourse, she pointed to Lincoln Center's earlier board ruling that the school chosen must teach all of the art forms. Curtis Institute and others had earlier lost out on the bid for this reason, she recalled; precisely because of this ruling, Juilliard had swiftly added a drama division in order to be eligible. She reasoned that in the same light, the study of ballet alone did not encompass all aspects of dance as an art form. Therefore, the single presence of the School of American Ballet violated Lincoln Center's mandate to the people.

President Mennin resolved the conflict by ordering the parceling off of two-thirds of the designated division dance space as an outright rental for the School of American Ballet. With the retention of at least some of the space for a future dance division, Martha had won an important battle, if not the war.

Mennin pleaded his case: "We are doing our damnedest to raise the money before we move downtown. The Dance Division has its space provided [two of six studios]. While the Dance Division was uptown in the old building it required less, was without comparable problems. It was under an umbrella. Downtown, it would become more of a separate division and have to be more self-sufficient."[7] Unable to eliminate the department, President Mennin begrudgingly admitted temporary defeat. And in the words of Joseph Polisi, Mennin "became host in his new building to more dancers than he could have imagined in his wildest dreams."[8]

In fact, holding on to classroom space for dance had always been difficult, even on Claremont Avenue. Dean Gid Waldrop dealt with the everyday operation of the school and was the administrator who answered a steady stream of memos from Martha over the years. In one response to Martha's complaint that percussionists were practicing "most disturbingly" in the hallway behind room 610 during dance classes (it was actually the xylophone players practicing their scales outside the studio door that drove José mad), Gid gently scolded, "You do know, Martha, that in the last few years, whenever there was some space available, the Dance Division got it. There just is no more space to give, and the problem of the percussionists is something that we will have to live with until we move downtown."[9]

Martha gave few interviews during this period, but one with Roger Kimball shows Martha typically skirting pertinent issues of funding and space. When asked how things looked now, she responded, "There is more dance today than ever. It's marvelous, and I don't know anyone who's giving up!" To the question, "What's next?" Martha replied "More of the same, we hope." Then she turned the interviewer's focus back to her day-to-day life at Juilliard. "We have a big student recital coming up next weekend and the annual benefit for our scholarship fund in less than a month, so we're all busy as bird dogs trying to get things in shape. . . . Once we start dancing we'd rather do almost anything than stop." "The message is clear," Kimball concluded, surely frustrated with Martha's lack of specifics about the future of dance at Lincoln Center.[10]

Once ballet technique was firmly established in the dance division's curriculum, Martha had talked both Tudor and Corvino into teaching "Ballet Arrangement" in an effort to improve the level of ballet choreography. She also joined Doris Hering, critic and *Dance Magazine* editor, who had set up a Manhattan office for the National Association for Regional Ballet (NARB) in 1965 as a service organization, teaching and lecturing at Craft of Choreography conferences across the United States. Martha happily observed the work of regional ballet companies as she traveled to the Pacific Sacramento and Fresno conferences, and then adjudicating its Southwest conference.[11] NARB was an organization that Martha wholeheartedly believed in.

Martha, along with José, also enjoyed serving on a special government committee to support young Native American artists. Beginning in 1969 they came up with a plan to invite three promising students into the dance division. As soon as they arrived, Martha took the two women to Lord and Taylor's for winter coats. "One chose black and the other dark brown!" she reported in disbelief, holding on to the romantic idea that they might choose colors more akin to the brightly colored serapes of the plains. José tried to look after the young male student, but had less success at integrating his charge into city life: drunken binges meant that the confused student missed weeks of school at a time. After a year on full scholarship, the three returned to their reservations—and *all* involved had learned a lesson or two.

To keep the momentum going, Martha knew the importance of producing the most effective showing of talent possible for the upcoming public concerts. The Juilliard Dance Ensemble's March 1969 program, with the Juilliard Repertory Orchestra conducted by Dennis Russell Davies, highlighted student performers in an equal number of ballet and modern pieces for what would be the department's last concert at 120 Claremont Avenue.

In the push, while preparing a new work, *Echoes*, Sokolow was her usual difficult self in the studio. Student Blake Brown remembered a special weekend rehearsal called during a blizzard that shut the city down for three days. "We got off the subway at West 116th Street and we couldn't see. Yet every person made that rehearsal because we knew Anna was going to be sitting in her chair!" Once there, Blake witnessed Anna's special ability to draw upon their personal lives:

> The night before, I went to a Grateful Dead concert at the Filmore East and there were a few substances going around. I got home around six in the morning and I had a rehearsal with Anna at ten. When I got there, I just felt like death. I was really suffering! We're doing this piece, and Anna stops the rehearsal and shouts, "I don't believe you!" And then she points at me. "Look at him! I believe HIM!" Which proved, go to a Dead concert, get three hours of sleep and you'd be ready for Anna.[12]

In contrast to the harshness of Sokolow's work, Limón's *La Piñata* (The saint's day), set to music commissioned by Juilliard (composed by Burrill Phillips), projected the innocence of a Mexican child's birthday party. Graduate Michael Uthoff created a lyrical ballet, *The Pleasures of Merely Circulating*, and Tudor directed Petipa's (with Ivanov) "languid and elegant" version of the peasant pas de trois from act 1 of *Swan Lake*. In her distinctive dancer-friendly style for the *Village Voice*, Deborah Jowitt (who less then ten years earlier had been a member of Juilliard Dance Theater), questioned Tudor's wisdom in his repertory choice: "It's like throwing them to the wolves, because these standard numbers are a formidable yardstick for technique and performing skill."

In the same article, Jowitt then broke the news that "because of pressure from all quarters, the Juilliard dance department will make the move to Lincoln Center with the rest of the school." She mentions that the use of two full-time studios and one part-time one for a year and a half had been "granted," adding, "Let's hope that the period will be extended indefinitely. Juilliard is our only real dance conservatory here; the time to abandon it is not now when it has shown that it is producing better and better students."[13]

Meanwhile at Columbia University, student protests were mounting over the January Tet Offensive in Vietnam. Rebellion erupted again on 23 April 1968, incited by the school's ties to the Defense Department and the plan to build a gym in Morningside Park over neighborhood objections. Students barricaded five buildings over three days; after failed negotiations, one thousand New York City police officers took over the uptown campus. By May, a second occupation ended with a police raid, where a reported seventeen officers and fifty-one students were injured. The events made Juilliard's administration even more anxious to complete graduation ceremonies and relocate away from the volatile Upper West Side.

With the upcoming association at Lincoln Center, a new conservatism seemed to have come over members of the dance division faculty. Student Risa Steinberg wanted to join in support of Columbia students. But her enthusiasm was abruptly quelled when she asked Limón if she might be excused from a rehearsal to attend a rally. Assuming that José was on the side of the protesters, she was dismayed by his response: "If you don't come to rehearsal, you're out of the work. Your art is your politics."[14] Risa quickly realized that José was as deeply embroiled in the political maneuvers of Lincoln Center as Martha Hill, and would be for years to come.

These turbulent times had also reached the shores of the Thames at Connecticut College, where local audiences were still struggling to understand what was going on in Palmer auditorium. In 1967, the School of Dance and ADF were roundly accused of "tired blood" with no one promoting new ideas and prompting significant changes. Strong criticism continued with even the more conservative Selma Jeanne Cohen (then teaching writing at ADF), admitting that the "festival's saint," José Limón had become "its scapegoat."[15]

Although distancing herself from the management of ADF, as its founder, Martha continued to keep a protective eye on the goings-on there. By the next summer (1968), she saw that change was inevitable. A letter from Martha to Pauline and José that summer expressed a touch of melancholy but definite relief at being out of the line of fire. "Dears," she wrote, "I'm thinking of you now as zero hour for the first new work approaches. How I wish I could be seeing it." Instead, she toured the Amish country with her brother and sister-in-law, noting, "I can't believe this exists in the same world with the Jefferson Airplane, student riots & mini-skirts."[16]

When her good friend Teddy Weisner resigned as director of ADF, Martha was back in Manhattan to chair a series of board meetings to find a replacement. Hill had tried to sustain a guiding position in the organization, but mounting difficulties made it clear that the board had lost its ability to run the school as an egalitarian body. Connecticut College President Charles Shain soon consented to a complete reorganization, appointing Charles Reinhart as director with Martha Meyers, a full-time college faculty dance person, at his side.[17]

In December 1968 Shain announced the merger of the School of Dance and the festival under the title of the Connecticut College American Dance Festival (CCADF), uniting the festival committee and advisory board to create a new administrative structure for the festival and its School of Dance. With these shifts, the feel of ADF definitely took on a more "with it" character. Reinhart decided against rehiring the majority of the dance faculty, whose firm beliefs seemed to weigh down the possibility of new ideas. "I had to decide whether to make changes gradually or to come in with a bang. I decided to come in with a bang," he told *Times* dance writer Jack Anderson.[18]

Reinhart's new direction meant enlisting avant-garde activity to match the earlier stir created by Merce's *Winterbranch*. Cunningham usurped Limón as the school's most venerated figure. Improvisation sessions replaced composition classes. One faculty member admitted to Doris Hering, "Our administration is all confused and nobody knows what is going on."[19]

Reinhart's concerted effort to revamp modern dance's image paid off. In winter 1969, modern dance suddenly became a hot item when presented as part of an avant-garde festival in Manhattan's Billy Rose Theater, under the umbrella of Richard Barr and Edward Albee's *Theater 1969*. The dance component featured a mix of old and new, with Cunningham, Graham, Hawkins, and Limón contingents mixing with the younger generation of choreographers, Meredith Monk, Rainer, Don Redlich, and Tharp. The project received the windfall of a Ford Foundation grant of $485,000—a seeming counter to the foundation's lopsided favoritism for ballet.

Reinhart also found monies from NEA to support choreographers Ailey, Rainer, Taylor, and Twyla Tharp and their companies at ADF for its 1969 season. "In residence" (a phrase used because the board refused to give Tharp the Doris Humphrey Choreographic Fellowship), Tharp created the site-specific work, *Medley*, for thirty-three students and her company; it covered the vast campus green. Yvonne Rainer, now considered the "furthest out" of the Judson avant-gardes, created a series of events titled *Connecticut Composite* for the Crozier-Williams Student Center. Jamie Cunningham made a zany flower child dancing-in-the-aisles piece he called *The Zoo at Night*. Even that caused a rumpus, bringing the New London police into Palmer auditorium to stop a brief bit of nude dancing.

In contrast to these antics, at a time when Martha might well have happily retired after a full career, homage came from many quarters as sturdy reminders of her illustrious past. Beginning at Adelphi University's 1965 commencement, she was awarded the first of many honorary awards, a doctorate of humane letters. Such occasions would become yearly events for the rest of her life with each one contributing to the collection of doctoral hoods, medals, awards, and citations that gathered in an out-of-the-way chest. The next year (1966), she received an honorary doctorate of fine arts from Mount Holyoke, and an Honor Award as a leading force in education from the Dance Division of AAHPER (The American Association of Health, Physical Education and Recreation), an acknowledgment—with seventy-two heartfelt letters of congratulations from generations of prominent colleagues—that seemed to bring Hill's career full circle.

In June 1969, Martha received her third honorary doctorate, this time, from Bennington College. The citation read: "As dancer, teacher, collaborator, and administrator, you have been the catalyst who has given vitality, structure, and style to modern dance here and abroad."[20] Graham sent a letter to be read at the ceremony, saying, "They are bestowing on you an honor you so richly deserve. You have been a key person in all that we have been able to do in dance and I feel that Bennington and your dream are largely responsible for the recognition and success that modern American dance has had today."[21] Martha was grateful for the honor at a time when she faced a troubled future at Juilliard.

Back in Manhattan, Martha methodically packed up her office on Claremont. With few moving companies willing to enter an area rampant with community demonstrations, student assistant Risa Steinberg enlisted her father, who was in the trucking business, to move the dance office on his off-hours.

With the move and the addition of a new drama center, the Juilliard School of Music officially changed its name to simply, The Juilliard School, with new importance given to the capitalized T. The building's ultramodern architecture, boldly supporting five stories above street level and four below, was impressively blocked in squares with a maze of wide corridors leading to and from the bank of elevators in the center of the building. The internal spaces of the boxlike structure from the third floor downward now held offices, public spaces, the Juilliard Theater, the recital hall, and the black-box drama workshop. The third floor also housed a large orchestra rehearsal studio with fifteen two-story outer wall studios designed for the dance, opera, and drama departments.[22] The fourth and fifth floors were reserved for smaller music studios, practice rooms, and classrooms on the east end, many facing a large light well. The east side of the fifth floor was designed to accommodate a spacious two-story music library. In its first decorating incarnation, bright grass-green carpeting held comfortable sofas that would soon offer a popular retreat for napping dancers.

The school's first design had two entrances: the unlocked one on Sixty-sixth Street had an imposing security desk superintended by familiar faces from the Claremont staff. Hesitant students and faculty were reassured when greeted by Nora with her lilting Irish brogue, just as she had done at the uptown building's coatroom. The old site's elevator operator, Bill, now stood by her side, at the ready with his trusty set of master keys. Their presence helped compensate for the coldness of the architecture and the uncertainty of its new occupants.

The second entrance, awkwardly placed on Sixty-fifth Street, was unlocked only for performances in the Juilliard Theater.[23] It opened, however, upon an elegant staircase and lobby, red-carpeted and grand in scale, revealing wide expanses of marble of pyramid proportions. Budding choreographers would quickly claim it as an impromptu practice space, setting up their battery-operated tape recorders to work out composition assignments in semidarkness.

A state of-the-art air circulation system, touted as a major scientific feat, was designed to control humidity levels for the sensitive throats of the singers and provide the perfect climate for pianos. Sealed high windows cast natural light while exposing only the outside skies. Almost immediately, everyone yearned for the windows of the old sixth-floor studios, overlooking Union Theological Seminary's amusing gargoyles and, to the north, Upper Manhattan and the 125th Street subway el—windows that could be opened for city air. The faculty noticed that a curiously lethargic feeling overtook anyone who stayed in the building for more than a few hours. A daily escape from the pristine catacombs to John's Coffee Shop across the street offered a much-needed reality check.

The two-thirds portion of the "dance wing" on the third floor (including six of the larger studios—complete with battleship linoleum flooring, dressing areas, and connecting spacious offices) went to Balanchine's School of American Ballet. The dance division was allotted two adjacent wood-floored studios (room 320 designated for ballet and 321 for modern, as well as part-time use of 314, a smaller multipurpose room) and fourth-floor dressing areas (originally designed for faculty use) across from a three-room administrative suite.

A small personal victory for Martha was that she would have an office of her own for the first time in her career. There Martha placed a cactus or two on the window ledge overlooking Broadway. She hung a pencil sketch of José Limón and an unusual Barbara Morgan collage painting on the walls. She was seldom at her desk, however, except to drop another sheet of paper on the mounting piles or to make a phone call. In contrast, once installed, Mary Chudick—with bouffant hair that seemed to expand in size over the years—proudly stationed herself in her own quarters. Her windowsill now held a bronze bust of Louis Horst (a gift of Elena Kapulas to the division) for which she had a special fondness. On more than one occasion she had good reason to look over at Louis and mumble private thoughts under her breath. When Mary needed a break she watered her collection of gloxinias that would now thrive in their eastern exposure. After a summer of reorganizing papers in the new row of filing cabinets, the two women were back in business, greeting students and faculty members, catching up on correspondence, and lunching at Lincoln Center's new underground Footlights Cafeteria. The Juilliard Dance Division had a new home.

30. *Martha Hill, Ben Belitt, 1939.*
Photo: Ralph Jester

31. *José Limón, Mills, 1939.*
Photo: Thomas Bouchard. © Diane Bouchard

32. *José Limón,* Danzas Mexicanas *1939. Photo: Barbara Morgan.*
(titled Mexican Suite, *"Conquistador")*

33. *Martha Graham and Erick Hawkins in* El Penitente, *1940. Photo: Barbara Morgan*

34. *Martha Hill, c. 1940. Courtesy of the Martha Hill Archives*

35. *Martha with brother, Bill Hill, 1941. Courtesy of the Martha Hill Archives*

36. *Mary Jo Shelly in uniform, 1941. Courtesy of the Martha Hill Archives*

37. *Martha Hill, far right, coaching students at NYU, 1941. Courtesy of the Martha Hill Archives*

38. *Thurston Davies, c. 1950. Courtesy of the Martha Hill Archives*

39. *Wedding photo. Back row: Bill Bales, Max Zera, Norman Lloyd, Ben Belitt, Bill Hill, Lefty's sister Letita Evans Frank and her husband. First row: Ruth Lloyd, Thurston Davies, and Martha Hill, Philadelphia, 1952. Courtesy of the Martha Hill Archives*

40. *Martha Hill, José Limón, Doris Humphrey, Connecticut College President Rosemary Park, c. 1956. Courtesy of the Connecticut College Archives*

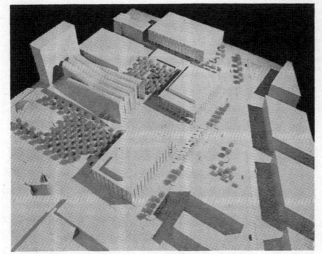

(Ezra Stoller)

Model of Lincoln Center for the Performing Arts. Clockwise from the left are the new Metropolitan Opera House, Repertory Theater and Library Museum, Juilliard School of Music, Philharmonic Hall, and Theater for the Dance.

41. Clipping from
Dance Observer,
December 1959
issue. Courtesy of
the Martha Hill
Archives

42. Walter Terry,
Martha Graham,
Martha Hill,
William Schuman.
Capezio Dance
Award to Graham.
1960. Photo:
Radford Bascome

43. *Eightieth birthday celebration for Ruth St. Denis, with Carl Van Vechten, Ted Shawn, Martha Hill. 1960. Photo: Hank Shulman*

44. *Humphrey's* Passacaglia and Fugue in C minor *(1938) rehearsal, Juilliard Studio 610. Pina Bausch,* foreground, *Mildred Hirsch, Nancy Lewis, Carla De Sola, Elizabeth Weil,* Back, Steve Paxton. *1960. Courtesy of the Juilliard School Archives*

45. *Pina Bausch and Kurt Stuyf in Tudor's* Choreographer Comments, *1960. Impact Photos, Inc. Courtesy of the Juilliard School Archives*

46. *Connecticut College School of the Dance faculty. 1961.*
Back row: *Norman Lloyd, Theodora Wiesner, Helen Priest Rogers, José Limón,* Standing: *Louis Horst.* Front row: *Ruth Lloyd, Pauline Lawrence Limón, Bessie Schönberg, Courtesy of the Connecticut College Archives*

47. *Merce Cunningham teaching at Connecticut College Summer School of the Dance, 1962. Photo: Philip Biscuti. Courtesy of the Connecticut College Archives*

48. *Jose Limón's* There is a Time, Juilliard Dance Ensemble, *1966, Photo: Milton Oleaga, courtesy of the Juilliard School Archives*

49. *Antony Tudor and Martha Hill on stage. 1967. Dancer, Maria Barrios,* left.
Photo: Elizabeth Sawyer

50. *Martha Hill receiving an honorary degree at Bennington College, 1969.*
Courtesy of the Martha Hill Archives

51. *Sylvia Yamada and Blake Brown, 1971. Courtesy of the Juilliard School Archives.*

52. *Martha Hill and Martha Graham. 1973. Photo: Bob Serating*

53. *President Gerald Ford greeting Martha Hill at White House "Medal of Freedom" granting to Martha Graham. 1976. Barbara Morgan,* far right. *Courtesy of the Martha Hill Archives*

54. *Anna Sokolow, 1979. Photo: © Peter Schaaf. Courtesy of the Juilliard School Archives*

55. Ride the Culture Loop. *Choreography, Anna Sokolow. Juilliard Dance Ensemble, 1975. Photo: Milton Oleaga. Courtesy of the Juilliard School Archives*

56. *Hanya Holm teaching at Juilliard, 1979. Photo:* © *Peter Schaaf.*
Courtesy of the Juilliard School Archives

57. *Author* right *teaching dance composition at Juilliard. 1979.*
Photo: © *Peter Schaaf. Courtesy of the Juilliard School Archives*

*58. Martha Hill, 1987.
Photo: Jane Rady. Courtesy
of the Juilliard School Archives*

*59. Martha Hill at Hong Kong
Academy for the Arts, 1990.
Courtesy of the Martha Hill
Archives*

PART IX

A Place for Dance

Juilliard at Lincoln Center, 1970–1972

Lincoln Center celebrated its official opening in January 1970 with festive nationally televised programs. The event also marked the beginning of a decade of remarkable growth for both ballet and modern dance companies and their audiences. Funding from the NEA bolstered touring opportunities: residencies for visiting choreographers formed new alliances with regional companies. Although the surroundings of the new Juilliard Dance Division were dramatically different from the old location, adjustments were made and within months everyone had settled in. But for Martha Hill, having navigated the uncertainties of the 1960s, the event marked only the beginning of another difficult decade.

With the help of an old friend, Baird Hastings (Juilliard's orchestra librarian as well as a music and dance historian), Martha scouted out available underutilized spaces, claiming several designated for the orchestra during seasonal concert times that could periodically be used for extra studio space. Another loyal colleague, Al Pischl, who advocated for dance whenever he could, now handled Juilliard's press office and managed the school bookstore.[1] And friend, chief librarian Ben Ludin, who was privy to administrative records, kept a lookout for signs of trouble.

Along with administrative offices, the corner cafeteria and lounge on the second floor was the one place where all students could gather. Between classes, dancers used the stairways to get there, avoiding the long walk to the central elevators. One of the first official memos to Martha from the dean's office made it known that Juilliard officials had new expectations for their students. Found traipsing between floors "inappropriately" dressed, the letter of complaint asked that they be reprimanded (just as the chagrined Benningtonites had demanded in 1934). SAB's dancers in the mix, on the other hand, were beyond the jurisdiction of the dean.

Although an occasional Balanchine sighting in the hallway was of passing interest to the Juilliard dancers, little interaction took place between the two groups of students. Only the after-school commotion caused by flocks of youngsters and their parents to and from SAB's afternoon classes hinted that a quite different environment existed next door. For students such as Blake Brown, the new building was an enormous improvement over the Claremont Avenue facility. Nonetheless, he was aware of a partition that went up "to separate us, and to separate the property" during the first year.[2] Risa Steinberg concurred, "We felt weird about that glass door."[3]

On the surface, Juilliard at Lincoln Center remained as removed from current events as it had on Claremont. But many students, having participated in marches and protest rallies in opposition to the escalating war in Vietnam, now sympathized with the gay liberation movement that had erupted since the Greenwich Village "Stonewall" rebellion in June 1969. Like Lefty at Town Hall during the McCarthy era, Martha had learned to sidestep any public stance on such issues while privately supporting the people behind the scenes.

Even as increased numbers of openly homosexual Juilliard students were becoming involved in gay pride rallies, Martha's colleagues still felt obliged to conceal their sexual preferences. Yet attitudes were changing; the American Psychiatric Association had recently removed homosexuality from its list of psychiatric disorders, and lesbian liberation was spreading.

Not all the men had an easy time adjusting to sexual innuendo within the conservatory. An ex-GI and percussionist before coming to Juilliard, dance student Bill Hug remembered resisting Tudor's overtures. Still, Bill longed for comments from the choreographer he most admired: after showing his work on a "one o'clock concert," he asked Tudor for feedback. "Why not come to my place tonight for dinner and we can talk," Tudor suggested. Bill replied, "I'm busy tonight." "Well, what about tomorrow night?" "I'm busy then, too." "I guess you're busy every night then," Tudor responded. "Yes, that's right," Bill told him, sorry that he was not able to handle the advance more diplomatically. "He didn't hold it against me," Bill explained. "During the next choreography class, he gave me wonderful advice that I really appreciated."[4]

Other protégés saw Tudor as their mentor and "as a role model for a young homosexual" in an environment where a good number of the faculty members and administrators were themselves homosexual. "While Tudor did nothing to deny or hide his sexual preference, neither did he make it an issue. . . . There were few such role models for young men who were struggling with their sexuality," Topaz recalled.[5] With quiet satisfaction, Martha saw some prejudices of the past begin to disappear.

If Martha dismissed certain actions among students as "childish" in private, she knew the importance of letting her charges vent their desire for trying new things. She willingly supported composition teachers (myself included) who fought for admissions and scholarships for the most creative entrants, although the conflict between creative talent and technical proficiency was particularly fierce among faculty members during this period. When composition students staged a series of "events in alternative spaces" Martha made sure the dean had a carefully worded memo about them beforehand. (In fact, the administration was far more troubled by the goings-on of the theater department, where naked actors periodically "streaked" through the corridors.) Along with a group of straggling viewers, Martha smiled as a parade of students rode tricycles in and out of elevators, romped under the library stairs, and created strange shapes around the Calder sculpture *Le Guichet* (the box office) on the plaza.

On 30 March 1970, division dancers Saeko Ichinohe (in kimono) and Jerome Weiss performed a more formal duet at the dedication of Mayasuki Nagare's giant black sculpture, recently installed at the school's plaza level. John D. Rockefeller III presided over the brief ceremony as the sculptor, members of the Japanese Embassy, and a few curious onlookers watched the event from the marble staircase.

Despite an appearance of calm, strains of tension among Juilliard students persisted. Gender issues were the new topics of conversation. Among Juilliard's "flower children," drug use for social "highs" became more common. Students smoked pot in the locker rooms between classes. Amphetamine use was on the rise. Yet among the scores of hopefuls that auditioned during this period, those entering Juilliard, if more individualistic in their artistic goals, were willing to work as hard as had those of past generations.[6]

Even as racial tensions smoldered outside of Juilliard's ivory tower, foreign students continued to be prized. Their lives outside the institution, however, had always been plagued with financial difficulties. But Martha continued to do what she could; as Ray Cook noted, "Not even God nor the President of the United States has done more for dance students from foreign shores. She was responsible for my being fed, tutored, and kept in pocket money."[7] Affordable housing was almost nonexistent owing to the rise of real estate costs on the West Side, and communal living (reminiscent of the 1930s) was back in style. Without student dormitories, the majority of Juilliard's students—many of whom were already on substantial scholarships—struggled to make ends meet. The undercurrent of rebelliousness that had torn Columbia University apart earlier became more evident among Juilliard students: beards and long hair became status symbols among the men. For his last two years of school, Blake Brown supported himself as a dancer with the Metropolitan Ballet. (Sylvia remembered that Blake "was committed to his hair," and he confirmed, "Even when I had to wear a short-haired wig when dancing at the Met, I used to wear my hair underneath in a bun!")[8]

Despite his chaotic schedule, Blake took part in a protest staged by Juilliard students against the war and the 4 May 1970 shootings Kent State (where four students were killed and nine wounded by Ohio National Guardsmen). "Everybody was upset and wanted to make some kind of statement, and Margie Fargnoli, who was the most outspoken, organized meetings in the student lounge. With some musicians and drama students in whiteface, we went over and did a little walk around Lincoln Center before our 'lie-in' around the fountain. We passed out protest flyers and the press was there," Blake recalled. Peter Mennin was livid and called Martha into the office. Margie was coming up to graduate and Mennin was going to throw her out, incensed that Fargnoli had put a bad mark on the Juilliard School. Stepping up to her guns, Martha argued, 'Don't you dare! The girl has fulfilled every class requirement and she is going to graduate.' Margie graduated."[9]

Now approaching her seventieth year, Martha had become one of the most revered dance figures in the country. Having served as a member of the National Council of the Arts and Government and on the dance panel of the National Council on the Arts (National Foundation on the Arts and the Humanities) and then as a panel member for the U.S. Department of State Bureau of Education and Cultural Affairs, Office of Cultural Presentations, she also continued to be a member of the Advisory Commission on the Performing Arts, for the School of Performing Arts, Board of Education of the City of New York. Martha accepted such assignments with a sense of civic duty and a certain amount of pride—they proved that she and her dance constituents were now recognized as an integral part of America's establishment.

A stronger environment was emerging for the arts, as federal funding from two endowments rapidly changed the economic situation, giving hope to many choreographers as grants began to flow toward major institutions. Allegra Fuller Snyder recalled sharing a hotel room in Washington with Martha when they served as evaluators for NEA's first awards to dance.[10] (She also recalled worrying about the amounts of vodka that room service delivered to their door.)

When President Nixon recommended that $40,000,000 be appropriated for the arts, it was Agnes de Mille who served as spokesperson before the Senate and House of Representatives hearings in February 1970, when two bills on authorization of funds for the National Endowment for the Arts were being considered. She argued:

> We are a romantic people, if violent, and we try to persuade ourselves and the rest of the world that we love art and cherish it, whereas in fact we have not cherished it. It is an historic fact that we have despised it. And if that were not so these hearings would not be necessary. . . . The art experience has been sidetracked. Our choreographers and dancers are . . . in demand elsewhere. They would prefer to stay here. This is their home. . . . What is

our image? What footsteps do we leave behind? The unchanging mark on a dead satellite? My Lai? Gentlemen, we deserve better."[11]

Appreciative of de Mille's outspoken stance, Martha invited de Mille's Dance Heritage Theater with its cast of twenty-five to perform at Juilliard. In a cleverly conceived format, Agnes moderated a kind of history lesson of dance in America. As she saw it, this was another way to educate audiences. Martha Hill was one of the most important behind-the-scenes players, but it was de Mille's flamboyance and way with words that made the difference in the public view.

Onstage performance opportunities were doled out by Mennin in a take-it-or-leave-it manner: for the May 1970 "informal" showings of new and repertory dance works in the Juilliard Theater, alumna Carolyn Brown, now a significant presence in Cunningham's company, presented her "work-in-progress" *West Country* (to Elgar's "Serenade for Strings in E Minor") as the ballet offering. The ambitious, if modestly produced program also included Limón's *The Unsung* (also listed as a "work-in-progress") and *There is a Time*; Sokolow's *Ballade* and *The Dove* (a "call for peace" at a time when some in the cast had skipped rehearsals for peace rallies in Washington, D.C.); and Graham dancer Helen McGehee's *Changes: I Am the Gate*.

As Mennin had specified two years earlier, prospective students were now informed that although efforts to secure funds were ongoing, the division might not be continued after the 1970–71 academic year. For Martha this meant that the president was still looking for an opportunity to disband the department altogether. That opportunity would soon come from an unlikely source within the ranks.

Without conferring with Martha, Tudor made an appointment with Mennin, suggesting an alternative scheme for the design of the dance division. Tudor had been increasingly frustrated over the division's prospects to maintain a ballet major, and he felt compelled to go directly to Mennin.[12] But the result was a near disaster (as Martha could have predicted). When his proposal was rejected, Tudor handed in a formal resignation for the 1971–72 year. He followed the meeting with a letter asking for a pension; it was denied. Furious that Tudor had done this behind her back, and feeling betrayed, Martha barely communicated with him over the next few months—a jarring reminder to the rest of the faculty that when someone crossed Martha it spelled the end of a relationship.

The result of Tudor's "proposed retirement" surfaced at a February 1971 board meeting, where Mennin took the opportunity to ask Juilliard's board of directors to discontinue "the degree with a major in ballet . . . in line with the understanding agreed to by the School of American Ballet." It was an understanding that Martha had long suspected, but was never told about.

For Tudor's last choreographic works at Juilliard, Martha arranged an informal afternoon showing in the Juilliard Theater on 27 May 1971 of *Sunflowers, Cereus,* and *Continuo,* works commissioned by the National Endowment for the Arts. The NEA's stipulation was that these pieces were designed for restaging in smaller companies, requiring less experienced dancers and simple production requirements. Told that he could bank the NEA money until the works were produced but would have to pay taxes on it, Tudor spewed out the works in rapid-fire succession, paying his student dancers stipends and giving the government back what was left. Tudor was also paying his choreographic debt to Martha for her sustained belief in him during what had proved to be the driest choreographic period of his life. The works were also a gift to a group of students that he loved, and ones who clearly adored Tudor. Although Tudor was often sardonic, even abrasive, many students remained devoted to him, Sylvia Yamada and Blake Brown among them. Blake recalled that when he began to study with Tudor, "everything just fell in place. I fell in love with ballet and got serious about technique. It was my life." A strong relationship with Sylvia and Blake developed to the point where Tudor even attended the couple's parties, inviting them to dinner at his place in return. Their close friendship continued after the couple's graduation and subsequent marriage.[13]

Martha knew the value of a hard-liner or two on the dance technique faculty, and Kazuko Hirabayashi, who graduated with a diploma as a dance major in 1962, played that role to the hilt.[14] Kazuko returned to teach at Juilliard in 1969 as a forceful teacher of Graham technique at the same time that she established her own dance company. (That year, she also joined Bill Bales on the Purchase College, SUNY, dance faculty.)

In contrast to Kazuko, Alfredo Corvino was gentle and self-effacing, a rock of Gibraltar for students wanting a solid technical base to survive their merciless schedule of classes and rehearsals. Hector Zaraspe replaced Tudor on the ballet faculty, along with an earlier hire, Genia Melikova of the Paris Opera Ballet.

When two dates opened up in the Juilliard Theater in November 1971, Martha was quick to request them: it would be the "first public performance" allowed by the administration at the new school, which was still fraught with Local 1 union problems and their fight to make the school's theater a union house. "Juilliard Dance Ensemble to make its Lincoln Center debut," a press release read, two and a half years after the school had opened its doors. Jowitt's *Village Voice* column commented, "an extremely important concert slid in and out of town last week in almost total silence." She called it "the most bollixed up public relations job I've known in some time. You'd think that the Juilliard School didn't want to publicize the debut"—not far from the truth.[15] Anna Kisselgoff wrote, "We should see this ensemble more often."[16]

During this period, José had been fighting prostate cancer. His wife, Pauline, had also been diagnosed with a rapidly spreading lung cancer. As her caregiver, José spent as much time as possible at their farm in Stockton, New Jersey, coming to New York City only for concentrated periods of rehearsal—a weekly schedule carefully orchestrated by Martha and Mary. All worked with demonlike energy to please the volcanic choreographer.

In one of the strongest concerts the division ever produced, Martha managed once again to get Graham's approval for *Diversion of Angels*. The program included a new work by Sokolow, *Scenes,* and featured Limón's *Revel* along with a final version of *The Unsung*, a suite of solos performed by eight men, evoking his (and Hill's) beloved Native American chiefs.[17]

A curious reunion of sorts took place on opening night in the lobby between Martha Hill and Erick Hawkins: "Martha said [*The Unsung*] was too long [and] you couldn't do that many solos in a row. . . . It showed me no wonder she didn't get what I did when I did something good." He concluded, "I guess the truth is that I am not very fond of Martha Hill." Erick had complained to José that she had "betrayed the whole modern dance," compromising it by bringing ballet into the curriculum at Juilliard. "If the modern dance was anything it had to be the whole principle," he now maintained.[18] Martha was not without her own critics.

Dissenters were a minority, however; the performances were a great success. Indeed, Mennin, from then on, scheduled a short block of time for the dance division in the theater—generally after the opera productions were finished, and the energies of the theater staff nearly spent. Any onstage performances for student works were wedged into this framework, always in "bare-stage, work light" conditions.

After a full fifteen months of employing a "wait and see" tactic, at the end of June 1972, Martha once more urged Mennin to "lift the ban you thought necessary in your January 1971 memorandum and re-establish a Dance Major." "In the interest of the Juilliard School," she asked for a change of Mennin's dance major policy as circulated by the school's office of admissions. "I suggest an unmodified or unqualified Major Study in Dance just as Juilliard lists in the catalog Major Study in Music, Major Study in Drama." The rationale was that "individual student emphases should be permitted through the administration of the Division and its major faculty members in line with the best practice of the art."

Martha's concession was that ballet would not be listed as a major area of study. Yet the dance style could not simply be eliminated from the division's training regimen; the obvious direction of dance training internationally precluded that. For hard evidence, she cited the loss of two "outstanding March admits to schools with double emphasis on ballet and modern dance," as well as one who withdrew to study ballet elsewhere, "whose father had recently contributed 7.5 million to Yale." How could she as director defend a "downgrading of ballet" when "funding agencies such as the National Endowment of the Arts and the State Councils of the Arts were now interested in inclusiveness rather than exclusiveness."[19]

Overwhelmed by additional responsibilities and worn down by Martha's refusal to take no for an answer, Peter Mennin allowed the department to continue its activities, largely because its coexistence with Balanchine's quarters seemed to be running smoothly. He insisted, however, that division dancers must be on call to participate in the main stage opera productions when needed. To serve this purpose, Martha hired Wendy Hilton, a baroque dance specialist who joined the faculty for the 1972–73 season.[20]

The spring 1972 Juilliard Dance Ensemble concerts were once again designed around a retrospective premise—the simplest solution in light of the pressure to avoid ballet repertory and the least expensive to produce. But it was also to support Limón who, because of failing health, had worked with faculty member and notator Billy Mahoney at his side to pull together Humphrey's *The Shakers, Lament for Ignacio Sánchez Mejías, Day of Earth*, and *Passacaglia*. These works were programmed with Sokolow's *Lyric Suite* and Limón's *The Winged*.

Although still presenting a positive outlook to students and faculty, friends knew that for Martha, José's physical deterioration was painfully similar to that of Lefty's last year. Her spirited front was infectious as she urged faculty members to join José for impromptu lunches where animated discussions shifted the focus away from his health to the dance goings-on around town.

Pauline Lawrence Limón passed away in July 1971. After her death José was more comfortable working with individual dancers in the studio in New Jersey, creating solos for the the women in his company. These solos were eventually titled *Dances for Isadora: Five Evocations of Isadora Duncan*. Martha communicated with José daily, organized assistants to cover his classes, and orchestrated his brief appearances at the school. Mary Chudick dealt with his medical payments and insurance coverage.

In the months before his death on 2 December 1972, he had managed to choreograph *Orfeo* and *Carlota* and set *Dido and Aeneas* for the Dallas Civic

Opera for eighteen dancers. Clive Barnes authored Limón's obituary for the *New York Times*, titling it "As a Dancer, an Eagle: a Gifted Choreographer, He Took His Leadership Seriously."[21] Although Limón had left no structure for company succession, for the next year, his sixteen-member company continued to fulfill important touring commitments, including government-funded performances in the Soviet Union and Paris.[22] Martha did whatever she could by guaranteeing teaching assignments at Juilliard, keeping "Limón technique" as an ongoing modern dance style, and seeing that Limón repertory remained central to student performances.[23]

Performances by the Juilliard Dance Ensemble in the school's theater were now annual events anticipated by New York critics. With limited resources for commissions (a grim reminder of Mennin's stifling hold), programs now relied on choreography by "in-house" faculty members, adding hours to their fixed teaching and coaching responsibilities. The May 1973 concerts featured Sokolow's *Three Poems*, a work with such "passionate integrity that it makes almost everything else I've seen recently seem false," Jowitt opined in the *Village Voice*. By comparison, she found Hirabayashi's *Black Angels* "full of empty virtuosity." Danny Lewis's work fared no better. She was displeased with the late Limón's "bowdlerized" version of Humphrey's classic *Ritmo Jondo*, adding, "It's too late to say how dare he."[1]

ADF's 1973 season was dedicated to Limón's memory; helping to make his company the first performing unit dedicated to a single choreographer's work after the death of its artistic director. Once the memorial concerts were completed, however, ADF's leadership was determined to move on to fresh vistas for the dance field.

Having lost control of the summer sessions once so important to her life, Martha was privately dismayed with the happenings at ADF. Reinhart had, in her eyes, discarded the tenets she had worked so hard to establish. Any rebellious upstarts—beyond the institution—were suspect. Although Hill readily admitted that she too had once been an "outsider," she refused to believe that being submerged in the Juilliard model had dimmed her ability to judge new directions in dance.[2] If many believed these new voices were energizing the field, for Martha, struggling to keep an open mind, the dance scene seemed to be clouded by raw, ill-mannered choreographers and dancers. Worse, this new generation was clearly able to get along without Martha's guardianship.

Yet others considered the new movement problematic. Hering complained in *Dance Magazine* that at ADF "self-indulgent choreographic junk [was] disguised by pretentious categories like structured improvisation, unstructured improvisation and inter-communal workshop."[3] Still, Martha gamely tried to keep up with new happenings on the choreographic scene; after seeing Rudy Perez's work in fall 1971, she recommended it as a "new wave" entry for ADF. (Rudy had begun a trend of choreographing for huge casts of people in mammoth collages. His *Steeple People* and *Countdown* were performed on a split concert with Charles Weidman's *Christmas Oratorio* for Dance Uptown. Seated on the "first come, first serve" bleachers in Barnard College's gymnasium, Martha thought back to the time almost forty years earlier, when in that same location, Robert Leigh approached her with an offer to consider Bennington.)[4]

Facing poor press notices, Reinhart used an interim tactic for the 1972 season. He regained Martha's support and that of other board members, along with funding, by agreeing to form a repertory company at ADF for its celebratory twenty-fifth anniversary—this time using the starting date, not of Bennington, but of its first residency at Connecticut College in 1948. This final effort to save the festival as the board wished it to remain was aided by the Rockefeller Foundation's willingness (through Norman Lloyd's urging) to plant the seeds for a more encouraging financial picture. The retrospective at ADF was soon fortified with grants from the NEA and the Ford Foundation for filming the works.

Martha served on an audition panel that spring of 1972 to select eighteen dancers for the project: eleven were from Juilliard (once more attempting to create the elusive modern repertory company). The board was enthusiastic about Charles Weidman's reconstruction of Humphrey's *New Dance,* calling it an example of "beautiful healthy dancing." Still, the job proved to be more difficult than anyone imagined. Company members from the original cast returned to the studio to rehearse with Charles and the dancers "remembering lots of feelings but not a single phrase." But the project did reawaken the convictions for those who were part of the original undertaking. Charles reflected, "Revolt is always good and will always be for a modern dance. One should never be satisfied with what you've done."[5]

For the opening festival performance that summer, Rosemary Park spoke of "the uniqueness of the school" as an indicator of "the temper of the country at large." Martha delivered brief reminiscences about her generation of dancers who "were really gypsies, with no federal, state or municipal backing, except for the short-lived WPA." She spoke of the need for "young people to carry on for the future . . . knowing the great talent among you [will produce] greater things in the next period."[6]

ADF's "dance classics" performed by the repertory company included Humphrey's *New Dance* alongside *With My Red Fires,* Limón's 1956 *Emperor Jones,* Weidman's *Flickers,* and Graham's *El Penitente.* Along with newcomer Rudy Perez, male choreographers began to take over the scene, with Alvin Ailey and Limón's protégé Louis Falco on board. Nikolais dancers Murray Louis and Don Redlich also presented works in the festival. But the effort to return the summer school to a mainstream focus was short-lived. Instead, these concerts were a gallant but brief step back to go ahead. It was time to move on.

For a Limón memorial in the Juilliard Theater on 14 December 1973, student dancers performed Humphrey's *Day on Earth*. Later, Martha summed up his legacy, drawn from an earlier lecture on Limón's biblical works she had delivered in Israel:

> José Limón loved life prodigiously, devouringly, passionately. To see him walk down Broadway on his way to The Juilliard School, to see him stride across a field at his New Jersey farm was to recognize instantly a heightened awareness of life, a super-vitality and a vigor endowed with beauty. . . . Born to be an artist, he was not only what Martha Graham has called in her wonderfully evocative way, "an acrobat of God," but he possessed the eye, the sensibility and the sensitivity to the meaning of movement that would inevitably lead him to become one of the greatest dancers and choreographers of all time.[7]

Limón's death, like Horst's, spelled an end of an era.

Along with standard repertory choices, the trend of "dancing for dancing's sake" created by these same choreographers continued on Juilliard's concert stage for the next few years, still meriting Barnes's comment, "The way the Juilliard School, year in year out, turns out fine modern dancers is something worth shouting about that is not shouted about enough." This review only aggravated Mennin further.[8]

For the 26 April 1975 performances, along with large ensemble premieres that included Hirabayashi's *Mask of Night* and Sokolow's *Ride the Culture Loop*, Danny reconstructed *Waldstein Sonata* for eight students (set to Beethoven's *Piano Sonata no. 21* and originally created for members of his company in the winter of 1971). Seeing the work prompted Agnes de Mille to send a personal note to Martha, saying that the piece moved her deeply, calling it "so beautiful, tranquil, so joyous, so refreshing and . . . so adequate to this unanswerable music. I thought how José had composed it . . . knowing he was doomed mortally, and what came out! Such a reaffirmation of life and human lovingness beyond sex, beyond event, beyond circumstances, a state of joy, a state of enduring peace. The tears poured down my cheeks. What a last word to have!"[9]

For the spring 1976 concerts, Sokolow again received praise for her *Ellis Island* in an assemblage of other dances that included Lewis's *Proliferation* and Hirabayashi's *Nowhere but Light*. Barnes noted the current trend of featuring "display vehicles for Juilliard's usual clutch of superbly trained dancers."[10] The 1977 program displayed even more "high dramatic intensity" with a revival of Limón's *Missa Brevis*, Hirabayashi's *Rounds*, and Sokolow's *The Holy Place* along with her now-classic *Rooms* created in 1955.

This repetitive pattern of the choreography presented at Juilliard sent the yearly events into a stasis that prompted McDonagh to write that he found them "almost divorced from the vital artistic currents of the day," though he would acknowledge, "Juilliard concentrates on producing dancers, and has from its beginning. The choice could be questioned, but the products speak for themselves."[11] Despite lukewarm reviews, Martha continued to admire Harabayashi's pieces that, for her, exuded a provocative mystique and a seriousness of purpose—qualities that had all but disappeared elsewhere on the concert scene. Sokolow's premiere, *Songs Remembered,* and *There is a Time* from Limón's repertory more than held their casts to a professional standard in 1978. The additions of Hilton's baroque *Divertissement from Les Fêtes Vénitiennes* (after Louis Pecour) and Helen McGehee's *Changes* gave what variety there was to the program from the year before. Although the quality of the division's performances far exceeded that of most around town, outsiders began to see her productions only as reminders of the past.

There was no stasis for Martha, however: the need to produce the most technically proficient students possible was even more critical. Mennin's constant questioning challenged Martha's artistic direction at every step. In Juilliard's 1976 *Student Handbook,* President Mennin's philosophy was clear: "In the performing arts today, we do not need more performers and composers, we need better performers and composers."[12] Weight problems among the department's female dancers were constantly at issue: Mennin hounded Hill to keep such students offstage. The pencil-thin Balanchine ballerina image was the ideal: any woman over a hundred and ten pounds was suspect, with the hormonal difference between an SAB teenager and a maturing college student never considered. It was a situation that only grew worse over the years.[13]

By 1979, Martha had convinced the dance world that the ensemble was able to handle many choreographic styles with élan, from modern classic repertory to baroque. (Later, Hector Zaraspe would create *Estancia, Goya meets Granados,* and *Paso a Cuatro,* cleverly enhancing classical vocabulary with Spanish overtones. Tudor's lovely [1971] *Cereus* would be revived and, for the first time, Paul Taylor's *Esplanade* performed by Juilliard dancers in 1981.) Martha circuitously found her way out of the doldrums of the 1970s, without seeming to compete with the Balanchine model.

Looking back at this period, Muriel Topaz sensed that it was almost as if Martha had lost her steam and simply grown tired of fighting for a production budget at Juilliard. With no guest artist budget available, in truth, Mennin simply starved the division, with funds going instead to theater, opera, and music festival productions.

Yet Martha's stature in the dance community was never higher. Awards continued to flow from institutions beyond the conservatory. She was given the American Dance Guild Annual Award for Service to the Profession in June 1974. The next year, Norman Lloyd presented the Association of American Dance Companies (AADC) Honor Award to Martha, saying, "I can think of no one who has been of more service to dance—all dance—than Martha Hill."[14] Alan M. Kriegsman, critic for the *Washington Post* praised her "self-effacing diligence" and for "laying the groundwork for many of the greatest creative achievements in American dance."[15] Graham's telegram lauded her "fanatic and sweet faithfulness to idea and friend."[16]

A Bennington fund-raiser in Hill's name started in 1969 had yielded enough revenue seven years later to build a dance studio complex on the campus. And by 1976, Bennington's Theater of the Visual and Performing Arts Center was dedicated, with the dance wing named the Martha Hill Dance Performance Workshop. The spacious facility was the model of all she had wished for during the school's rich period of productivity in the 1930s.

For Martha, it was somewhat ironic that so much had been created with so few resources during the Bennington years. When the dance space was in full operation and Martha went to visit classes and showcases performed by Bennington's dance majors, she could only express dismay at the lack of discipline. The school had maintained its progressive ideologies, but the tide had shifted dramatically: the dance department faculty now preferred the philosophies of the newly labeled "postmoderns." "Everything is contact improvisation in sweatpants," she lamented when she returned to her Juilliard digs where triple turns and high athleticism in a range of styles were still requisites for her students.[17]

The honors bestowed upon her notwithstanding, Hill was the first to acknowledge that it was Martha Graham who was America's foremost dance icon. On 14 October 1976, President Ford presented Graham with the Medal of Freedom; the ceremony included a White House reception and dinner, and Martha Hill was among the guests. The event was a strong public gesture in support of American dance: Graham would be the first dancer and choreographer awarded the medal as a "National Treasure." (Hill became one of the "100" at a later date.) Graham had performed for or visited the last seven presidents and took this event in stride, but Hill found her first invitation to the White House exciting beyond words. For the occasion Hill donned a hand-painted silk jersey evening dress, and her favorite Mexican silver necklace that had been a gift from José.

Betty Bloomer Ford, now the First Lady, had attended Bennington's summer school in 1936 and 1937, later describing the experience as "a movable feast that stays with you whereever you go for the rest of your life." In the receiving line, Martha shook the president's hand while commenting that she had enjoyed the privilege of being his wife's dance teacher at Bennington. The event gave Martha the opportunity to connect once more with Betty, who had participated in the dedication ceremony of the new dance wing at Bennington the previous spring.

Once so private and intensely focused on her work in the studio, Graham's famous profile (complete with face-lifts) was now photographed as part of the disco/Studio 54 scene with celebrities such as Liza Minnelli, Halston, Madonna (who had earlier studied at her studio), and Rudolf Nureyev. With Ron Protas ever at her side, Graham, like these celebrities, was her own invention. Although a formidable costumer herself, Graham's image as a diva of high fashion began with designer Halston outfitting her for special occasions and then creating costume designs for the company (beginning in 1975 with *Lucifer*, starring Margot Fonteyn and Nureyev, through her *Night Chant* in 1988). Graham's thrilling company continued to perform regular seasons at City Center. After her last stage appearance on 20 April 1969, her bows at the end of every performance brought the audience to its feet.

According to Hill, Graham reveled in publicity and always had a special ability to present a public image and raise funds. "If anybody can raise money, it's Martha," Hill sighed. In one ad spot for the Blackgama mink campaign "What becomes a legend most?" Graham appeared, photographed with Fonteyn and Nureyev. It was all for the good of the field. If Graham's tactics were questionable to those "that knew her when," Martha Hill never ceased to acknowledge Graham's greatness.

Both Marthas were geniuses at maintaining their images, but of the two, Graham was a zealot who continued to demand the spotlight.[18] As others turned away, Hill continued to phone Graham to chat or reminisce when the occasion arose; more and more, however, her messages were not acknowledged by the "indisposed" legend. But with her leading dancers continuing to teach at Juilliard, Graham's distinctive technique remained essential to the curriculum; a number of Juilliard students continued to go directly into her company.[19]

To the outside world, Martha was always on the go, managing her whirlwind calendar of meetings and dance events with ease. Few knew about a troubling left knee from "an old dance injury"; in truth a knee brace was prescribed for a linear fracture of the patella. Recovery slowed her down for several summer months, giving her time to deal with another personal problem.

Landlord Reto Badrutt had long pressed for Martha's eviction from 210 Columbia Heights, and now wanted her apartment for his daughter. Martha quickly contacted her lawyer (who happened to be Edith Issacs's son) and, after months of haggling, Reto finally offered her a downstairs apartment and guaranteed the transfer of rent-controlled status. In retrospect, she admitted, the move to the elegant first-floor apartment meant fewer stairs to climb. Reto, himself living in the garden apartment, soon became a trusted neighbor and frequent dinner guest.

Martha's fondness for hosting Sunday brunches in Brooklyn Heights returned a few years after Lefty's death. Her students with their families and friends were invited for a postgraduation celebration each year to everyone's delight. Casual weekend get-togethers with a wide array of dance people were often on the docket. Martha served Bloody Marys, set out a roasted chicken, and fried up single orders of omelets on request. Sometimes her next-door neighbors joined the mix along with out-of-towners such as Marion Van Tuyl and her psychiatrist husband Douglas Campbell from San Francisco, or Bethsabée de Rothschild, who now actively produced seasons of contemporary dance on Broadway.

Martha's gatherings often had an ulterior motive, as was the case with the party including Bill Bales and his actress wife, Jo Van Fleet, and the actress Kim Hunter. Here the motive was to reunite the estranged actresses: Jo had recently lost a lead role to Kim and they were no longer on speaking terms.

For years, many had encouraged Martha and Mary Jo to write a definitive book on Bennington. The idea was tempting, but both were too busy to contemplate the venture until challenged by an unexpected source. Sali Ann Kriegsman—an assistant editor at Lincoln Center when American Dance Theatre "was attempting to become established as a constituent of the arts complex"—became aware of Bennington as "a persistent but elusive nexus" in modern dance history. According to Kriegsman, "Among ADT's goals was the restoration of 'classics' of modern dance. . . . I proposed that ADT develop a catalogue raisonné of modern dances, as there was—and is—no such tool. When ADT collapsed in 1966, the catalogue project was left on the drawing board without institutional sponsorship."[20]

Sali Ann had begun to work on the Bennington materials in 1967, writing to Bill Bales and President Jacob Bloustein for permission to examine the cartons of documents at Bennington. She recalled, "Bales informed me that Martha Hill and Mary Jo Shelly . . . were planning to write a history of Bennington and he proposed that I abandon my plans. . . . I reluctantly put aside my research and preliminary chronology in 1968." She nonetheless published her own book on the topic in 1981: "Martha Hill had not produced her book [on Bennington], though she stated that she intended to do so, so I reasoned that even if she carried out her intentions, it seemed likely that her book would be a personal memoir, an insider's account, while mine was to be written from an outsider's perspective."²¹ (Kriegsman's struggle aside, her book *Modern Dance in America: The Bennington Years* to this day remains a primary reader on dance at Bennington.)

With the news of Kriegsman's project, and encouraged by historian Thomas Brockway's recent *Quadrille* articles on Bennington's history, Martha and Mary Jo set to work on their own manuscript in earnest, bringing the couple together again as working partners. Although their friendship had cooled considerably after Martha's marriage, they now often met for Sunday dinner or the theater, with a reunion every summer at ADF and Shelly's house on Block Island. Mary Jo developed a narrative draft that grew to more than fifty pages (some is quoted in this book), while Martha worked on chronologies, brief descriptions, and outlines. Both refused to acknowledge Kriegsman's continuing efforts.

Mary Jo's sudden death on 5 August 1976 was a blow not only to the project but also to Martha in the loss of her most loved confidante. Stricken by a viral infection, Mary Jo was hospitalized in Manhattan on 2 August and placed in intensive care: Martha was at her bedside when she passed away three days later. The following day, she consoled Mary Jo's partner, Gin, and helped with final arrangements, delivering an obituary notice to the *New York Times* herself. Martha's final notations about "MJS" in her Week-at-a-Glance calendar end with a final visit to Block Island for a memorial service, after which she traveled to Bennington with Ben and Becca for a week of reminiscences and shared sorrow. As executor of Mary Jo's estate, Martha found herself looking back on Shelly's own illustrious career and the directions their lives had taken.²²

After legal matters were settled, Martha sorted through Mary Jo's personal effects at 10 Mitchell Place. To the contents of her own bedroom chest, Martha added Mary Jo's family photographs, papers, and personal notebooks of poetry, and mused over the manuscript pages they had worked on together at different times in their lives.

Mary Jo's death went largely unnoticed by the dance community, but upon seeing the obituary in the *Times,* Barbara Morgan sent a condolence note to the one person she knew was most important to Mary Jo's life: "My very dear Martha, To dear Mary Jo I send my love and appreciation for all the human warmth and good to people that she has generously given throughout her affirmative, creative life. I remember the wonderful creation of the Bennington Dance activities that you built together. I am overwhelmed in this context by the vast and continuing outflow of inspirational good, anchored in practical study, that Martha Hill's generous life's bounty has given to the world—and *is* giving to people daily. Blessings to Mary Jo. Blessings to Martha Hill, Love—Barbara Morgan."[23]

The following August, Ben Belitt expressed his grief in a postcard from Block Island, the place that he had earlier grown to love on his visits to see Mary Jo. "I'm back on the island again, feeling strangely bereaved, seeing ghosts in the rose-hips and thinking of Josephine's little lunches of cucumber sandwiches, and still counting myself lucky to be here at all!"[24] Two years later, in another postcard to Martha, he wrote, "A little memento from Block Island, which is always an imaginary visit to Josephine, over which she specially hovers in her floppy hat and adobe colored slacks. Love, Benji."[25]

Martha gathered materials for what was to be the Bennington manuscript for Selma Jeanne Cohen (then editor of *Dance Perspectives*). After reading this first draft of the Hill-Shelly Bennington story, Cohen suggested that Martha might look for another coauthor. Martha tried to interest Nancy Reynolds in the project without success. Later, as they traveled to Washington, D.C., on their way to an NEA panel meeting, she tried to convince Francis Mason to join the project.

With no prospect of a coauthor, Martha's enthusiasm waned. But Sali Ann's did not: she sought out interviews with those who had been part of the Bennington story and revisited Bennington College. By 1978, Martha initially agreed to clarify "a few questions of fact put to her in writing." She did so with a collect call that February during which, Kriegsman recorded, she was "gracious but firm about not contributing anything."[26] Soon after, Martha demanded an all-out boycott of Kriegsman, personally calling everyone on Sali Ann's probable list to insist they refuse to be interviewed on the subject. Graham complied outright; some who had already been interviewed refused to sign Kriegsman's release form.

Another contentious point over the publication took place when Bennington applied for a $44,000 grant from the National Endowment for the Humanities. It was awarded in 1978 to the Columbia Oral History Library in association with the Bennington School, with Nancy Goldner slated to write the book. (During a year's stretch from 1979 to 1980, seventy-three people were interviewed.)[27] Although Goldner eventually pulled out of the project and the search for another writer never came to fruition, Martha continued her angry campaign against Kriegsman, steadfastly refusing to acknowledge her "unauthorized" chronicle on the Bennington years.

After "turbulent and unduly attenuated" interruptions, Sali Ann resumed her work for a new dance book series to be published by Marcel Dekker. Mary Ann Leibert of the book company then attempted to go before Congress because she saw the NEH grant as "clear competition between the federal government and the private sector," Kriegsman wrote to Erick Hawkins, who lent a sympathetic ear.[28] The rocky road to final publication was again foiled when Dekker suspended its dance book series in 1979. The manuscript was later transferred to G. K. Hall in 1980 and at last published in 1981 to everyone's—but Martha's—appreciation.

By the late 1970s, much had changed in the continually evolving, and better-funded world of concert dance. A congressional allocation of $1,900,000 for NEA's Dance Program went to support extensive tours by four companies during 1977 and 1978. Production grants going to choreographers—including Ailey, Cunningham, Graham, Nikolais, and Paul Taylor—helped spur the phenomenal growth of the modern dance field.

But money had become an insurmountable issue for Connecticut College, the newly appointed President Ames found ADF to be in "a legal and financial mess." After a disagreement concerning the responsibility for operating costs, he determined that the summer school would be charged a base rental fee of $15,000. Instead of complying, Reinhart made his move, now armed with non-profit status for ADF and a "boardless" administrative arrangement that made it possible for ADF to seek out another sponsor and location for the summer school.[29] In 1978, Duke University in North Carolina, with seed monies from the Liggett Group and local supporters, placed the highest bid for ADF's move. The agreement with Duke was for a $14,000 rental fee and the promise of the school's mounting a multimillion-dollar campaign for the festival.

The relocation to Durham was celebrated with a gala event in June 1978 to illustrate ADF's "rich heritage," beginning with Bennington's first summer of 1934. Martha was invited as guest of honor for the occasion. Delighted, she traveled to North Carolina to receive an onstage award amid speeches, film clips of Charles Weidman, the Limón company performing *The Moor's Pavane*, and works by Paul Taylor and Pilobolus. Martha was duly impressed with the new locale, objecting only to the oppressive heat and draining humidity. She soon headed out to a drier climate and her favorite town, Santa Fe, New Mexico, for an extended stay with Tish Evans Frank in "Indian Country."

In a move to pursue dance styles beyond those of Limón and Graham, Martha hired Hanya Holm, by now a legend not only as Wigman's leading proponent and one of the "big four," but as an important musical theater choreographer. Hanya, at the remarkable age of eighty-six, demanded that the dancers "want something" and take "responsibility."[1] She expected students "bewildering their way through diagonal walks with nuanced body facings" to know why they were moving, making their Wednesday sessions an interesting break from the rote learning of their technique sessions. Dressed in black dance clothes with a signature scarf tied around her neck, Hanya charmed students as she taught a kind of improvisation technique–composition class that she had developed in Colorado.

Martha enjoyed visits on "Hanya's day" at Juilliard. Even so, Hanya and Martha shared (and some say, competed for) the same dinner and concert-going escort: Kenneth French, a retired actor and theater librarian, who had known Hanya for many years. When he met Martha at Juilliard, he struck up a friendship with her as well.

Another concert companion for Martha was recently retired CBS film editor Irwin Denis. "I met her at a Christmas party," he recalled. Enamored with dance and a Graham devotee since the 1950s, Irwin took up Martha's offer to visit Juilliard. Arriving early the next morning, he watched classes until Martha came in to retrieve him at noon. "Watching dance is like eating peanuts," she warned him, "Once you start you can't stop! Let's go to lunch." From then on, Irwin would be Martha's most loyal admirer, "I tell people, there are three great figures in dance: Louis the Fourteenth, Diaghilev, and Martha Hill!"[2]

Aided dramatically by its association with Lincoln Center and the explosion of similar cultural institutions across the country, Juilliard was fast becoming one of America's leading models for dance training. Hill's curriculum from the Bennington years had significantly impacted other college departments across the United States. Now dance units such as those at Purchase College, SUNY (designed by Bill Bales), sported a program very much like Juilliard's in 1972. New York University's Tisch School with Stuart Hodes as head, and other schools would soon adopt the Juilliard curricular model as well. But it was the Juilliard Dance Division that Robert Coe in the *Village Voice* praised most highly: "As the quintessential professional school, one that can sustain itself against the liveliest innovations in its field, Juilliard has become the Harvard of the dance world." Still, he could not help noticing the school's obsession with technique: "narcissism, self-consciousness, and a superficiality that rarely challenges basic assumptions are negative Juilliard distinctions," even with "conscientiousness and competence, its virtues." Coe managed to catch an "ironic smile" from Martha as she confided, "Nobody at Juilliard knows anything about dance but us."[3]

The last decade's "phenomenal growth" of modern dance, bolstered by support from corporations and foundations, now seemed to have reached a plateau. A distinctly international flavor was now present in the dance division's third-floor studios, with Martha ever anxious to make connections for her students. With more attention on cultural diversity in the arts in general, Martha began to revamp her thinking about the best possible training for a life in the profession. Long before the buzzwords of multiculturalism hit universities, Martha had been fascinated by the rich cultural heritages of countries beyond America. She believed they could offer a corrective to what she perceived as the empty messages now being delivered by a new generation of choreographers.

Her appreciation for dance from other cultures had been greatly deepened by her Town Hall and World's Fair experiences with Lefty. Although Martha had added style classes in tap and jazz to the Juilliard curriculum on occasion (mainly to help students prepare for Broadway auditions), in 1972, she hired Gloria Marina and embraced her teaching of classic Spanish dance for the assertiveness it gave young dancers. Soon after, she included the study of classic Indian dance, taught by the charming authority Indrani. These forms embodied self-confidence and theatricality, in contrast to the more trendy explorations in contact improvisation and "release" technique finding their way into other dance scenes. Martha dismissed these emerging ideas as motivated by the dreaded "me" generation, with no cause beyond self-promotion.

Australia and Israel were countries building new frontiers for modern dance and Martha encouraged their advocates. These burgeoning dance environments recalled that of the 1930s in the United States, Martha believed, and they were important in expanding the international community of dance. Having nurtured a number of students from these places, she had developed a strong network of friends and associates in both countries.

Martha was first invited to Armidale, Australia, for its December and January 1975–76 Choreographic Conference, visiting regional companies in Papeete, Auckland, Melbourne, and Sydney before returning through Fiji, Hawaii, and the West Coast. In the summer of 1977, she traveled to the University of South Wales to direct their conference. In July 1981 Martha took part in meetings of the International Dance Council of Australia, serving on the advisory committees in Adelaide and Victoria, and then as consultant for a composer-choreographer conference at the Victorian College of the Arts in Melbourne. (She would return to Adelaide and Melbourne in 1985.)[4]

Martha's newfound love for Australians and every aspect of their culture amused her secretary, Mary Chudick, as she received flurries of postcards with photographs of koala bears. In Martha's correspondence with the head of dance at the South Australian College of Advanced Education, she expressed her "high hopes and interest" in taking part in the development of dance education there: "I sometimes say we fly the Australian flag outside my office!"[5] The admiration was reciprocal: Anne Woolliams of Victorian College of the Arts wrote that when Martha visited Melbourne in 1981, "something happened! You are the yeast in our dough. The spring in our cartilages. The studio floors bounce even better and the dancers remember you with love and a light in the eye. You *are* dance and we are enriched. Thank you for coming."[6]

An earlier trip to Israel, as visiting professor at the Rubin Academy in Jerusalem, began a close association there as well. (After that stint in 1977, she vacationed in Mykonos, Greece, and toured Italy.) Martha would return to Israel two more times. In the summer of 1979 she went with Anna Sokolow for three weeks concluding with her participation in the International Seminar on the Bible in Dance.[7] Martha's enthusiasm for travel continued with her return to Europe and Greece in 1981, this time with friend Helen Knight. She returned to Israel in July 1982. In between these journeys, Martha visited her adored Santa Fe in 1978, 1980, 1983, and 1985, each time scouting out Native American dance festivals.

Martha now took on writing assignments when urged, producing "Antony Tudor: The Juilliard Years" for the Harwood Press. In 1980, for the republishing of Morgan's now classic book of her photography of Graham, Martha was asked to write a brief statement for its cover. She quoted photographer Cartier-Bresson as having said that only two things exist: "the moment—and eternity." She added, "All dancers know this—it is a prime bond between us as well as with that superb artist-photographer, Barbara Morgan, who holds 'the moment' for us in her beautiful, true photographs of Martha Graham."[8] (Barbara signed a thank-you note with "always love and faith in 'integrity' that 'rare element.'")[9] But though Martha had the ability to write out her own story, or even Bennington's, she no longer had the will. "I can't think about the past," she told Irwin Denis, who nagged her to begin such a project. "I have young dancers to train! That's where the dance future lies."[10]

With age, "Miss Hill" (as Juilliard students now called her) had grown more pragmatic and honest to the point of mercilessness—qualities that struck in varying degrees depending on the time and place. Still, all understood her unswerving dedication. Backstage to congratulate a Juilliard alumna, she minced no words: "You are a good dancer, but that was terrible choreography." And her comments did not stay within the boundaries of Juilliard. She often gave her wholehearted support to talented strangers, as when she singled out Sandra Kaufmann after a showcase at the Graham studio, telling her, "You are a wonderful dancer with fine choreographic ideas." Months later in a theater lobby, Martha astoundingly greeted her by name. Having recently joined the Graham company, Sandra asked whether Martha thought she should go back to school for a master's degree. Martha surprised her by replying, "No! You are a dancer with special talent. You must dance!"[11] As Dennis Nahat (a 1965 alumnus who cofounded the Cleveland Ballet and was now its artistic and executive director) explained, "In Martha Hill's world the worst must become better, the better must become brilliant, and the brilliant must strive for perfection. Miss Hill has always sought out talent, guided it, and nurtured it. It takes talent to recognize talent."[12]

During this period, President Mennin's mission statements in Juilliard's yearly student handbook, continued to serve as a harsh reality check. For the 1982 edition he wrote, "Our job is to teach people how to do it, not how to enjoy it," giving pause to those who had begun to question the impossibly high demands of the conservatory. But in widening dance circles, high technique and passion were plainly moving out of style: Elizabeth Zimmer complained in *Dance Magazine* that Juilliard was now the "chief supplier to the dance community of performers trained to disappear into a dramatic role."[13] But for Martha, the ability to take on any role was key to her students' survival in the field.

Throughout, Martha had "hung on to her job by her fingernails." Material gain was never important to Martha. Though modest, her financial situation was secure.[14] Her days at Juilliard were what she lived for now, with the school the center of her universe.

Martha's decision to stay on at Juilliard for as long as possible was confirmed when she dug out the school's pension booklet handed to her in 1951 where it was written that she was "automatically" included in the school plan. After a call to the controller in April 1978, however, she discovered that the old pension plan no longer existed and that any retirement compensation was at the discretion of the school's president. She was told, "President Mennin handles and decides this matter."[15]

In a twist of fate, her generations-younger adversary, Peter Mennin, died at age sixty on 17 June 1983, a little more than a year after undergoing an operation for stomach cancer. With administrators preoccupied with carrying out

Mennin's duties, the subject of Martha's retirement was overlooked for another school year.

When Gid Waldrop took over as Juilliard's acting president (after a brief period with Wriston Locklair managing the institution), the question of a replacement for Martha once again surfaced. The two men called in alumnus Paul Taylor "to continue discussions initiated by the late Peter Mennin relative to your possible association with the Juilliard School." It was apparent that Locklair and Waldrop were just as anxious to see a new head of the dance division as Mennin had been.

In a letter to Taylor dated 1 November 1983, Waldrop mentions a "long and very helpful meeting yesterday with Martha Hill"—the first in which she was involved—where she "concurs completely that Paul Taylor is the ideal choice to be the future artistic director of the Dance Division." It continues, "so far as most of us are concerned, you are the only candidate." Waldrop also acknowledged Paul's candid response that he was "incredibly busy." Although promising to visit the department, he warned that he would not feel comfortable in making day-to-day administrative decisions. To this, Gid assured him that Martha would be "willing and delighted to serve as a consultant during an interim period."[16]

It is clear that Paul, if flattered by the offer, had only a passing interest in the position; he had always insisted that it was his own company and his own school to which he was fully committed. Some believed that this was his way of holding off Martha's retirement. If this was his tactic, it worked.

Hill and Taylor had long been devoted to each other, with Martha sending him notes of praise and encouragement after each of his New York seasons and Paul responding to her words that "meant so much. . . . With such loving pats on my back as yours, who could give up?"[17]

Another who felt that devotion was Carl Wolz: without doubt, a person Martha had recommended for her job. Carl had relied on her advice throughout his years at the University of Hawaii and, after 1983, at the Hong Kong Academy for the Arts; as the dean of dance, he was responsible for establishing the dance department. Each time he came to town, he took Martha to dinner. Sometimes he went to her apartment where he found her "always a very gracious host and always happy to see me." He joked, "Both of us were workaholics. We used to call each other 'Mr. And Mrs. 7–11'—on duty from seven in the morning to eleven at night at our respective institutions."[18]

Martha returned to Juilliard from Israel's Rubin Academy (where she conducted choreographic workshops in the summer of 1982), to find that of eighty-three students, thirty-four of them were men. Some professed they had been encouraged to audition because of films such as *Hair* and *West Side Story* where men "danced" as real characters to which they could relate.

Along with increased respect for the male dancer, gay liberation had become a new battle cry. A growing number of closeted men and women who were "coming out" at the time faced an escalation of the AIDS epidemic. By 1984 the most devastating threat to the department and to the field came with the spread of the HIV virus among young, urban homosexuals. With this catastrophic event, men who danced professionally and who were only recently perceived as superlative athletes once again became victims of social mistrust. Several young men from the department became infected. Over the next years, Martha watched with horror as AIDS took the lives of so many she had encouraged to enter the field, often against the wishes of protesting parents.

Martha felt a deep responsibility once they *did* commit to the profession. But it is a fact that she had always favored her male "children" with as much ardor as had Humphrey, who had shifted her legacy to Limón. (After years of fighting an emotional power struggle with Erick Hawkins, Martha Graham, too, would cave in to the dictates of an admiring philanderer, Ron Protas.)[19] In the past, Hill had defended Bales, Limón, Taylor, and Tudor, with the fierceness of a mother cat, seeing to it that leadership jobs went their way. Her example helped increasing numbers to become directors of regional ballet companies. When asked where he learned his administrative skills, one former observer said, "I just watched Martha Hill."

David Briggs and Joel Schnee found jobs in opera houses in Germany, Eric Hampton went to Holland (Netherlands Dans Theater), Sheldon Schwartz to Switzerland (Baslertheater), and she encouraged Francis Patrelle and Michael Uthoff to go into America's "provinces." Uthoff became artistic director of the Hartford Ballet and would later hold the same position with Ballet Arizona. To him, Martha "was full of objectivity. . . . She understood more than anyone where you were coming from. . . . It was never the same advice for anybody else."[20] Her brother Bill saw it from another perspective: "Martha always tried to point people in the direction they were going, but if she felt they weren't capable, she'd point them in another way."

Danny Lewis was already in Limón's company when he graduated from Juilliard in 1963, then joining the dance faculty as José's assistant. A rebel by Juilliard standards, he grooved into the emerging culture of "sex, drugs, and rock-and-roll." Having become acting director of José's company for a brief time before establishing his own company, Contemporary Dance System, which performed many of Sokolow's works, Lewis would also become one of Martha's dearest "sons" and her part-time "assistant" after Limón's death. Student Dianne McPherson describes him in her memoir manuscript, "Door for a Dervish," as a faculty member "who wasn't gay" and who "socialized and selected lovers from his student ranks" and "looked like Jim Morrison walking down the hall in faded bell-bottom blue jeans, a work shirt, his long dark hair tossed back. Unlike other teachers who changed into special outfits to teach, Danny taught in his jeans and desert boots. A sheaf of keys clipped to his belt jingled when he landed from demonstrating a jump or came smoothly out of a turn. Then he ran his fingers through his hair to put it off his face. He was a little dangerous, keeping us all on the flirting edge."[21]

Ever savvy, Martha knew her own survival depended on keeping abreast of the times. With students resisting authority from any source, as "the man around the house," it was Lewis who proved to be very useful to Martha (just as Bill Bales had been at Bennington). "Danny was very allegiant and he had an 'in' to the students," Muriel Topaz explained, "Closer to their age, he was their buddy. If something was going on among the students, he was the informant." Lewis became Martha's way of bridging a generation gap that had become very pronounced.

Blessed with good health, save periodic bouts with flu, an occasional bronchial infection, or stomach ulcer flare-up, Martha "listened to her body." The octogenarian carried her trim, lanky frame with an air of well-being that inspired her colleagues, who were more often plagued with aching limbs then she was. But Martha's hearing problem was becoming more evident. "Wax," she confessed to Mary back in the office after a doctor's visit. Refusing to acknowledge the real problem, it was not unusual for her to insist that students "speak up." Even Martha's most sympathetic friends noticed that she was even less inclined to listen to the ideas of others. Coaxed into being outfitted with a hearing aid, she never felt comfortable wearing it.

In short, Martha had become increasingly dictatorial, a common behavior among the hard of hearing. Whenever possible, frustrated students and faculty now routed their problems through Mary, who was almost always able to handle her boss's increasingly abrupt manner. Phone conversations with the volume raised in Brooklyn Heights had become the best means of communication with Martha.

The dance field was becoming increasingly aware of its fragile dependency on aging leaders. In the spring of 1982, a special event celebrating the fiftieth anniversary of the Department of Dance and Dance Education at NYU honored Martha Hill with its Presidential Citation. Speeches, a special banquet, and a concert of dance, featuring guest artists Pearl Lang and Daniel Nagrin, filled the university auditorium on West Fourth Street. In publicizing the event, a *Times* feature by Anna Kisselgoff titled, "The Innovations of Martha Hill," spelled out the honoree's wide array of accomplishments. George Balanchine would die the following April, after five years of declining health, and the future of NYCB without him was dubious. For these leaders, the subject of succession, though hotly debated in private, was carefully concealed from the public.

A different celebration of sorts was hosted by the Dance Notation Bureau in Martha's honor in the form of a Distinguished Service Award ceremony. The elaborate occasion took place on 9 April 1984 in the marble canyon of Juilliard's main lobby. The fund-raiser's stated purpose was to endow a studio at the notation bureau in Martha's name; in truth the returns barely covered DNB's recent indebtedness. Arranged by DNB's director, Muriel Topaz, with Acting President Gid Waldrop's full cooperation, the elegant party drew hundreds who came to celebrate Martha's accomplishments. After the pretheater buffet, hosted by Carol Channing, Robert Joffrey, and Paul Taylor, all attended a performance of *Sunday in the Park with George* on Broadway. Tudor gave the presentation speech. By then, Martha had had enough whiskey sours to cover her fear that the elaborate affair was her farewell event. And, under the guise of a DNB fund-raiser, it was.

Ironically, Martha was fighting off replacements for others on other fronts. Having brokered the liaison between Holm and Colorado College in 1941, Martha now witnessed Hanya's forced retirement from the project envisioned by Lefty as a center for the arts in the West. Martha wrote an angry letter about Hanya's forced retirement after forty-three years: "One can only conclude that Colorado College has seceded from the ranks of those institutions which support the best in American education for the arts and, further, has little realization of the supreme value of its most creative major figure, Hanya Holm."[22] (She could have been writing a similar report to Waldrop on her own behalf.) But Lefty's idea for promoting the college and creating regional patriotism when World War II began had finally played itself out. Hanya was as obstinate at holding on to her summer directorship as Martha was in her Juilliard position. The letter did little to change a difficult situation at Colorado College. Likewise, Gid had already made up his mind about new leadership for the dance division. With Taylor's definite refusal to become associated with Juilliard, Waldrop asked Muriel Topaz to take over Martha's position.

Determined to go out with flying colors, Martha produced one of the most challenging concert series of her career. Within four days, the Juilliard Dance Ensemble's 1984 spring season presented world premieres by Hector Zaraspe and Hirabayashi, and Wendy Hilton's reach back into dance with *Celebration of the French Baroque*. Matched with Tudor's *A Choreographer Comments*, Alvin

Ailey's 1980 *Streams* (set by Mari Kajiwara and rehearsed by Judith Jamison and alumna Sylvia Waters), Sokolow's powerful *Dreams*, Taylor's *Esplanade*, and Limón's *Missa Brevis*, the remarkable depth and diversity of this accomplishment would be unmatched for years to follow.

On 10 June 1984, the American Dance Festival celebrated its fiftieth anniversary, dedicated officially to Balasarwati, Hill, Horst, and John Martin. But at the opening night ceremony, it was Hanya Holm who received the most attention, as the recipient of the $25,000 Samuel H. Scripps American Dance Festival Award.[23] When Hanya and Martha flew to Durham together for the occasion, much attention was paid to Martha as well. Now it was Charles Reinhart who held the powerful position of artistic director and president of its board of directors. Remarkably and to his credit, Charlie had removed the school from its troublesome and mistrusted position at Connecticut College and transformed it into a multimillion-dollar enterprise at Duke University.[24]

ADF's founder observed it all, graciously acknowledging ADF's ongoing contribution to dance. Martha marveled at the way Reinhart seemed to manipulate the system to everyone's advantage (though she was quietly unnerved by the dance school's relationship with Duke itself). His management style, with his wife Stephanie now part of the team, was dramatically different from Martha's, although much like her own in outcome. Martha said little and kept her visit to Durham brief, but she had to admit she enjoyed being fussed over. Yet she firmly agreed with dance historian Susanne Shelton's commentary in a special publication accompanying a photographic exhibit at ADF that summer: "However it soars in innovation, however [modern dance] redefines itself, it still seems identifiably American. Today in modern dance change is the norm, and the frontier is the imagination."[25]

A few months later, on 28 November 1984, Martha would again be honored with the City of New York's "Mayor's Award for Art and Culture," presented by Mayor Koch "for lifetime achievement." The other award recipients were dance's brilliant bundle of contradictions, Twyla Tharp; alongside set designer Ming Cho Lee; and critic and writer on architecture, Ada Louise Huxtable. At the ceremony, Koch read from the citation, "Martha Hill continued to champion . . . all kinds of dancing. Her contribution to the dance field was significant . . . linking different generations, differing aesthetics, divergent skills to create a richer and more various art form."[26] Martha graciously accepted, even if the word "was" struck a decidedly discordant note. Public acknowledgment that her own career was nearing its end was all the more painful with the tenacious Tharp at her side.

Bill Hill had come to town to be her escort at Gracie Mansion. He marveled that his sister was still driven "to get things done. Then she'd get accolades. She wanted it but then she'd be very modest about it." Sensing the tension between the two dance honorees, he admitted, "Martha was very ruthless in a kind of no nonsense way. How do you separate judgmental from ruthless after you hit a certain level? It's there."

In the fall of 1984, Joseph Polisi, a man of striking good looks (equal to Mennin's) and quiet wit, became the next president of Juilliard. His meteoric career began when he became dean of the Conservatory of Music at the University of Cincinnati, and then continued to rise as dean at the Manhattan School of Music. Polisi's father served as a principal bassoonist for years with the New York Philharmonic. His mother, a French teacher, and his sister had both been interested in a career in dance. "He is family," Martha told the dance faculty, pleased with the hire.

With high expectations, the dance faculty looked forward to a meeting with the new president during the last week of 1984. The invitation was the first since the one Mennin had held to relate the School of American Ballet news nineteen years before. Ethel Winter and choreography teacher Doris Rudko decided it was to be an intimate Christmas celebration, but Martha was solemn. "It's important that you go," is all she offered to the dozen or so dance colleagues (some in the school's service for the past two decades and longer, such as Corvino, Winter, and the author). Once all were assembled, Polisi read a short statement announcing Martha Hill's replacement. It was clear that even Martha was unprepared for so swift a coup. No one moved. "Are there any questions?" he offered. After a long pause, Polisi confessed, "The decision was made before my arrival. It is final." A long silence followed. "But why?" someone asked. Polisi responded as gently as he could manage, "Martha is eighty-four years old! The board has appointed a new director for the dance division, to begin July first." The faculty, with no inkling of the decision, was stunned, not just by the dismissal, but by the information that Martha was actually eighty-four. Impossible!

Led to believe that Martha wanted to retire, Polisi had been presented with the decision as finalized by Waldrop. Surprised by the tension in the room that day, he recalled realizing immediately that it was "not a done deal in Martha's mind." The solemnity of the occasion contrasted with the sound of a trumpeter's Christmas carol serenading the corridors outside. The president tactfully shoed him away.[27]

Polisi mercifully waited until the new year to announce the new directorship, and Martha would be granted her request of emeritus status. The release from the president's office on 15 January 1985 read, "Martha Hill's extraordinary contribution to the art of the dance through her position at Juilliard has established a tradition of excellence in the training of a complete performer.... I know that this tradition of excellence at Juilliard will continue under the direction of Muriel Topaz, who brings . . . a clear vision of the needs of the profession in the future."[28] To the dance faculty Polisi wrote simply, "After many years of extraordinary leadership as head, Miss Martha Hill will be retiring from her present position at the end of this academic year and will continue her association with the Juilliard School as Artistic Adviser Emeritus."[29]

Dance Magazine announced Martha's new position that May, quoting Topaz as saying, "I'll be very much continuing in Martha's tradition," and reminding readers that she was in the first class of the division at Juilliard. (Martha added an impersonal comment, "Our goal has always been to train students for professional careers.")[30] Topaz later explained that she had been hired six months earlier, with the proviso that she first come into the division as a consultant for the spring 1985 semester: "I was approached by Gid Waldrop in the spring of 1984 after Peter died. I don't think that Martha knew." Gid offered me a job. Period. It was right after we did the Dance Notation Bureau party for Martha where he saw me operate as an administrator. . . . I said I wouldn't take the job unless Juilliard kept Martha on the faculty and gave her an office and at least a small pension." With her title confirmed, Martha Hill used it and the office, and drew a pension for another decade.

To ease herself into the position, Topaz was first hired as a consultant for the department beginning in January 1985. It was then that Muriel discovered that there were certain things Martha did "magnificently and there were other things she just didn't do. The first thing I asked to see was the budget, and Gid said, 'What budget?' And he got Charlie [the bursar] to show me whatever figures they could pull together. But they didn't have a separate Dance Division budget." It was then that Topaz realized that under Mennin, Martha had had to "beg for every penny."

Among a full roster of works, the season's March 1985 concerts included Taylor's 1976 *Cloven Kingdom*, rewarding Martha's earlier maneuvers to incorporate his work and his technique into the curriculum. As a surprise gesture during the last week of classes, students planned a noon event in the large orchestra room "for Miss Hill in loving appreciation for your love and understanding." It ended with a specially composed grand finale, the "Juilliard Galliard," danced by everyone in the department. Six weeks later, Martha was off to Hong Kong.

Throughout the international community, dance institutions were coming into being. Martha was a popular and enthusiastic source of professional advice. As an adviser sponsored by Arts America, an organization in Washington, D.C., Martha had helped Carl Wolz secure funding to help develop the Hong Kong Academy of the Arts, and agreed to serve as an outside examiner. Her first extended visit to Hong Kong (followed by four more over the next six years) offered this eighty-five-year-old a myriad of duties that gave her a much-needed new lease on life.

"Officials were very much into strategic planning and all that sort of rationalization," Carl explained. "Along with a whole stream of people coming in, Martha read our basic plan where dancers were slated to study ballet, modern, and Chinese dance, with each choosing one major with two second areas of study."[1] Carl recalled Martha's determination when she met with Hong Kong officials; she insisted on a tour of the building. "The complex was not finished. I had a big row with the dean of the School of Technical Arts because Martha wanted to go inside. We finally got in with hard hats and, of course, she loved the building." Carl served as Martha's city guide each day. "I took her to all kinds of places as well as my favorite Chinese vegetarian restaurant. She loved Chinese food and ate everything. She was in fine shape, walked everywhere, and was fascinated by all the different types of transportation in Hong Kong. We took the double-decker buses, the little open-air trolleys, and the fourteen passenger buses called Siubas, subways, the Star Ferry, and the trams going up to the peak. She had to try everything."

One of the school's faculty members, Janice Meaden, an American, spent many hours with Martha at that time. "She was a model for me," Janice remarked, recalling Martha's exuberance. "She really did care and listened to young people. She was always in the present, letting the picture unfold with each piece as it came along." At a particularly long diner at the Regent Hotel, they discussed the sometimes overwhelming frustrations in building a new program, and Carl's intense political battles with administrators, mirroring Martha's earlier struggles at Lincoln Center. To Martha it was all worth it. "You never know when life offers an unexpected opening. You have to be willing to walk through the door," Janice remembered her saying, while thinking to herself, "That's how I want to be as I grow older."[2]

From Hong Kong, Martha flew to Melbourne, Australia, where she again visited the Victorian College of the Arts; she then went on to Adelaide to meet with directors of colleges as an adviser to the Australian government's newly formed Council on the Arts. On her return to the United States, she made her usual stopover in San Francisco for a visit with Marion Van Tuyl (Campbell) at her home overlooking the city. Anxious to recount her adventures, she was shocked when Marion exclaimed, "Martha, I've just found out I have cancer." For the next few days, they shared stories, not of Martha's international doings, but of the tragedies that had struck their lives. Sobered by the experience, Martha conveyed the sad event to close friends when she arrived back East.[3]

Later that summer, when she gave an informal talk at Bennington to faculty and students at a special session in dance, Martha was in a contemplative mood: "Our dance is characterized by . . . the body as center, whereas Germany['s] dance, drawn from Laban and Wigman ideas, [is] taught from a sense of space around us, reacting to space, or making it one's own." She mused that her recent trip reminded her "that we need to recognize our [own] debt to the American Indian. In Australia, aboriginal names "are on the land, just as you can't go one hundred miles [in the United States] without coming across an Indian name on a signpost. We don't realize how much we're affected [by that] or [can] use the riches of what that can be."

Phyllis Lamhut, choreographer and former Nikolais dancer who had traveled to many universities throughout her career, asked Martha to explain why "even today intelligent people in academe don't understand what we do." Lamhut wondered if dancers would ever get away from the burden of pioneering. Martha responded firmly: "You're never going to get away from it, dear! 'It's always all over again,' is what John Martin and I would say to each other." Martha then referred to Paul Taylor's recent flyer and an inside quote that caught her eye:

It said, "I had rather hoped the dances would speak for themselves." I thought back fifty years, when Martha Graham [performed] *Dance* to Honegger, in a red dress on a platform. [It was] her credo of the moment. People didn't like it, calling it ugly and angular. Graham said, "I will open every program with this until it's accepted." It was grudgingly accepted, so she could leave it off. I thought, true. True. True.

We are still missionaries. We need to be kinesthetic or we are not doing our job. Give something we want to look at. We shouldn't pander to the audience. As Jay Nash from NYU used to say, "What makes a leader? One follower." What makes a performer? One person in the audience looking. . . .

[But today] there is too much dancing for oneself. I'm not interested. At Juilliard a student said, "I don't want to do other people's dances, I only want to do my own." I said, "Try them out without trying your audiences. Try to say something that is important, as any artist wants to."

She then confessed, "There's an awful lot of bad dancing in the world these days," and worried "whether we'll ruin or kill our audience off. . . . I [wonder] where we've been, where we are, and where we are going." Martha then ended the session with "That's enough," leaving her audience with far more to contemplate than they had anticipated.[4]

For the start of the fall 1985 semester, the most dramatic change for faculty and students was that Miss Hill was nowhere in sight. She was given a new office that had been a small practice room (up one flight and down a long corridor, it was as great a distance as Topaz could have hoped for). But Martha was soon back in the main dance office, giving visitors explicit instructions on how to find her unmarked door.

The division's student head count was seventy-one total—thirty-nine returning and thirty new—figures that revealed the school's fairly high attrition rate. Topaz began her first semester as dance division director with enthusiasm: "I fussed with the program, but I didn't change Martha's philosophy, because I believed in it. I thought it was the right way to train." But other things were handled differently. File cabinets holding years of records were emptied. Mary Chudick was asked to retire.

Polisi had warned Martha that she should not interfere with Topaz's decisions in any way. The first few months revealed the likely pattern of an incoming director continuing in the footsteps of a legacy. Topaz admitted, "Occasionally I wanted to wring her neck because she had ideas of her own and was not afraid to express them. With Martha around, there were no secrets. If there was friction, you saw the friction."

Topaz's initial difficulties lay in her limited expertise in handling young artists (while at the same time maintaining the respect of the older ones). Saner student-friendly scheduling—actual dinner breaks!—were ideas that Martha felt bordered on the gratuitous.[5] Because faculty members were generally paid an hourly wage, these busy professionals much preferred Hill's more accommodating administrative style.[6] Topaz soon learned it would have been a struggle for anyone to succeed Martha.

Intent on a fresh start, Topaz promptly set in motion the creation of works by five alumni for a November 1985 Juilliard Theater concert series. She then announced that, contrary to Martha's modus operandi, she would no longer be commissioning works from the dance faculty. Taylor's *Aureole*, Lar Lubovitch's *Whirligogs*, Martha Clarke's trio *Haiku*, along with ballets by David Briggs (*Suite Italienne*) and Eric Hampton (*Nocturne*), constituted a forward-looking program. That spring of 1986, a second concert series comprised Petipa's Spanish-flavored pas de trois from *Paquita*, Michel Uthoff's *New England Triptych* (to William Schuman's 1956 score), and modern dance offerings of David Parson's *The Envelope*, with Sokolow's *Rooms* and Limón's *The Traitor*—another strong program. Martha, now teaching a single seminar for seniors, busied herself with arranging master classes with the Kibbutz Dance company, Juan Carlos Copes and María Nieves (the lead couple from Broadway's latest hit, *Tango Argentino*), and with visiting dancers from the Central Ballet of China.

That spring of 1986, at the graduation ceremony for Teachers College, Columbia, Martha was presented a Medal for Distinguished Service. On another occasion, she fondly embraced Antony Tudor for his Capezio Award. But perhaps the greater tribute for both of them was that the American Ballet Theatre planned an entire program dedicated to the choreographer's work in May 1987. Martha was in the audience. (Sadly, Tudor died two days before the opening.)[7] She was back in Hong Kong that July, once again sitting in on exams and meetings with officials as they planned ways to open horizons for the arts in China. This time Martha returned to New York City via Taipei and Hawaii.[8]

But if widely acknowledged throughout the 1980s, Martha and her associates continued to have their detractors. She had cultivated a more expansive view of dance in the world, but her counterpart, Kirstein, now an icon in the arts, had not, and his harangues against modern dance continued. Having won the State Theater and Juilliard studios for his flagship NYCB, he had stopped virtually every person who attempted to block his master plan, save Martha Hill. To Kirstein, only Graham had transcended "the curse of Isadora." "Ballet is a serious craft that possesses a lexicon developed over four centuries, comparable to the corpus of law, medicine or architecture," he wrote in 1986. In contrast, he called modern dance "a three-ring circus; free-form dance is a side-show with its oddballs, freaks and phonies."[9]

Martha took Kirstein's comments in stride, tending to business as usual at Juilliard. On occasion she would meet him in the Juilliard elevator. One afternoon, he quietly acknowledged his nemesis by showing her the Renaissance cross he was wearing. "It means sacrifice," Kirstein told her. "This represents you and me, Martha."[10]

In March 1987 the dance division celebrated its thirty-fifth anniversary with a special preconcert gathering in Hill's honor. A mixed bill of choreography followed, with "A Special Homage to Martha Hill" (a lively potpourri of balletic waltzes and tangos choreographed by Marina, Michael Maule, Melikova, and Zaraspe), Taylor's *Diggity*, a revival of Tudor's *Cereus*, and Limón's *There is a Time* delighted the audience.

For Juilliard administrators, and most definitely, for Muriel Topaz, Martha's long goodbye must have seemed endless. Nonetheless, they were very much aware that she had single-handedly created a reputation for the school as the major training ground for dance, whether Juilliard's successive board members and presidents wanted to admit it or not. Juilliard was now as impressive in its scope as Bennington had been and the American Dance Festival continued to be.

On 21 May 1987, the day before the graduation ceremony where Martha was to receive an honorary doctorate from Juilliard (along with John Housman, Itzhak Perlman, Leontyne Price, Mrs. John D. Rockefeller III, and William Schuman), Martha tripped and fell on her way to the subway. She wound up in the hospital dealing with a fractured collarbone. Polisi graciously spoke about the things Martha Hill's vision had made possible. These public words and her unusual absence were all the more poignant because they were about someone who was actually "in house," perhaps more than any other faculty person in Juilliard's history. A Martha Hill Dance Scholarship was awarded for the first time.

Anxious to get back home, Martha refused to have the bones reset and resisted the little rehabilitation offered at her local Brooklyn Hospital. With limited range of motion in her right shoulder, she could no longer comb her hair into its usual topknot. At eighty-six, the injury was a chronic daily reminder of encroaching old age.

This series of events prompted Clive Barnes, now with the *New York Post*, to write kind words in her behalf:

> For as long as anyone can remember, American dance has had two Marthas. One, of course, is Martha Graham, and the other, perhaps lesser known but scarcely lesser valued, is Martha Hill. . . . Miss Hill is one of God's teachers, but she will leave her mark on dance as a prophet—a prophet of reconciliation. There was classic ballet on the one hand, and there was modern dance on the other. . . . The velvety smiling, iron-gloved Miss Hill cut through the nonsense, deciding that there were only two kinds of dance, the good and the bad, or possibly the quick and the dead. She brought together on her faculty, dancers and teachers from every discipline—fish and fowl, lambs and lions, all higgledy-piggledy . . . and dance—virtually everywhere and anywhere—was never precisely the same again.[11]

For the next years, Martha reigned over her monarchy, holding court during hours that suited her at Juilliard. Generations who owed their careers to her marveled as her own continued with extraordinary courage. Her schedule still included evenings of concert-going each week, often accompanied by a bevy of friends, colleagues, and former students who delighted in her company.

In a production that bravely claimed the Juilliard Dance Division could hold its own in the ballet field, the March 1988 Juilliard Dance Ensemble program featured ballets by the English master choreographer Kenneth McMillan and Americans Eliot Feld and Dennis Nahat. Perhaps a misstep on Topaz's part, George Balanchine's 1934 *Serenade* (taught through Labanotation rather than by a Balanchine expert) was also presented. This choice, signaling an attempt at compromise, found a cold shoulder from the "enemy camp" twenty-five feet down the hall at SAB's headquarters. (Peter Martins and Jerome Robbins as "Ballet Masters in Chief" were now at the helm of NYCB with Kirstein soon to announce his own retirement.)[12] The move backfired: critics were fascinated with this repertory mix, but Polisi was more than ever convinced that the division's performances were substandard.

For the faculty and students, Topaz's directorship was a pale imitation of what the role had been. Holding on to the importance of ballet within the curriculum, she, too, was losing favor with the administration. Topaz was soon asked to step down.

In the summer of 1988, Martha once more traveled to Hong Kong Academy for its First International Dance Festival, this time with the Juilliard Dance Ensemble. As the one who knew the area the best, Martha became a kind of ring-leader for the contingent's sightseeing trips. She settled in comfortably at her usual residence, the modern YMCA located conveniently next to the school. The group enjoyed rounds of shopping along the rows of stalls at Stanley Market amid a nonstop schedule of dinner engagements and concert-going. She also introduced her colleagues to her favorite tailor, Harry Chang, at the Hilton where she herself was measured for a camel hair–blend coat— "for longer wear."

Martha returned to the United States via San Francisco to San Jose, this time to visit her stepdaughter Judy and the Dilts family. She then journeyed to Carmel where friend Shirley Wimmer tried to talk Martha into buying a condominium apartment.[13] Seriously considering the prospect, Martha contemplated such a move while enjoying the California sun on Shirley's gardened terrace. (On an earlier trip to Santa Fe in the summer of 1980, while staying with Tish Evans Frank, she had toyed with the idea of retiring at the El Castillo Retirement Residence, only to discover that they had a three- to five-year waiting period.)

That fall when Carl was back for a brief visit in New York City, he recalled, "Martha arranged a dinner party at the Princeton Club for several of us from the Hong Kong group as a kind of thank you. After a very nice dinner in this old boy's club setting, Martha insisted on paying. We all knew that she couldn't afford it." Once back in the city, she decided that the idea of retiring in California did not really suit her. No matter how beautiful the California coast, she couldn't live without the vitality of New York City.

Still, she continued to pursue her passion for travel, stuffing postcards into her well-organized tote bag at every stop. Whenever she had the opportunity to walk along the shores of Hawaii, the West Coast, or Australia, she picked up varieties of seashells that she returned to a huge collection jar in her den.

On Martha's next visit to Hong Kong in the summer of 1990 for the Fifth International Conference of Dance, she was a guest of the academy for the month of July with the proviso that she consent to an archival videotaping of interviews with various Americans who were also attending. The sixteen sessions ranged from discussions with Madeleine Nichols about New York City's invaluable Dance Collection to informal conversations with a favorite Juilliard alumnus, Australian Ray Cook, critic Marcia Siegal, and longtime associates Topaz, Wolz, and myself. For each session, the ninety-year-old crisply fielded rounds of questions as incisively and as properly as she was dressed.

Martha Graham's ninety-six years of life and Hanya Holm's almost one hundred were causes of celebration in the dance community: when Graham passed away on 1 April 1991 and Hanya Holm on 3 November 1992, their lives were widely commemorated.

Hill was again reminded of the thinning of the ranks of her generation when another lifelong colleague, John Martin, who had continued to write on dance for the *Times* until 1991, died in Saratoga, New York, where he had retired. He had helped carve the shape of dance for nearly sixty-four years. When complimented for his weekly essays in the Sunday *Times* over the years, Martin wryly replied, "I was afraid that if I ever stopped, they might discontinue them."[14] No one was more thankful for his influence than Martha Hill.

Martha dutifully attended each memorial service. But once back in her office, she was immediately preoccupied with the living. Martha believed in "celebrations of life," she told others (now concealing the fact that she herself was receiving treatment for a recently diagnosed, but slow-growing ovarian tumor).

Martha would not be patronized. She had anxiously watched Bill Bales's rapid deterioration from Alzheimer's; he was forced to retire from his job as head of the Purchase College dance division. Teddy, too, had retired from Brooklyn College to a kind of dotage that Martha dreaded would someday happen to her.

Martha was still a regular on the Capezio Dance Award nomination board. Inevitably someone would suggest her, an idea she dismissed immediately.

Only after she was no longer a voting member, did she receive official recognition. At the 1991 event, after cocktails and congratulations all around, an envelope containing a small honorarium and a bouquet were presented to her. Capezio President Ben Somers, paid tribute to Martha as "an extraordinary educator; [Martha's] standards are high and no one is in doubt as to what they are, yet she doesn't impose answers. It is with questions that she tempts those who listen to become explorers who may discover something new and true about themselves. Surprisingly often, they have found something new, true and beautiful about the world and then—in their dancing, dancers or thinking about dance—they created new vistas for us all."[15] Irwin Denis remembered that at the presentation Martha held the flowers for only about ten minutes before she gave them over to Natalia Markova, who was there to receive the primary award. Some thought it a gesture of humility, but more likely the ever-practical Martha was thinking ahead: she had a subway ride to Brooklyn ahead of her.

As artistic adviser emerita, the nonagenarian observed dramatic changes within the Juilliard Dance Division. After Topaz's eight years as head, Ben Harkavy (founder of the Netherlands Dance Theater whom Topaz had hired to join the ballet faculty in 1990) became its next director in 1992. The *Juilliard Journal* reported Polisi's announcement that Topaz had "decided to step down." Martha could see the move coming as Harkavy initiated discussions with the president about the needs of the department. His eloquent if long-winded remarks promised a high level of entering talent, with stricter rules governing body type and prerequisite proficiency in ballet. Since Harkavy's (and Polisi's) major interest was in developing performers rather than well-rounded dance artists, his revised selection process would now honor uniformity at the expense of individuality.[16] But Harkavy's strong background in ballet (similar to that of his successor in 2000, Lawrence Rhodes) assured the continuation of Martha's vision of a program where modern and ballet complemented each other.

When Lincoln Center's Rose Building was completed and able to offer space to the School of American Ballet in 1990, to his credit, Polisi negotiated the return of the quarters for dance—much to Kirstein's chagrin. It was a "gift-in-kind," more valued than any other Martha Hill had ever received. Now in its rightful home, the division could now produce, arguably, the finest dancers in the field.

There would be several more years of going to Juilliard two or three times a week, before Martha began to limit her daily activities. Moving the idea of a biography one step further, I arranged a luncheon date with my editor from Duke University Press to meet Martha. A clear mismatch of personalities surfaced.

The notion was to interest Duke in a biography of this great woman—an idea extinguished from the moment we sat down at Alfredo's, a cozy Italian restaurant on Broadway at Sixty-eighth Street. Martha's first remark was, "I am not a feminist! I hate the term *Ms.*" The young editor, who had recently acquired several feminist theory authors, listened carefully before discreetly turning the conversation to the glories of Italian cooking. Martha regained her composure, enthusiastically recommending the house special as a best bet. I silently rethought the project.

In May 1993, Martha received another honorary doctorate, this time from Purchase College, SUNY, as a "pioneer at the dawn of the golden age of modern dance, the art form which America exported to the rest of the world."[17] A month later, amid excited greetings when Ethel Winter and her husband, Charlie Hyman, came to pick her up for a trip to Bennington, Martha stumbled as she reached for the car door. The fall cracked the tip of the femur at her left hip. At Columbia Presbyterian Hospital, Martha refused an operation, opting instead for extended hospital care.

This time, getting her back to Brooklyn Heights would be more difficult. I supplied her with a stack of legal pads, pens, and pencils, hoping that writing would be good therapy, and she filled pages with lists of things to do and people to call. Another of Martha's favorite former students, Allen Maniker, paid her a Sunday afternoon visit. Now a neurosurgeon, he broached the serious questions others had avoided. She did have a will, Martha stated firmly, and her brother, as principal beneficiary of her estate, would handle financial matters.[18] Hortie Zera would supervise the distribution of her personal effects, and Janet Soares should have her personal papers, "for the biography."

Nervous about returning to her apartment alone, Martha somehow managed to stay at the hospital for an unheard-of total of three months, defying administrators anxious to release her to home care. Each day she looked forward to her work with a young therapist who loved to go out dancing. "Martha's been trying to recruit me into the profession since I first started working with her," he told visitors.

Martha surprised Hortie with her comment as she showed off a gingerly gait with her walker: "Not bad for a ninety-two-year-old." In Hortie's memory, this was the first time Martha had ever mentioned her age. Faced with mortality and in a rare moment of spiritual questioning, she then asked Hortie if she thought there was a God. Satisfied with Hortie's answer of "I've always believed that," the discussion was over.

By the last month, even walking the hospital corridors became a social activity, as Martha made daily rounds, cheering on amputees and patients with severe back injuries. Bill Hill, as next of kin, made the decision to put his sister in an assisted-care home in Florida close to where he and his wife had now retired.

Max and Hortie Zera packed Martha into their car for the drive to La Guardia Airport. Bill met her plane, and then drove his disgruntled sister directly to Winter Haven Nursing Home. Once there, Martha refused to sign any formal papers, insisting on a weekly bill. "This all happened after she got off the plane!" Within weeks, "every one of her three chairs was stacked with newspapers and correspondence. She was such a pack rat!" her sister-in-law, Mary Ann, recollected.

"The only thing to recommend Florida—a very dull place—is its cloud formations," Martha declared. Watching the birds interested her, as did several cats who roamed the grounds—all moving things. When Danny Lewis visited he couldn't believe how "in control" she was of the situation, literally directing wheelchair traffic in the hallways with her cane, and making calls on the public phone to avoid charges on a personal one since her stay would be "so brief."

"Martha's goal was to get back to Juilliard in time for graduation, and she did!" Mary Ann recalled, frankly relieved when she departed. By spring of 1994, Martha phoned her longtime Thursday housekeeper, who had maintained her apartment, to announce her plan to return to Brooklyn. But her call to the Juilliard dance office brought more trepidation. Assuming she would not return, Martha's office had been taken over by the school psychologist. That news did more to set her demise in motion than anything else, friends observed. She was devastated. But once settled in her Brooklyn apartment, Martha resumed her daily chores, determined to regain her independent life. Lining up phone numbers for food deliveries, her taxi service, and resuming her *Times* delivery, she was home at last.

It was Max Zera's sudden death in May that most visibly unnerved Martha. His loss was a culmination of all the others that had gone before him. In August 1994, Sylvia and Blake Brown, in town from Hawaii, set up a luncheon date with Martha. Her frailty shocked them as she answered the door. Each taking an arm for support, they made their way to Shorties. The couple knew this would be their last visit to 210 Columbia Heights. Over the next year, others attempted short phone conversations and sent notes to their ever more reclusive, homebound friend.

On 16 September 1995, on his way through New York City, Carl phoned Martha. "I kept calling and couldn't get an answer." He then contacted the landlord. "Reto found Martha collapsed behind the front door. When I arrived, she was very disoriented. She kept saying, 'I want to go! I want to go!' She was ready." By the next week, Martha rallied somewhat but, having contracted pneumonia, she was still going in and out of focus. Carl remembered, "She didn't even recognize me. After about thirty minutes, she suddenly said, 'You're Carl!' Soon after that she didn't recognize me again." Arrangements were made to take Martha back home with round-the-clock nursing.

Martha was now bedridden in her shuttered front bedroom and fighting fluid in her lungs. Nurses worked to calm her difficult moods. Visitors were co-ordinated for different afternoons. Some brought flowers from the Brooklyn Heights subway exit stall; others, her favorite chicken noodle soup. They chatted on for a few minutes about any news that came to mind while Martha's own thoughts drifted back into childhood memories. She recalled her sister Katherine and how beautiful her mother had been as a young woman. Sometimes she asked to have her silky fine hair brushed. As she lay on the bed, Martha stretched her legs upward, anxious to move whatever she could. Visiting the day before flying off to Paris, I asked, "What can I bring you?" After a thoughtful moment, Martha replied, "Ribbon. A lovely piece of French velvet ribbon for my hair!" Two weeks later, on 19 November 1995, Martha died, of "natural causes."

"Martha was cremated," Mary Ann recalled. "The box came in the regular mail. We opened it up, and it was in a plastic bagful of ashes. We didn't know what to do with it. We knew she wanted to be buried in Ironton, Ohio, so we contacted the cemetery and a funeral home there. We had Martha's records so we called the same company and they made a matching tombstone. We sent the ashes to the cemetery." As with her brother Gene's burial, no graveside service was held. The final resting place in the Davies burial lot at Woodland Cemetery placed Martha with generations of Lefty's ancestors in plot number 10 next to Thurston Jenkyns Davies.

Few had any idea of these arrangements. Kazuko lamented that she had wanted to accompany Martha's ashes to the burial site, as was her custom in Japan. When Mary Ann and Bill were able to travel north, they spent a week at 210 Columbia Heights sorting out Martha's belongings, the genial Reto filling endless bags to be donated to the local church or hauling trash to the street.

A number of memorial services and events honoring Martha's life would take place over the next several years. The first, held at Juilliard, was an informal reception for its faculty and students and invited guests. A woman in her fifties quietly signed the guest book upon entering the dance studio. She introduced herself as Eugene Hill's daughter and Martha's niece. She had read about the event in the paper, she explained, and although she had never met Martha, she wanted to be introduced to those who knew her. Saddened that she had never known her "dancing aunt," she was reminded that Martha, too, had a dancing aunt who had inspired her—a woman who had performed on a showboat on the Missouri River.[19]

Bennington held an exhibition, program of remembrances, and reception in Hill's honor in March 1996. Gathered in the Martha Hill Wing of its arts center, Ben Belitt said, "Nothing was more characteristic of Martha than her capacity to magnify talent in the act of serving an unruly art in search of its American prerogatives. . . . Her presence has made the difference between an era of scarcity and anarchy in contemporary dance and furnished the spiritual cornerstone for that 'school of dance' whose truest measure is an era's enlightenment."[20] On 30 September 1996, Juilliard held an elaborate one-day affair, upholding the tradition of honoring its illustrious faculty after death, with panels, an exhibition in the library, speeches, and a concert in the Juilliard Theater to a capacity audience. Appropriately, the works of Graham, Limón, and Taylor filled the bill.

In 2000, a Martha Hill Committee formed, with Irwin Denis as its head. With the creation of a nonprofit Martha Hill Dance Fund, a prize in her name would be presented annually to honor her legacy as mentor, educator, and leader for dance. The first fund-raising event was attended by 131 contributing guests who dined together on seven courses of Martha's "favorite foods" in Chinatown. The party began with the proclamation by Mayor Rudolph Giuliani of "Martha Hill's One Hundredth Birthday Celebration Day." Emceed by actress Marion Seldes, speeches were given by Bennington's president, Elizabeth Coleman, and an array of former students and colleagues. When the last ones said good night to the owner of the Harmony Palace, he replied that it had been one of the most wonderful evenings it had been his pleasure to serve. He was delighted that Martha's dance children honored their ancestor so reverently in the Chinese tradition—even with a huge birthday cake with candles! It was an event that made up for all the birthday celebrations Martha had refused in her lifetime.

All who attended gave assent to Anna Kisselgoff, who averred, "When one looks at what is happening in dance now, the branches in the family tree more often than not lead back to Martha Hill. . . . And if times have changed, Martha had something to do with it."[21]

In her own summation of her life's accomplishments, Martha had mused, "It is difficult to say whether it was through wisdom, insight, clairvoyance, determination, or sheer happenstance." Asked to explain the dance phenomena that took place during her lifetime, Martha quoted Shakespeare: "There is a tide in the affairs of men, which, taken at the flood, leads on to fortune; Omitted, all the voyage of their life is bound in shallows and in miseries." To this she added, "Today I feel no tide. Neither flood, nor a riptide. Rather a channel with white water, taking courage and good fortune to shoot those rapids."

Today, dance as a separate but equal art form enjoys the acceptance of the government, press, and public in the United States.
It is this book's thesis that a great deal of credit for this goes to the
Herculean efforts of Martha Hill and her twentieth-century colleagues. If other
cultures had long revered dance throughout their history, American culture
had not. Within her lifetime, Martha and her colleagues sought to establish a
tradition that is rich and all-inclusive. It was Martha's determination and stead-
fastness that helped carve a niche for dance, paving the way for a newfound legitimacy.

Martha Hill's influence continues to permeate the thriving Juilliard Dance
Division (still an uneasy constituent of New York City Ballet's School of American Ballet), which produces some of the finest dancers anywhere. Today, many
other schools are wellsprings for dancers and choreographers, delivering a
kind of dance that is disciplined, yet expansive. And the burgeoning summer
program American Dance Festival at Duke University continues as a leading
force in modern dance.

American-made dance now maintains a stunning presence in the arts, not
only because of its influence on theater and other dance forms, but because it
supplies so much vitality to the field as a whole. The repertory concept (with
guest choreographers in shared bills with classic works) holds strong for up-
and-coming regional and major ballet companies alike. The New York City
Ballet remains the resident company at Lincoln Center's State Theater carrying
on the Balanchine-Kirstein legacy. Antony Tudor's aesthetic is at the heart of
American Ballet Theatre, and the company maintains a presence at Lincoln
Center with an annual season on the Metropolitan Opera stage. But on the professional scene, the umbrella concept of shared concerts among contemporary
choreographers has not fared as well.

Although New York City is still the "dance capital" in some minds, a number of other cities throughout the world now challenge its preeminence. And
with the proliferation of dance centers internationally, the breadth and depth
in the globalization of dance has multiplied many times over. Today, the Cunningham, Graham, Limón, and Taylor companies live on. If the major works
of Humphrey, Holm, Sokolow, Tamiris, and Weidman are seldom viewed in
the mainstream, their ideas nonetheless permeate important work on the current scene. Julliard-trained artists Pina Bausch of Germany and Ohad Naharin

of Israel, both exemplify the caliber, sophistication, and the popularity of cutting-edge dance.

Isadora Duncan asked that our children "come forth with great strides, leaps, and bounds, with lifted forehead and far-spread arms, to dance the language of our pioneers. . . . That will be America dancing."[1] For the generations that follow her, Martha Hill did her fair share in furthering that cause.

As I was going through her personal papers one last time, a fragment of paper fell to the floor. On it, Martha had written, "I condemn you to Freedom. Freedom of choice."[2] The battles she fought and won have produced an open environment for dancemaking: one that champions aesthetic demands common to the other arts, yet rests on the caveat of individualism. In writing this biography I have come to learn that Martha's life choices were determined by her powerful sense of duty and honor—in the name of dance. These choices were always hers. And on behalf of dance lovers everywhere, I thank her.

Choreographer's name precedes ch:
Composer's name appears in parentheses
For repeated works, only the main title is given
Premiere is indicated by *
First New York performance is indicated by **
Sources: DULL:ADF, SA; CC:SLA
    (A list of abbreviations appears on pages 339–340.)

WORKS PRODUCED DURING MARTHA HILL'S DIRECTORSHIPS AT BENNINGTON COLLEGE, CONNECTICUT COLLEGE/ADF, AND JUILLIARD

BENNINGTON COLLEGE, BENNINGTON, VERMONT

1934

College Theatre
20 July *Martha Graham Solo Recital*
    Graham ch: Dance Prelude (Nikolai Lopatnifov), Lamentation (Zoltán Kodály),
    Dithrambic (Aaron Copland), Satyric Festival Song (Irme Weisshaus), Ekstatis:
    Two Lyric Fragments (Lehman Engel), Primitive Canticles: a. Ave, b. Salve (Hector
    Villa-Lobos), Sarabande from "Transitions" (Lehman Engel), Frenetic Rhythms
    (Wallingford Riegger, voice, Norman Lloyd), Harlequinade: a. Wonder,
    b. Renunciation, c. Action (Ernst Toch).

27 July *Doris Humphrey and Charles Weidman*
    Humphrey ch: Three Mazurkas (Alexander Tan), Counterpoint No. 2 (Harvey Pollins),
    Two Ecstatic Themes: a. Circular Descent (Nikolai Medtner), b. Pointed Ascent (Gian
    Francesco Malipiero). Weidman, ch: Memorials: a. To the Trivial b. To the Connubial
    c. To the Colossal (Jerome Moross), Kinetic Pantomime (Colin McPhee). Humphrey
    and Weidman ch: Rudepoema (Villa-Lobos), Alcina Suite a. Introduction Pomposo
    and Allegro b. Pantomime c. Minuete, Musette, Minuet (Handel).

1935

College Theatre
13 July *Tina Flade Solo Recital*
    Flade ch: Dance in the Early Morning (Henry Cowell), Paeans (Dane Rudhyar),
    Obsession of the Spiral (Crawford), Sinister Resonance (Cowell), Two Sarabandes
    (Arcangelo Corelli), Elegy (Alejandro Caturia), Fire Cycle a. Fire Preservation b. Fire
    Torture c. Fire Purification (Cowell).

28 July *An Evening of Revolutionary Dance New Dance League*
    Miriam Blecher ch: Three Negro Poems a. Poems (Frank Horne, Langston Hughes),
    b. Woman, from The Disinherited (Parnas). Jane Dudley ch: Time is Money

(S. Funaroff), Dilemmas a. Aesthete b. Liberal (Arthur Honegger, Prokofiev). Merle Hirsh ch: Affectations a. Ennui b. Sentimentale (Alexander Scriabin, Maurice Ravel). Lil Liandre ch: American Sketches, One of the West, Two of the South, One of the East (Louis Gruenberg). Marie Marchowsky ch: Agitation (Gyorgy Kosa). Sophie Maslow ch: Themes from a Slavic People (Béla Bartók), Forward (Alex North). Lily Mehlman ch: Fatherland a. Persecution b. Defiance (Honegger, Sergei Prokofiev). Anna Sokolow, ch: Greeting (Shebalin), Impressions of a Dance Hall (Louis Gruenberg).

3 August *Doris Humphrey and Charles Weidman*
Humphrey ch: New Dance* (Riegger), Life of the Bee (Pauline Lawrence, comb and wax paper). Weidman ch: Traditions (Lehman Engel), Studies in Conflict (Dane Rudhyar) Alcina Suite.

Vermont State Armory
14, 15 August *Martha Graham and the Workshop Group*
Graham ch: Celebration (Horst), Sarabande, Frontier from Perspectives (Horst), Panorama 1.Theme of Dedication, 2. Imperial Theme, 3. Popular Theme* (Lloyd), décor: Isamu Noguchi, mobiles: Alexander Calder, setting: Arch Lauterer.

1936

College Theatre
17, 18 July *Ballet Caravan*
Lew Christensen ch: Encounter (Mozart), Pocahontas* (Elliott Carter). William Dollar ch: Promenade* (Ravel). Eugene Loring ch: Harlequin for President (Scarlatti), Divertissements: Mazurka, Morning Greeting, Pas de Deux, Gitana, Can-Can, Pas Classique, Rhapsody, Valse, March.

26 July *New Dance League*
Eva Desca ch: Transition (Elizabeth Gottesleben). Fara Lynn ch: Hunger (Prokofiev). Bill Matons ch: Well Fed (Brown). Matons and Edith Orcutt ch: American Rapsody (Scriabin). Sokolow ch: Histrionics (Paul Hindemith), Romantic Dances a. Illusion b. Desire (Scriabin), Speaker (North), Four Little Salon Pieces a. Debut b. Elan c. Reverie, d. Entr'acte (Dmitri Shostakovitch), Ballad in Popular Style (North).

31 July, 1 August *Martha Graham Solo Recital*
Graham ch: Praeludium (Paul Nordoff), Imperial Gesture (Lehman Engel), Building Motif from Horizons (Horst), Act of Piety from American Provincials (Horst), Lamentation, Frontier, Satyric Festival Song, Sarabande, Harlequinade, Ekstasis.

7, 8 August *Hanya Holm and Group of the New York Wigman School of Dance*
Holm ch: Salutation (Cowell), In a Quiet Space (Franziska Boas), Drive (Harvey Pollins), Dance in Two Parts: A Cry Rises in the Land, New Destinies (Riegger), Dance Stanzas (Jurist), Sarabande (Pollins), City Nocturne (Riegger), Four Chromatic Eccentricities (Riegger), Primitive Rhythm (Lucretia Barzun). Note: Concert first performed at Mills 25 July. In November 1936, Holm severed her affiliation with Wigman.

Vermont State Armory

12, 14 August *Humphrey-Weidman with Concert Groups and Students from Workshops of the School*

Humphrey ch: Part I: Theatre Piece, Part II: New Dance. Weidman ch: In the Theatre and third theme of New Dance (Riegger). Humphrey ch: With My Red Fires* (Riegger). Weidman ch: Quest: A Choreographic Pantomime (Lloyd, Clair Leonard also credited).

1937

Vermont State Armory

20, 31 July *Martha Graham Solo Recital*

Graham ch: Opening Dance* (Lloyd), Immediate Tragedy: Dance of Dedication* (Cowell), Spectre 1914 from Chronicle (Riegger), Lamentation, Satiric Festival Song, Imperial Gesture, Act of Piety from American Provincials, Harlequinade.

24 July *Ballet Caravan*

Christensen ch: Encounter (Mozart), Erick Hawkins ch: Showpiece (Robert McBride), Loring ch: Yankee Clipper (Paul Bowles)

12 August *Esther Junger, José Limón, Anna Sokolow, Fellows of the Bennington School of the Dance*

Junger ch: Dance to the People* (Moross), Ravage* (Pollins), Festive Rites* (Morris Mamorsky) Limón ch: Danza de la Muerte* (Clark), Junger, Limón ch: Opus for Three and Props* (Dmitri Shostakovitch) Sokolow ch: Façade-Esposizione Italiana (North), Speaker, Ballad in a Popular Style.

13, 14 August *Hanya Holm and her Concert Group with Students of the School Workshop*

Holm ch: Festive Rhythm (Lucretia Wilson), Prelude (Riegger), Trend* (Riegger and Edgard Varèse). Salutation, City Nocturne.

1938

Vermont State Armory

4, 8 August *Eleanor King, Louise Kloepper, Marian Van Tuyl, Fellows of the Bennington School of the Dance*

King ch: Ode to Freedom* (arranged by John Colman, Lloyd), American Folk Suite a. Bonja Song* (arranged by Esther Williamson), b. Hoe-Down (Reginald Forsythe), c. Horn-pipe (traditional). Kloepper ch: Romantic Theme* (Pollins), Statement of Dissent* (Gregory Tucker), Earth Saga* (Williamson). Van Tuyl ch: Directions, a. Flight b. Indecision c. Redirection* (Nikolai Lopatnikow), Out of One Happening* (Tucker), In the Clearing: Variations on a Theme (Tucker).

5, 9 August *Hanya Holm and Group; Doris Humphrey and Group*

Holm ch: Dance of Work and Play* (Lloyd), Dance Sonata* (Harrison Kerr). Humphrey ch: Passacaglia in C Minor* (J. S. Bach), Variations and Conclusion from New Dance (Riegger for two pianos and percussion).

6, 9 August *Charles Weidman and Group; Martha Graham and Group*
    Graham ch: American Document* (Ray Green). Weidman ch: Opus 51* (Vivian Fine).

1939

Mills College, Oakland, California, Lisser Hall
4 August *School of the Dance at Mills: A Concert of Modern Dance by Ethel Butler,*
Louise Kloepper, José Limón, Katherine Manning
    Butler ch: Ceremonial Dance* (Ralph Gilbert), The Spirit of the Land Moves in the
    Blood* (Carlos Chávez) Limón ch: Danzas Mexicanas Indio, Conquistadore, Peón,
    Caballero, Revolucionario* (Lionel Nowak) Cancion y Danza (Mompou), Danza
    (Prokofiev), Limón and Katherine Manning ch: Suite in B minor: a. Polonaise b. Rondo,
    c. Badinerie (J. S. Bach), Kloepper ch: Romantic Theme, Statement of Dissent

1940

College Theatre: First Session of the Bennington School of the Arts: Dance Division
13 July *Erick Hawkins in a Program of Dances*
    Hawkins ch: Liberty Tree* (Gilbert), Insubstantial Pageant* (Engel), Yankee
    Bluebritches (Hunter Johnson).

10, 12, 14, 16 August *The King and the Duke: A Melodramatic Farce from*
Huckleberry Finn*
    Martha Hill ch: (Tucker), sets and light: Arch Lauterer

11, 13, 15, 17 August *Martha Graham and Dance Group*
    Graham ch: El Penitente* (Horst), Every Soul Is a Circus A Satire (Nordoff), sets and
    light: Lauterer, Props: Philip Stapp, Letter to the World* (Johnson), sets and light:
    Lauterer.

1941

College Theatre: Second Session of the Bennington School of the Arts: Dance Division
19 July *Erick Hawkins with Jean Erdman and Jane Dudley*
    Dudley ch: The Ballad of Molly Pitcher (Earl Robinson), Harmonica Breakdown
    (Sonny Terry, Oh Red: recording) Hawkins ch: In Time of Armament* (Johnson),
    Trailbreaker-Kentucky (Gilbert), Trickster Coyote (Cowell), Mask: James W. Harker,
    Chaconne: The Pilgrim's Progress (Riegger), Set: Stapp, Yankee Bluebritches.

General Stark Theatre, Bennington, Vermont
3, 4 August *The School for Wives*
    Martha Hill ch: (Mozart, Molière), director: Francis Fergusson, music director: Otto
    Luening.

College Theatre
9, 11, 13, 15, 17 August *Doris Humphrey–Charles Weidman and Company*
    Humphrey ch: Decade: A Biography of Modern Dance from 1930–1940

(Nowak: arranged sections by Bach, Aaron Copland, Debussy, Herbert Elwell, Fine, Gluck, Lloyd, Nikolai Medtner, Riegger, Winthrop Sargent, Scriabin).

10, 12, 14, 16 August *Martha Graham and Dance Company*
Graham ch: Punch and the Judy* (McBride) sets and light, art collaboration: Lauterer, El Penitente, Letter to the World.

1942

College Theatre: Bennington College Summer Session: Dance
1 August *A Program of Dances: Jean Erdman, Nina Fonaroff, and Merce Cunningham*
Cunningham ch: Credo in Us* (John Cage), Renaissance Testimonials Profession, Confession* (Maxwell Powers) Erdman ch: The Transformations of Medusa Maid of the Sacred Isle, Lady of the Wild Things, Queen of Gorgons*, Cunningham and Erdman ch: Ad Lib* (Tucker), Seeds of Brightness* (Lloyd) Fonaroff ch: Theodolina, Queen of the Amazons (Fantasy of a little creature) a. Theodolina, the huntress b. Theodolina dances for joy c. Theodolina has a thought d. Theodolina flies through space (Horst), Hooker on a Fiver (Tcherepnin), Cafe Chantant-Five A.M. (Larmanjat).

9 August *Martha Graham Dance Company*
American Document.

13 August *Jane Dudley, Sophie Maslow, William Bales: Program of Dances Assisted by Members of the Martha Graham Dance Company*
Bales ch: To a Green Mountain Boy (Paul Creston), Black Tambourine (Zoe Williams). Dudley, Maslow, Bales ch: Suite: a. Scherzo, b. Loure,* c. Gigue (Bach). Dudley ch: Two Dust Bowl Ballads: a I Ain't Got No Home in This World Anymore, b. Dusty Old Dust (Woody Guthrie), Short Story (Creston). Sophie Maslow ch: Folksay Excerpts (folk songs sung by Burl Ives; words from Carl Sandburg's "The People Yes"), Harmonica Breakdown.

1946

College Theatre
11 July *José Limón Dance Company* (debut of company)
Humphrey ch: Lament for Ignacio Sanchez Mejias* (Lloyd; text Frederico García Lorca), The Story of Mankind * (Nowak).

CONNECTICUT COLLEGE, NEW LONDON, CONNECTICUT

1948

Connecticut College—New York University Summer School of the Dance, American Dance Festival, Palmer Auditorium

13–22 August

Martha Graham Dance Company
Graham ch: Wilderness Stair (Diversion of Angels)* (Norman Dello Joio), Appalachian Spring (Copland), Night Journey (William Schuman), Hérodiade (Paul

Hindemith), Dark Meadow (Chávez), Errand into the Maze (Gian-Carlo Menotti), Cave of the Heart (Samuel Barber). Erick Hawkins ch: The Stangler: A Rite of Passage* (Bohuslav Martinu), design: Lauterer, poetry: Robert Fitzgerald.

Dudley-Maslow-Bales Trio Ensemble
Bales ch: The Lonely Ones (Williams, arranged sound effects), Soliloquy (Herbert Haufreucht), Peon Portraits (traditional). Dudley ch: Song for a Child (Brahms), Spanish Suite a. Cante Flamenco, b. Llanto (traditional), Harmonica Breakdown, New World a 'Comin', Short Story. Maslow ch: Dust Bowl Ballads, Partisan Journey (Guerill Song), Champion, Folksay.

José Limón and Company
Humphrey ch: Corybantic* (Bartók), Day on Earth, Lament for Ignacio Sanchez Mejias, Story of Mankind, With My Red Fires. Pauline Koner ch: Voice in the Wilderness (Lucas Foss), Limón ch: Sonata No. IV a. Adagio, b. Andante, c. Un poco (Bach), Vivaldi Concerto, Chaconne in D Minor.

1949

Palmer: Connecticut College—New York University Summer School of the Dance (Ruth Bloomer and Martha Hill: co-chairmen)
13, 16 August *Dudley-Maslow-Bales Trio and New Dance Group Company*
Bales ch: Judith* (Hazel Johnson), set: Charles Hyman, William Sherman. Dudley ch: Out of the Cradle Endlessly Rocking* (Beethoven), set: Hyman, Sherman Vagary* (Bartók). Maslow ch: Festival* (later part of the Village I Knew) (Tucker, Samuel Matlowsky).

17 August *José Limón and Company*
Limón ch: The Moor's Pavane: Variations on the Theme of Othello*(Henry Purcell, arranged by Simon Sadoff), La Malinche. Humphrey ch: Invention (Lloyd), Corybantic, Story of Mankind.

14, 18 August *Valerie Bettis and Company*
Bettis ch: Domino Furioso* (Bernado Segall, script: John Malcolm Brinnin), It's Always Farewell* (Irwin Bazelon), Yerma (Segall), As I lay Dying (Segall), The Desperate Heart (Segall), The Earth Shall Bear Again (Segall).

1950

Connecticut College School of the Dance
4–6 August *Dudley-Maslow-Bales and Company*
Bales ch: Impromptu* (Erik Satie), The Haunted Ones* (Leon Kirchner), Peon Portraits, Lonely Ones, Bach Suite. Dudley ch: Passional* (Bartók), Family Portrait (Meyer Kupferman), set: Milton Wynne, Vagary. Maslow ch: The Village I Knew* (Tucker, Matlowsky), Four Sonnets, Bach Suite, Folksay, Champion, Dust Bowl Ballads, Harmonica Breakdown.

4–6 August *José Limón and Dance Company*
  Humphrey ch: Day on Earth. Koner ch: Concerto in D Major (K. P. E. Bach arranged
  by Trudy Rittmann), The Visit (Ernest Bloch). Limon ch: The Exiles* (Arnold
  Schoenberg), set: Anita Weschler, Concert* (Bach arranged by Sadoff), The Moor's
  Pavane, La Malinche, Chaconne in D Minor.

11–13 August *Merce Cunningham, Katherine Litz*
  Cunningham ch: Two Step (Satie), Root of an Unfocus (Cage), The Monkey Dances
  (Satie), Before Dawn (unaccompanied). Litz ch: Suite for a Woman (Corelli, arranged
  by Sadoff), Twilight of a Flower (Ravel), Fire in the Snow (Beethoven), Daughter of
  Virtue (Rachmaninoff, Sousa).

18–20 August *Nina Fonaroff, Pearl Primus*
  Fonaroff ch: Mr. Puppet (words by Fonaroff). Primus ch: Prayer, Chants of Africa,
  Fanga: Dance of Welcome, Spirituals, Drums of Africa and Haiti (Helen Tinsley),
  Shouters of Sobo (traditional).

1951

Palmer Auditorium
16–19 August *José Limón and Dance Company Charles Weidman, Pauline Koner*
  Humphrey ch: Quartet No. I (Night Spell) * (Priaulx Rainier), set: Thomas Skelton,
  Passacaglia and Fugue in C Minor. Limón ch: The Moor's Pavane, Tonantzintla,
  (Antonio Soler), Dialogues, La Malinche. Weidman ch: A Song for You* (Brazilian
  songs recorded by Elsie Houston) Koner ch: Amorous Adventure (Freda Miller),
  story and designs: Abner Dean.

1952

Palmer Auditorium
21–24 August

José Limón and Dance Company
  Limón ch: The Queen's Epicedum* (Purcell), The Visitation* (Schoenberg),
  Tonantzintla (Antonio Soler), Concerto Grosso. Humphrey ch: Fantasy and Fugue
  in C Minor* (Mozart), Day on Earth, Story of Mankind, Variations and Conclusion
  from New Dance.

Dudley-Maslow-Bales and Company
  Bales ch: The Haunted Ones* (Leon Kirchner). Dudley ch: Family Portrait* (Meyer
  Kupferman), Sonata. Maslow ch: Four Sonnets (Robert Schumann). Maslow ch:
  Snow Queen * (Prokofieff), Four Sonnets, The Village I Knew.

Guest artists: *Ronne Aul, Emily Frankel and Mark Ryder, Pearl Lang*
  Aul ch: Mostly Like Flight* (Stravinsky), Street Musician, The (Possible), Hunter,
  Caller of the Wind, Movement Dance (Konrad Wolff, accompanist). Frankel, Ryder
  ch: Biography of Fear, And Jacob Loved Rachel, The Misfits.* Lang ch: Song of
  Deborah (Richard Winslow), Legend (Morton Feldman), Moonsung (Bartók),

Windsung (Samuel Barber). Note: 1953 to 1958: Ruth Bloomer and Martha Hill (on leave), co-directors. Hill served on advisory or administrative boards until 1969 and on festival committees through 1972.

JUILLIARD SCHOOL OF MUSIC, DANCE DEPARTMENT PRODUCTIONS, NEW YORK, N.Y.

1952–1969
Julliard Concert Hall

April 1952 *Martha Graham Dance Company*
Graham ch: Canticle for Innocent Comedians* (Thomas Ribbink), The Triumph of Saint Joan** (Dello Joio), Judith (Schuman), El Penitente, Errand into the Maze, Lamentation.

December 1952 *José Limón and Dance Company*
Limón ch: El Grito (The Shout)**(Silvestre Revueltas), The Exiles**, The Queen's Epicedium**, The Visitation** (Schoenberg), La Malinche, The Moor's Pavane. Humphrey ch: Fantasy and Fugue in C Minor** (Mozart), Night Spell** , Desert Gods from Song of the West (Roy Harris), Day on Earth.

May 1953 *A Demonstration in Dance*
Tudor, Lecture Demonstration: Let's Be Basic, Tudor ch: Exercise Piece* (Juan Crisóstomo de Arriaga y Balzola), Lecture Demonstration: What Dances Are Made Of (Humphrey and Students). Humphrey ch: Desert Gods from Song of the West.

December 1953 *Ballet Evening*
Tudor ch: Brittania Triumphans: Five Anti-Masques Entry, Descent and Dances of the Grand Masquers (William Lawes), Elizabethan Dances* (Orlando Gibbons, Thomas Morley, Anthony Holborne, William Byrd, Thomas Tomkins).

January 1954 *José Limón and Dance Company*
Limón ch: Ode to the Dance* (Barber), set: Paul Trautvetter. Humphrey ch: Ritmo Jondo, Ruins and Visions, Night Spell, Day on Earth, Lament for Ignasio Sanchez, Variations and Conclusion from New Dance Koner ch: Cassandra (Copland)

April, May 1955 *Juilliard Dance Theater*
Sokolow ch: Primavera* (Domenico Cimarosa, Arthur Benjamin). Humphrey ch: The Rock and the Spring* (Frank Martin), Day on Earth, Life of the Bee (Hindemith). Limón ch: Study for Scherzo* (John Barracuda, Stoddard Lincoln, Lucy Venable: percussion improvisation). Note: Scherzo premiere at ADF, August 1955 to a Hazel Johnson score.

April 1956 *Juilliard Dance Theater*
Limón ch: Variations on a Theme (later, There is a Time)* (Dello Joio), Kings' Heart* (Stanley Wolfe), Symphony for Strings* (Schuman). Humphrey ch: Dawn in New York* (Hunter Johnson), Theatre Piece No. 2 (Luening), The Race of Life (Vivian Fine).

December 1956
Lecture Demonstration, José Limón assisted by members of his company.
Wednesday One O'Clock Concert Series: Limón ch: Excerpts from There Is a Time,

The Traitor (Gunther Schuller), The Emperor Jones (Heitor Villa-Lobos), Concerto in D Minor after Vivaldi (J.S. Bach), Rhythm Study* (self-accompanied).

January 1957 *Juilliard Dance Theater*
Humphrey ch: Dawn in New York (Hunter Johnson), Descent into the Dream* (Goffredo Petrassi), Life of the Bee (Hindemith)

April 1958 *Juilliard Dance Theater with members of the José Limón Company*
Limón ch: Missa Brevis* (Kodály). Humphrey ch: Descent Into the Dream* (Goffredo Petrassi), Partita No. 5 (Bach). Sokolow ch: Session '58 (Teo Macero). Donald McKayle ch: Out of the Chrysalis* (Ernest Bloch).

May 1959 *Juilliard Dance Theater*
Bettis ch: Closed Door* (Anton Webern), The Desperate Heart. Humphrey, in collaboration with Ruth Currier ch: Brandenburg Concerto No. 4 in G Minor* (Bach). Limón ch: The Traitor, Missa Brevis (Kodály). Helen Tamiris ch: Dance for Walt Whitman* (David Diamond).

April 1960 *Juilliard Dance Ensemble*
Ruth Currier ch: Toccanta* (Cowell). Humphrey ch: Passacaglia and Fugue in C Minor (Bach). Limón with Koner ch: Barren Sceptre* (Gunther Schuller). Tudor ch: A Choreographer Comments* (Franz Schubert), Little Improvisations** (Schumann). Raoul Feuillet ch, set by Helmut Kluge: Ballet de Neuf Danseurs (anon.). La Meri ch: The Seasons** (Antonio Vivaldi). Pécour ch:Trois Entrées Espagnoles (André Campra, from L'Europe Galante). Gilbert Reed ch: The Clowns* (Benjamin Britten).

April 1961 *Juilliard Dance Ensemble*
Humphrey ch: Passacaglia and Fugue in C Minor Limón ch: Performance* (Variations on a theme by Schuman by Hugh Aitken, William Bergsma, Jacob Druckman, Vittorio Giannini, Lloyd, Vincent Persichetti, Robert Starer, Hugo Weisgall)

March–April 1962 *Juilliard Dance Ensemble*
Gradus ad Parnassum* Margaret Black ch: Enfantines. Alfredo Corvino ch: Scenes d'Enfants (Mompou). Fiorella Keane ch: Suite Française (Francis Poulenc). Tudor ch: From Musick's Hand-maid (Purcell), Passamezzi (Antonio Gardano). Michel Fokine ch: Le Carnaval, excerpts (Schumann). Lucas Hoving ch: Suite for a Summer Day* (Peter Schickele). Helen McGehee ch: Incursion* (Ramiro Cortés). Jack Moore ch: Opticon (a Vaudeville of the Mind)* (Jean Middleton). Tudor ch: Dance Studies (Less Orthodox)* (Elliott Carter), Trio Con Brio* (Mikhail Ivanovich Glinka), Little Improvisations.

March, April, May 1963 *Juilliard Dance Ensemble*
Humphrey ch: Variations and Conclusion from New Dance. Limón ch: Concerto in D Minor after Vivaldi* (Bach), (Restaging of Concerto Grosso 1945). Tudor ch: A Choreographer Comments, Dance Studies (Less Orthodox) (Elliott Carter).

Ethel Winter ch: The Magic Mirror* (Arthur Murphy). Sokolow ch: Opus '63 (Teo Macero). Grant Strate ch: House of Atreus* (Alberto Ginastera).

March, April 1964 *Juilliard Dance Ensemble*
Kevin Carlisle ch: Part-time Invention* (Schickele), Paul Draper ch: Sometimes* (Barber), Ray Harrison ch: Espial* (Gerald Cook), Humphrey ch: Ruins and Visions Excerpt (Britten), Lev Ivanov ch: Swan Lake Pas de Deux (Tchaikovsky) Limón ch: Two Essays for Large Ensemble* (Bach) Note: These are sections for A Choreographic Offering that premiered August 1964 at ADF. Concerto in D Minor after Vivaldi* (Bach) (Restaging of Concerto Grosso 1945), The Demon* (Hindemith) Scenery: Malcolm McCormick Sokolow ch: Session for Six* (Macero), The Question* (Webern) Tudor ch: A Choreographer Comments

February 1965 *Juilliard Dance Ensemble*
Humphrey ch: Ritmo Jondo (Surinach) re-arranged. Limón ch: Variations on a Theme by Paganini* (Brahms), Sokolow ch: Ballade* (Scriabin), Odes* (Varèse)

May 1966 *Juilliard Dance Ensemble*
Fredbjorn Bjornsson ch: Badinage (Johan Halvorsen), Richard Englund ch: Jigs'n Reels** (Malcom Arnold), Limón ch: There is a Time (Dello Joio) Sokolow ch: Night* (Luciano Berio)

April, May 1967 *Juilliard Dance Ensemble*
Graham ch: Diversion of Angels (Dello Joio) Limón ch: MacAber's Dance* (Druckman), Sokolow ch: Memories* (Macero), Tudor ch: Jardin aux Lilas (Ernest Chausson) Graham ch: Diversion of Angels

March 1968 *Juilliard Dance Ensemble*
Limón ch: La Malinche (Lloyd) Tonantzintla** (Soler) Tudor ch: Fandango (Soler), Little Improvisations Graham ch: Diversion of Angels

March 1969 *Juilliard Dance Ensemble*
Limón ch: La Pinata (The Saint's Day)*(Burrill Phillips) Petipa (with Ivanov, direction by Tudor) ch: Swan Lake Pas de Trois (Tchaikovsky), Sokolow ch: Echoes* (John Weinzweig), Michael Uthoff ch: The Pleasures of Merely Circulating* (Handel)

THE JUILLIARD SCHOOL, LINCOLN CENTER, NYC. NY.

1970–1985
The Juilliard Theater

May 1970 *Juilliard Dance Ensemble*
Carolyn Brown ch: West Country* (Edward Elgar) work-in-progress. Helen McGehee ch: I Am the Gate* (Hindemith), Limón ch: The Unsung* (in silence), work-in-progress There is a Time. Sokolow ch: The Dove* (Cristóbal Hailffter), Ballade.

May 1971 *Juilliard Dance Ensemble*
Limón ch: Revel* (Elizabeth Sawyer) work-in-progress. Sokolow ch: *Scenes from the Music of Charles Ives** (Charles Ives). Graham ch: Diversion of Angels.

May 1971 *Informal Showing*
Tudor ch: Continuo* (Johann Pachelbel), Sunflowers* (Leos Janácek), Cereus* (Geoffrey Grey).

November 1971 *Juilliard Dance Ensemble*
Graham ch: Diversion of Angels. Limón ch: Revel (Sawyer) first complete performance, The Unsung* (in silence) first complete performance. Sokolow ch: *Scenes from the Music of Charles Ives.*

May 1972 *Juilliard Dance Ensemble*
Humphrey ch: The Shakers (traditional), Day on Earth, Lament for Ignacio Sanchez Mejias, Passacaglia, and Fugue in C Minor. Limón ch: The Winged (Hank Johnson). Sokolow ch: Lyric Suite (Alban Berg).

May 1973 *Juilliard Dance Ensemble*
Kazuko Hirabayashi ch: Black Angels* (George Crumb). Daniel Lewis ch: Irving the Terrific* (sound collage: Pia Gilbert, Saul Goodman, Joseph Lyons, Rolling Stones). Sokolow ch: Three Poems* (Joel Thome). Night Humphrey ch: Ritmo Jondo.

May 1974 *Juilliard Dance Ensemble*
Hirabayashi ch: Night of Four Moons with Lone Shadow* (Crumb). Limón ch: A Choreographic Offering (Bach), Missa Brevis. Sokolow ch: Come, Come Travel with Dreams* (Scriabin).

April, May 1975 *Juilliard Dance Ensemble*
Hirabayashi ch: Mask of Night* (Crumb). Limón ch: The Waldstein Sonata* (Beethoven) reconstructed by Daniel Lewis. Sokolow ch: Ride the Culture Loop* (Macero).

May 1976 *Juilliard Dance Ensemble*
Hirabayashi ch: Nowhere but Light* (Takemitsu). Lewis ch: Proliferation* (Goodman). Sokolow ch: Ellis Island* (Ives).

May 1977 *Juilliard Dance Ensemble*
Hirabayashi ch: Rounds* (Macero). Sokolow ch: The Holy Place* (Bloch), Rooms (Kenyon Hopkins). Limón ch: Missa Brevis.

March 1978 *Juilliard Dance Ensemble*
Wendy Hilton, after Pécour ch: Divertissement from Les Festes Vénitiennes** (Campra). Hirabayashi ch: Concerto* (Bach), Dark Star* (Takemitsu). McGehee ch: Changes* (Benjamin Britten). Sokolow ch: Songs Remembered* (Diamond). Limón ch: There is a Time.

February 1979 *Juilliard Dance Ensemble*
Hirabayashi ch: The Stone Garden* (Ryohei Hirose, Marilyn Rosenberger). Lewis ch: Mostly Beethoven* (Beethoven). McGehee ch: El Retablo de Maese Pedro** (Manuel de Falla). Hector Zaraspe ch: Bolero* (Giuseppe Verdi), Debussyana, excerpts (Claude Debussy).

March 1980 *Juilliard Dance Ensemble*
Hilton, with Anthony L'Abbe ch: An Entertainment for His Majesty George II **
(Handel). Limon ch: The Winged. Sokolow ch: Magritte, Magritte (Scriabin, Liszt,
Douglas Finch). Zaraspe ch: Estancia (Ginastera).

April 1981 *Juilliard Dance Ensemble*
Hirabayashi ch: The Darkening Green* (Crumb). Limón ch: Tonantzintla, La
Malinche. Sokolow ch: Los Converso* (Richard J. Neumann), Magritte, Magritte
(Scriabin, Liszt, Satie). Paul Taylor ch: Esplanade (Bach). Tudor ch: Cereus. Zaraspe
ch: Paso a Cuatro* (Solar, Albeniz, Rodriquez, Galles).

March 1982 *Juilliard Dance Ensemble*
Lewis ch: Moments: A Tribute to José Limón* (Edgar David Grana). Sokolow ch:
Everything Musts Go* (Macero), Ballade, Odes. Taylor ch: Aureole (Handel),
3 Epitaphs (American folk music), Esplanade. Tudor ch: Soirée Musicale (Britten,
after Rossini). Zaraspe ch: Goya Meets Granados* (Enrique Granados).

March 1983 *Juilliard Dance Ensemble*
Hilton ch: Celebration of Lully (Lully). Lewis ch: Moments: A Tribute to José Limón.
Michael Maule ch: Carib Pedlar (Darius Milhaud). Sokolow ch: Deserts (Varèse), Four
Preludes* (Sergei Rachmaninoff). Taylor ch: Esplanade. Tudor ch: A Choreographer
Comments (excerpts), Soirée Musicale. Zaraspe ch: Fantasy* (Franz Schubert).

March 1984 *Juilliard Dance Ensemble*
Alvin Ailey ch: Streams (Miloslav Kabelá). Hirabayashi ch: Mudai II * (Takehisa
Kosugi). Hilton ch: Celebration of the French Baroque (Lully, Campra, Jean-Philippe
Rameau). Limón ch: Missa Brevis. Sokolow ch: Dreams (Bach, Macero). Taylor ch:
Esplanade. Tudor ch: A Choreographer Comments (excerpts). Zaraspe ch: Of Sun,
Moon, Stars* (Dvořák).

March 1985 *Juilliard Dance Ensemble*
Hilton ch: Celebration of the French Baroque II (Lully, Campra, Rameau).
Hirabayashi ch: On Land* (Kosugi). Lewis ch: Women* (Martin Swerdlow). Limón
ch: The Emperor Jones (Villa-Lobos). Maule ch: Brahms Sextet* (Brahms). Genia
Melikova ch: Vivaldiana* (Vivaldi). Sokolow ch: Magritte, Magritte. Taylor ch:
Cloven Kingdom (Corelli, Cowell, Malloy Miller). Tudor ch: Continuo.

AAHPR	American Association for Health, Physical Education, and Recreation.
BC:WLA	Barnard College, Wollman Library Archives, New York City.
BCA	Bennington College Library Archives, Bennington, Vermont. Catalogues, publications, papers.
CC:SLA	Connecticut College, Charles E. Shain Library, New London, Connecticut. American Dance Festival Papers.
CU:OHRO	Columbia University, Butler Library Rare Book and Manuscript Library and the Oral History Research Office, New York City. Bennington Summer School of the Dance Project. Interviews with Teresa Bowers, supervised by Nancy Goldner.
DULL:ADF	Duke University, Durham, North Carolina. Rare Book, Manuscript, and Special Collections Library, Lily Library, American Dance Festival Papers, marked "1930.0001."
EPMPL	East Palestine Memorial Public Library, East Palestine, Ohio.
FHSU:FL	Fort Hays State University, Forsyth Library, Hays, Kansas.
JSA	Juilliard School Archives, the Juilliard School Library, New York City. Juilliard Dance Division and Martha Hill Archives, General Administrative Records, 1947–1991, Faculty applications and correspondence 1951–1959. President, Office of the: General Administrative Records, 1932–62; Dance Department, 1951–61; Dance Department, Early History 1951–1952; Dance Division Scrapbooks; Thurston Davies, Agnes de Mille, Martha Hill, Barbara Morgan, Antony Tudor files.
LCPAA:OHP	Lincoln Center for the Performing Arts, Inc., Archives, New York City. Oral History Project: Dunbar, Lowry, Schuman, interviewed by Sharon Zane. June Dunbar Folder. Boxes 34–43. Box 42: Lincoln Center Dance, 1957–61, plans for dance center. Box 49: Dance Council, 1957–58. Box 62: Lincoln Kirstein, Lincoln Center. Box 68: Repertory Theater of Lincoln Center. JDR III, Lincoln Center Dance Concerts, 1956–58. Box 5: E. P. Young, negotiations with City Center, 1965–66.
LOC: MD	Library of Congress, Music Division, Washington, D.C. S. A. Kriegsman Collection: Bennington. Boxes 26–44. Including interviews with Erick Hawkins, Martha Hill, Norman Lloyd, and Mark Ryder.
MCA	Olin Library, Mills College, Oakland, California. Marian Van Tuyl Collection, Bennington at Mills file.
MHA	Martha Hill Archive. Willed to the author as biographical heir by Martha Hill. Placed in the New York Public Library for the Performing Arts, Astor, Lenox, and Tilden Foundations, Jerome Robbins Dance Division: New York City, by the author, 26 September 2007.

NYPL:DC	New York Public Library for the Performing Arts, Astor, Lenox, and Tilden Foundations. Jerome Robbins Dance Division: New York City. Martha Graham: Misc. Manuscripts Scrapbooks: Articles on Dance 1937–1966; Doris Humphrey Collection. Lincoln Kirstein Papers. Arch Lauterer Papers. Pauline Lawrence Papers. José Limón Papers. W. Terry, Dance Scrapbook: *New York Herald Tribune.* Clippings files: American Dance Theater. Hong Kong Oral History Project: Interviews with Martha Hill, 1990, three videocassettes.
NYPL:HL	New York Public Library, Humanities Library, Forty-second Street Branch, New York City. Town Hall Archives.
NYPL:MD	New York Public Library at Lincoln Center. Music Division: New York City. Town Hall Archives.
NYU:BL	New York University, New York City. Archives of the Sales Library.
PC	Personal collection of the author. Includes photographs, Dilts family papers, clippings, and so forth.
RFA	Rockefeller Foundation Archives, Pocantico Hills, New York. Edgar B. Young Papers. Lincoln Kirstein Papers. Family JDR III. Lincoln Center Council Files: Box 59. Kirstein-Young correspondence, Fol. 529.
SL	Salem Library, Salem, Ohio.
TCA	Teachers College, Columbia University, Gottesman Library Archives, New York City.
UOL	University of Organ Library, Eugene, Oregon.
WAA	Wadsworth Atheneum Archives, Hartford, Connecticut.
WL	Willard Library, Battle Creek, Michigan.

PREFACE AND ACKNOWLEDGMENTS (pp. xi–xv)

1. Martha Hill to Janet Soares. From interviews with the author in preparation for a biography on 21, 22, 28 January 1993, the Juilliard School, New York City. All subsequent quotes by Martha Hill are from these 1993 interviews, unless noted.

2. Rebecca Godwin, "Martha Hill on Early Dance at Bennington," *Quadrille* 25, no. 1 (Winter 1992–93), 19.

3. Ben Belitt, "Wilderness Stair. Dance Piece," *This Scribe, My Hand: The Complete Poems of Ben Belitt* (1955; reprint, Baton Rouge: Louisiana State University Press, 1998), 151. The fourth stanza of the poem is: "And the terrible gift / Of the gaze, blind on its zenith, the wreath / Of the throat, the body's unwearied uplift, / Unmaking and making its death."

INTRODUCTION (pp. xvii–xx)

1. See Isadora Duncan, *My Life* (1927; reprint, New York: W.W. Norton, 1955); see also Ann Daly's *Done into Dance* (Bloomington: Indiana University Press, 1995).

2. Linda J. Tomko, *Dancing Class: Gender, Ethnicity, and Social Divides in American Dance, 1890–1920* (Bloomington: Indiana University Press, 1999), 69.

3. Ibid.

Part I: Bible Belt to Academe

GROWING UP IN OHIO, 1900–1922 (pp. 3–11)

1. Information drawn from various papers on the family genealogy collected by Martha and her brother Lewis (known as Bill), and sister-in-law, Mary Ann. MHA.

2. William B. McCord, *History of Columbiana County, Ohio* (Chicago: Biographical Publishing, 1905), 2.

3. Bill Hill to author, 9 April 2002, Lakeland, Florida. All subsequent quotes by Bill (with his wife, Mary Ann Hill) are taken from this interview, unless noted.

4. Bill Hill added, "Uncle Charles, who played the organ at the Masonic Temple, had the dry goods, and Uncle Fred, who was the borough secretary for years and years, had the grocery. John A. had the hardware." Ibid.

5. Years later, McGeary, a student at Juilliard in Martha Hill's Dance for Musicians class (he later became Louis Horst's accompanist at Connecticut College Summer School of the Dance), discovered his connection with Martha's relatives. After that the two loved to exchange Leechburg stories. George McGeary to JS, 8 December 2003, New York City.

6. Martha Hill to Tom Brown, Hong Kong Oral History Project, Hong Kong Academy for Performing Arts (video recording, Hong Kong, July 1990). NYPL:DC.

7. Ann Wagner, *Adversaries of Dance: From the Puritans to the Present* (Urbana: University of Illinois Press, 1997), 240.

8. Philip Graham, *Showboats: The History of an American Institution* (Austin: University of Texas Press, 1951), 96. According to Graham, while her husband served as captain, Olive continued to manage the entertainment, selecting melodramas that emphasized female roles such as "Nellie the Sewing Machine Girl," with specialty numbers presented between acts. In 1928 she was left in charge while Price took a tow of coal down the Mississippi, contracted pneumonia, and died before returning home. The *Columbia* was sold soon after.

9. "High Students Organize Two Bible Classes," *Reveille Echo*, East Palestine, Ohio, 9 March 1916. Archives, EPMPL.

10. "Francis Mason interviews Martha Hill," audiotape, 1965. NYPL:DC.

11. "Agnes de Mille interviews Martha Hill," audiotape, 30 March 1983. NYPL:DC.

12. These exercises often reflected the glories of ancient Greek and exotic Eastern cultures and were incorporated into physical education programs. In America, the programs were popularized by Genevieve Stebbins, whose students used "statue posing and tableaus" to connect to the classical world and commune with the divine through the body. By the early 1900s, specially built outdoor amphitheaters sprouted up on American college campuses to display "free" dancing in Greek tunics. Delsarte (1811–71) developed this training for singing, declamation, and aesthetic purposes; it was not adapted for performance reasons until the end of the nineteenth century. Ted Shawn had studied with Henrietta (Crane) Hovey and later championed the principles of movement she taught based on relaxation, balance, and natural breathing.

13. At the University of Chicago and then Columbia University, Dewey had led a vigorous turn toward professionalism in higher education that included the fields of physical education and dance. By 1918 Columbia University's Teachers College physical education program introduced Duncan-inspired dance courses called "natural dancing." Physical health advocates had become dissatisfied with borrowed ideas of physical culture such as Germany's group drills and the calisthenics of Swedish gymnastics.

14. Barbara Page Beiswanger to Sali Ann Kriegsman, 15 May 1977, S. A. Kriegsman Collection, Bennington. LOC:MD. When Kellogg traveled out of Battle Creek, he also wore a white felt hat and a white wool coat.

15. According to local history records, the school of physical education had been in existence since 1909. It was not until 1923 that the school offered a four-year liberal arts program. During those fourteen years, Battle Creek College existed on the doctor's earnings from his food creations. In interviews, Hill breezed over those years with few details, leading one to wonder if her undergraduate experiences weren't more akin to T. Coraghessan T. Boyle's fictional account in his book *The Road to Wellville* (New York: Viking, 1993).

16. According to a 1891 handbook by Hartvig Nissen, *The ABC's of Swedish Educational Gymnastics*, this system of increasingly difficult progressions of exercises was executed to staccato commands by the instructor. Designed for mastery of one's own will, and subordination as "part of a great totality," part of the class was devoted to "games" that consisted of running, pulling ropes, and dancing.

17. Martha Hill to Teresa Bowers, interviews on 21 and 29 March 1979, New York City. CU:ORHO.

18. Barbara Page Beiswanger to Theodora Wiesner, 10 February 1975, Atlanta, Georgia. NYPL:DC.

1. Edna L. McRae, letter in *Portfolio of tributes presented to Martha Hill*, Heritage Luncheon, Dance Division, AAHPER, Chicago, 20 March 1966. MHA.

2. Lucile Bogue, *Dancers on Horseback: The Perry-Mansfield Story* (San Francisco, Calif.: Strawberry Hill Press, 1984), 53.

3. An example is "A Baby Dance for Two or More Very Small Girls" that describes steps measure by measure, such as "facing each other, they join R hands, pointing the R ft. forward as in Figure 2," matched to accompanying photographs. "Sweet Forget-Me-Nots," *The Dance Magazine* 8, no. 6 (October 1927), 36.

4. Interviewed by Charles Curtiss. "Bright Days Ahead," *The Dance Magazine* 6, no. 2 (July 1926), 42. Vestoff prophesied, "In this country . . . dancing has a tremendous future. Someday New York will be the dancing capital of the world. Education will make it so."

5. See my *Louis Horst: Musician in a Dancer's World* (Durham, N.C.: Duke University Press,1992).

6. Program, "The Dance," 4 May 1925. FHSU:FL.

7. *1925 Reveille*, 94. FHSU:FL.

8. Beginning with Mary Wood Hinman, who taught at Hull House, dance specialists regularly joined communities of women reformers working with immigrant children.

9. Louis H. Chalif, *The Chalif Textbook of Dancing* (New York: Isaac Goldman Coy, 1916). The "Chalif Method" of merging ballet's barre exercises and positions with folk dance movements and rhythms had become popular in women's physical education programs.

10. Harry Moss, "What the Dance Teachers Say," *Dance Lovers Magazine* 1, no. 2 (December 1923), 27.

11. Ibid., 4.

12. Curtiss, "Bright Days Ahead," 42.

13. "Agnes de Mille interviews Martha Hill."

14. MH to T. Bowers.

15. M.S., "The Dance Reviewed," *The Dance Magazine* 6, no. 3 (July 1926), 25.

16. MH to T. Bowers.

17. Teachers College School of Practical Arts, 1926–27 catalogue. TCA.

18. M.S., "The Dance Reviewed," 58.

19. Knowing that she taught "in the gymnasium," Louis gave Martha a copy of Schluter's *Schule der Rhythmischen Gymnastik*, a book of dance exercises and accompanying scores that he had purchased during his 1926 stay in Germany. MHA.

20. After fifteen years as Denishawn's music director, Horst left to study composition in Vienna. Although he had initially planned to stay for two years, he returned instead to help Graham with her first concert, admitting that he loved her "no matter what."

21. Martha Graham, *Blood Memory* (New York: Doubleday, 1991), 160.

22. 26 January 1927; noted in Diana McLellan's *The Girls: Sappho Goes to Hollywood* (New York: LA Weekly Books/St. Martin's Press, 2000).

23. McLellan writes more about this situation and its repercussions, not only in filmmaking but also on campuses of women's colleges, quoting one dean as warning his students of "the dangers of a reprehensible attachment"; ibid., 86.

24. MH to T. Bowers.

25. Having graduated from the University of Wisconsin, H'Doubler began her teaching as a coach of women's basketball and baseball teams in 1912. By 1918 the "Wisconsin Idea" of the service university came about. In 1921 a studio devoted to dance opened on campus, and she developed a movement fundamentals course. She wrote of the course (in *A Manual of Dancing*, 1921) that it was "not dancing; it is merely getting at the things which make dancing possible." She formed a student-run ensemble that she labeled Orchesis, a name that stuck as college student dance groups multiplied across the country. By 1923 she had established a dance minor, having made the case for dance as a discipline. In 1927 a specialized major in dancing within the School of Education's physical education department admitted its first university major in dance, later that year expanding the curriculum to include an M.A. in physical education with a specialized major in dancing. See Margaret Newell H'Doubler, *The Dance and its Place in Education* (New York: Harcourt, Brace, 1925).

26. For a comprehensive overview on H'Doubler, see Janis Ross, *Moving Lessons: Margaret H'Doubler and the Beginning of Dance in American Education* (Madison: University of Wisconsin Press, 2000).

27. The summer session also gave Hill a fuller sense of H'Doubler's popularity and the state of dance in education during that period. It also informed her decision a few years later to invite Wigman's exponent, Hanya Holm, to become one of Bennington's "Big Four." "H'Doubler had never liked Graham, and always suggested that her students study with Mary Wigman in Germany," according to Wisconsin graduate Theodora (Teddy) Wiesner. Later, when "Wisconsin graduates came East, they chose to study with Hanya because hers was the technique with which they were more familiar." Theodora (Teddy) Wiesner to T. Bowers (1979). CU:OHRO.

28. Beiswanger to Wiesner.

29. D. Jowitt, "A Conversation with Bessie Schönberg. American Modern Dance: The Early Years," *Ballet Review* 9, no. 1 (1981), 33.

30. Bessie Schönberg to Rose Anne Thom, Bronxville, 6 December 1976, New York. audiotape, Cassette 1. National Initiative to Preserve American Dance Oral History Project. NYPL:DC.

31. " A Study of the Nature of the Dance," manuscript, 28 August 1928, 12 and 13. MHA.

Part II: New Dance

DANCING WITH GRAHAM, 1929–1931 (pp. 27–38)

1. D. Jowitt, "A Conversation," 41.

2. See McLellan, *The Girls*, 150, for an explanation of lesbians during this period suggesting that ideas of same-sex relationships were still firmly rooted in class.

3. Martha's name is not in the Lincoln School faculty listings until 1930–31.

4. MH to T. Bowers.

5. Ibid.

6. Ibid.

7. Alice Helpern quoting Dorothy Bird (Villiard), "The Evolution of Martha Graham's Dance Technique" (Ph.D. diss., New York University, 1981), 88. Bird joined the company shortly after Hill.

8. Louis Horst to Jeanette Roosevelt (notes taken by author from transcription of interviews, 1960–1961). PC. In Soares, *Louis Horst*, 83, 84. See chapter 5 for more about Horst during this period.

9. R. Garland, "New Dance Theatre Scores a Success," *New York Telegram*, 6 January 1930, clipping files. NYPL:DC.

10. Martha Graham, "Seeking an American Art of the Dance," in *Revolt in the Arts*, ed. Oliver Sayler (New York: Brentano's, 1930), 249.

11. Chronologist Christena L. Schlundt notes at least ten different billings for the Humphrey-Weidman company over the years. See Selma Jeanne Cohen, ed., *Doris Humphrey: An Artist First*. (Middletown, Conn.: Wesleyan University Press, 1972), 271.

12. Ibid., 90.

13. L. Horst to J. Roosevelt.

14. Tobi Tobias, "A Conversation with May O'Donnell," *Ballet Review* 9, no. 1 (Spring 1981), 79.

15. Martha Hill to JS, 15 February 1991.

16. Professor Thomas Alexander was key to formulating the educational philosophy for the school. (It closed after the 1938–39 academic year.) See Soares, "Barnard's 1932 and 1933 Dance Symposiums: Bringing Dance to the University," SDHS (Minneapolis: University of Minnesota, 1997).

17. MH to T. Bowers.

18. Ibid.

19. Helen Knight to T. Bowers, March 1979. CU:OHRO.

20. "Pop Nash had a great reputation in recreation and also in Indian affairs," Hill recalled about her colleague. "This was a crossover for us because I'd always been interested in Indian arts, Indian dance, a great deal of it derived from my association with Martha Graham. I used to go into the dean's office and say, 'Here's your tip sheet for the week,' getting Jay to go to see Hanya because he would understand, whereas something abstruse in content might not have been as attractive to him. He served on the advisory board to the Bennington School of the Dance 1934 and 1935, and later organized American Indian communities in relation to the war effort."

21. Ruth Lloyd to JS, 10 January 2002, Farmington, Connecticut.

22. Ibid.

23. Ibid.

24. Lillian Faderman, *Surpassing the Love of Men: Romantic Friendship and Love Between Women from the Renaissance to the Present* (1981; reprint, New York: Perennial/HarperCollins, 2001), 187.

25. Beth Olson Mitchell to JS, 22 August 2002, Bloomfield, Connecticut.

26. Mary Jo Shelly, "Bennington and the Dance in America or, the Dance and Beginnington. The improbable made real or Turning Point." Unpublished manuscript, c. 1957. MHA. All subsequent quotes by Shelly are from this source, unless noted.

27. Aired on a PBS special on MOMA, 2 May 2002. The expression "modern dancing," generally referring to ballroom routines, can be found in the pages of *Dance Lovers Magazine* as early as 1924 (as in Nada MacLean's article, "Too Much Freedom in Modern Dancing?"). The January 1925 cover of *Dance Lovers Magazine* pictures Valodia Vestoff performing barefoot (the mark of a modern dancer in the 1930s). This had not been un-

usual among ballet dancers a decade earlier; by 1930, however, barefoot dancing had become a distinctive modern dance feature.

28. Martha Hill, with Mary Jo Shelly, "Sources and Characteristics of the New Dance," manuscript, seventy-two pages. (corrected version signed June 1933). MHA.

BENNINGTON, 1932–1933 (pp. 39–47)

1. MH to T. Bowers.

2. After working as assistant educational director for the U.S. Public Health Service during World War I, Leigh received a Ph.D. from Columbia in 1927; he taught at Reed and then at Barnard College. Beginning in 1932 he served on the advisory board of the Progressive Education Association, having recently published *Federal Health Administration in the United States*. He remained active with that association for the next decade, inviting Hill to join a panel discussion group on drama and dance in conjunction with the Museum of Modern Art on 19 March 1941.

3. "Agnes de Mille interviews Martha Hill."

4. MH to T. Bowers.

5. According to Thomas Brockway, that first year Grace King was hired as director of sports in charge of a recreation program. But after "a lively year of modern dance, Miss King's sports programs had a limited appeal and she was not reappointed." Thomas Brockway, *Bennington College: In the Beginning* (Bennington, Vt.: Bennington College Press, 1981), 127.

6. Ben Belitt to JS, 25 August 1997, Bennington, Vermont. All subsequent quotes by Belitt are from this source, unless noted.

7. See 110–111 of Soares's *Louis Horst: Musician in a Dancer's World* for a fuller description of the event.

8. MH to JS, 10 January 1986, New York City.

9. Mildred Leigh, a classmate at Teachers College, had also received an M.A. in education from Columbia.

10. MH to T. Bowers.

11. Ibid. Leigh would remain an influential spouse, ever guarding the moral fiber of the Bennington community. The president also gave his wife administrative responsibilities when he could. He had a "particular fondness" for husband-wife combinations, because in his view "the educated but unemployed faculty wife was likely to become neurotic and be generally troublesome." Brockway, *Bennington College*, 93.

12. Mary Jo Shelly with Martha Hill, *Bennington Newsletter* 2, no. 3 (Winter 1934), 1. MHA.

13. R. Lloyd to JS, 10 January 2002, Farmington, Connecticut.

14. *The Early Years: The Bennington Years*, video recording, 9–12 April 1981, Purchase, New York. Festival director, Patricia Kerr Ross; video producer, Daniel Labeille. NYPL:DC.

15. B. Belitt to JS, 15 March 1996, Bennington, Vermont.

16. Norman Lloyd and R. Lloyd to T. Bowers, 1979. CU:OHRO. All subsequent quotes by Norman and Ruth Lloyd from this source, unless noted. Norman added, "This was not true of José Limón or Letitia Ide, who were the first two who became Broadway successes, [but] never thought of leaving Doris or Charles."

17. Walter Terry, moderator: "Charles Weidman: A Celebration," 6 October 1975, Majestic Theatre, New York City. NYPL:DC.

18. B. Belitt to JS, 15 March 1996.

19. "Agnes de Mille interviews Martha Hill."

20. Marked in pencil on yellow tablet paper: "for American Dance Symposium, August, 1968," 1. MHA.

21. Air script, revised 17 November 1965, 1. MHA. (MH was a consultant for this project.)

A SUMMER SCHOOL FOR DANCE, 1934 (pp. 48–57)

1. Shelly and Hill, *Bennington College Bulletin* (February 1934), 1. Throughout, the first prospectus promised, the groups would participate in formal and informal discussions, centering on "questions and topics growing out of the work of the School and those current in the contemporary dance." A series of "forum laboratory recitals" would also take place during the last three weeks of the session.

2. Bessie Schönberg to T. Bowers, c. 1979. CU:OHRO.

3. Bennington handout, single sheet. MHA.

4. Martha Hill, "Reflections and Memories. Comments about Hanya Holm," *Choreography and Dance* 2, part 2 (1992), 93.

5. Hanya Holm, dialogue on film, "Four Pioneers," air script, 2. MHA.

6. Charles Weidman, ibid, air script, 3.

7. Bessie Schönberg to T. Bowers. Also called fleshlings, these body suits were often worn under costumes.

8. José Limón, *An Unfinished Memoir*, ed. Lynn Garafola (Hanover, N.H.: University Press of New England/Wesleyan University Press, 1999), 78.

9. Brockway, *Bennington College*, 129.

10. John Martin to S. A. Kriegsman, letter, 23 January 1977, S. A. Kriegsman collection, Bennington. LOC:MD.

11. Limón, *Memoir*, 63.

12. MH to T. Bowers.

13. Viewed in "Martha Hill technique demonstrated by the students of the Bennington School of the Dance." 1934 (video of film, 2001). Silent, approximately eight minutes. American Dance Festival Archives, Durham, N.C.: Duke University. DULL:ADF. In another sequence the camera focuses on Hill performing a leg-swing pattern, accented by a sudden drop and hold, before swinging arms regain momentum as she relevés in second position. She then performs a sequence on the diagonal of parallel runs in low attitude, revealing finely pointed feet, arms outstretched and reaching forward.

14. *Bennington Banner*, 11 August 1934, clipping. MHA.

15. Tucker was a member of the Bennington College winter music faculty. According to Norman Lloyd, he was a dear friend whom he had known "since the age of five in Pennsylvania."

16. Janis Ross. *Moving Lessons: Margaret H. Doubler and the Beginning of Dance in American Education* (Madison: University of Wisconsin Press, 2000), 165. Claxton moved on to Wayne State University in Detroit two years later to become chair of its art department. The long-distance marriage remained a convenient arrangement for both of them.

17. Hanya was married to artist Reinhold Kuntze from 1917 to 1921. Klaus Kuntze was born in 1920. When Hanya came to the United States in 1931, Klaus was placed in boarding school in Germany, with Mary Wigman (then involved in a relationship with one of Hanya's former lovers) contributing toward Klaus's education. See Claudia Gitelman, *Dancing with Principle: Hanya Holm in Colorado, 1941–1983* (Boulder: University Press of Colorado, 2001), 14 (quoting letter to Holm from Mary Wigman).

Part III: Private Lives and Common Goals

PANORAMA, 1935 (pp. 61–76)

1. Sali Ann Kriegsman, "notes from telephone conversation." S. A. Kriegsman Collection, Bennington. LOC:MD. This comment reveals the attitude of producing institutions at a time when commissions claimed no ownership (as they often do today).

2. Rebecca (Becca) Stickney to JS, 27 August 1997, Bennington, Vermont. All subsequent quotes by Stickney are from this source, unless noted.

3. Brockway, *Bennington College*, 144. Fergusson and his wife Marion had been associated with the American Laboratory Theatre in New York, itself modeled after the Moscow Art Theatre.

4. After teaching a course in dance at Springfield College, Shawn had established his first all-male company, first presenting lecture-demonstrations in colleges advocating dance for men in 1931–32, and then touring with his company from 1933 to 1940.

5. Limón, *Memoir*, 63.

6. Marcia Siegel, "A Conversation with Hanya Holm," *Ballet Review* 9, no. 1 (Spring 1981), 24.

7. Katherine Vickery, "The Summer at Bennington," *Dance Observer* 2, no. 7 (October 1935), 77.

8. Notebook of Helen Mendel Levy (later Lyons). Dated "1935, Bennington," this gift to the author was given by her daughter Louise Coons. After her Bennington experience, Helen returned to a suburb of Philadelphia, Elkins Park, and opened a dance studio.

9. Joseph Arnold Kaye, *American Dancer* 9, no. 1 (October 1935), 10, 11; qtd. in Sali Ann Kriegsman, *Modern Dance in America: The Bennington Years* (Boston: G. K. Hall, 1981), 52.

10. See Ellen Graff, *Stepping Left: Dance and Politics in New York City, 1928–1942* (Durham, N.C.: Duke University Press, 1997); and Lynn Garafola, "Writing on the Left: The Remarkable Career of Edna Ocko," in her *Legacies of Twentieth-Century Dance* (Middletown, Conn.: Wesleyan University Press, 2005).

11. T. Wiesner to T. Bowers.

12. For a fuller description, see Marcia B. Siegel, *Days on Earth: The Dance of Doris Humphrey* (New Haven, Conn.: Yale University Press, 1988), 77.

13. Eleanor King, *Transformations: A Memoir by Eleanor King: The Humphrey-Weidman Era* (Brooklyn, N.Y.: Dance Horizons, 1978), 142.

14. The same score was orchestrated by Stanley Sussman and reused by the Graham company many years later for a reconstruction of her *Steps in the Street* when the original score by Riegger could not be located.

15. Cohen, *An Artist First*, 137.

16. Limón, *Memoir*, 66.

17. Humphrey quoted in Cohen, *An Artist First*, appendix, "New Dance" [1936], 238.

18. Martha Graham, 15 November 1976, letter read at Bennington's Martha Hill Workshop inauguration. MHA.

19. Alexander Calder and Jean Davidson, *Calder: An Autobiography with Pictures* (New York: Pantheon Books, 1966),127.

20. T. Wiesner to T. Bowers.

21. Ibid. (Her memories, and Norman Lloyd's that follow, give a whole other impression of *Panorama* compared to Yuriko's much abbreviated 1992 reconstruction for the Graham company now in its repertory.

22. For Graham's *Horizons* the following spring the enthusiastic Calder "supplied circles and spirals that spun around on an empty stage to set the mood of each section, and blocks for the dancers to dance among" that Graham found so unsatisfactory that she never again collaborated with him; Don McDonagh, *Martha Graham: A Biography* (New York: Praeger, 1973), 114.

23. Graham and Horst would perform these solos at the White House for the president and Eleanor Roosevelt after a dinner party on 26 February 1937. By then, *Frontier* had become symbolic as a dance expression of the American spirit.

24. According to Ruth Lloyd, Martha always rehearsed her solos in three different tempos—slow, medium, and fast—as she did when working with Louis at the keyboard. Discovering that the tempo depended on how Louis felt, as a soloist she learned to do a sarabande very slowly, with control, or twice as fast. (The joke was that if Louis played very fast, he was usually worried about catching a train, or had a date.) This range made Graham very sensitive to the music, and very versatile as a performer. R. Lloyd to JS.

25. "A Brief Summary of the Proceedings of a FORUM ON THE MODERN DANCE Conducted at the Bennington School of the Dance August 16, 1935." Nine pages typed and stapled. No authors listed. MHA.

26. "Announcement for Fourth Year 'Fields of Study.'" *Bennington College Catalog* (M. Hill, unnamed author), 28. BCA.

WINTER, 1936 (pp. 77–87)

1. "Davies 1934–1948," *Colorado College Magazine*, clipping, 22, Dilts Papers. The article added sardonically, "Davies had his crack-up in 1947."

2. Judy Dilts to JS, letter, 25 August 1997, with attached documents.

3. Davies had kept up with the dance scene through his Princeton classmate, dance filmmaker Julian Bryan.

4. See Gitelman, *Dancing with Principle*.

5. R. Lloyd to JS.

6. Bales performed with the Humphrey-Weidman company until 1940, when he became a full-time faculty member at Bennington in the dance department. In 1943, Bales formed a trio with Jane Dudley and Sophie Maslow that toured the United States through the early 1950s. His association with Bennington continued until 1966, when he became dean of the new dance wing at the State University of New York at Purchase. He, and his tempestuous actress wife, Jo Van Fleet, remained Martha's close friends.

7. Larry Warren, *Anna Sokolow: The Rebellious Spirit* (Princeton, N.J.: Dance Horizons, 1991), 60.

8. Having marched in May Day parades and performed in Communist pageants, New Dance League members continued a passionate involvement in the political arena (with the help of Hallie Flanagan, the national director of the Federal Theatre Project) that led to the establishment of the Federal Dance Project in the spring of 1936. It was the fifth project to be formed in Roosevelt's Works Progress Administration (WPA) to provide government employment to out-of-work Americans.

9. In 1958 Martha hired Sokolow to serve on the Juilliard faculty as a resident choreographer; she stayed on for the next thirty years. As her biographer Larry Warren points out, Sokolow was one of the most demanding personalities in the modern dance world.

10. See Naomi M. Jackson, *Converging Movements: Modern Dance and Jewish Culture at the Ninety-second Street Y* (Middletown, Conn.: Wesleyan University Press, 2000) for a history of the organization's importance to dance.

11. Lincoln Kirstein to Chick Austin, letter, 16 July 1933. WAA.

12. While a student at Harvard, Kirstein created and edited the journal *Hound and Horn* (1927–34). By 1940 he had established the dance archives at MOMA, donating his personal collection of more than five thousand pieces as the centerpiece of the holdings. See Nicholas Fox Weber, *Patron Saints: Five Rebels Who Opened America to a New Art, 1928–1943* (New York: Knopf, 1992). See also Martin Duberman, *The Worlds of Lincoln Kirstein* (New York: Knopf, 2007).

13. As described by biographer James R. Mellow, *Walker Evans* (New York: Basic Books,1999).

14. See Eugene R. Gaddis, "We've Got to Get Them!" in *Magician of the Modern: Chick Austin and the Transformation of the Arts in America* (New York: Knopf, 2000) for a description of events surrounding the Hartford incident.

15. Martin Duberman's *The World of Lincoln Kirstein* (New York: Knopf, 2007) is a superlative, in-depth portrait of Kirstein.

16. Mary Jo Shelly, "Art and the Three R's," *Dance Observer* 2, no. 1 (January 1935), 9.

17. Nicholas Jenkins, "Reflections. The Great Impresario," *New Yorker*, 13 April 1998, 48, 61. At her retirement as artistic adviser emeritus in 1985, Martha's Juilliard salary had barely reached $30,000 a year—very different circumstances from Kirstein's inherited wealth and social advantage.

18. Martha Graham, *Blood Memory* (New York: Doubleday, 1991), 171.

19. Lincoln Kirstein, transcription to Merle Armitage, Box 6, folder 102, Lincoln Kirstein Papers. NYPL:DC.

20. Don McDonagh, *Martha Graham: A Biography* (New York: Praeger, 1973), 107. Armitage, a theatrical agent and connoisseur of the arts, owned a ranch that became Graham's favorite Southwestern retreat in Santa Fe, New Mexico. Graham had begun a brief but passionate affair with artist Carlos Dyer, who was responsible for the artwork of *Martha Graham: The Early Years*, ed. Merle Armitage (1937; reprint, New York: Da Capo Press, 1978). Armitage was Kirstein's love interest—and Dyer, Graham's. As the two plotted their course of action, Graham and Kirstein exchanged intimate thoughts, revealing their as yet unrequited passions to each other.

21. M. Graham to L. Kirstein, letters, n.d. Folder: Correspondence with Martha Graham, Kirstein Papers. NYPL:DC.

SUMMER, 1936 (pp. 88–94)

1. Frances Hawkins had been an administrative assistant at Bennington in 1934 and was now serving as Graham's and Kirstein's concert manager.

2. Lincoln Kirstein, *The New York City Ballet* (New York: Knopf, 1973), 49.

3. Lincoln Kirstein, American Dance Festival 1967 program note, 41–42.

4. Louis Horst to J. Roosevelt.

5. Limón, *Memoir*, 77.

6. In letter from Doris Humphrey to Charles Woodford, 12 July 1936, Doris Humphrey Collection. NYPL:DC.

7. Press release draft, Bennington Papers. MHA.

8. Kriegsman, "Interview with Walter Terry," *Modern Dance in America*, 141.

9. Limón, *Memoir*, 75, 76.

10. John Martin, *America Dancing: The Background and Personalities of the Modern Dance* (1936; reprint, New York: Dance Horizons, 1968), 239, 240. Weidman's outpouring of works included *The Happy Hypocrite, Paul Bunyan,* and *Atavisms: Bargain Counter, Stock Exchange, Lynchtown. Traditions, Flickers,* and *Ringside* were all noted for their wit and social comment. They were, for the most part, theater pieces.

11. Shelly added that his work "was made even more interesting by the first full recognition of the gift possessed by the leading member of Charles's concert group, José Limón." If Charles was able to see his world in a humorous light, José was determined to make a name for himself in a more serious vein.

12. Martha Hill, speech, "Charles Weidman: A Celebration," video recording. NYPL:DC.

13. Nona Schurman to S. A. Kriegsman, letter; Kriegsman, *Modern Dance in America*, 305.

14. Bouchard's photographs of Hill, although first exhibited in 1938, were shot in 1936. He returned to campus the next summer of 1937. Barbara Morgan replaced him in 1938. Both came back as official photographers at Mills in 1939. Without their photographs little visual record of these years would exist, save the one Mills film production, amateur snapshots, and brief film clips taken by students.

15. See "Thomas Bouchard," *U.S. Camera* 2 (February 1939), 14–17. His first subjects were Helen Tamiris and then Doris Humphrey, who invited him to shoot during her studio dress rehearsals. Doris later called upon Bouchard to film *The Shakers* in her studio on West Sixteenth Street in 1939.

16. For Horst, preclassic meant preromantic, or pre-Beethoven. It was his way of escaping romanticism and teaching his students about "going back [to simpler forms] to go ahead" as contemporary artists had done.

17. These women found a supportive environment in which to work as young composers. Many made careers as accompanists and composers connected to university teaching. Hazel Johnson recalled her rigorous training as "essential" to her lifetime vocation as did Ruth Lloyd on the Sarah Lawrence faculty. Hazel Johnson to JS, 6 April 2002, New York City. All subsequent quotes by Johnson are from this source, unless noted.

18. Virginia Mishnun, "Bennington Festival," *Brooklyn Eagle*, 23 August 1936. In Kriegsman, *Modern Dance in America*, 56.

19. The school "plant" was rented for $5,000. The Armory "fee" to the school for thirty-six days cost $108. Extra expenses included $337.50 for Ballet Caravan's debut, with Graham receiving $221.46, and Hanya $137.54. Arch Lauterer was given another $100 for additional construction materials, the source notes.

20. First initiated as a way to escape the harsh Vermont winter, the recess was later lengthened when the wartime fuel shortage increased. It was renamed the non-resident term under President Jones.

21. Brockway, *Bennington College*, 128.

22. Hortense (Hortie) Zera to JS. 12 September 1997, New York City. All subsequent quotes by Zera are from this source, unless noted. To the end of her life, Martha counted the couple among her most loyal friends. Hortie Zera became a leading force in setting up the Martha Hill Dance Fund, Ltd, established in 2001 to give annual awards to outstanding leaders in the dance field.

23. R. Lloyd to JS.

Part IV: The Late Thirties

IMMEDIATE TRAGEDY, 1937 (pp. 97–106)

1. Bill was clearly reluctant to reveal this information to the author, but nonetheless, spoke candidly.

2. There is conjecture among family members that Gene's association with Chiang Kai-shek began with a network that had been illegally shipping arms to China from the Philippines during his service there. During this period many Americans sympathized with the Chinese cause. Almost every day in October and November 1937 the Japanese-Chinese conflict was front-page news in both the *Wall Street Journal* and *New York Times*.

3. A decade later, when Beth Olson Mitchell told of a suicide in her family, Martha spoke of her continuing grief over the loss of her brother. Beth Olson Mitchell to JS, 22 August 2002, Bloomfield, Connecticut. All subsequent quotes by Mitchell are from this source, unless noted.

4. Martha Hill speech at Hanya Holm birthday celebration, Video recording, 1993. NYPL:DC.

5. Gitelman, *Dancing with Principle*, 10. Gitelman telephone interview with Martha Hill, 3 September 1993.

6. *The Early Years: The Bennington Years*, Video recording, 1981. NYPL:DC.

7. "Agnes de Mille interviews Martha Hill."

8. Limón, *Memoir*, 74.

9. Cowell was arrested in May 1936 on a charge involving a seventeen-year-old boy. He agreed to serve four years; anticipating probation, he pleaded guilty to spare his friends publicity. However, he was not released until 1940.

10. "Kirstein 1937," in Armitage, *Martha Graham: The Early Years*, 33.

11. His texts *New Musical Resources* (1930) and *American Composers on American Music* (1933) made Cowell a respected champion for new music during this time. His unorthodox approaches to musical composition and performance had influenced Horst and

others such as Lou Harrison and John Cage (both working at Mills during this period), especially his advocacy of non-Western techniques.

12. Sokolow had earlier premiered a solo *Opening Dance* at the YMHA in April 1936. The duplication of titles seemed not to concern Graham.

13. John Martin, *New York Times*, 15 August 1937. Qtd. in Kriegsman, *Modern Dance in America*, 154, 155.

14. Limón, *Memoir*, 83.

15. Norman explained, "This is why we did *Inquest* later on [1944] in the middle of these horrible things. When the newspapers reported thousands of people killed . . . we could pinpoint tragedy happening to one individual. A hundred thousand people dying is beyond comprehension, but a little man who starves to death as in *Inquest*, is just a John Ruskin report of the many society ignores. That's the kind of thing Doris would do."

16. Norman Lloyd, "Sound Companion for Dance," *Dance Scope* 2, no. 2 (Spring 1966), 10–12.

17. The previous February (1937), Sokolow had presented a first version of *Façade* at the YMHA called *Excerpts from War Poem* based on F. T. Marinetti's poem, "War is Beautiful." *Façade* was reworked to become *New Masses* for its New York premiere in 1939.

18. Kriegsman, *Modern Dance in America*, 264.

19. Ibid., 164.

20. Holm also added Varèse's *Octandre* for *Trend*'s New York premiere, 28 December 1937, at the Mecca Auditorium (now known as New York City Center). The whole work was performed to sound recorded under Lloyd's direction (see description in Kriegsman, *Modern Dance in America*, 164). Norman Lloyd explained his working relationship with Pollins. "Harvey was anti-union, so anytime Hanya did anything with union musicians in New York City, she couldn't use Harvey" (N. and R. Lloyd to T. Bowers). Ruth and Norman Lloyd filled in for him whenever Hanya needed union people. Amazingly, the husband-and-wife team accompanied each of the "Big Four" at one time or another.

21. Unsigned, *Dance Observer* 4, no. 7 (August–September, 1937), 74.

22. Mary Jo Shelly and Martha Hill, 1936 report, page titled, "Summing Up." MHA.

23. Martin, *America Dancing*, 178, 179.

24. Lincoln Kirstein, "The Ballet: Sad but Hopeful," *Dance Observer* 5, no. 9 (November 1937), 113. Kirstein had taken lessons with Fokine on his return from Europe in 1933. That year he became enamored by Diaghilev's legacy as a ballet impresario. Discovering George Balanchine, he felt "as close as one might get to the prime spring of things. . . . I knew I could not myself be a dancer, but there was a possibility as a scholar, perhaps even as some sort of participant. I did not yet dare think of myself as anything so unlikely an impresario. But . . . maybe, perhaps . . . in time?" Lincoln Kirstein, "The Great Conspiracy," in *Ballet: Bias & Belief. Three Pamphlets Collected and Other Dance Writings of Lincoln Kirstein* (1937; reprint, Brooklyn, N.Y.: Dance Horizons, 1983), 226.

25. Lincoln Kirstein, "The Ballet: Tyranny and Blackmail," *Dance Observer* 4, no. 10 (December 1937), 129.

26. Kirstein, "The Great Conspiracy," *Ballet: Bias & Belief*, 229.

27. In a conciliatory move, Martha invited Kirstein back to Bennington for a lecture series on theatrical dancing in the summer of 1940.

28. Leigh had organized the college with no ranks conferred in the appointment of fac-

ulty members, removing the usual academic hierarchy as "not appropriate in the informal Bennington College community." Instead, two-, then three-, then five-year appointments were put into place with eight months' leave after five years of service. Salaries, too, held to his strict guidelines with a basic salary ranging from a minimum of $2,000 a year and a maximum of $5,000 for full-time work by 1939; see *Bennington College Bulletin*, 8, no. 2 (December 1939).

29. Limón, *Memoir*. 79.

30. Ibid.

CULMINATION OF A PLAN, 1938 (pp. 107–115)

1. "The quality of the dancing improved dramatically," although the level of compositional experience was "still low," among incoming students, Norman Lloyd observed.

2. Anna (Schuman) Halprin to Sali Ann Kriegsman, letter, 25 February 1977; S. A. Kriegsman Collection, Bennington, Box 31. LOC:MD. (Also qtd. in Kriegsman, *Modern Dance in America*, 267.) Anna was a student at Bennington during the summers of 1938 and 1939.

3. Eleanor King, *The Early Years*, video recording.

4. Marian Van Tuyl, *The Early Years*, video recording.

5. Ibid. This rare admission from Graham hints at why the yin and yang nature of her relationship with Horst was so successful: he guarded the formal structure of each new collaboration while she concentrated on the how and why of the content.

6. See Soares, *Louis Horst*, for more on this subject.

7. B. Beiswanger to T. Wiesner.

8. See Soares, *Louis Horst*, 140–141.

9. Martin Duberman. *The Worlds of Lincoln Kirstein*, (New York: Knopf, 2007), 318.

10. Erick Hawkins to Kriegsman, *Modern Dance in America*, 260.

11. Joseph Campbell to Kriegsman, *Modern Dance in America*, 274.

12. John Martin, "The Dance: Cycle's End: Bennington Festival Concludes Five-Year Schedule," *New York Times*, 14 August 1938, 134.

13. Erick Hawkins to Sali Ann Kriegsman, 13 August 1976; S. A. Kriegsman Collection, Bennington, Box 31, transcript 6. LOC:MD.

14. "Agnes de Mille interviews Martha Hill."

15. Statement in Festival Program, August 1938. BCA.

16. *Bennington College Bulletin*, May 1939. BCA.

CALIFORNIA AND BACK, 1939–1940 (pp. 116–129)

1. H. Knight to T. Bowers.

2. Martha Hill to JS, 10 January 1986.

3. Soares, *Louis Horst*, 144.

4. T. Wiesner to T. Bowers.

5. H. Knight to T. Bowers.

6. Alfred Frankenstein, "A Program of Percussion," *San Francisco Chronicle*, 28 July 1939, Bennington at Mills file. MCA.

7. Cohen, *An Artist First*, letter, D. Humphrey to C. F. Woodford, n.d., 155–156.

8. See Brockway's chapter, "Leigh's Resignation," in his *Bennington College*. Accreditation was given in 1941 after Jones made substantial changes in the curriculum.

9. Crane's inspiration was "the marvelous beauty of Brooklyn Bridge . . . and the constant stream of tugs, liners, sail boats, etc in procession before you on the river" that he viewed from his room in Brooklyn at 110 Columbia Heights; letter to his mother in 1924, in *Letters of Hart Crane and His Family*, ed. Thomas S. W. Lewis (New York: Columbia University Press, 1974), 305. It would be a similar expanse that so thrilled Martha and Lefty from their apartment a block away when they settled at 210 Columbia Heights.

10. Clive Fisher, *Hart Crane: A Life* (New Haven, Conn.: Yale University Press, 2002), 278, 289.

11. MH to R. T. Godwin, "Martha Hill on Early Dance at Bennington," *Quadrille* 25, no. 1 (Winter 1992–1993), 19.

12. Limón, *Memoir*, 92.

13. Ibid.

14. His earlier American Ballet had produced concerts for several years following the opening in 1934 of the School of American Ballet, with Balanchine at its head as ballet master and choreographer. Ballet Society gave its first performance in November 1946. The company name was changed to the New York City Ballet in 1949.

15. Lincoln Kirstein, "Our Young Dancer's Ideal," from "The Great Conspiracy," in *Ballet: Bias & Belief*, 246, 247.

16. Jenkins, "Reflections," 51.

17. Hazel had returned to Vermont in the summer of 1942 as an accompanist before joining the full-time Bennington faculty. Moving to New York in 1946, she played for Martha at NYU, also joining her staff at Connecticut College American Dance Festival every summer for the next twenty years. Hazel then worked with Hill at Juilliard.

18. H. Knight to T. Bowers.

19. Erick Hawkins would later reverse his stance on the need for ballet technique for modern dancers. When he established his own company in the late 1950s, he ruled out the wearing of tights and shoes and forbade his dancers to take ballet classes.

20. Norman Lloyd added, "Now we're wed to it . . . seeing Rochenberg, Cage and Cunningham and Andy Warhol working together."

21. McDonagh, *Martha Graham*, 146.

22. *Dance Observer's* August–September 1940 issue, with four separate articles on the festival, avoids any mention of the concert.

23. Martha Graham, letters to Kirstein, n.d., Lincoln Kirstein Papers; Box 6, folder 101. NYPL:DC.

24. Horst's YMHA 14 April 1940 and 12 January 1941 lecture-demonstrations with the Martha Graham Group, further solidified the notion that his courses were basic to every future choreographer's education.

25. This hexagon-shaped prototype ("fabricated industrially . . . deliverable in 24 hours" and "primarily a machine in which to live," as described in an invitation letter), had been fostered by the executive committee of the Harvard Society of Contemporary Art in 1929, and was one of Kirstein's and E. E. Warburg's first promotions. It was Fuller's lectures and exhibit that attracted fellow student, Philip Johnson, where he met Kirstein for the first time; see Nicholas Fox Weber. *Patron Saints: Five Rebels Who Opened America to a*

New Art, 1928–1943 (New York: Knopf, 1992), 62, for more details. The house ended up at Bennington as a gift; Fuller's daughter, Rebecca, was a student who studied dance at the summer sessions, graduating as a dance major from Bennington in 1951.

26. Graham, *Blood Memory*, 162.

27. See Soares, *Louis Horst*, 146.

28. John Martin, "Dance Premieres at Bennington, Vt.; Martha Graham Is Seen in 'El Penitente' and 'Letter to the World' at Festival," *New York Times*, 12 August 1940, 10.

29. "I said 'Cut, cut, cut. It's too long. The dance wasn't good—the music wasn't good. So I did cut. We just ended it earlier and it's been cut ever since," Louis explained. Soares, *Louis Horst*, 148–149.

30. Elizabeth McCausland, "Martha Graham and Letter to the World," *Dance Observer* 7, no. 7 (August–September 1940), 97. Later, Jean Erdman took over the role.

31. Dances should be constructed from movement and idea not from music, the musician taught and displayed in his own collaborations with Graham.

32. Levy notebook, marked "Pre Classic Forms. Louis Horst," 1935.

33. Martha Graham writing on Martin, possibly for a tribute statement after his death, 9 June 1985; Lauterer folder. NYPL:DC.

34. Fergusson comment in Kriegsman, *Modern Dance in America*, notes from 23 May 1977 interview. S. A. Kriegsman Collection, Bennington. LOC:MD.

35. Vida Ginsberg Deming, in Brockway, *Bennington College*, 69.

Part V: The Forties

"THE WAR EFFORT HIT US ALL, 1941–1942" (pp. 133–145)

1. Doris Humphrey, "A Home for Humphrey-Weidman," *Dance Observer* 7, no. 9 (November 1940), 124, 125.

2. See Claudia Gitelman, *Dancing with Principle: Hanya Holm in Colorado, 1941–1983* (Boulder: University Press of Colorado, 2001).

3. Mary Gadd. "Country Dancing with the Services," *Dance Observer* 10, no. 8 (October 1943), 89.

4. "Music at Bennington," *Dance Observer* 8, no. 7 (August–September 1941), 97.

5. Doris Humphrey to Julia Humphrey, letter, n.d., Doris Humphrey Collection. NYPL:DC.

6. Margaret Lloyd, *Christian Science Monitor*, 30 August 1940 (qtd. in Kriegsman, *Modern Dance in America*, 106).

7. Margaret Lloyd, "The New Martha Graham," part 1, *Christian Science Monitor*, 21 March 1942. (See collection of comments in Kriegsman, *Modern Dance in America*, 224.)

8. Robert Horan, "The Recent Theater of Martha Graham," in *Chronicles of the American Dance*, ed. Paul Magriel (New York: Henry Holt, 1948), 239.

9. V. Deming, in Brockway, *Bennington College*, 135. (Twenty years later, on the faculty of Juilliard, teaching dramatic literature, she observed, "Martha still electrified her dancers so that they were eager and open to learning . . . endowing her students with the respect for discipline and dedication and the love of an art that she had given us." Ibid.)

10. Brockway, *Bennington College*, 131.

11. Hudas Liff (quoting a letter from Peter F. Drucker), "Martha Hill Centennial," *Ballet Review* 29, no. 4 (Winter 2001), 90.

12. Graham, *Blood Memory*, 162, 163. Curiously, this is the only time Graham mentions Martha Hill in her entire autobiography. She also omits Hill from the acknowledgments at the end of her book, naming instead Bianca Jagger, Calvin Klein, Madonna, and Rudolf Nureyev among her "dear friends and colleagues."

13. Ethel Winter to JS, 3 December 2001, New York City. All subsequent quotes by Winter are from this source, unless noted.

14. Lois Balcom, "College Demonstrations," *Dance Observer* 9, no. 6 (June–July 1942), 76.

15. Thurston Davies, "From this Earth," *American Dancer* (April 1942), 17, 39.

16. Mary Jo Shelly, "Bennington—1942," *Dance Observer* 9, no. 4 (April 1942), 53.

17. José Limón, "Young Dancers State their Views," *Dance Observer* 13, no. 1 (January 1946), 7.

18. Limón, *Memoir*, 113.

19. George Beiswanger, "Doris Humphrey and Company, with José Limón," *Dance Observer* 10, no. 2 (February 1943),15.

20. Gitelman, *Dancing with Principle*, 24.

21. For Belitt, the draft in 1942 seemed a very welcome alternative.

22. Nona Schurman to Sali Ann Kriegsman, letter, 26 March 1978; in Kriegsman, *Modern Dance in America*, 117.

23. "Agnes de Mille interviews Martha Hill."

24. George Beiswanger, "Martha Graham: A Perspective," in *Martha Graham: Sixteen Dances in Photographs*, by Barbara Morgan (1941; reprint, Dobbs Ferry, N.Y.: Morgan Press, 1980), 148.

25. Martha Graham, "1980 Perspectives," in Morgan, *Martha Graham: Sixteen Dances*, 8.

26. That summer Shawn hosted Helen Tamiris on his "Second Generation of American Dance" program (with Shawn still reigning as a leader of the first generation).

27. Presenting these dances in a fall concert at the Humphrey-Weidman Studio Theatre, their New York debut was a "happy occasion" and called a "companion success" to the earlier Dudley-Maslow-Bales trio the previous year. George Beiswanger, "Jean Erdman, Nina Fonaroff, Merce Cunningham," *Dance Observer* 9, no. 9 (November 1942), 120.

28. Lois Balcom, "Bennington in 1942," *Dance Observer* 9, no. 7 (August–September 1942), 87.

29. Gervase N. Butler. "A Little Bell Called Wyron," *Dance Observer* 9, no. 8 (October 1942), 115.

30. R. Stickney to JS.

WAR YEARS AND RECOVERY, 1943–1947 (pp. 146–158)

1. T. Wiesner to T. Bowers. Teddy explained, "Mary Jo knew that they had asked me for a test for officer qualification. I got a call from her. 'You passed with flying colors and they are going to offer you an ensign's commission. Don't take it. I want you with a higher rank than that. Tell them no, you won't come in for less that a lieutenant junior grade.' I got my orders as lieutenant jr. grade and a 48-hours notice. I want to Saks and had my hair cut and sublet my apartment. I was in the Navy. Hortense didn't make it. Minimum height, [they said]."

2. H. Knight to T. Bowers.

3. Martha Hill, "Implications for the Dance," *Journal of Health and Physical Education* 13, no. 6 (June 1942), 348.

4. Walter Everett, "The Dance Goes to War," *Dance Magazine* 17, no. 9 (August 1943), 10.

5. Martha Hill, "Martha Hill Reminisces about Bennington," video recording by Billie Mahoney, 25 July 1985. Martha Hill lecture, Bennington College, Vermont, "José Limón Company Summer Dance Program at Bennington College." NYPL:DC.

6. Jack Anderson, *The American Dance Festival* (Durham, N.C.: Duke University Press, 1987), 3.

7. Among her dance majors at Bennington, Hill found Carol Channing, "very rhythmic and totally convincing in movement." Carol's intention had been to devote her studies to work with Graham but, dazzled by the Broadway stage, on her return to school for the spring semester, Carol promptly changed her major from dance to drama.

8. Always supportive of new talent, Louis placed a photograph of Ethel Winter and Welland Lathrop (his teaching assistant at the Neighborhood Playhouse) on the cover of the March 1943 issue of *Dance Observer*.

9. For Beth Olson Mitchell, it was Martha's advice that sent her to graduate school at Mills, and a job leading to twenty-five years as head of dance at the exclusive Ethel Walker School in Simsbury, Connecticut.

10. Hudas Liff to JS, 5 February 2002, New York City.

11. "College Performance," *Dance Observer* 10, no. 6 (June–July 1943), 71. Ethel Winter was one of those special students. Spotted as "the most promising young dancer seen in these parts in many a moon," she also won an audition for an upcoming YMHA subscription series. By December 1944 Ethel was touring with the company and in the spring of 1945 was dancing in Graham's New York season.

12. Ad, "Bennington College, 1943," *Dance Observer* 10, no. 6 (June–July 1943), 71.

13. Martha Graham to Arch Lauterer, letter, 4 August 1943, Lauterer Papers. NYPL:DC.

14. Arch Lauterer to M. Graham, letter, n.d., Lauterer Papers. NYPL:DC. Lauterer went on to earn a living in academia, moving on to Sarah Lawrence College, and finally, to Mills College where he was director of drama "without peer or rival"; see Brockway, *Bennington College*, 151.

15. Graham to Lauterer, letter, 4 August 1943.

16. G.M.G., "The New Summer Plan With New Works at Bennington College," College Correspondence, *Dance Observer* 10, no. 8 (October 1943), 91.

17. Then an NYU student, Muriel Topaz remembered the coincidence of once being on the same train to Philadelphia with Martha, "which was a little awkward. After a while it became so obvious that she admitted that she was going to see Lefty. She was very embarrassed that I, as a student, discovered that about her." Muriel Topaz to JS, 12 June 2002, Milford, Connecticut. All subsequent quotes by Topaz are from this source, unless noted.

18. Mary Ann confessed that she was awed by Martha's presence from then on.

19. M.S., "Bennington College and Sarah Lawrence College Dance Groups," *Dance Observer* 12, no. 1 (January 1945), 9.

20. Hill suggested circulation of the best dissertations, theses, and projects to extend the literature in the field. She pointed to examples by some of her students, such as "Dance in Negro Colleges and Universities" and "A Survey of Dance Repertories and Festivals in the United States," and suggested that such a periodical might serve as a center for infor-

mation. "Research in Dance," *Dance Observer* 11, no. 7 (August–September 1944), 81. Bruce King was one of three graduate students Hill sent to Oswald at the main branch of the New York Public Library. (Put in charge of the dance archives that had accumulated in the music division, Oswald's first assignment was to look through materials Kirstein had earlier deposited at the MOMA collection.)

21. Martha Hill with Genevieve (Gigi) Oswald, 13 December 1990, New York City. (Filmed as an addendum to the Hong Kong Oral History Project, Hong Kong Academy for Performing Arts.) NYPL:DC.

22. Martha understood the importance of reciprocity. "Later, when Carlton's wife Elizabeth wanted to present Indian dancers Swati and Shanta Rao at MOMA, I made Juilliard available," Hill recalled.

23. Joseph Campbell, "The Jubilee of Content and Form," *Dance Observer* 12, no. 5 (May 1945), 52.

24. Margaret H'Doubler. "A Question of Values and Terms," *Dance Observer* 12, no. 7 (August–September 1945), 83.

25. Dilts papers, J. Dilts to JS, letter, 25 August 1997. MHA:PC.

26. Ibid.

27. Angela Gibbs, "The Absolute Frontier," *New Yorker*, 25 no. 45 (27 December 1947): 35.

28. Dated ADF papers, Box 1. DULL:ADF.

29. Joe Nash to Martha Hill, memo, 31 November 1946. MHA.

30. Martha Hill to Joe Nash, letter, 26 November 1946. MHA.

31. Martha Hill to Joe Nash, "More freedom . . . ," n.d. MHA.

32. Rosemary Park, *A Decade of Dance, 1948–1957*, souvenir program of the 10th American Dance Festival, 1957, 3. (Park had also been enlightened by Susanne Langer, then a professor of philosophy on campus who was very much a presence at dance events sduring the 1950s and 1960s.)

33. Emily Coleman, "Martha Graham Still Leaps Forward," *New York Times Magazine*, 9 April 1961, 49.

34. Rosemary Park, American Dance Festival Program, 16 August 1956, Connecticut College. CC:SLA.

35. While working at Bennington, Hazel Johnson recognized Martha's complete trust in Bales and noticed that she gave him everything he asked for, without question. To Hazel, this favoritism toward men become more pronounced over time.

36. Rosemary Park to Martha Hill, letter, December 1947, Box 1. DULL:ADF.

AN AMERICAN DANCE FESTIVAL, 1948 (pp. 159–168)

1. In the original budget, as well as free room and board, Graham, Holm Humphrey, Horst, Lloyd, Bales, and Limón were all to receive $700; Belitt, $500; Hill, $400 (plus an administrative fee of $300; Bloomer, $600 as assistant administrative director; and Shelly, $700 as administrative director. Five accompanists were to receive $500 each. A revision gave Graham $1,250, with $750 each for Humphrey and Limón, and $700 for musicians. Budget proposal sheet. MHA.

2. Doris Humphrey files. DULL:ADF. (She also reminded Martha that she hadn't requested teaching a section of dance repertory. "Am undecided about the value of it.")

3. Martha Hill to Rosemary Park, letter, 18 February 1948. DULL:ADF.

4. The list included Patricia (Patsi, or Pat) Birch, New York City, and Helen Knight, Saint Louis, Missouri.

5. Walter Terry, "A New Modern Dance Venture Is Instituted at New London," *Herald Tribune*, 22 August 1948, section 5, 4.

6. Mark Ryder to S. A. Kriegsman, 26 May 1977, S. A. Kriegsman Collection, Bennington, Box 40. LOC:MD.

7. Agnes de Mille, *Martha* (New York: Random House, 1991), 350.

8. Martha Hill and Louis Horst, personal communications to JS, c. 1961–1964.

9. Of that group, it was Limón who continued to teach on the summer faculty until his death in 1972, presenting new choreography on the festival programs each year.

10. This included head, shoulder, elbow, palm of the hand, rib cage, hip, knee, and heel isolations, used as distinct accents, and in combination, that some felt were influenced by similar vocabulary in Peter Hamilton's jazz work.

11. José Limón, "Young Dancers State Their Views," *Dance Observer* 13, no. 1 (January 1946), 7.

12. Thora McCready, "Miss Martha Hill, chairman of the Administrative Board of New York University-CC School of the Dance," ? ? ? ?. 1, no. 1 (26 July 1948).

13. The newsletter also reported: "Mr. Belitt, a roller-skating enthusiast, spent his first evening skating at Ocean Beach which he claims has one of the finest rinks in the U.S." Ibid.

14. Before their deaths, both published books on their teaching methods that would become important resources for teaching dance composition in the United States. See Humphrey's *The Art of Making Dances* (1959; reprint, Princeton, N.J.: Dance Horizons, 1987), and Horst's *Modern Dance Forms in Relation to the Other Arts* (1961; reprint, Princeton, N.J.: Dance Horizons, 1987), as well as his 1937 *Pre-Classic Dance Forms* (1937; reprint, Princeton, N.J.: Dance Horizons, 1988).

15. American Dance Festival, 1967 festival program note. MHA.

16. These outreach programs became part of the school's publicity efforts. By 1961, a more formal touring company of students, Dance Advance was created under the author's direction, performing in ten to twelve neighboring communities each summer for the next three years in such places as the Danbury Arts Festival, a school picnic at Mystic Seaport's gazebo, in art galleries, and at local summer camps.

17. Nik Krevitsky, "Review of American Dance Festival," *Dance Observer* 15, no. 8 (August–September 1948), 84.

18. Limón had officially debuted his new company at Bennington on 11 July 1946.

19. Dello Joio's next project at Sarah Lawrence (while in residence there with Schuman and Lloyd) would be an extravagant production based on Joan of Arc. Other configurations of his music for that particular production found its way into another score for Graham, first as the solo *The Triumph of St. Joan* (1951) and later as the group work *Seraphic Dialogue* (1955).

20. Joseph Wiseman to JS, 21 February 2002, New York City.

21. See Soares, *Louis Horst*, chap. 9.

22. De Mille, *Martha*, 283.

23. McGeary to JS.

24. Nik Krevitsky, "New York City 'Dance Theatre' at the N.Y. City Center," *Dance Observer* 17, no. 1 (January 1950), 10.

25. Walter Terry, "The Dance World. A Dance Orphan is Adopted, Named The New York City Dance Theater," *Herald Tribune*, 18 December 1949, scrapbooks. NYPL:DC.

26. From that group, Pat Birch would soon become a member of the Graham company, and Allegra Fuller (Snyder), Buckminster Fuller's daughter, would go on to direct the University of California at Los Angeles's Department of Dance, working extensively as a dance filmmaker.

CHANGES, 1949–1950 (pp. 169–176)

1. "Message from Denny: Town Hall Morning Lectures, 1948–49," Series IB, Folder 14, Town Hall Archives. NYPL:MC. Denny went on to devote most of his time to the development of *America's Town Meeting of the Air*, designed to broadcast "informed public opinion." (From 1954 to 1956, Davies is listed as its executive director.)

2. Series IB, Folder 24, Town Hall Archives. NYPL:MD.

3. Martha Hill Archives. NYPL:HL.

4. Correspondence between Martha Hill and Rusty Bloomer. MHA.

5. Carl Miller, "The N.Y.U. Connecticut College Second Summer Session," *Dance Observer* 16, no. 7 (August 1949), 98.

6. One was for special Bennington student Harvey Lichtenstein as a backstage apprentice. "He is very attractive, boyish, masculine, and a very honorable person," Martha wrote to Rusty. MHA. (Years later he became executive director of Brooklyn Academy.)

7. John Martin, "'Pavane': Impressive Work by Limón on Theme of Othello," *New York Times*, 28 August 1949. New York Times Scrapbooks: Articles on Dance 1937–1966. NYPL:DC.

8. Nik Krevitsky, "José Limón and Company," *Dance Observer* 16, no. 7 (August–September 1949), 68.

9. B. Mitchell to JS.

10. Louis Horst to JS, c. 1962.

11. José Limón, "Young Dancers State their Views," *Dance Observer* 13, no. 1 (January 1946), 7.

12. N. Krevitsky, *Dance Observer* 16, no. 7 (August–September, 1949), 98.

13. Ibid. 99.

14. *Creative Leisure* (1951), 16 mm film, U.S. Department of the Army. Producer, Herbert Kerkow.

15. The film was screened the next summer at ADF to everyone's delight.

16. For an insightful overview, see Tom Borek's "The Connecticut College American Dance Festival 1948–1972: A Fantastical Documentary." *Dance Perspectives* 50 (Summer 1972).

17. Associate Dean Ralph E. Picket, then director of Education Summer Sessions, explained that from the beginning the "central administration let it be known that the New York State Board of Regents did not . . . look with favor, on the affiliation of an institution chartered under New York State and one chartered under the rules of another." Qtd. in *Fifty Years of Dance in Higher Education*, NYU Publication for Gala Events, 2 April 1982, 3. NYU:BL.

18. Rusty Bloomer to Martha Hill, letter, 25 August 1949. DULL:ADF.

19. John Martin, "The Dance: Futures with Uday Shankar," *New York Times*, 8 January 1950, 77.

20. Among Grace's papers, Martha found a small pamphlet, "The Dancing Question," by preacher W. B. Boies, Alcula, South Carolina, that confirmed her mother's continuing resolution against dance. Boies writes, "The explanation of your wanting to dance is probably that Satan is seeking to drown and smother the desires that the Holy Spirit is seeking to put into your heart, for higher and holier things." MHA.

21. Martha Hill to Isadora Bennett, letter, 19 April 1950. MHA.

22. Martha's student from NYU, Trinidadian Pearl Primus, first aspired to be a physician, but took her first dance lesson at the New Dance Group in 1941. She then studied with the "Big Four" and presented a debut concert at the YMHA in 1943. By 1944 she had developed dances based on African and West Indian styles—*Strange Fruit* and *The Negro Speaks of Rivers*—describing the downtrodden conditions of black people. After several Broadway stints, she traveled to Africa to study its indigenous dance, returning to found the Pearl Primus School of Primal Dance. The 1950 performance was a disappointment— some thought it haphazardly presented—but Hill remained an ardent supporter (encouraging the ANTA dance panel to fund her in 1960). She particularly admired Primus's later efforts as an educator and anthropologist.

23. See Claudia Gitelman, ed., *Liebe Hanya: Mary Wigman's Letters to Hanya Holm* (Madison: University of Wisconsin Press, 2003), 111–112. In a letter to Hill at ADF, Wigman wrote, "I want to thank you, all of you, for your great kindness and loyalty. You cannot imagine what it means to me not to be forgotten in your country and to be wanted again."

24. Martha Hill, "José Limón and his Biblical Works," in *Choreography and Dance*, vol. 5, part 3 (London: Harwood Academic, 1992), 59. *The Exiles* was a dance that Limón later released to Israel's Batsheva Company as well as to the Royal Swedish Ballet.

25. "The Festival" (three-page report). MHA.

26. Lloyd joined the Juilliard faculty in 1949. In 1963 he became dean of Oberlin's music conservatory and later, director of the arts program of the Rockefeller Foundation.

27. Roger Kimball, "Martha" (unpublished draft for article, n.d.). MHA.

28. William Schuman interviewed by Sharon Zane. LCPAA:OHP. All subsequent quotes by Schuman are from this source unless noted. In this interview the terms *dance department* and *dance division* are often interchanged.

29. During this time, Graham was going through her own emotional crisis: Erick had left her, and the tumultuous relationship was over; They divorced in 1954. Graham's twenty-minute dance, *Legend of Judith* (the first of three versions)—a solo that retold the myth of the biblical heroine who removes her "garments of sadness" and puts on "garments of gladness"—was an attempt to purge her despondency over the breakup. Erick recounted, "Martha believes, you see, that one's life is for the art, and I believe the art is for one's life, and that's where we differ." Hawkins to Kriegsman, *Modern Dance in America*, 260. Graham knew the split was inevitable when Erick asked their analyst, Frances Wickes, "if she could make him a better dancer and choreographer than I was. Mrs. Wickes said, 'No, I cannot.' . . . Erick said, 'therefore I break my analysis.' And he walked out, not only from analysis, but gradually, from our marriage as well"; Graham, *Blood Memory*, 180.

30. Vera C. Michaelson, manuscript sent to Martha Hill, 1968, Dance Division General Administrative Records, 1947–1991, Box 1, Fol. 12. JSA.

31. William Schuman to Martha Hill, letter, 6 February 1951. MHA.

Part VI: Dance within the Conservatory

JUILLIARD, 1951–1952 (pp. 179–188)

1. Robert Tracy, "Martha Hill," in *Goddess: Martha Graham's Dancers Remember* (New York: Limelight Editions, 1997), 17.

2. Hill to Kimball, "Martha." MHA.

3. Martha Hill to Katherine Tatge, video recording and transcript. Interview for documentary, *Martha Graham: An Artist Revealed*. MHA.

4. See Muriel Topaz's biography on Tudor, *Undimmed Lustre: The Life of Antony Tudor* (Lanham, Md.: Scarecrow Press, 2002).

5. June Dunbar, Oral History Project, June Dunbar Folder. LCPAA:OHP. All subsequent qotes by Dunbar are from this source, unless noted.

6. Until this point, within other dance conservatories, only Kurt Jooss had attempted this—a dream crushed by the World War II. Aware of Jooss's work, Martha did hire two former Jooss company dancers, Alfredo Corvino (from Montevideo, Uruguay) and Lucas Hoving for the Juilliard faculty. The Opera Theatre department was directed by Fritz Cohen (composer for Jooss's *The Green Table*) and his wife Elsa Kahn, originally from that company as well.

7. Throughout his lifetime, Tudor suffered silent criticism about his "humble origins" and his name change. His first choice had been Stuart, but because there was already a Stuart in the Rambert company, he chose Tudor and dropped the "h" in Anthony for "more uniqueness." P. W. Manchester, "Reflections After Reading *Shadowplay*." *Ballet Review* 20, no. 1 (Spring 1992), 75.

8. Anna Kisselgoff, "Contrasting Tudor and, at Season's End, Balanchine," *New York Times*, 6 November 2001.

9. Tudor gave up his position as artistic director of the company in 1963 and directorship of the school in 1966.

10. Donna Perlmutter, *Shadowplay* (New York: Viking Penguin, 1991), 236.

11. Martha Hill, "Antony Tudor: The Juilliard Years," in *Antony Tudor: The American Years, Choreography and Dance*, ed. Muriel Topaz (New York: Routledge, 1989), 43.

12. Although Balanchine's choreography remained the company's main staple, this unusual interest in expanding the repertory was heartening to those who favored a broader repertory concept for a company receiving significant funding from a city of wide demographics.

13. Though generally keeping their emotions at bay, their mutual distrust was obvious to both their colleagues and the students, particularly when they sat on juries and exams together at Juilliard.

14. Weidman had long challenged his dancers to think of movement, not steps. Following suit, Limón defined modern dance as a style that "permitted choice for gesture in movement, not limited by the formalities of ballet." Outtakes from the film *Festival of the Dance*, audiotaped interview excerpts, 1971. NYPL:DC.

15. Drawn from author's notes of Elizabeth Sawyer's comments at "On Dance" lecture series, March 2003, Barnard College, New York City.

16. Elizabeth Sawyer, "Notes on *Dark Elegies*," *Dance Chronicle: Studies in Dance and the Related Arts* 28, no. 1 (2005), 7.

17. Martha Hill to Muriel Topaz, Hong Kong Oral History Project, Hong Kong Academy for Performing Arts (video recording, Hong Kong, July 1990). NYPL:DC.

18. In the same year, Limón's company was sent abroad on a cultural mission by the U.S. government under the auspices of the American National Theatre.

19. HH to T. Bowers.

20. Topaz added, "In the beginning the department was clearly an experiment, and it took Martha a few years to really weld it together into the school. First of all, the faculty had no idea how to behave. They'd never taught in that kind of a school. There were strong disagreements among faculty members in the early years. Eventually it all pulled together."

21. Yasuko Toganaga, a Juilliard alumna now directing the dance division at Boston Conservatory, equated Martha's explanation into movement analysis "effort-shape" analysis terms used as a basis for study in the Boston school. Yasuko Toganaga to JS, 14 September 2003, Tucson, Arizona.

22. Martha told an interviewer in 1979: "Because every choreographer you dance with is different, if you are imbued with one approach and one aesthetic, unless you are a very unusual person, you're limited. That's one reason our Juilliard dancers are very much in demand. They are very versatile." MH to T. Bowers.

23. Marshall McClintock, "Song and Dance College," *Collier's* (10 May 1952), 39.

24. Martha Hill to William Schuman, letter, 4 November 1954, president's records, Box 5, Fol. 1. JSA.

25. Paul Taylor, *Public Domain* (New York: Knopf, 1987), 42.

26. "Martha Hill Centennial," *Ballet Review* 29, no. 4 (Winter 2001), 91.

MARRIAGE, 1952–1955 (pp. 189–196)

1. Lefty's first wife, Joyce Davies, died in November 1953.

2. A favorite student of Hill's, first at the Lincoln School of Teachers College, Columbia, then at Bennington, Tish Evans is the granddaughter of Mabel Dodge Luhan. Tish later taught at Juilliard in the mid-1950s. The author took her first dance composition course with Evans in 1956–57.

3. MH to J. Dilts, letter, n.d. (c. 1952), Dilts papers. MHA.

4. Note, 2 August 1954, Davies files, Town Hall Archives. NYPL:HL.

5. Town Hall Archives. LCPA:MC. (Dame Ninette De Valois also gave a lecture on ballet in October 1956.)

6. José's good luck at making connections coincided, not surprisingly, with Lefty's "people to people mission" with the various government officials. In 1950, Limón began a two-year relationship with the Mexican government's newly formed National Institute for Arts under composer Carlos Chávez's direction. See "José Limón and *La Malinche* in Mexico," Margarita Tortajada Quiroz, in *José Limón and La Malinche*, ed. Patricia Seed (Austin: University of Texas, 2008), 119–153. If such collaborations helped José produce the work, dancers were not that well rewarded. Each received a check for $10 handed to

them by Pauline after the last performance, according to Eric Russell, who willingly rehearsed all autumn for the event (personal conversation, 21 January 2004, New York City.)

7. Natasha Derujinsky, "The New Dance Department: An Interview with Miss Martha Hill," *Stretto*, no. 1 (January 1952), 1.

8. Robert Sabin, "José Limón and Company," *Dance Observer* 21, no. 3 (March 1954), 41.

9. Doris Hering, "Preview of a New Dance Company," *Dance Magazine* (April 1955), 27.

10. With somewhat casual academic objectives for her already overworked students, rather than adhering to any chronological study of history, Martha began by discussing the present state of dance. She then pressed her senior students to consider their personal objectives in preparation for the future. The required research project usually produced practical, immediate benefits, such as a chronology of Limón's works, or the notation of pieces by Tudor or Humphrey currently in rehearsal. Some of these documents became invaluable.

11. Sweigard, with Betty Jones assisting her, conducted laboratories (with leather belts strapped together bent knees and rolled towels braced turned-in feet). When her book *Human Movement Analysis: Ideokinetic Facilitation* was released in 1962, Martha celebrated its arrival for weeks in the dance office, making sure there were stacks for sale in the Juilliard Book Store.

12. Doreen Vallis to Martha Hill, letter, n.d. JSA.

13. Martha's own politicizing more often took place behind closed doors at ANTA meetings, or in advocating for honorees of her choice for the yearly Capezio Awards. That year, honoring Isadora Bennett, press agent for dance, the official photograph for the 1953 event shows John Martin, Walter Terry, the young Anna Kisselgoff (later to become chief dance critic for the *New York Times*) the ever-smiling Hill, and sponsor of the award, Capezio's president, Ben Sommers.

14. Martha Hill to Ruth (Rusty) Bloomer, letter, n.d. DULL:ADF.

15. Although the school made a profit of $1,904.84, the festival budget income reached just more than half of its projected $6,000 intake.

16. Rosemary Park to José Limón, letter, January 1954, José Limón Papers. NYPL:DC.

17. As director of the YMHA's Dance Center since 1945 under Dr. Kolodney, Doris had recently been appointed artistic head of the Y's School of the Dance and the Dance Theatre, causing Terry to complain of her newest title as "a form of benevolent despotism"; Walter Terry, "New Theatre Policy at the Y.M.H.A.," *Herald Tribune*, 1 November 1953. The plan, according to Naomi M. Jackson's research about the Y's dance activities, was to develop the Y as a performance outlet for Humphrey so that, beginning in January 1954, she might establish a company to showcase her work. Kolodney had received $4,000 from the Baron de Rothschild Foundation for the Arts and Sciences to set the project in motion. But Humphrey evidently saw Juilliard as a more attractive opportunity. Money from the foundation was switched to Juilliard, and Martha had her company. See Jackson, *Converging Movements: Modern Dance and Jewish Culture at the Ninety-second Street Y* (Middletown, Conn.: Wesleyan University Press, 2000), for an overview of the institution's dance activities.

18. See Naima Prevots, *Dance for Export: Cultural Diplomacy and the Cold War* (Middletown, Conn.: Wesleyan University Press, 1998), 37–40, for a comprehensive history of ANTA.

19. "Dance Critic Declines to Serve on Advisory Panel of International Program," *Dance News* (January 1955), 1; qtd. in Jackson, *Converging Movements*, 43.

20. Cohen, quoting Humphrey, *An Artist First*, 208.

PLANS FOR LINCOLN SQUARE, 1955–1956 (pp. 197–205)

1. Jenkins, "Reflections," 48, 61.

2. Martin L. Sokol, *The New York City Opera: An American Adventure* (New York: Macmillan, 1981), 166.

3. Ibid., 167.

4. Kirstein to Morton Baum and Newbold Morris, memorandum, 28 December 1953; qtd. in Sokol, *New York City Opera*, 167.

5. Sokol, *New York City Opera*, 170.

6. David Rockefeller, the forty-year-old grandson of JDR III, was at this time vice president of Chase Manhattan Bank. By coincidence, Thurston Davies would soon be part of negotiations for what would become the World Trade Center, giving Martha an insider source for the Rockefeller family's dealings. That project began on 31 October 1955 after a meeting with David Rockefeller and Robert Moses who needed Davies's salesmanship and savvy for their proposed five million square feet of office space in Lower Manhattan. Lefty's involvement with the Port Authority and the Lower Manhattan Project is noted in the 1961 article "Mierow, Davies, Former College Presidents, Die," *Colorado College Magazine*. MHA.

7. See Robert A. Caro, *The Power Broker: Robert Moses and the Fall of New York* (New York: Knopf, 1974), chaps. 43–46.

8. Papers and personal correspondence of the committee were found on this subject in the Lincoln Kirstein and Edgar Young files at the Rockefeller Foundation Archives. Subsequently referenced here as Kirstein Papers or Young Papers. RFA.

9. Kirstein was invited at the recommendation of JDR III's brother, Nelson A. Rockefeller, who would become vice president, after serving four terms as New York State's Republican governor. Nelson, who was soon to become a strong foe of Robert Moses, had written a personal note to Kirstein expressing his appreciation of "the full flowering of your great dream. No one but you could have or would have seen this through"; Nelson Rockefeller to Lincoln Kirstein, letter, 22 June 1955, Kirstein Papers. RFA.

10. George Beiswanger, transcription of Martha Hill lecture at Connecticut College, "Summary: The Education of a Dancer, Connecticut College School of the Dance." MHA. (Beiswanger directed the lecture series as part of his new course "Backgrounds and Aesthetics of Dance," given in the summer of 1955 with help from a Rockefeller Foundation grant.)

11. Jenkins, "Reflections."

12. Sokol, *New York City Opera*, 170. Kirstein had to give a solid argument because of the company's attachment then to the New York City Center of Music and Drama. Only after having secured a place for the New York City Ballet on the plaza, did Kirstein return to his alliance to the New York City Center of Music and Drama. At the time, NYCB's non-profit association was with Ballet Society, Inc., founded in 1947 for the express purpose of creating new works for the lyric repertory: a Kirstein document states, "As of 1956, all new works produced by the *New York City Ballet* company are the property of *Ballet Society* . . . although not yet activated as a public institution . . . that had received personal and foun-

dation grants amounting to about $475,000 in the past ten years." This document contains a section on physical requirements with at least 2800–3200 seats needing powerful architectural support for the "warmth, splendor and excitement of the event," with an orchestra pit seating "at least 60 men," a proscenium opening of at least fifty by fifty, a slightly forward apron, and a partly hidden pit, a slightly raked stage, for an auditorium to enhance the "human scale of action" so important to dance. Box 59, Fol. 529, Kirstein to Young, correspondence. RFA.

13. Kirstein also stated that NYCB had become "the ranking organization of its kind in the Americas, and recognized, after four European tours as one of the representative companies of the world, to be equated with the British Saddler's [sic] Wells, and the Russian Bolshoi." Ibid.

14. Jenkins, "Reflections."

15. An Edgar Young to JDR III letter, dated 7 December 1956, frets over "what to do about the letter from Ballet Theatre" and Lucia Chase's request for a conference with JDR III. In it he encloses a drafted letter to be sent to Lucia Chase's son, Ewing. It states, "The real issue underlining the request is whether Lincoln Center wants to take on as a major participating institution a second ballet company. Perhaps this issue should receive some discussion at a board meeting. My own feeling is that it would be unwise to do so and that we should regard the New York City Ballet as the primary institutional participant in the field of dance. If this is to be our position, then there is not too much to be served by having a conference." Young Papers. RFA.

16. Memo, 13 December 1956, Young Papers. RFA.

17. Kirstein Papers. RFA. Kirstein again reminds the committee, "Tudor is now in charge of the Ballet School of the Metropolitan Opera Association which is a lucrative operation."

18. Ibid.

19. Town Hall Archives. NYPL:HL.

20. Each season more responsibilities were assumed by Bloomer, including the management of a lecture series for which she formally invited such personalities as Aaron Copland, Kirstein, and Schuman. Offered a stipend of $50, they each responded with polite but firm rejection letters.

21. Jack Anderson, *American Dance Festival*, 57.

22. Schlottman's successor at Connecticut was Martha's close friend, Teddy Wiesner, who assumed the running of the summer school while continuing to teach at Brooklyn College during the academic year. To some, this hiring once more demonstrated Martha's need to control. (In 1966, when Teddy resigned from ADF, I was asked by the board to take the job. Though flattered—I was only 28—I quickly lost interest, as Martha insisted that the position would be easy because all of the decisions would be made by "the board." I was anxious to "paddle my own canoe"—as Martha had earlier—and said no.)

23. Thurston Davies and Martha Hill to Judy Dilts, letter, 9 February 1957. MHA.

24. Found among Davies's papers was a seven-year $85,000 Brooklyn–Port Authority Pier and upland area development plan to replace obsolete shipping facilities on the Brooklyn waterfront. This plan included removing the warehouses along the Brooklyn Heights Esplanade to give unobstructed views of the "magnificent harbor panorama"— coincidently, directly in front of Martha and Lefty's apartment.

25. Bill Hill's job there was with Smucker's. "He was in charge of selecting the best strawberries for their jams," Martha proudly explained.

26. Martha Hill, "José Limón and his Biblical Works," 57; quoting Robert Frost, "Quantula," in *Robert Frost: Collected Poems, Prose, & Plays* (1949; reprint, New York: Library of America, 1995), 329.

27. *New York Times*, 30 January 1957, Thurston Davies file. JSA. This would prove to be the largest universal fair since the New York World's Fair of 1939.

28. "World's Fair 1958: A Preview," *Time*, 4 February 1957, clipping, Davies file. JSA.

Part VII: Between Two Worlds

TIME AWAY, 1958 (pp. 209–218)

1. Letters, n.d., c. 1957, José Limón folder. NYPL:DC.

2. Ibid. Limón had choreographed to Chávez's music in 1951, creating *Los Cuatros Soles* and *Anatigona* in Mexico. (See note 6, page 364)

3. 24 July 1957, letters, c. 1957, José Limón Papers. NYPL:DC.

4. MH to JS, 10 January 1986.

5. Martha Hill donated copies of eighty-four films of dances produced at Juilliard from 1954 to 1985 to the New York Public Library for the Performing Arts.

6. June Dunbar to MH, letter, n.d. JSA. Having first taught Limón's classes while he was on tour in 1953, June was well aware of how the department functioned.

7. Acknowledging Schuman's role, June later wrote, "José the artist was unstintingly sustained by this team and we are the richer for their belief in his vision." Dunbar, *José Limón*, 128.

8. Kirstein to Young, letter, 16 December 1957, Kirstein Papers. RFA. He also discussed the design of a new theater component for Juilliard, much to Schuman's chagrin. (Young Papers, RFA.) In November 1956 Kirstein was asked to suggest a plan for the future operation of the Phoenix Theater. (He was then a producer with John Houseman for two of the company's Shakespeare Festival plays in 1957.) Not surprisingly, it would be Houseman who became the final choice as director of the theater division at Juilliard. Kirstein advocated a "host-house" for the theater. "What New York badly needs . . . [is] a place in which to perform," his document concludes.

9. Duberman, *The Worlds of Lincoln Kirstein*, 541.

10. William Schuman to Young, Young Papers. RFA. Schuman continues, "Martha Graham is elite, meaning the best quality, a highly specialized quality. I'm not afraid of the word, if it's used in its broadest context. It's not anti-democratic; it's a qualitative term, and that's the only way in which I use it." Ibid.

11. Stoddard had been president of the University of Illinois for seven years and served as the commissioner of education of New York. He chaired a self-study for NYU in 1953, and by 1960 had became the school's academic chancellor and executive vice president.

12. Stoddard to Young, memorandum, Young Papers. RFA.

13. John D. Rockefeller III, Edgar B. Young Papers, meeting of advisory council, minutes, 13 January 1958. RFA. The members were Reginald Allen, Lucia Chase, Belvins

Davis, Doris Duke (the only one not present), Hallock DuPont, Julius Fleischmann, Martha Graham, Lincoln Kirstein, William Kolodney, Joseph Martinson, William Schuman, and Edgar B. Young, with George Stoddard acting as temporary chairman. (He eventually requested that Allen assume the chair.)

14. Marcia Siegel, *Days on Earth: The Dance of Doris Humphrey* (New Haven, Conn.: Yale University Press, 1988), 247.

15. Meeting of advisory council, minutes, 11 February 1958, Young Papers. RFA.

16. W. McNeil Lowry, "The Ford Foundation Dance Grants Revisited," in *On the Edge: Challenges to American Dance*. Proceedings of the 1989 Dance Critics Association Conference (San Francisco, Calif., 1989), 88.

17. NYCB and SAB would be the recipients from the Ford Foundation. Walter Terry, "Ford Blows Up a Storm," *New York Herald Tribune*, 12 January 1964, in Walter Terry, *I Was There* (New York: Marcel Dekker, 1978), 451, 454.

18. Minutes of advisory council, 6 March 1958, Young Papers. RFA.

19. Minutes of advisory council, 22 April 1958, Young Papers. RFA. These minutes reveal that Philip Johnson was paid a $1,500 fee for preliminary conferences and then $100 for a first meeting on 22 August 1957. At the next meeting with eleven present, Johnson described his preliminary designs for the dance theater. Young noted that from as early as 31 December 1956, Johnson's preliminary sketches and models for both ballet and light opera had been discussed, noting that "the requirements of the house for Ballet usage had already been outlined to Mr. Johnson by LK"; ibid. In the fall of 1958, the executive committee proposed to the city a plan to make Lincoln Center the new home for City Center of Music and Drama (with the city providing half the cost of the dance theater), therefore involving the whole City Center, rather than a dance constituency alone. By January 1959, the newly elected governor of New York, Nelson Rockefeller, entered the discussions concerning City Center. Moses objected to any implication that the city would pay the costs: as the date for groundbreaking approached, the question of a dance constituent was still unresolved. In the meantime, the New York State World's Fair commission met on 15 December 1960 for the proposed use of the theater for the World's Fair, although seven miles from the actual Queens fairgrounds. A contract provided for purchase by the state of the completed New York State Theater building for $15 million, with Lincoln Center as the owner, leasing it to the state for the two years of the World's Fair. On 24 April 1959, the city council gave final approval to provide $4,383,000 toward the cost of the New York State Theater building and its land.

20. William Schuman, minutes of advisory council, 22 April 1958, Young Papers. RFA.

21. Louis Horst, "Juilliard Dance Theater," *Dance Observer* 25, no. 6 (June–July 1958), 86.

22. José Limón, "Dancers are Musicians are Dancers," reprinted from the *Juilliard Review Annual, 1966–67*, in *José Limón*: ed. J. Dunbar, 18.

23. June Dunbar to Martha Hill, letter, n.d. MHA.

24. Agnes de Mille, "Dance: 'We Deserve a Fair Showing,'" *New York Times*, 23 September 1962, 287. She later recalled her visit: although impressed by the rich assortment of concert activity Lefty had put into place, she felt a lack of identity with a nation so diverse culturally, and so emerged in popular art, rather than substance. She most admired the Finnish building, where the first pages of the score of Sibelius's *Finlandia* were on dis-

play: "On those pages rested a cast of the master's hand, the imprimatur of Finland." Why, she wondered, was the United States so lacking in national identity?

25. Thurston Davies to Martha Hill, letter, 25 September 1958. MHA.

BRUSSELS RESPITE, 1959 (pp. 219–227)

1. Arthur Todd, "Which Direction for Dance at Lincoln Center?" *Dance Observer* 26, no. 9 (November 1959), 107.

2. Harry Bernstein, *Dance Observer* 26, no. 9 (November 1959), 133.

3. Helen Tamiris to Young, "Statement of Purpose" (8 pages), Young Papers. RFA. Tamiris also compiled a two-page list of outstanding dance centers for modern dance in the United States and calculated an audience figure of 45,000 for 1956–57 for modern dance in New York, Connecticut, and Massachusetts.

4. Ibid. Tamiris names "Doris Humphrey, Martha Graham, Hanya Holm, Charles Weidman, and herself, along with a second generation—such as José Limón, Valerie Bettis, Anna Sokolow, and Sophie Maslow" as those choreographers.

5. Young to Allen and Stoddard, memorandum, 14 October 1958, Young Papers. RFA.

6. Doris Humphrey to MH, letter. JSA.

7. Important work was, however, being created down the block at the Columbia-Princeton Music Laboratory in the Prentis Building on West 125th Street.

8. Margo Mink (Colbert) to JS, 14 January 2002, New York City. A favorite of Tudor's because of her quick wit, Margo would become an avant-garde choreographer before joining the University of Nevada faculty.

9. Quoting a M. Hill letter to Wolz, he responded, "How could I not hire this person!" Carl Wolz to JS, 22 August 2001, New York City. All subsequent quotes by Wolz are from this source, unless noted.

10. Davies to MH, letter, 1 October 1958. JSA. Telegram, 3 October 1958. MHA.

11. Davies to MH, letters, 11, 14, 17, October 1958. MHA.

12. Davies to MH, letter, 28 October 1958. MHA. Lefty's correspondence also concerned Martha's communications with his daughters. Judy and her family were considering a possible move to the East and his second daughter, Mary Louise, was struggling with bouts of alcoholism and deepening mental illness: Martha made an effort to spend time with Mary Louise, who stayed with her in Brooklyn for a brief period. "She likes you & says she understands and appreciates," Lefty wrote to Martha, but warned that she "lives ups and downs—part of the time in a sort of dream world in which everything is wonderful & then goes off completely." But Lefty's fatherly duties stopped there. "You might tell Judy—and Mary Louise, if necessary—what a burden this is to me as well as to you," he added; letter, 4 November 1958. MHA.

13. Davies to MH, letters, 3 October 1958 and 11 November 1958. MHA.

14. Jerry Bywaters (Cochran) to JS, e-mail, 12 June 2003.

15. Davies to MH, letter, 14 November 1958. MHA.

16. Dunbar to MH, 6 January 1959 (Dunbar letters: Dance Div. General admin. 1951–71. Box 1, fol. 5). JSA.

17. Coincidently, the new company member was the author: Janet Mansfield "doing a superb job of picking up the material." It was shocking to find one's own name attached to such an emotional event. Then a second-year student, I was called in to join the Juilliard

Dance Theater to replace an injured dancer a week before the showing that June describes. My recollection was of simply trying to keep up while not looking conspicuously out of place.

18. Shortly before her death, Doris completed her book *The Art of Making Dances*, fulfilling her 1949 Guggenheim Fellowship obligation.

19. Months later, I realized that more than likely Leo was present because he had begun an amorous relationship with company member Joyce Tristler, who had been Doris's protégé. (They married the next year.)

20. Dunbar to MH, letter, 6 January 1959 (Dunbar letters: Dance Div. General admin. 1951–71. Box 1, fol. 5). JSA. (The company toured that spring under the name Doris Humphrey Dance Theatre; for legal reasons the Juilliard name could not be placed on any representative company that performed without live music.)

21. After difficult years of coexistence, by 1967 June was given other administrative responsibilities as Juilliard's Lincoln Center Student Program (LCSP) director, with an office of her own in the new building.

22. June continued, "I think she's been proven ahead of her time in that the most prestigious people have graduated from Juilliard in the intervening forty years. It's amazing. . . . It was a way-breaking department."

23. As a dancer in that work, I remember Tamiris's showgirl look with golden curls and sparkling eyes, and the stories about Hollywood that she told. For her audition, we simply walked on the diagonal across the floor one by one. "I can see everything I need from your walks," she explained.

24. Now more in sympathy with Tamiris's work, Martha also arranged for a commission for ADF for the summer of 1959 where Tamiris premiered *Memoir*.

25. Thurston Davies' 1959 engagement calendar. MHA.

26. Taylor, *Private Domain*, 88. See pp. 88–95 for Taylor's full description of *Episodes*.

27. Ibid., 93.

28. De Mille, *Martha*, 348. See pp. 344–351 for a full account.

29. Louis Horst, "12th American Dance Festival," *Dance Observer* (August–September 1959,) 101. Other contributions at ADF included solos by Sybil Shearer and Pauline Koner. *Memoir*, Tamiris's dramatic reworking of an earlier work, *Chrysalis*, was based on growing up poor in an Orthodox Jewish family; it was paired with a small ensemble work, *Theatre for Fools*, by the charismatic Daniel Nagrin (now Tamiris's husband), who also performed his own solos.

30. See Prevots, *Dance for Export*, 56, 57.

Part VIII: The Sixties

STUDENTS AND MASTER TEACHERS, 1960–1961 (pp. 231–238)

1. José Limón to JS, c. 1965.

2. "Alumni Profiles," *Dance Drama Music: 100 Years of the Juilliard School*. Special commemorative magazine (Tampa, Fla.: Faircount, 2005), 144.

3. Danny Lewis remembered that on more than one occasion, when tallying audition results, Martha vetoed faculty consensus outright, saying, "Can't they tell talent when they see it?" Yet at other times, she could reject a student outright. "I never completely under-

stood why," he admitted. Daniel (Danny) Lewis to JS, 13 September 2002, Tucson, Arizona.

4. Carl stayed on as a special student for three years. When he received a fellowship at the Pacific Institute, he worried that he should stay another year at Juilliard in order to graduate instead, Martha told him, "You already have a B.A. Don't worry about the diploma. You just go." He went to Hawaii "for two years, and stayed for twenty," developing a dance program for the University of Hawaii.

5. Blake Brown, who graduated from the division in 1972, recalled that the situation didn't really bother him. "No one really wanted me that much that I recall. I was straight for one thing. If you were not vulnerable, they would let you alone." Blake Brown to JS, 1 February 2002, Honolulu, Hawaii. All subsequent quotes by Brown are from this source, unless noted.

6. L. Horst to JS, c. 1962.

7. The cast included Bruce (Kevin) Carlyle, Rina Gluck, Joel Schnee, and Charles Wadsworth.

8. The Swedish Ballet later commissioned Tudor to make a new work; he served as their artistic director from 1962 to 1964. Martha found teaching replacements during his leaves.

9. The original cast for its premiere at Jacob's Pillow in 1953 was Yvonne Chouteau and Gilbert Reed.

10. My own story was not unusual among students who endured sometimes torturous teasing. Tudor was determined to fix "Miss Providence"'s problem, for fifteen minutes after class, he insisted that I continue one poorly executed turn after another down the line of males anxious to leave. Although I had entered the school as a potential ballet dancer, I soon appreciated Limón's brand of off-balance fall and recovery techniques, and quickly became a "Limón major."

11. See pages 234 and 235, *Shadowplay: The Life of Antony Tudor*, chap. 26, "School Days," for another full description of Tudor at Juilliard.

12. "Dance Division 35th Anniversary Memoriam" scrapbook, letter, 1987. JSA.

13. Mercedes Ellington to JS, 27 November 2001, New York City.

14. Dilts papers, MH and TD to Judy Dilts, letter, 23 July 1960. MHA.

15. Pearl Primus to Martha Hill, letter, 20 September 1961. MHA.

16. Jerry Bywaters Cochran to JS, e-mail, 12 June 2003.

17. When Martha got wind of a birthday celebration several friends were secretly planning, she decreed, "No birthday! Absolutely not. I don't want my birth date spread around Juilliard"; Hortense Zera to JS.

STANDING FIRM, 1962–1965 (pp. 239–247)

1. William Schuman to Edgar B. Young, letter, 6 June 1961. RFA. (Young responded, "It is my feeling that we must retain an open mind about the nature of training in the field of the dance and about any financial support from L.C. for this purpose until the program needs and opportunities are much clearer than they are today"; E. B. Young to Schuman. RFA.

2. William Schuman to Edgar B. Young, letter, 16 June 1961. To this, Young answered, "In the course of these conferences I feel we must think through very carefully the future of a dance training program in the J School at L.C. In all of our previous discussions I have

felt we had a mutual recognition of the fact that it is difficult to reach conclusions on this matter until L.C. has resolved all doubt about its constituent organization in the field of the dance. [Signed] EBY, Acting pres. L.C. Dance Council"; memorandum, 20 June 1961. RFA.

3. *Time*, "Composer's Curriculum," 22 June 1962, President, Office of the General Administrator Recorder, 1933–62. JSA. At twenty-four, Mennin had joined the composition faculty at Juilliard. An Oberlin graduate, he received a doctorate from the Eastman School, and at thirty-five he became the director of the Peabody Conservatory in Baltimore, one of the youngest heads in its history. Four years later, he was selected to succeed Schuman at Juilliard.

4. "Peter Mennin (1923–1983)," *Juilliard News Bulletin* 22, no. 1 (October/November 1983), 1.

5. Joseph W. Polisi, "An Unsettled Marriage: The Merger of the School of American Ballet with the Juilliard School," manuscript, courtesy J. Polisi, 2004, 15.

6. Ibid., 15.

7. Ibid., 11.

8. From their Sarah Lawrence days, Schuman and the Lloyds saw Martha Hill as the most knowledgeable voice in devising a plan to come to the aid of dance. (Ruth Lloyd gave details of the group's close friendship. A Greenwich millionaire and arts patron, who wanted his arts friends as his neighbors, gave Schuman the opportunity to purchase land at a greatly reduced price for a home there. In turn, the Lloyds were "invited" to do the same. Ruth reflected that without that financial backing, they would never have been able to live as well as they did. Martha and Lefty had been regular visitors in Greenwich where much of the conversation centered on ways to claim theater space for dance.

9. Martha Hill, charts, handwritten on legal pad. JSA. (The "Met" column is the least developed, and filled with question marks; at this point, Martha and Tudor knew that the Metropolitan Ballet School, originally developed as a feeder for the Metropolitan Opera Ballet Company might not survive the move to Lincoln Center.)

10. This included a chart for how the Dance Division might be the center for the Metropolitan Opera's ballet school, holding rehearsals of its ballet company and housing rehearsals and previews for the dance theater company. MHA.

11. Eugene Palatshy, "Myron Is a Senior," *Dance Magazine* (May 1963), 44.

12. The terms of the lease of the State Theater to Lincoln Center were for the duration of the fair, giving the Center full responsibility for operating the theater and determining what the public would be offered from its stage.

13. A search of the Lincoln Center Archives uncovered the following details: the precise financial terms became the subject of prolonged negotiation, with one after another offer and counterproposal. The Ballet was to receive the first $65,000 of each week's box office receipt (from an estimated gross of $89,000 at capacity). In addition, the Ballet was to have a grant of $2,000,000 from the Fund for Education and Creative Artistic Advancement to underwrite the expenses of new productions and to augment student admissions.

14. Lincoln Center's August 1963 Fanfare series presented a earlier trial run concerts of modern dance: with Paul Taylor and Donald McKayle, 6 August; Merce Cunningham, 13 August; and Limón's company, 13 August.

15. In the meantime, rehearsals began for a rather oddly programmed Juilliard dance production that included a new ballet, *The House of Atreus* by guest choreographer Grant Strate (from the Canadian National Ballet), which included professionals Carolyn Brown playing Electra, Limón dancer Chase Robinson as Agamemnon, and Tudor's assistant, Margaret (Maggie) Black (now doing a great deal of subbing for Tudor to the students' delight) as the Leader of the Chorus—a clear indication of the questionable technical level of the school's own ballet students in the minds of Hill and Tudor.

16. Martha Graham, n.d., Arch Lauterer Papers. NYPL:DC. Printed in *Dance Observer* 25, no. 10 (December 1958), 152. See Soares, *Louis Horst*, for more details.

17. Louis Horst to Martha Hill, as told to JS.

18. Don McDonagh, *The Rise and Fall and Rise of Modern Dance* (1970; reprint, Pennington, N.J.: a cappella books, 1990), xi.

19. *Rockefeller Panel Report on the Future of Theatre, Dance, Music in America: The Performing Art Problems and Prospects*, Rockefeller Brothers Fund, Inc. (1965) and *The Performing Arts Problems and Prospects: The Rockefeller Panel Report* (March 1965). In the fall of 1963, the Rockefeller Brothers Fund asked a group of "citizens . . . from all parts of the country to join in a study." They were Alvin Ailey, Samuel Barber, Isadora Bennett, William Kolodney, Congressman John Lindsay, John Martin, Peter Mennin, Paul Taylor, and Gid Waldrop (dean of Juilliard)—mostly New York City residents. Under President Lyndon Johnson's administration, the National Foundation for the Arts and the National Foundation for the Humanities were created and began to give government grants to nonprofit organizations. ABT received one of NEA's first awards of $350,000 in 1965. By comparison, $4,000,000 of the Ford Grant was allocated to NYCB and SAB.

20. "Martha Hill Reminisces," videotape, Bennington, 25 July 1985. NYPL:DC.

21. Allen Hughes, "Festival Problems; Dance Events Turned toward the Past," *New York Times*, 23 August 1964, Sunday section x8.

22. Although able to fill theaters on Broadway or City Center, Graham most likely had been forewarned against involvement by Kirstein—who, of course, was the first to relate low turnout figures to the Lincoln Center board.

23. Martha Graham, *Dance Observer* 25, no. 10 (December 1958), 152.

24. P. J. Manchester, "Creating Tradition: On American Dance Theater," *Christian Science Monitor,* 23 November 1964, Dance Division scrapbook. JSA.

25. Michael Hollander, "Mazurkas: Origins, Choreography, Significance," in *José Limón: The Artist Re-viewed*, ed. June Dunbar, 93.

26. Leonard Harris, *New York World Telegram*, Dance Scrapbooks, clippings file. NYPL:DC.

27. Douglas Watt, "Modern Dancers take over N.Y. State Theater," *Daily News*, 3 March 1965, 66. (Nikolais, who had been a favorite student at Bennington, had gone on to create his own dance theater under the auspices of the Henry Street Settlement Playhouse in Lower Manhattan.)

28. Allen Hughes, "Dance: At Lincoln Center. American Theater Troupe Performs 4 works as part of week's Series," *New York Times*, 5 March 1965, 36.

29. "Thorn[y] Evangelists." 15 March 1965. Dance Division Scrapbook, clipping. JSA.

30. José Limón to Martha Hill, letter, 21 April 1965. MHA.

31. Memo from Schuman to Robert Englander, Peter Mennin, et al., (D), 2, Office of the President, General Administrative Records, 1033–1985, Series I, Box 4, fol. 15. JSA.

32. Polisi, "An Unsettled Marriage," 21.

33. Clive Barnes, "Dance: A Case for Blackmail," *New York Times*, 28 August 1966. With somewhat naïve enthusiasm, Barnes goes on to propose that perhaps Graham's school could "be enlarged" and "brought into the Juilliard School to represent Modern dance just as the School of American Ballet represents classic dance"—an idea that made Martha Hill smile knowingly.

34. Thomas P. DeGaetani, "Building for the Arts. A House Is *Not* a Home," *Dance Magazine* (November 1966), 39.

CONTRASTS AND CONFLICTS, 1965–1968 (pp. 248–257)

1. When the book was published in 1973, it enraged both José and Martha with its tacit message that modern dance was outmoded.

2. Alma Guillermoprieto, "Dancing in the City," *New Yorker* (10 February 2003), 70, 73.

3. DTW was set up in the early sixties and run by Art Bauman and Jack Moore, along with Jeff Duncan, who gave over his living space for performances. (Moore had been on the Juilliard faculty as assistant to Horst from 1959 to 1961 and now held a faculty position at Bennington and Bauman was a Juilliard extension division student in 1959 and 1960. Duncan, a favorite of Doris Humphrey's, was an early member of Juilliard Dance Theater.) Later DTW moved into Jerome Robbins's American Theatre Laboratory space to become "DTW at ATL." By 1969 there were seven organizations supporting new choreography in Manhattan.

4. See McDonagh, "Some Thoughts After the Revolution," *Rise and Fall*, 202–212.

5. William Schuman to Peter Mennin, letter, 16 October 1964. JSA.

6. Polisi, "An Unsettled Marriage," 12.

7. Ibid., 17.

8. "School of American Ballet to join Juilliard at Lincoln Center," *Juilliard School of Music News Release*, 2 November 1965, Office of the President, Administrative Papers, The Juilliard School.

9. Lowry continued, "The modern dance people were better [than the ballet people]. Martha Hill cared about it, modern dance. So Pete had all this to contend with as well as the music thing." Lowry to Sharon Zane, 11 January 1990. LCAA:OHP.

10. Janet Sumner Prieur to JS, 14 September 2002, Tucson, Arizona.

11. Barnes, "Dance: Enterprising Juilliard Program: Works by Sokolow and Limón in Debut. Pieces by Graham and Tudor Revived," *New York Times*, 21 April 1967, 48.

12. Walter Terry, "A closing bravo," *World Journal Tribune*, 16 October 1964, clipping. Scrapbook. NYPL:DC.

13. Peter Mennin to MH, memorandum, n.d. JSA.

14. Polisi, "An Unsettled Marriage," 12.

15. Mennin to faculty, memorandum, n.d. JSA.

16. Vera Michaelson, undated draft, 2. JSA.

17. Martha Hill to Gid Waldrop, memorandum, 25 March 1968. JSA.

18. Sylvia Yamada to JS, 1 February 2002, Honolulu, Hawaii.

19. William Bales to Peter Mennin, copy of letter. MHA.

20. Risa Steinberg to JS, 9 December 2002, New York City.

"GOOD GUYS VS. BAD GUYS," 1968–1969 (PP. 258–267)

1. Douglas Turnbaugh, "Good Guys vs. Bad Guys at Lincoln Center," *New York* (20 May 1968), 51.

2. Robert Sabin, "Juilliard on the Crossroads," *Dance Magazine* (July 1968), 32.

3. Robert Commaday, "The Squeeze-out at the Juilliard," *San Francisco Chronicle* (27 October 1968), 26–27. Robert Commaday to Martha Hill, letter, 25 October 1968, Box 4, Fol. 4. Lincoln Center Folder: "Future of Dance Dept. 1967–68." JSA.

4. Martha Hill to Commaday, letter, 15 November 1968, Gen. Admin., Records, 1947–91. JSA.

5. At one point, the Lincoln Center board responded with an offer to support the theater department on condition that no fund-raising be undertaken, so as not to collide with Lincoln Center's own massive fund-raising project.

6. Glenn Lowry referred to Nelson Rockefeller as a "one-man democracy" from his knowledge of earlier dealings with Kirstein at MOMA.

7. Peter Mennin to Martha Hill, memorandum, n.d. JSA.

8. Polisi, "An Unsettled Marriage," *Ballet Review*, 34, no. 1 (Spring 2006), 82.

9. Gid Waldrop to Martha Hill, letter, 24 June 1966, Box 2. JSA.

10. Hill to Kimball, "*Martha.*" MHA.

11. NARB later became Regional Dance America. Having made important strides in supporting America's professional regional companies over the years, the organization dissolved in 1987.

12. Blake Brown to JS.

13. Deborah Jowitt, "Dance. Veterans & Newcomers." *Village Voice* (27 March 1969), 32.

14. Risa Steinberg to JS. After graduation from Juilliard she joined the José Limón Company.

15. Selma Jeanne Cohen, qtd. in Anderson, *American Dance Festival* (Durham, N.C.: Duke University Press, 1987), 121.

16. Martha Hill to Pauline and José Limón, 4 August 1968, Limón papers. NYPL:DC.

17. Martha had been the one consistent member from its inception. Reinhart began as a box office manager at Jacob's Pillow, and had worked as an office temp for press representative Isadora "Izzy" Bennett. He joined Al Pischl's festival staff in 1963, also working backstage and hanging out with the company whenever possible. That fall he became tour manager for Taylor.

18. Jack Anderson, *American Dance Festival*, 128.

19. Doris Hering, "Next Year, Keep the Baby," *Dance Magazine* (October 1969), 40–41 (qtd. in Anderson, *American Dance Festival*, 130; for a full description of these events, see chap. 6).

20. Bennington College citation statement. MHA.

21. Brockway, *Bennington College* (quoting Martha Graham), 138.

22. Alice Tully Hall, carved into the east end of the building and originally designed as Juilliard's music hall, now had its own entrance and separate management.

23. This area was later redesigned to serve as the main entrance at the plaza level of West Sixty-fifth Street.

Part IX: A Place for Dance

JUILLIARD AT LINCOLN CENTER, 1970–1972 (pp. 271–279)

1. For years, fellow Brooklynite Al Pischl, also spent his summers managing the box office at ADF, while directing the small press Dance Horizons and editing the journal *Dance Perspectives*.

2. Blake Brown to JS. Blake added, "Miss Hill never said anything derogatory about Balanchine or the school. She was very careful about that. But she would talk about those 'other' people, and you knew she meant those people through the door."

3. Risa Steinberg to JS.

4. Bill Hug to JS, 13 September 2003, Tampa, Florida. Although most advances were not acknowledged, some clearly were. The stunning modern dancer Bruce Marks was invited by Tudor to travel with him to Greece "to do research for the choreography," according to biographer Topaz. Marks went on to study ballet seriously.

5. M. Topaz, *Undimmed Lustre*, 200, 201.

6. Among recent graduates, Dalienne Majors and Hannah Kahn created their own companies, and Dianne McPherson and Mark Haim became two very promising choreographers on the scene. Sylvia and Blake Brown performed extensively in Europe beginning at the Cologne Opera House for two years, then with Ballet Rambert in London, and later, in Australian companies.

7. From Dance Division 35th Anniversary Memoriam scrapbook, March 1987. JSA.

8. S. Yamada and B. Brown to JS.

9. Ibid. Soon after, Mennin scoffed at a suggestion broached by Waldrop in an effort to move Hill's possible retirement forward, answering, "I see little reason to celebrate Hill's 70th birthday." Attached to the 30 October 1970 memo is a note that Hill's pension would be $118.38 a month should she retire then; President's Papers. JSA.

10. Coincidentally, another government assignment in October 1974, for the Office of Cultural Presentations in Washington, D.C., took Martha to see the Hartford Ballet and evaluate the new director's work. Commenting positively on Ben Harkarvy, an American who had built his reputation as founder-director of the Netherlands Dance Theater in Amsterdam, she would never have suspected that in 1992 he would take over the position of director of the Juilliard Dance Division.

11. Agnes de Mille, "Agnes de Mille speaks to Congress on the State of the Arts," *Dance Magazine* (May 1970) 34, 35. JSA.

12. Tudor was particularly depressed about the situation, as he felt that he had groomed the finest group of ballet dancers in his career. Sylvia Yamada recalled that Martha urged him to stay for another year in order to receive the pension he deserved. It would also have given her time to find a replacement for him. "And he said, 'No. This is the best class that I will ever have, and there's no reason to keep teaching.'" S. Yamada to JS. Because he had not yet reached the retirement age of 65, Mennin told him he was not eligible. Peter Mennin to Antony Tudor, letter, 3 October 1970. Tudor folder. JSA.

13. Tudor told Brown and Yamada that the longest and most complex of the three ballets, *Cereus*—a trio—was inspired by what he observed at the party they had invited him to at their Brooklyn apartment.

14. At Martha's suggestion, Kazuko first took a job for three years at Randolph-Macon and another three at Kirkland College, where she honed her skills as a teacher—much as Hill herself had done in her own life. Kazuko performed with Graham's extended company for the reworking of *Primitive Mysteries* at the American Dance Festival.

15. Deborah Jowitt, "An extremely important . . . dance," *Village Voice* (18 November 1971), 15.

16. Anna Kisselgoff, "Juilliard Group Gives Premiere of Limón and Sokolow Dances," *New York Times*, 15 November 1971, 53.

17. Solos represented Melacomet, Pontiac, Tecumseh, Red Eagle, Black Hawk, Osceola, Sitting Bull, and Geronimo.

18. Erick Hawkins to S. A. Kriegsman, 13 August 1976, transcript, S. A. Kriegsman Collection. LOCC:MD.

19. Martha Hill to President Mennin, 30 June 1972, Dance Div. General admin., 1951–71, Box 1, fol. 3. JSA.

20. Mennin had established the Juilliard American Opera Center in 1969; under his leadership, opera productions were the most costly events of the year. Juilliard's costume shop, housed in two entire subfloor levels, employed the best designers draping the finest imported fabrics. In-house dye specialists and wigmakers were available, and the costume shop's budget more than matched the dance division's.

21. Clive Barnes, "As a Dancer, an Eagle: A Gifted and Fluent Choreographer, He Took His Leadership Seriously," *New York Times*, 3 December 1972, 86.

22. One of his most intimate friends, costume designer Charles Tomlinson, worked to ensure that the company would survive, setting up a management plan. Danny Lewis became "acting artistic director" for eight months before Ruth Currier took over for five years beginning in 1973.

23. To suit Juilliard's dance exam requirements, Limón and his teachers worked to codify his technique as Graham had done, drawing from the Humphrey-Weidman exercises with added emphasis on patterned isolations combined like "instruments in an orchestra." To accomplish this, materials were cobbled together from phrases developed in Limón's choreography (already the primary resource for his and Doris's technique classes). His merging of isolated movements with Humphrey's succession and breath phrases, along with her use of swing and fall and rebound techniques, were now combined with distinctive arm gestures and torso actions, often in legato phrasing that complemented ground bass traveling patterns.

AN EVEN KEEL, 1973–1978 (pp. 280–289)

1. Deborah Jowitt, "Clinging Together in the Dark," *Village Voice*, 7 June 1973, 38.

2. At Juilliard, Hill never produced Merce Cunningham's or Nikolais's work because their nonacoustic musical choices and offbeat ideas were seen as contradictory to the conservatory's aims.

3. Doris Hering, "Fourteenth American Dance Festival," *Dance Magazine* (October 1971), 61.

4. The gymnasium had changed little, with Greek Games columns, cyclorama drapes, and bleachers still intact.

5. "Festival of Dance," audiotaped interview excerpts, 1971. MGZTC 31099 outtakes from the film, *Festival of the Dance*. NYPL:DC.

6. Park and Hill remarks qtd. in *Connecticut College Bulletin* (September 1972).

7. Martha Hill, "José Limón and his Biblical Works," 57.

8. Clive Barnes, "Dance: Juilliard Ensemble presents 3 New Works," *New York Times*, 29 April 1975, 39.

9. Agnes de Mille to Martha Hill, letter, 11 May 1975, Agnes de Mille file. JSA.

10. Barnes, "Dance: Juilliard Ensemble presents 3 New Works," *New York Times*, 29 April 1975, Dance Division Scrapbooks. JSA.

11. Don McDonagh, "Juilliard Ensemble Gives 'Ellis Island,' A Sokolow Dance," *New York Times*, 11 May 1976, 26.

12. Peter Mennin, *Juilliard Student Handbook*, 1976.

13. When Muriel Topaz became the director of the dance division in 1985, she argued over the same problem: "[Mennin] drove me crazy if any one was onstage who was a little overweight. And he didn't want them around the school where by chance the board of directors might see them. He didn't want to train people like SAB, but in fact, it was what he did want." M. Topaz to JS.

14. Norman Lloyd, presentation speech for AADC Honor Award. MHA.

15. Alan M. Kriegsman, *Washington Post*, S. A. Kriegsman Collection, Bennington, Box 31, fol. 3. LOC:MD.

16. Martha Graham, telegram. MHA.

17. MH to JS.

18. Another to drop his fortune in Graham's path was Englishman Robin Howard, who converted an abandoned firehouse into The Place near Euston Station, the first contemporary dance school in London, with Graham technique the requisite. Howard—a very tall and charming gentleman with a pronounced limp from a war injury—was a frequent visitor to the new dance division facilities. It was Hill he grilled for information on how to set up the school as well as whom to hire, and she encouraged him to consider early Graham dancers Jane Dudley and Nina Fonaroff. Additionally, her support of American Robert Cohen for Howard's newly established London Contemporary Dance Theater was significant in spreading American modern dance to Great Britain.

19. Among them were Janet Eilber (now artistic director of the Martha Graham Dance Company), Joyce Herring, Peter London, Bonnie Oda, Peter Sparling, and Shelley Washington.

20. Kriegsman, preface to *Dance in America*, xii. Kriegsman continued, "If I passed up this opportunity and Martha Hill did not succeed in producing her book, the field would be left with neither."

21. Ibid. Stickney remembered that it was a delicate situation; she worried about giving access to Sali Ann because of Martha's impending book. Bloustein felt, however, that legally they could not bar access to the papers, or prevent the use of photographs from their archives. B. Stickney to JS. Another interesting development arose in 1986 when Sali Ann, despite being married to the arts reviewer for the *Washington Post*, became head of the Dance Division of the NEA.

22. In 1951, during the Korean War, Mary Jo went on to command the Women in the Air Force as an Air Force colonel. She returned to Bennington College to hold various positions in its admissions and development departments. Shortly before her death, she had retired as the public relations director of the Girl Scouts of America.

23. Barbara Morgan to MH, letter, c. August 1976, Barbara Morgan file. JSA.

24. Ben Belitt to MH, postcard, 25 August 1977. MHA.

25. Ben Belitt to MH, postcard, 20 July 1979. MHA.

26. Sali Ann Kriegsman, notes, 15 February 1978, "Bennington; Hill, "Martha," Box 31, S. A. Kriegsman Collection, Bennington. LOC:MD.

27. Sali Ann contended that although the grant was received and work "conducted after my manuscript was completed," she was not allowed to see the interviews because they were "closed to scholars until publication of Martha Hill's book" (xii). (A few of these interviews actually remained unavailable until the deaths of the interviewees.)

28. Sali Ann Kriegsman to Erick Hawkins, letter, 14 May 1979, Box 31, S. A. Kriegsman Collection, Bennington. LOC:MD.

29. See Anderson's *American Dance Festival*, chap. 6. To substantiate the move, Reinhart organized a panel to discuss the possibility with a group of dance leaders including Robert Joffrey, Stuart Hodes (then head of dance at NYU), and Rhoda Grauer (executive director of Tharp's Dance Foundation), proving that there were other capable decision-makers in the field beside Hill's clutch of associates.

MATRIARCH, 1979–1984 (pp. 290–300)

1. Gitelman, *Dancing with Principle*, 125.

2. Irwin Denis to JS, various communications, 2000–2003.

3. Robert Coe, "Old School Tights," *Village Voice*, 9 March 1979, 1–3.

4. Among dance students who came from Australia to study at Juilliard were Ray Cook, Nanette Haskell, and Leigh Warren. Of those Americans she sent to Australia, Carol Johnson went to work with the Aboriginals, and Francine Landes and Dianne McPherson joined the guest artist faculty at Victoria College.

5. Martha Hill to David Roche, letter, 10 July 1984. MHA.

6. Anne Woolliams to Martha Hill, letter, 1987, Dance Division 35th Anniversary Memoriam scrapbook. JSA.

7. For the event Hill delivered a paper on José Limón's choreography based on biblical themes (including *There is a Time*, which drew from Ecclesiastes, and *The Traitor*, inspired by the Judas story). Both dances had premiered at Juilliard.

8. Martha Hill to Barbara Morgan, letter, 11 August 1980. JSA.

9. Barbara Morgan to MH, letter, n.d., Barbara Morgan file. JSA.

10. Irwin Denis to JS; often repeated in conversations from 2000 to 2003.

11. Sandra Kaufmann to JS, e-mail, 4 April 2000.

12. Letter, March 1987, Dance Division 35th Anniversary Memoriam scrapbook. JSA.

13. Elizabeth Zimmer, "Reviews: Juilliard Dance Ensemble," *Dance Magazine* (November 1982), 35–36.

14. In 1984, Martha's rent was $663 a month: her yearly salary was $23,980. She had more than $40,000 invested in stocks and bonds and had accumulated TIAA annuity benefits of almost $14,000. She also received $1,500 monthly in Social Security checks.

15. President Mennin's office to MH, memorandum 7 April 1978. MHA.

16. Gid Waldrop to Paul Taylor, 1 November 1983. Martha Hill Archives. JSA.

17. Paul Taylor to MH, letter, 17 August 1982. MHA.

18. Carl Wolz to JS.

19. When asked what she thought of Protas's influence on Graham's life, company, and school—an influence that had distressed many in the dance community—Martha offered a surprisingly subdued answer: "What will complaining about it change?" Graham was still producing works with a company and maintaining an international reputation as a great artist, she said. It was a sympathetic comment from a woman who faced her own life in her declining years alone.

20. Michael Uthoff, "Martha Hill Centennial," 92.

21. Description drawn from Dianne McPherson's 2006 manuscript, *Door for a Dervish*, 22.

22. Gitelman, *Dancing with Principle*, note 15. Holm papers.

23. In 1989, a Martha Hill Scholarship was set up at ADF.

24. In North Carolina, money flowed into ADF's till from the tobacco industry, the Doris Duke Foundation, and the National Endowment for the Arts. With a summer rental arrangement, ADF physically disappears from the university days after the festival closes. The ADF staff returns to its office in Washington, D.C.

25. Susanne Shelton. ADF 50th Anniversary Photographic Exhibition, "Made in America—Modern Dance Then and Now," in *The Aesthetic and Cultural Significance of Modern Dance, American Dance Festival 1984, 50th Anniversary Program*, n.p.

26. Ed Koch, Mayor's Award for Art and Culture, 1984. MHA.

27. Joseph Polisi to JS, 22 November 2004, New York City.

28. Press release from the president's office at Juilliard, 15 January 1985. Dance Division Archives. JSA.

29. Joseph Polisi to members of the Juilliard faculty, memorandum, 19 January 1985. MHA.

30. Yvette Louis, "Juilliard Head Changes Hats," *Ballet News* (May 1985), 120.

LAST YEARS, 1985–1995 (pp. 301–312)

1. From Carl's perspective, a new integrated Hong Kong dance style would be the result.

2. Janice Meaden to JS, telephone interview, 19 November 2004.

3. "To think that Marion gave constant care to her invalid husband for ten years. Now she was dying herself," she lamented.

4. "Martha Hill Reminisces about Bennington," video recording of Martha Hill lecture, 25 July 1985, Bennington College, Vermont, NYPL:DC.

5. This scheduling became easier with the rise of the Rose Building on the plaza guaranteeing a cafeteria. Topaz also set up a student government of sorts to air complaints and created opportunities for more one-on-one advising sessions.

6. As with other conservatories, Juilliard had no tenure system or union in place. Each faculty member received a yearly letter of agreement from the president quoting the amount to be received per class. (During the Mennin presidency, my letters of agreement spelled out the amount I was to receive per class [$35 in 1969] and included annual fifty-cent raises.) Teaching multiple classes in a row meant that a faculty member could make

a good day's wages. But with Topaz's spread-out scheduling, only one or two sessions per day were possible—a definite hardship for professionals with busy careers.

7. Mikhail Baryshnikov, then the director of ABT, said, "We do Tudor's ballets because we must. Tudor is our conscience." David Vaughn, "Antony Tudor," *International Encyclopedia of Dance* (Oxford University Press: New York, 1998), 6:203.

8. With the Chinese takeover of this British colony slated for the year 1990, the rush to get things accomplished was becoming more urgent, particularly for Americans like Carl Wolz who did not know what their future in that city held.

9. Lincoln Kirstein, "Dance and the Curse of Isadora," *New York Times*, 23 November 1986, 1.

10. Martha Hill to JS. Personal communication, c. 1986.

11. Clive Barnes, "Juilliard Honors a Prophet in Her Time," *New York Post*, 30 March 1987, 24.

12. In contrast to limited access at the time, Balanchine's repertory is now handled by the Balanchine Trust and performed regularly throughout the world.

13. While staying with Shirley, Martha and Allegra Fuller Schneider visited Helen Knight. Helen pulled a collection of films out from under her bed of footage from Bennington she wanted Martha to have. (When Helen died in 1991, her papers and $15,000 were willed to Martha.)

14. Jack Anderson, "John Martin Is Dead at 91; *Times* Critic 35 Years," *New York Times*, 21 May 1985, B6.

15. Ben Somers, Capezio Award statement. MHA.

16. Judith Kogan wrote in her appraisal, *Nothing but the Best: The Struggle for Perfection at the Juilliard School* (New York: Limelight Editions, 1989): "Juilliard does not care whether [its students] can tie their shoes, crack an egg or boil a pot of water. Juilliard does not care whether they can screw in a light bulb, mend a fence or feed a cat. Juilliard does not seem to care whether they can put an English sentence together either. Juilliard cares about whether they can do one thing: perform" (11).

17. Doctor of Fine Arts degree citation, Purchase College, SUNY, 16 May 1993. MHA.

18. Over the years Hill had rewritten her will several times: the first in 1954 gave everything to her husband. The second, after Lefty's death in 1962, was the most elaborate with 28 percent of her securities and cash going to her brother-in-law, the Reverend Robert Gearhart; 28 percent to her brother; 28 percent to her stepdaughter Judy Dilts; 4 percent each to the Bennington and Juilliard dance departments (pegged as student funds for living expenses), and to Princeton in memory of Lefty. She then specified 3 percent to go to "her good friend" (and cleaning lady) and 1 percent to their housekeeper in Brussels, Belgium. June Dunbar and William Bales were given discretion to distribute her books, photographs, music, and memorabilia; and Mary Jo Shelly, her personal possessions. Martha revised her will again in 1975, giving the bulk of her estate to her brother. MHA.

19. After Martha's death, memorabilia that had belonged to Eugene Hill was sent to his children. Bill and his wife Mary Ann would be the only ones to meet their nephew David years later, when as a young adult he sought out his father's relatives.

20. Ben Belitt, "Martha Hill: Homage." Speech, Hill Memorial, Bennington, Vermont. Documented by Belitt, 17 March 1966.

21. Anna Kisselgoff, "Dance View: The Innovations of Martha Hill," *New York Times*, 28 March 1982, D6, 30.

EPILOGUE (pp. 313–314)
1. Duncan, *My Life*, 245.
2. "I condemn you to freedom." Note, handwritten by Martha Hill. MHA.

Anderson, Jack. *The American Dance Festival.* Durham, N.C.: Duke University Press, 1987.

Armitage, Merle, ed. *Martha Graham: The Early Years.* 1937. Reprint, New York: Da Capo Press, 1978.

Banes, Sally, *Terpsichore in Sneakers: Post-Modern Dance.* Middletown, Conn.: Wesleyan University Press: Scranton, Pa. (distributed by Harper and Row), 1987.

Brockway, Thomas. *Bennington College: In the Beginning.* Bennington, Vt.: Bennington College Press, 1981.

Brown, Carolyn. *Chance and Circumstance. Twenty Years with Cage and Cunningham.* New York: Knopf, 2007.

Cohen, Selma Jeanne, ed. *Doris Humphrey: An Artist First.* Middletown, Conn.: Wesleyan University Press, 1972.

Dewey, John. *Art as Experience.* New York: Capricorn Books, 1934.

Dunning, Jennifer. *"But First a School." New York: Viking, 1985.*

Daly, Ann. *Done into Dance: Isadora Duncan in America.* Bloomington and Indianapolis: Indiana University Press, 1995.

de Mille, Agnes. *Martha.* New York: Random House, 1991.

Duberman, Martin. *The Worlds of Lincoln Kirstein.* New York: Knopf, 2007.

Dunbar, June, ed. *José Limón.* (2000) New York: Routledge, 2002.

Garafola, Lynn. *Legacies of Twentieth-Century Dance.* Middletown, Conn. Wesleyan University Press, 2005.

Gitelman, Claudia. *Dancing with Principle: Hanya Holm in Colorado, 1941–1983.* Boulder, Colo.: University Press of Colorado, 2001.

Graff, Ellen. *Stepping Left: Dance and Politics in New York City, 1928–1942.* Durham, N.C.: Duke University Press, 1997.

Graham, Martha. *Blood Memory.* New York: Doubleday, 1991.

Jackson, Naomi M. *Converging Movements: Modern Dance and Jewish Culture at the 92ND Street Y.* Middletown, Conn: Wesleyan University Press, 2000.

H'Doubler, Margaret Newell. *Dance: A Creative Art Experience*, Madison: University of Wisconsin Press, 1940.

Hill, Martha. "Antony Tudor: The Juilliard Years." In *Antony Tudor: The American Years*, ed. Muriel Topaz. *Choreography and Dance*, vol. 1, part 2. London: Harwood Academic, 1989.

———. "José Limón and His Biblical Works." In *Choreography and Dance*, vol.5, part 3. London: Harwood Academic, 1992.

Humphrey, Doris. *Doris Humphrey: An Artist First.* Middletown, Conn: Wesleyan University Press, 1972.

Jowitt, Deborah. *Time and the Dancing Image.* New York: W. Morrow. 1988.

Kendall, Elizabeth. *Where She Danced.* (1979) Berkeley: University of California Press, 1984.

Kirstein, Lincoln. *Ballet: Bias & Belief. Three Pamphlets Collected and Other Dance Writings of Lincoln Kirstein.* (1937) Brooklyn, N.Y.: Dance Horizons, 1983.

Kogan, Judith. *Nothing but the Best: The Struggle for Perfection at the Juilliard School.* New York: Limelight Editions, 1989.

Kriegsman, Sali Ann. *Modern Dance in America: The Bennington Years.* Boston: G. K. Hall, 1981.

Limón, José. *An Unfinished Memoir*, ed. Lynn Garafola. Hanover, N.H.: Wesleyan University Press and University Press of New England, 1999.

Lowry, W. McNeil. *The Performing Arts and American Society.* Englewood Cliffs, N.J.: Prentice-Hall, 1977.

Martin, John. *America Dancing: The Background and Personalities of the Modern Dance.* (1936) New York: Dance Horizons, 1968.

McDonagh, Don. *Martha Graham: A Biography.* New York: Praeger, 1973.

———. *The Rise and Fall and Rise of Modern Dance.* (1970) Pennington, N.J.: a cappella books, 1990.

Morgan, Barbara, and Martha Graham. *Sixteen Dances in Photographs.* (1941) Dobbs Ferry, N.Y.: Morgan and Morgan Press, 1980.

Prevots, Naima. *Dance for Export: Cultural Diplomacy and the Cold War.* Middletown, Conn.: Wesleyan University Press, 1998.

Purlmutter, Donna. *Shadowplay: The Life of Antony Tudor.* New York: Viking Penguin, 1991.

Reynolds, Nancy, and Malcolm McCormick. *No Fixed Points: Dance in the Twentieth Century.* New Haven, Conn.: Yale University Press, 2003.

Ross, Janis. *Moving Lessons: Margaret H'Doubler and the Beginning of Dance in American Education.* Madison: University of Wisconsin Press, 2000.

———. *Anna Halprin: Experience as Dance.* Berkeley: University of California Press, 2007.

Ruyter, Nancy Lee Chalfa. *Reformers and Visionaries: The Americanization of the Art of Dance.* New York: Dance Horizons, 1979.

Shelton, Susanne. *Divine Dancer: Ruth St. Denis.* (1981) Austin: University of Texas Press, 1990.

Siegel, Marcia B. *Days on Earth: The Dance of Doris Humphrey.* New Haven, Conn.: Yale University Press, 1988.

Soares, Janet Mansfield. "The Landscape of Dance: 5 Professionals Assess the Field." *The Juilliard Journal* 21, no. 6 (March 2006): 14–15.

———. "In Music's Domain: 50 Years of Dance at Juilliard." On-line exclusive. *The Juilliard Journal* 17, no. 8. (May 2002).

———. "Martha Hill: The Early Years." *Ballet Review* 28, no. 4 (winter 2000): 66–94.

———. "Martha Hill: Visionary for Dance in the Conservatory Against All Odds." *The Society of Dance History Scholars 22nd Annual Conference Proceedings*, June 10–13, 1999. Albuquerque: University of New Mexico, 1999.

———. "Remembering Martha Hill, Juilliard's Dance Legend." *The Juilliard Journal.* (September 1996): 9.

———. *Louis Horst: Musician in a Dancer's World.* Durham, North Carolina: Duke University Press, 1992.

———. "With the Future in Mind." *The Juilliard Journal.* (April 1987): 4–5.

Sokol, Martin L. *The New York City Opera: An American Adventure.* New York: Macmillan, 1981.

Taylor, Paul. *Private Domain.* New York: Knopf, 1987.

Tomko, Linda J. *Dancing Class: Gender, Ethnicity, and Social Divides in American Dance, 1890–1920.* Bloomington: Indiana University Press, 1999.

Topaz, Muriel. *Undimmed Lustre: The Life of Antony Tudor.* Lanham, Md.: Scarecrow, 2002.

Vaughan, David. *Merce Cunningham: Fifty Years.* New York: Aperture, 1997.

Wagner, Ann. *Adversaries of Dance From the Puritans to the Present.* Urbana: University of Illinois Press, 1997.

Warren, Larry. *Anna Sokolow: The Rebellious Spirit.* Princeton, N.J.: Dance Horizons/Princeton Books, 1991.

Young, Edgar B. *Lincoln Center: The Building of an Institution.* New York: New York University Press, 1980.

Beerhohm, Max, 44

Beethoven, Ludwig van, xviii, 19, 90, 282

Beiswanger, Barbara Page, 9, 11, 22, 109

Beiswanger, George, 66, 141, 143

Belitt, Ben: Bennington College, work at, 40, 43–46, 102, 105; Bennington summer school, work at, 48; Bennington's culminating festival, work on, 110, 114; and changes, 170; and Gene's suicide, 98; and Hill and Shelly's alliance, 75; and Hill's death, 312; and Shelly's death, 287–88; summer at Connecticut College and ADF, 159; summer at Mills and return to Bennington, 117, 119, 122; and World War II, 138, 142, 147, 149

Belluschi, Pietro, 215

Bennett, Isadora, 167, 174

Bennington Armory, 69–70, 72–73, 90–92, 101–2, 107, 110, 112–13

Bennington College: Bales at, 168, 296; beginnings of Hill's work at, 39–47, 200; Bloomer at, 284–85; book about, 286–88; Connecticut program modeled after, 157, 161–62, 165, 167, 173; dance explosion of the 1960s, 249, 253–54, 257; festivals at, 100–101, 107–15, 281; fundraiser, 284; and Graham's *Immediate Tragedy*, 98–105; and Graham's *Panorama*, 61–68, 70–71, 73–75; group splitting up, 170; Hill and Graham friends since days of, 190; and Hill as matriarch of modern dance, 290, 292; Hill's honorary doctorate from, 265; and Hill's last years, 302, 305, 309; Hill's resignation from, 179–80; and Hill's struggle for balance, 281; Juilliard program modeled after, 185–86; Juilliard staff at, 201; Juilliard students at, 184; memorial for Hill, 312; Mills, summer at and return to, 116, 118–26, 128; modern dance, start of at, 203–4; NYU program modeled after, 1936 work at, 81, 83–85, 87–94; 159–60; Olson's work at, 171; reunion at funeral,

225; Shelly's work at, 179; students, expectations of, 271; summer programs, end of, 152; Summer School of the Dance, 43, 48–57, 61–63, 86, 89, 92, 107; and World War II, 133–43, 145–51, 153–56, 158

Berio, Luciano, 253

Bernstein, Harry, 219

Bettis, Valerie, 167, 172–73, 225–26

Biehle, Martha, 69

"Big Four," the: Bennington summer school, work at, 49, 57; Bennington's culminating festival, work on, 108–9; Graham as last with a company, 151; and Graham's *Panorama*, 62, 64; Holm's legend as one of, 290; summer at Connecticut College and ADF, 167

Billy the Kid, 143

Birch, Patricia (Patsy), 162

Bird, Bonnie, 116

Bird, Dorothy, 30

Black, Margaret (Maggie), 183, 234

Black Angels, 280

Blake, William, 31, 89

Blood Wedding, 128

Bloomer (Ford), Betty, 101, 284–85

Bloomer, Ruth: Bennington College, work at, 88, 92; Bennington summer school, work at, 48; and changes, 170, 173–74; Connecticut College, work at, 195, 202; and Hill leaving Connecticut College, 179; and World War II, 156–58

Bloustein, Jacob, 286

Blue Roses, 209

Bluebird, The, 6

Bolm, Adolph, 13

Bolshoi Ballet, 217, 225–26

Bouchard, Thomas, 91–92, 112, 118

Bowles, Paul, 209

Brahms, Johannes, 16

Brandenburg Concerto No. 4, 225

Bridge, The, 121–22

Briggs, David, 295, 304

Brinnin, John Malcolm, 172

Britannia Triumphans, 233

Britten, Benjamin, 193
Broadway: ANTA series on, 225; dancers under investigation, 195; de Mille choreographer on, 183; De Rothschild on, 286; farewell to Hill performance on, 297; Graham Company on, 248; helping students audition for, 291; Holm choreographer on, 151, 167; Lang on, 148; Limón on, 122; Tamiris on, 220; *Tango Argentino* on, 304
Brockway, Thomas, 52, 287
Brown, Blake, 262, 271, 273–74, 276, 310
Brown, Carolyn, 188, 275
Brown, Sylvia Yamada. *See* Yamada (Brown), Sylvia
Brussels: Davies's move to, 209, 211; Hill's respite to, 219–27; Hill's time in, 214; return from, 226; World's Fair in, 203–4, 216–18, 237, 291
Butler, Ethel, 119, 124–25
Bywaters (Cochran), Jerry, 223, 237

Cafe Chantant—Five A.M., 144
Cage, John, 119, 144, 250
Calder, Alexander ("Sandy"), 68–70, 72, 127, 273
Campbell, Douglas, 286
Campbell, Joseph, 111, 152
Campbell, Marian Van Tuyl. *See* Van Tuyl (Campbell), Marian
Canticle for Innocent Comedians, 185
Capezio Dance Award, 195, 304, 307–8
Career, Hill forging a, 12–24
Carlota, 278
Carmines, Al, 250
Carousel, 148
Carpenter, John Alden, 16
Carter, Bill, 161
Carter, Elliott, 89
Cartier-Bresson, Henri, 292
Cassandra, 193
Cassidy, Rosalind, 114, 116
Castle, Irene and Vernon, xix
Catalano, Eduardo F., 215
Cave of the Heart, 164

Cecchetti, Enrico, 182–83
Celebration, 73, 124
Celebration of the French Baroque, 297
Century (Club) Association, 198
Cereus, 276, 283, 305
Chaconne in D Minor, 141, 163
Chalif, Louis H., 13, 17, 255
Champion, 163
Changes: I Am the Gate, 275, 283
Channing, Carol, 122, 297
Chase, Lucia, 181, 196, 200, 212, 243
Chopin, Frederic, xviii
Choreoconcerts, 249
Choreographer Comments, A, 233, 297
Choreographic Conference, 291
Choreographic Offering, A, 244–45
Choreography: award for, 284; of Balanchine, 82, 122, 166, 181; ballet/modern dance controversy, 242, 245; of Clarke, 231; collaboration with other artists, 62; combination of ballet and modern dance, 213; of Cunningham, 144, 289; dance explosion of the 1960s, 248–49, 255; of de Mille, 183; controversy, 264; of Graham, 71, 110, 125, 164, 185, 289; grants, 289; of Hawkins, 111, 125, 161; of Hill, 13–15, 20, 85, 103, 105–6, 124, 126, 128; and Hill as matriarch of modern dance, 290–94, 299; Hill studying others', 55–56; Hill's continuing influence today, 313; and Hill's last years, 302, 304, 306; and Hill's struggle for balance, 280–83; and Hill's work with Graham, 29–32; of Holm, 99, 109, 141, 151, 167; Horst's influence on, 125, 143–44, 162, 201; of Humphrey, 44, 67, 109, 171, 181, 185, 193, 195, 203, 224–25; at JDT, 225; at Juilliard, 192, 271–72, 274, 276–77; of Junger, 101; of Limón, 119, 171, 185, 193, 216, 279, 282; of New Dance League, 66; of Sokolow, 81, 253–54; starting career through, xvii, xix; of Tamiris, 225; of Taylor, 289; teaching, 54, 88, 92–93, 108, 125–26, 150, 231, 261; of Tudor, 181–83, 185–86,

Feminism, Hill and Shelly front-runners of, 123–24

Fergusson, Francis, 63, 105, 121, 124, 126, 128

Fernández, Felix, 195

Festivals: Bennington's culminating, 100–101, 107–15; *Dance International: 1900–1937*, 104; end of, 128; Festival of British Music, 233; First Green Mountain Festival of the Arts, 137; First National Dance Congress and, 82; First series in 1936, 89; Hill's first, 13–14; International Dance Festival, 306; Juilliard's fiftieth anniversary, 203; none at Mills, 116; planned for 1940 summer, 124; of Shawn, 144; Spoleto Festival, 234; tenth anniversary of summer school, 209. *See also* American Dance Festival (ADF)

Festive Rhythm, 102

Feuillet, Raoul, 233

Findlay, Elsa, 30, 35

Fine, Vivian, 56, 108–9, 112, 203

Fiorella, 234

First Green Mountain Festival of the Arts, 137

Fisher, Clive, 121

Fisher, Nelle, 125

Fitzgerald, F. Scott, 27, 77, 153

Fitzgerald, Robert, 164

Fivefold Mesh, The, 159

Flade, Tina, 64–66, 114

Flanagan, Hallie, 94

Flickers, 281

Fokine, Michel and Fokina, Vera, 11, 104

Folksay, 163

Fonaroff, Nina, 77, 111, 125, 136, 144

Ford, Betty Bloomer. *See* Bloomer (Ford), Betty

Ford, Gerald R., 192, 284

Ford Foundation, 192, 213, 243–44, 253, 256, 264, 281

Forum on the Modern Dance, 75

Four Hundred, New York City, xviii

Four Little Salon Pieces, 81

Four Pioneers, 255

Four Seasons, 233

Four Soviet Songs, 81

Franco, anti-, 89, 101

Frank, Letitia (Tish) Evans. *See* Evans (Frank), Letitia (Tish)

Frank Loomis Palmer auditorium, 161, 163, 167, 172, 209, 245–46, 263–64

French, Kenneth, 290

Frontier, 73, 124, 143

Frost, Robert, 203

Fuller, Buckminster, 125

Fuller, Loie, xvii, xix, 6, 77

Gadd, May, 135

Gavers, Mattlyn, 183

Gearhart, Robert, 189–90

Gentry, Eve, 99, 143

Gershwin, George, 128

Gibbs, Angela, 154

Gilbert, Ralph, 125

Gilbert and Sullivan, xviii

Gluck, Christoph, 45

Gluck, Rina, 166

Godwin, Dwight, 210

Golden Gate International Exposition, 118

Goldner, Nancy, 288

Goya Meets Granados, 283

Gradus and Parnassum, 234

Graham, Martha: age of, 238; ANTA, work at, 227; ballet/modern dance controversy, 239, 244; Bennington College, work at, 87–88, 90–91; Bennington summer school, work at, 52–53, 55–56; Bennington's culminating festival, work on, 108–13; bohemian lifestyle of, 51, 288; and changes, 170, 173, 175–76; choreography grants for, 289; combination of ballet and modern dance, 205; company of, 33, 241, 248–49, 256, 275, 293, 313; and "curse of Isadora," 304; as a dance icon, 284–85; dance explosion of the 1960s, 254; and Davies's death, 237; death of, 307; family of, 87;

followers of, 81–82, 84–86; controversy, 264; and Hill as matriarch of modern dance, 290; and Hill receiving honorary doctorate from Bennington College, 265; Hill's association with, 200–201; as Hill's contemporary, xvii, xix; as Hill's influence, 19–24; and Hill's marriage, 190; Hill's power struggle with, 295; and Hill's receiving dance award, 284; Hill's support of, 196; and Hill's time away, 209; and Hill's work at Bennington College, 44; Horst as mentor of, 46; and Horst's death, 242–43; imitation of, 45; and *Immediate Tragedy*, 97–106; Juilliard, work at, 180–82, 184–88; and Juilliard at Lincoln Center, 277; Limón, opinion of, 282; Lincoln Center, work on, 212–14; NYCB, work at, 226–27; as one of the "Big Four," 49, 57, 62, 64, 108–9, 151, 167; as the "other Martha," 305; and *Panorama*, 61–76; as part of dance history, 199; performance at Radio City Music Hall, 40–41; performance in Colorado Springs, 80; photography book of, 292; relationship with Hawkins, 110–11, 118, 164–65, 189; relationship with Horst, 15, 20, 77, 80, 118; residency at Sarah Lawrence, 42; resignation from festival, 179; student performances of, 253; summer at Connecticut College and ADF, 161, 163–65, 167–68; summer at Mills and return to Bennington, 116–20, 122, 124–28; technique of, 235, 248, 276; Town Hall, work at, 192; work with Hill, 27–39; works of, 192, 281, 302, 312; and World War II, 133–39, 141–45, 148–49, 152, 154–56
Granados, Enrique, 16
Green, Ray, 108, 112, 133
Greenhood, Henrietta. *See* Gentry, Eve
Greenwich Village, 34, 51, 138, 253, 272
Grieg, Edward, 14
Griffith, D. W., xix

Grito, El, 192
Guichet, Le, 273
Guiliani, Rudolph, 312
Guthrie, Woody, 163

Haiku, 304
Hail and Farewell, 233
Halprin, Anna, 107
Hamilton, Peter, 141, 171
Hampton, Eric, 295, 304
Handel, George Frideric, 14
Happy Hippocrite, The, 44, 136
Harkavy, Benjamin (Ben), 308
Harkness, Rebecca, 200, 243, 256
Harlequin for President, 88
Harmonica Breakdown, 163
Harris, Roy, 67, 126, 141, 193
Harrison, Lou, 119, 136
Hastings, Baird, 271
Hawkins, Erick: Bennington's culminating festival, work on, 110–13; book about Bennington, 289; controversy, 264; Hill's power struggle with, 295; and Juilliard at Lincoln Center, 277; relationship with Graham, 110–11, 118, 164–65, 189; summer at Connecticut College and ADF, 161, 164–65; summer at Mills and return to Bennington, 118, 124–26, 128; and World War II, 134–35, 142, 144
Hawkins, Frances, 82, 88
H'Doubler (Claxton), Margaret (Marge) Newell, 22, 35, 42, 56, 106, 143, 152
Heald, Henry, 198
Hellebrandt, Beatrice, 92
Heretic, 28–29, 31–32, 56
Hering, Doris, 193, 261, 264, 280
Hero of the Grid Iron, The, 7
Herodiade, 164
Hicks, Lewis, 4, 7
High School for the Performing Arts (HPA), 166, 184
Hill, Betty Phelps, 97–98
Hill, Bill: death of father, 203; death of mother, 174; family memories of, 97;

Hong Kong Academy for the Arts, 294, 301, 306

Hoofer on a Fiver, 144

Horan, Robert, 136

Horst, Betty, 80, 111, 118

Horst, Louis: at ADF, 227; ADF dedicated to, 298; ballet/modern dance controversy, 239; Bennington College, work at, 81, 88–90, 92; Bennington summer school, work at, 52–54, 56; Bennington's culminating festival, work on, 108–9, 112–13; bohemian lifestyle of, 51; bust of, 267; and changes, 172–73; clash with Holm, 99; combination of ballet and modern dance, 205; death of, 242–43, 282; dog of, 87, 154; Dunn as pianist for, 250; as editor of *Dance Observer*, 104, 219; and Graham's *Panorama*, 61, 63–67, 71–72, 74–75; and Hill forging a career, 15; Hill's association with, 200; and Hill's work at Bennington College, 46; and Hill's work with Graham, 27–28, 30–34, 36; importance to Hill, 156; Juilliard, work at, 180–82, 187, 201, 215; performance at Radio City Music Hall, 41; and politics, 82; relationship with Fonaroff, 111; relationship with Graham, 15, 20, 77, 80, 118; residency at Sarah Lawrence, 42; social life of, 100; students and master teachers, 233; summer at Connecticut College and ADF, 161–67; summer at Mills and return to Bennington, 117–18, 120, 125–28; and World War II, 134, 136–37, 139, 142, 144–45, 148–49, 154–55

Hoving, Lucas, 171, 179

Hug, Bill, 272

Hughes, Allen, 242, 244, 246

Humphrey (Woodford), Doris: ANTA, work for, 196, 209; Bennington College, work at, 88–92; Bennington summer school, work at, 56; Bennington's culminating festival, work on, 99–102, 108, 112; and changes, 170–74; combi-

nation of ballet and modern dance, 205; as contemporary of Hill, xvii, xix; *Dance International: 1900–1937*, 104; dance theatre of, 232; death of, 224; family of, 87; fellowship of, 264; first independent concert of, 24; and Graham's *Panorama*, 61–68, 75; Hill's association with, 200; and Hill's work at Bennington, 44; and Hill's work with Graham, 28, 31–32, 35–36; illness of, 220–21; influence on dance today, 313; JDT, work for, 196; Juilliard, work at, 180–81, 184–85, 193, 195, 203, 210, 215–16, 225–26; legacy of, 295; as Limón's mentor, 195; marriage of, 45, 77; as one of the "Big Four," 49, 57, 62, 64, 108–9, 167; as part of dance history, 199; and politics, 82; retirement as a dancer, 150; summer at Connecticut College and ADF, 159, 161–63, 167; summer at Mills and return to Bennington, 116, 119–20, 124–25; tribute to, 227, 244, 246; Weidman, work with, 45, 50; works of, 179, 278, 280–82; and World War II, 133–34, 136, 139, 141–42, 152. *See also* Humphrey-Weidman Dance Company

Humphrey-Limón technique, 184, 187

Humphrey-Weidman Dance Company: Bennington's culminating festival, work on, 108; disbanding of, 150, 171; and larger ensembles, 66; focus on company, 88–91; style of, 162; and World War II, 135–37, 141. *See also* Humphrey (Woodford), Doris; Weidman, Charles

Humphrey-Weidman School, 81

Hunter, Kim, 194, 286

Hutchinson, Ann, 184

Hyman, Charlie, 309

Ichinohe, Saeko, 273

Ide, Letitia, 171, 175

Imago, 246

Immediate Tragedy: Dance of Dedication, 97–106

Leigh, Robert Devore (*continued*)
  Panorama, 61; and Hill's struggle for balance, 281; summer at Mills and return to Bennington, 120–21; wife's death, 225; and World War II, 140, 156
Let's Take a Trip, 210
Letter to the World, 126–28, 136, 141
L'Europe Galante, 233
Levy, Helen Mandel, 64–65
Lewis, Daniel (Danny), 280, 282, 295–96, 310
Leyenda de José, La, 233
Liberty Tree, 125
Liebert, Mary Ann, 288
Lieberthal (Zera), Hortense ("Hortie"): Bennington College, work at, 93; Bennington Festival Series, 101; and Gene's suicide, 98–99; and Hill's last years, 309–10; and Hill's marriage, 189–90; students and master teachers, 235; summer at Connecticut College and ADF, 159; summer at Mills and return to Bennington, 119–20; and World War II, 142, 146; at World's Fair, 217
Life of the Bee, 44, 66, 196, 216
Lilac Garden, 181–82, 254
Limón, José: ANTA, work for, 209, 227; ballet/modern dance controversy, 239, 241–42, 244–47; Bennington College, work at, 87–90; Bennington summer school, work at, 51, 53–54; and changes, 170–75; combination of ballet and modern dance, 205; company of, 161, 163, 170, 241–42, 256, 289, 295, 313; Connecticut College, work at, 195; dance explosion of the 1960s, 253–54; controversy, 261–64, 266; and Graham's *Immediate Tragedy*, 100–101; and Graham's *Panorama*, 64, 67, 74; and Hill as matriarch of modern dance, 290; and Hill leaving Connecticut College, 179; Hill's defense of, 295; as Hill's replacement teacher, 105; and Hill's struggle for balance, 284; Hill's support of, 196; homosexuality of, 45; illness

and death of, 277–79; interpreting music, 216; Juilliard, work at, 182, 184–87, 192–93, 203, 215, 225; and Juilliard at Lincoln Center, 275, 278; legacy of, 280, 282, 295; Lincoln Center, work on, 215, 219; idea for *Missa Brevis*, 211; performing Humphrey's works, 227; students and master teachers, 231, 233, 236; summer at Connecticut College and ADF, 161–63, 167; summer at Mills and return to Bennington, 118–22; technique of, 184, 187, 248, 279; on tour, 195, 221; works of, 281, 283, 298, 304–5, 312; and World War II, 133, 140–41, 152
Limón, Pauline Lawrence: ballet/modern dance controversy, 242, 246; Bennington College, work at, 45, 90, 105; Bennington summer school, work at, 51, 56; and changes, 171; controversy, 263; and Graham's *Panorama*, 64, 66; and Hill's time away, 209; and Juilliard at Lincoln Center, 277–78; and World War II, 133, 141
Lincoln Center for the Performing Arts: agreement between SAB and Juilliard, 253; ballet/modern dance controversy, 239–47; battle for modern dance at, 219–20, 225–26; dance explosion of the 1960s, 248, 251, 255–56; controversy, 258–63, 267; and Hill as matriarch of modern dance, 290; Hill's continuing influence today, 313; and Hill's last years, 308; Hill's struggles at, 286, 301; and Hill's time away, 212–16; at Juilliard, 232, 271–79
Lincoln Square Dance Theater, 214
Lincoln Square, plans for, 197–205, 215, 219
Lindsay, John, 257
Little Improvisations, 234
Little Theodolina, 144
Litz, Katherine, 88
Lloyd, Margaret, 67, 136, 220
Lloyd, Norman: at ADF, 195; ballet/modern dance controversy, 243–44;

Bennington College, work at, 45, 85, 88–90; Bennington summer school, work at, 48, 52–54, 56; Bennington's culminating festival, work on, 102, 108–9, 112–13; bohemian lifestyle of, 51; and changes, 170, 173, 175; and Graham's *Immediate Tragedy*, 99–101; and Graham's *Panorama*, 67, 70–75; and Hill's marriage, 189; and Hill's struggle for balance, 281, 284; and Hill's work with Graham, 36; Juilliard, work at, 192–93; marriage of, 80; and politics, 82; students and master teachers, 236; summer at Connecticut College and ADF, 161–62, 167; summer at Mills and return to Bennington, 117, 120–21, 123–26, 128; and World War II, 134–36, 142, 144, 148, 152

Lloyd, Ruth: at ADF, 195; Bennington College, work at, 44, 79, 90, 94; Bennington summer school, work at, 50, 53; Bennington's culminating festival, work on, 109, 112–13; bohemian lifestyle of, 51; and Graham's *Immediate Tragedy*, 100–101; and Graham's *Panorama*, 67, 71–72, 74–75; and Hill's marriage, 189; and Hill's work with Graham, 36–37; marriage of, 80; and relationship between Hill and Davies, 86; summer at Connecticut College and ADF, 161–62; summer at Mills and return to Bennington, 117, 120; and World War II, 134–35

Locklair, Wriston, 294
Lonely Ones, The, 163
Loring, Eugene, 88, 181, 199
Louis, Murray, 281
Louther, William, 234
Lowry, Glenn, 37
Lowry, W. McNeill, 213–14, 239, 253
Lubovitch, Lar, 304
Lucifer, 285
Ludin, Ben, 271
Luening, Otto, 72, 111, 124, 128
Lynchtown, 134
Lyric Suite, 278

MacAber's Dance, 254
Macero, Teo, 254
Macy, Gertrude, 246
Maeterlinck, Maurice, 6, 66
Malinche, La, 192
Malloy, Henry Edward, 14–16, 21
Malraux, André, 27
Manchester, P. W., 181, 245
Maniker, Allen, 309
Mansfield, Brydon, 204
Mansfield, Portia, 13, 15
Marina, Gloria, 291, 305
Marks, Bruce, 233
Marseillaise, La, xviii
Martha Graham Center for Contemporary Dance, 248
Martha Hill Dance Fund, 312
Martha Hill Dance Performance Workshop, 284
Martha Hill Dance Scholarship, 305
Martin, John: ADF dedicated to, 298; ANTA, opinions about, 196; ballet merger unsuccessful, 214; ballet/ modern dance controversy, 246; Bennington College, work at, 78, 87–89, 91–92; Bennington summer school, work at, 48, 53; Bennington's culminating festival, work on, 112; *Dance Observer*, work at, 104; death of, 307; defining modern dance, 37–38; and Graham's *Immediate Tragedy*, 100; and Graham's *Panorama*, 61, 63, 66–67, 74–75; and Hill's last years, 302; and Hill's work at Bennington College, 41, 45–46; Lincoln Center, work on, 212; review for *Letter to the World*, 128; review of *The Moor's Pavane*, 171; start at *New York Times*, 24; students of writing reviews, 103; summer at Connecticut College and ADF, 166–67; summer at Mills and return to Bennington, 126; and World War II, 137, 155
Martin, Louise, 63
Mask of Night, 282

Schuman, William: agreement between SAB and Juilliard, 253; ballet merger unsuccessful, 214; ballet/modern dance controversy, 239, 241, 244–47; and changes, 175–76; creation of dance company, 195; conflict, 211; dance explosion of the 1960s, 251; filming dance concerts, 210; controversy, 260; and Hill's last years, 304–5; and Hill's position at Juilliard, 191; and Hill's time away, 214; JDT, work for, 196, 221; Juilliard, work at, 180–82, 185, 188, 192, 217; Lincoln Center, work on, 212–13, 215–16, 225; Lincoln Square, plans for, 198, 201, 204; students and master teachers, 236; and World War II, 148

Schumann, Robert, 234

Schurman, Nona, 91, 142–43

Scriabin, Alexander, 19

Seeds of Brightness, 144

Segall, Bernardo, 172

Serenade, 83, 306

Serova, Sonia, 14–15, 18

Session '58, 215

Shadowplay, 254

Shain, Charles, 246, 264

Shakers, The, 44, 134, 167, 278

Shakespeare, William, 312

Shawn, Ted, xix, 45, 63, 77, 111, 144. *See also* Denishawn

Shelly, Mary Jo: Bennington College, work at, 83–85, 87–94; Bennington summer school, work at, 48–51, 54, 57, 103; Bennington's culminating festival, work on, 107, 110–13; book about Bennington College, 286–88; and changes, 172; death of, 287–88; first meeting with Hill, 12; friendship with Hill, 19, 27, 29, 34–35, 37–38, 80, 105, 123–24; and Graham's *Panorama*, 61–64, 66, 68–69, 73–75; and Hill forging a career, 21–23; and Hill's move to Mills, 114–15; and Hill's work at Bennington College, 39, 42–47; and Hill's work at Juilliard, 179;

lesbianism of, 157; and male dancing, 81; move of, 100; relationship with Hill and, 29, 105, 123–24; replacement for, 240; summer at Connecticut College and ADF, 160; summer at Mills and return to Bennington, 116, 118–21, 124; and World War II, 134, 136, 138–40, 142, 144–47, 150, 157–58

Showpiece, 111, 125

Shurr, Gertrude, 30–31, 133

Siegal, Marcia, 213, 307

Sketches from the People, 31–32

Sleeping Beauty, 236

Smith, Carlton Sprague, 151

Smith, Oliver, 200

Snyder, Allegra Fuller, 274

Soaring, 44

Social Mores Reflected in Dance, 128

Society for the Suppression of Vice, 21

Sokol, Martin L., 197–98

Sokolow, Anna: ballet/modern dance controversy, 244–45; Bennington College, work at, 81–82; Bennington Festival Series, 101; as choreographer, 253–54; and Graham's *Panorama*, 66, 71–72; and Hill as matriarch of modern dance, 292; and Hill's work with Graham, 30; influence on dance today, 313; JDT, work for, 196; Juilliard, work at, 215; and Juilliard at Lincoln Center, 275, 277–78; student performances of, 253; students and master teachers, 231; as a teacher, 254, 262; works of, 280, 282–83, 295, 298, 304

Sommers, Ben, 246, 308

Song of the West, 193

Songs Remembered, 283

Speaker, 81

Spender, Stephen, 193

Spirit of the Sea, 91

Spofford, Charles M., 197–98

St. Denis, Ruth: dance ancestor, xvii–xix; *Dance International: 1900–1937*, 104; as Graham's influence, 20; and Graham's *Panorama*, 63, 65; and Hill's work with

Graham, 31; Humphrey as assistant to, 44; marriage of, 77; Weidman performing work of, 45. *See also* Denishawn
Starer, Robert, 236
Steeple People, 280
Steig, William, 163
Steinberg, Risa, 257, 263, 265, 272
Stevens, Wallace, 117
Stickney, Rebecca (Becca), 62, 105, 114, 145, 153, 287
Stoddard, George, 212, 220
Stone, Ed, 204
Story of Mankind, The, 152, 163
Strangler, The, 164
Stravinsky, Igor, 15, 30, 192
Streams, 298
Streetcar Named Desire, A, 194
Streng, Marian, 48–49
Stuart, Muriel, 70
Students and master teachers, 231–38
Suite Italienne, 304
Suite of Soviet Songs, 81
Summer 1936, happenings in, 88–94
Summer School of the Dance, Bennington, 43, 48–57, 61–63, 86, 89, 92, 107
Sumner, Janet, 254
Sunday, Billy, 6
Sunday in the Park with George, 297
Sunflowers, 276
Surinach, Carlos, 193
Swallow Book, The, 136
Swan Lake, 262
Sweigard, Lulu, 19, 194

Tamiris, Helen: *Dance International: 1900–1937*, 104; at festival, 82; first solo of, 24; and Hill forging a career, 20; and Hill's work with Graham, 31; imitation of, 45; influence on dance today, 313; Juilliard, work at, 224, 226; Lincoln Center, work on, 216, 220, 225; summer at Connecticut College and ADF, 167; and World War II, 147
Tap dancing, 194, 291

Taylor, Paul: choreography grants for, 289; company of, 256, 313; controversy, 264; and Hill as matriarch of modern dance, 297; Hill's defense of, 295; and Hill's last years, 302; as Hill's possible replacement, 294; Juilliard, work at, 188, 193; NYCB, work at, 226–27; works of, 283, 289, 298, 300, 304–5, 312
Taylor, Ralph, 46
Tchaikovsky, Peter, 14, 83
Teachers, students and master, 231–38
Ted Shawn and His Men Dancers, 63
Temple of Terpsichore, 17
Tenebrae 1914, 227
Terry, Sonny, 163
Terry, Walter: ANTA, work for, 196; ballet, rise of, 214; ballet/modern dance controversy, 241; Bennington College, work at, 90; as dance critic, 67; dance explosion of the 1960s, 254; Lincoln Center, work on, 212, 220; summer at Connecticut College and ADF, 160, 167
Tet Offensive, 263
Tharp, Twyla, 264, 298
Theater 1969, 264
Theatre Piece, 89–90
There is a Time, 192, 203, 275, 283, 305
Thirteen Ways of Looking at a Blackbird, 117
Three Arts Club, 17, 148
Three Poems, 280
Time Table, 182
Todd (Hill), Grace. *See* Hill, Grace Todd
Todd, Mabel Ellsworth, 19, 194
Todd, Martha, as stage name, 33
Toller, Ernst, 136
Tonantzintla, 179
Topaz, Muriel ("Mickey"): As DNB director, 297; and Hill as matriarch of modern dance, 296; and Hill's last years, 303, 305–7; and Hill's struggle for balance, 283; as Hill's successor, 300, 308; Juilliard, work at, 180, 184–85, 187–88, 193; and Juilliard at Lincoln Center, 272

About the Author

Janet Mansfield Soares began her career as a dancer with Juilliard Dance Theatre and the José Limón Dance Company before creating work for her own company, DANCES/Janet Soares. She served as a Lincoln Center Institute artist-in-residence for New York City schools, artistic director for Juilliard Student Touring Programs, director of Dance Advance, a touring company for the American Dance Festival, and founder-director of the concert series Dance Uptown from 1967 to 1990. She is professor of dance emerita from Barnard College, New York City, where she was chair and artistic director of the department of dance. A graduate of the Juilliard School (where she taught dance composition from 1964 to 1987), she holds a doctorate from Columbia University. Her biography, *Louis Horst: Musician in a Dancer's World* was published by Duke University Press in 1994. She now divides her time between Tucson, Arizona, and Lyme, Connecticut.